EUROAMERICAN SETTLEMENTS
IN THE
OREGON COUNTRY

MISSIONS
M Methodist
C Catholic
CP Congressional
Presbyterian
o Other settlements

FORTS
RAC Russian-American Co.
PFC Pacific Fur Co.
NWC North West Co.
HBC Hudson's Bay Co
AFC American Fur Co.

Trails

Drawn by H. Guzewska. Cartographic Office.
Department of Geography. York University.

The Lifeline of the
Oregon Country

James R. Gibson

The Lifeline of the Oregon Country

THE FRASER-COLUMBIA BRIGADE SYSTEM, 1811-47

UBCPress / Vancouver

Printed in Canada on acid-free paper ∞
ISBN 0-7748-0642-7

Canadian Cataloguing in Publication Data

Gibson, James R.
    The lifeline of the Oregon Country

    Includes bibliographical references and index.
    ISBN 0-7748-0642-7

    1. Northwest, Pacific – Discovery and exploration.   2.
Transportation – Northwest, Pacific – History.   3. Fur trade –
Northwest, Pacific – History.   4. Hudson's Bay Company –
History.   I. Title.
F880.G52   1998   979.5'03   C97-911049-1

This book has been published with a grant from the Social Sciences Federation of Canada, using funds provided by the Social Sciences and Humanities Research Council of Canada.

UBC Press also gratefully acknowledges the ongoing support to its publishing program from the Canada Council for the Arts, the British Columbia Arts Council, and the Multiculturalism Program of the Department of Canadian Heritage.

Set in Stone Serif by Brenda and Neil West, BN Typographics West
Copy editor: Andy Carroll
Proofreader: Dallas Harrison
Printed and bound in Canada by Friesens

UBC Press
University of British Columbia
6344 Memorial Road
Vancouver, BC V6T 1Z2
(604) 822-5959
Fax: 1-800-668-0821
E-mail: orders@ubcpress.ubc.ca
http://www.ubcpress.ubc.ca

For Brian and Lara
may your journey be as adventurous as that of the brigaders

and for John Stuart (1779-1847),
the first and the best of the brigaders

*The extension of the [fur] trade across the northern
half of the [North American] continent and the
transportation of furs and goods over great distances
involved the elaboration of an extensive organization of
transport, of personnel, and of food supply.*

– HAROLD A. INNIS, *The Fur Trade in Canada*

Contents

Maps

Preface

When the district [New Caledonia] was first settled [by the NWC in 1805],
the goods required for trade were brought in by the winterers [wintering partners]
from Lac la Pluie [Fort Frances on Rainy Lake], which was their dépôt. The
people left the district as early in spring as the navigation permitted, and returned
so late that they were frequently overtaken by winter ere they reached their
destination. Cold, hunger, and fatigue, were the unavoidable consequences; but the
enterprising spirit of the men of those days – the intrepid, indefatigable adven-
turers of the North-West Company – overcame every difficulty. It was that spirit
that opened a communication across the broad continent of America; that
penetrated to the frost-bound regions of the Arctic circle; and that established a
trade with the natives in this remote land, when the merchandise required for it
was in one season transported from Montreal to within a short distance of the
Pacific. Such enterprise has never been exceeded, seldom or never equalled. The
outfit is now [middle 1830s] sent out from England by Cape Horn, to Fort
Vancouver, thence it is conveyed in boats to [Fort] Okanagan, then transported
on horses' backs to Alexandria, the lower post of the district, whence it is
conveyed in boats to Fort St. James.

– CHIEF TRADER JOHN MCLEAN, ca. 1837[1]

In his seminal study of the Canadian fur trade, the late Harold A. Innis emphasized – mostly implicitly – the constraining role of logistics, what he saw as the high overhead costs of distance. This overhead became especially significant as trade was extended across Rupert's Land along the main river and lake waterways farther and farther to the west of the entrepôts of the Hudson's Bay Company (HBC) and the North West Company (NWC) on the northern and southern edges of the Canadian Shield at, respectively, York Factory on Hudson Bay and Fort William on Rainy Lake.[2] On the "west side the [Rocky] Mountains," the supply lines were stretched to the breaking point, particularly in Western, or New, Caledonia (essentially the upper basin of the Fraser River above the Thompson River forks). Only the Peace River breached the Rocky Mountains to the north, as Alexander Mackenzie found in 1792 en route to the Pacific.[3] Moreover, unlike the waterways of the Great Plains, those of the Cordillera trended north-south, not east-west; furthermore, these mountain and plateau rivers were turbulent, not sluggish, with tight gorges or rocky rapids sometimes necessitating arduous cordelling or portaging. Nevertheless, unlike the Fraser River, which in 1808 proved "impracticable" for navigation to its namesake, comprising "a dreadful chain of difficulties apparently insurmountable,"[4] the Columbia River in the southern half of the Columbia Department, or Oregon Country, was found by Lewis and Clark in 1805 to be descendable by canoe or boat to the Pacific, as well as enterable by ship (as both Captain Robert Gray and Lieutenant William Broughton determined in 1792), despite the perilous Columbia Bar.[5] So at least this milder part of the Pacific Slope could export its returns and import its supplies by sea more easily and more cheaply than overland. This advantage eventually resulted in the logistical linking of the New Caledonia and Columbia Districts by means of the Fraser-Columbia brigade system, the linkage following the Okanagan trench between the upper Thompson and the middle Columbia Rivers. This transport system of North canoes, Indian pack horses, and Columbia batteaux, moving beaver pelts to the coast and trade goods to the interior, was the lifeline of the fur trade of the Columbia Department from 1826 to 1847, when it was severed by the extension of the 1818 international boundary along the forty-ninth parallel from the Rockies to the Pacific under the terms of the Treaty of Washington (1846). Even before 1826 it had always served the Columbia District and in some years the New Caledonia District. The lifeline was an integral part of what Harris has termed "a minimal construction of nodes and circuits intended to facilitate trade in an isolated corner of the world and to make connections to distant managers and markets"; it was also a feature of the "politics of fear" of the European fur traders as they "sought to reconfigure an alien territory and discipline its peoples so that an ordered, profitable trade was possible" in the Cordillera.[6]

The vital role of the brigade system became evident to me while writing a book on the beginnings of agriculture in the Oregon Country,[7] and I soon concluded that the subject deserved monographic treatment. Surprisingly, given the obvious importance of the brigade system, as well as the abundant and accessible records,[8] no comprehensive study of what was called the "main communication" has hitherto appeared.[9] Whatever the reasons for this oversight – the unpopularity of transport history, the parochialism of local history, or the presumptuousness of historical geography in taking the basic role of transport for granted – I hope that this book will help to correct it. My study is very much an empirical, even documentary, treatment; it does not pretend to be theoretical or philosophical (and certainly not "creative non-fiction"), but it may well serve as a source or basis for such approaches.

I am grateful to the following archives and libraries for the use of their collections: Bancroft Library of the University of California (BLUC), Berkeley; Beinecke Rare Book and Manuscript Library (BRBML) of Yale University, New Haven; British Columbia Archives and Records Service (BCARS), Victoria; Hudson's Bay Company Archives (HBCA) of the Provincial Archives of Manitoba, Winnipeg, especially Keeper Judith Beattie; Oregon Historical Society (OHS), Portland; National Archives of Canada (NAC), Ottawa; and Public Records Office (PRO), London. Many of their holdings were made available to me via the resource sharing service of York University's Scott Library under Mary Lehane, whose assistance has been much appreciated. I am also indebted to the Social Sciences and Humanities Research Council of Canada and to York University for grants that allowed me to spend less time teaching and more time researching and writing this book. Finally, I am thankful to Carolyn King of the Cartographic Office of the Department of Geography of York University for making the maps.

PART I

Introduction

This part of the country [Columbia Department] has many
charms to fascinate ... the eye can fix on no one object, which is
not directly the reverse, of what it has been accustomed to, on the
east side of the [Rocky] Mountains – the Trees, Birds, Insects, &
herbage wear a foreign aspect.

– CHIEF FACTOR DUNCAN FINLAYSON, 1832
in G.P. de T. Glazebrook, ed., *The Hargrave Correspondence*
1821-1843 (Toronto: Champlain Society 1938), 88.

CHAPTER I

Opening the Oregon Country

Furs is what brings us to this country.
— CHIEF FACTOR JOHN STUART, 1823[1]

THE NWC ON THE FRASER

From the middle 1780s the North West Company (NWC) and the Hudson's Bay Company (HBC) vied for dominance of the continental fur trade of the northern and western halves of North America.[2] With its shorter supply line from Montreal via Fort William, its "grand depot and headquarters,"[3] and perhaps a willingness to take more risks, the "Canada Company" (as the NWC was sometimes called), following the 1793 lead of one of its "wintering partners" (field agents), Alexander Mackenzie, crossed the Rockies a dozen years later to preempt New Caledonia. In 1805 – just as Americans Lewis and Clark were poised to descend the lower Columbia to its mouth and winter at Fort Clatsop – another NWC partner, Simon Fraser, likewise Pacific-bound down what he thought was the Columbia River in a search for a supply route from the sea, founded McLeod's Lake (his Trout Lake Post) on the "carrying place" between the Peace and Fraser river systems. It became the "place of embarkation" for eastbound voyages via the Peace from what became known as New Caledonia from its resemblance to the Scottish Highlands. In 1806 the district's headquarters, Fort St. James (Nakazleh), or, more commonly, Stuart's Lake, was established by Fraser's second-in-command and canoe maker, John Stuart, a young clerk who was destined to spend nearly two decades as the "bourgeois" (superintendent), or *homme d'affaires*, of what he termed "the worst side of the Rocky Mountains."[4] But it had more furs than the other side, and "furs is what brings us to this country," he understated.[5] Fraser's Lake (Natleh) was founded temporarily in the same year as Stuart's Lake, and permanently in 1814. Fort George was established in 1807 at the junction of the Nechako and Fraser Rivers as a place for the building of canoes for Fraser, who was accompanied by Stuart in his voyage downriver in the following year. It was abandoned in 1808, reoccupied in 1821 (the year of the NWC-HBC merger), abandoned again in 1824, and reoccupied again in 1829. Fort Alexandria, or, more commonly, simply Alexandria, was erected in 1821 on the left (eastern) bank of the Fraser just below its junction with the West Road (Blackwater) River, which Mackenzie had followed to the Pacific; in 1836 the post was moved to the Fraser's right (western) bank. Additional posts were founded at Babine Lake (Fort Kilmaurs) in 1822, Connolly's (Bear) Lake in 1827, and Chilcotin's Lake (Fort Chilcotin) in 1829 in accordance with the HBC's policy of extending the trade northwards and westwards in a vain attempt to intercept the flow of furs from the interior to the coast.

Having opened New Caledonia, the NWC resolved to cross the Fraser-Columbia interfluve and open the "Columbia quarter." Accordingly, in 1807-11 the "surveyor" (geographer) David Thompson – *Koo-Koo-Sint,* the "man who looks at the stars," in the words of the Nez Percé Indians[6] – reconnoitred the Columbia River system. In the summer of 1811 Thompson with nine men (including two Indians) embarked at Kettle Falls "to explore this River, in order to open out a Passage for the Interiour Trade with the Pacific Ocean."[7] That same summer the annual meeting of the NWC had passed a resolution "for entering into adventure and a Trade from England, and China to the North West Coast of America – provided a suitable licence to that Effect is obtained from the East India Company."[8] The plan envisioned tapping the furs of the Pacific Slope via the Columbia and shipping them directly to the Chinese market at Canton, where, however, permission to trade would have to be purchased from the British East India Company (EIC), which enjoyed a monopoly (until 1834) on British trade with China. Fulfilment of this plan would realize Mackenzie's dream of securing the "entire command of the fur trade of North America" through a transcontinental-transoceanic strategy based upon the "great river of the west."[9]

THE PFC ON THE COLUMBIA[10]

However, when on 15 July 1811 Thompson, "northwest-like, came dashing down the Columbia in a light canoe" to the river's mouth,[11] he found that he had been preceded by the Astorians of John Jacob Astor's Pacific Fur Company (PFC). Astor had also conceived a plan – to drive the British from the Oregon Country trade by cooperating with the

Russian-American Company (RAC) at New Archangel (Sitka) and by linking the Columbia corridor, the Pacific sea lane, and the Chinese market. He regarded the Columbia with Astoria at its mouth as the "key to a vast country."[12] Astor recruited mostly British subjects, especially disgruntled former Nor'Westers, reasoning that they would give the British authorities "less offence" in the disputed territory; at least thirty-nine Canadians, including twenty-four boatmen, were hired. "No place like Montreal for hardy and expert voyagers!" declared Astor's lieutenant, Wilson Price Hunt.[13]

One party of seventeen under Hunt proceeded overland, and another of thirty-three under Alexander McKay sailed round Cape Horn on the *Tonquin*, Captain Thorn. From the outset the venture was plagued by misfortune. All of the livestock on the *Tonquin* were lost at sea during a storm between the Sandwich (Hawaiian) Islands and the Northwest Coast, and eight crewmen were drowned when Captain Thorn misread the Columbia Bar; subsequently, the tyrannical Thorn lost his life, crew, ship, and cargo to the Indians on the coast of Vancouver Island. Another supply ship, the *Lark*, Captain Northrop, was wrecked off Maui in the summer of 1813. Hunt's overland party did not arrive until early 1812, a year after the overseas party, having been delayed by starvation, desertion, and dissension. Meanwhile, it had taken the Astorians two months to clear an acre of the thick rainforest for their post on the left bank of the river at its mouth. The "emporium of the west" was dedicated on 18 May 1811, just two months before Thompson's arrival.

The Nor'Wester was warmly received, for in fact he arrived in the belief that the Astorians were collaborators, not competitors. The NWC's wintering partners had agreed in 1810 to a joint venture with the PFC on the Columbia, and they had sent Thompson to protect their interests. So he "raced" to the river's mouth to meet, not beat, the Astorians.[14] However, the NWC had no intention of ultimately sharing the Pacific Slope with the PFC, so Thompson took "great pains" to describe the difficulties and dangers facing the Astorians on the Columbia in the hope of discouraging them.

Astor's men may have believed Thompson, but they did not heed him, quickly putting the river to use to convey both the "outfit" (a post's or district's yearly supply of goods, including those for consumption by the traders and those for bartering to the natives) to the interior and the "returns" (a post's or district's yearly take of furs) to the coast. Their first brigade[15] – one canoe with nine men and from fifteen to twenty "pieces" (bales or bundles of freight, each weighing from eighty-five to ninety pounds) under David Stuart, Astor's partner – left Astoria on 22 July, accompanying Thompson's party of eleven men (including two ex-Astorians) on its return upriver. The two canoes proceeded together for mutual safety; the undermanned and undersupplied Astorian party was "too small to attempt anything of the kind by itself."[16] Between the Cascades, where the river breached the Cascade Range, and the long rapids of the Dalles, the two parties separated, Thompson's going ahead. At the beginning of September the Astorian party founded Fort Okanagan at the forks of the Columbia and Okanogan Rivers. During its first six months this post traded £35 worth of goods for 1,550 beaver skins worth £2,250 at Canton.[17]

The second Astorian brigade was not dispatched until 1812. It left with supplies on 22 March under Robert Stuart, David's nephew, reached Fort Okanagan on 24 April, stayed four or five days, left in four canoes under David Stuart with 2,500 beaver skins, and reached Astoria on 12 May.

Following the arrival of the supply ship *Beaver* on 15 May 1812, the third brigade of sixty-two men under John Clarke left Astoria on 29 June and made Fort Okanagan on 12 August. Two weeks later David Stuart, who had opened the Okanagan trench route in late 1811-early 1812, left Fort Okanagan for the Shuswap Country to establish Shewaps Post in the fall at the junction of the North and South Thompson Rivers; it was quickly duplicated by the NWC's Fort Cumcloups (Kamloops), which became commonly known as Thompson's River. Stuart returned to Astoria with furs in the spring of 1813. Meanwhile, in the summer of 1812 Clarke had established another PFC post at Spokane, which duplicated the NWC's Spokane House.

The fourth and final Astorian brigade, possibly under David Stuart, left on 5 July 1813 and reached Fort Okanagan on 15 August.

By 1 June 1813 – after two years of operation – the PFC had obtained 24,281 furs (including 10,782 beaver and 12,105 muskrat skins),[18] not a large catch. But its fate had already been decided. Undermanned (during its existence the PFC lost sixty-one lives, including forty-six at sea[19]), undersupplied, mismanaged, and threatened (by the War of 1812 between the United States and Great Britain), the company's partners had already decided at their second council in the summer of 1812 to abandon the Columbian venture by 1 June 1813. They rendezvoused for the last time at the Columbia-Snake forks on that date and reached Astoria two weeks later. It was deemed a "safer speculation" to sell the PFC's remaining goods and furs to the NWC than to try to convey them overland to St. Louis. On 16 October in the words of a Nor'Wester, his company "purchased from the Pacific Fur Co. what Furs they had traded as well as all the Goods they had remaining on hand, and the People who ...

choose to remain in this Country for those who bought them out."[20] All of the Astorian goods and furs were sold to the Nor'Westers at 10 percent above gross value for a total of $80,500, payable in bills of exchange in Canada.[21] The NWC was expecting the arrival at the Columbia of the *Isaac Todd*, outfitted as a British ship of war or a letter of marque, either of which could seize the PFC's property as a prize. Instead, the more formidable *Racoon*, a sloop of war of twenty-six guns, appeared, and on 12 December Captain William Black took formal possession of Astoria and – appropriately for what the Chinook Indians called a "King George ship" – renamed it Fort George. Most of the Astorians (Astoria numbered seventy-two men in November 1813[22]) entered the service of the NWC, becoming what Astorian Alexander Ross derisively termed the "strutting and plumed bullies of the north."[23]

The NWC on the Columbia and the Fraser[24]

Even before buying the PFC's property, of course, the NWC had been energetically countering its rival on the Columbia, and not without reason. In a memorandum of 1812, Colin Robertson, an ex-Nor'Wester, noted that Rupert's Land was "exhausted" of beaver, which, however, still commanded high prices, so that expansion of the trade west of the Rockies was necessary to maintain profits.[25] In the same year the NWC complained that the "great scarcity" of beaver east of the Rockies had been felt for two years; more importantly, because the PFC had already begun operations on the Columbia, it was "absolutely necessary" for the NWC to confront it there "for the defence of our only remaining Beaver country." The NWC's council cautioned, however, that "we know from dear bought experience the impossibility of contending from this side of the mountains with people who get their goods from so short a distance as the mouth of the Columbia is from the mountains."[26] Until 1813 the Columbia's Nor'Westers annually conveyed their returns in four or five canoes to Fort William and returned with their outfits (from Montreal) via Athabasca Pass across the Rockies between the headwaters of the Athabasca and Columbia Rivers.[27]

With the NWC's takeover of the PFC, the higher cost of overland supply of the Columbia became less crucial, but the Nor'Westers were still keen to decrease costs and increase profits. And they still wanted to market directly at Canton. So they tried to service both the New Caledonia and Columbia Districts overseas via the Columbia. In July 1812 at its annual meeting, the NWC authorized John Stuart "to take charge of the Department of New Caledonia & combine his Plans &

operations with the Gentlemen [chief factors and chief traders] on the Columbia, & ... to proceed next Spring as early as possible down to the Sea, and there to ... meet the Ship intended to come to the Columbia," a licence having been obtained from the EIC for the China trade.[28] In the fall Stuart was sent from Fort Chipewyan to Stuart's Lake to winter, and in the spring he and his men were to make "their way to the Columbia River down which they will descend to the Pacific Ocean in company with J[ohn]. G. McTavish [from Fort Okanagan]," and "at the Sea it is expected they will meet Donald McTavish Esqr. [bourgeois of the Athabasca District] etc. who last October [1811] were to sail from England round Cape Horn to the entrance of the Columbia River."[29] On 13 May 1813 a party of nine men in two canoes under Stuart with enough provisions for one and a half months left Stuart's Lake to open a brigade route from the Fraser to the Columbia. Stuart was to meet John McTavish and his Spokane men at Fort Okanagan and "with them proceed down to the Sea."[30] The significance of this experiment did not escape another veteran Nor'Wester and New Caledonian, Daniel Harmon: "should Mr. Stuart be so fortunate as to discover a water communication between this [Fraser River] and the Columbia, we shall for the future get our yearly supply of Goods from that quarter, and send our Returns out that way, which will be shipped there directly for the China Market in Vessels which the Concern intends building on that Coast."[31]

Stuart descended the Fraser until, after eight days, he "was obliged to leave his Canoes and take his property on Horses" to Okanagan Lake via Fort Kamloops, which had been established by the NWC in the fall of 1812 but abandoned in the spring of 1813, just before Stuart's arrival.[32] It is unknown whether the brigade followed the waters of the North and South Thompson Rivers, Okanagan Lake, and the Okanagan River in canoes or their banks and shores on horses. From Fort Okanagan Stuart and McTavish proceeded together downriver in a combined brigade of ten canoes with seventy-five men, not reaching Astoria until 7 October (but in time to participate in the purchase of the PFC).[33] Stuart reported that it was possible to go from Okanagan Lake to the sea by water "by making a few short Portages"; he also reported that he had "met with every kindness and assistance from the Natives he saw along the way."[34] Thus Stuart was able to recall a decade later that in 1813 "I first opened the communication between New Caledonia and the Columbia."[35]

However, having opened the Fraser-Columbia brigade route, the NWC chose not to use it after 1814, when a second brigade of eleven men in two canoes under Joseph Laroque reached Stuart's Lake "laden with Goods from the mouth of the Columbia River (Fort George) which place they left the latter end of August last."[36] The route continued to be used by the express (post) but evidently not by the brigade, the reason presumably being that it returned to New Caledonia so late in the season that it was difficult or impossible to distribute the goods from Stuart's Lake to the district's other posts before freeze-up. And the later the receipt of goods, the fewer the furs that could be traded from the Indians before the onset of winter. Indeed, Stuart had reached the sea so late (middle of October) that he could not possibly have returned to his post before freeze-up.

Thus, New Caledonia continued to be served from Fort William via the Peace River route, while the Columbia District – what Fort George regarded as the "upper country" (the interior beyond the Cascade Range as far north as Thompson's River and as far east as the Flathead Post) – continued to be served via the Columbia. The first NWC downriver brigade on the Columbia – two canoes with twenty-three men under John McTavish – went from Spokane House to Astoria in the winter of 1812-13 to meet the *Isaac Todd*. McTavish's return upriver in the spring of 1813 was presumably the first NWC upriver brigade. In January 1814 the inward brigade of two canoes with twenty men under James Keith and the express for Fort William left Fort George together, but they were ambushed and plundered by natives at the Cascades; on 4 April the reinforced brigade – ten canoes with sixty men and two passengers, again under Keith – was redispatched from Fort George.[37] On 1 May, following the arrival of the *Isaac Todd*, a brigade of ten canoes with seventy-eight men and three families, accompanied by an express of two light canoes with twenty-four men, left Fort George for the interior.[38]

From 1815, apparently, round-trip brigades plied the Columbia twice each year, once in the spring and once in the autumn,[39] each coming downriver to the depot with returns to meet the annual supply ship and going upriver with goods for the inland posts. The 1816 spring upriver brigade supposedly comprised twelve boats with 102 men and departed Fort George after a stay of fifteen days, following the arrival of the *Colonel Allan*, which left for Canton with furs in August;[40] the fall downriver brigade consisted of nine canoes with seventy men and on 1 October reached Fort George, which it left on 5 October.[41] And the 1817 spring outward brigade stayed at Fort George for eight days and left with only forty-five men, little more than half the usual complement; half of this brigade remained at Fort Okanagan and half proceeded to Thompson's River and Spokane House.[42]

Meanwhile, according to Astorian-cum-Nor'Wester Alexander Ross, because its Columbian enterprise "fell greatly short of their expectations,"[43] owing to "apathy and want of energy," "extravagance," and "old habits," the NWC in 1815 decided upon a "change of system." The Columbia quarter would be divided into two districts, one coastal and one inland, each with its own bourgeois (James Keith for the coast and Donald McKenzie for the interior); operations would be extended southwards into California and eastwards into the Rockies by means of trapping parties rather than trading posts; Iroquois would be introduced from Montreal as exemplary hunters and trappers; and the "costly" mode of conducting the express would be abandoned and entrusted to natives, with the exception of the annual general express ("by this means of conveyance a voyage which employed forty or fifty men was abolished, consequently saving the risk of lives, the loss of time, and heavy expenses, and the charges incurred were a mere trifle"). Fort Nez Percés, or often simply Walla Walla, "being more central for the general business of the interior," was founded in 1818 near the Columbia-Snake forks to replace Spokane House, which was well-known as a "delightful place" with "no hostile natives," "handsome buildings," "fine women," and "fine horses" – all in all, "a retired [retirement] spot" but inconvenient and expensive.[44] Also, the NWC soon stopped shipping furs to Canton in its own vessels and instead sent them on American ships in return for a percentage of the proceeds "in consequence of the East Indian Company's debarring the bulk of British subjects from sailing in the Indian Ocean."[45]

The changes do not seem to have had much impact, the extravagance, complacency, and mismanagement apparently continuing. In 1818 mishaps in the Fort George area alone (chiefly clashes with the natives) reduced the NWC's annual returns by four thousand beaver pelts worth £6,000.[46] Four years later an ex-Nor'Wester recalled that the Columbia quarter had been "but a lossing concern to the N.W. Company, owing to the great number of people setting themselves free."[47] In other words, the NWC – for whatever reasons – had difficulty retaining its employees. Many of them became freemen (*lachés*) in the region itself rather than return to the Canadas or Britain, and many of these freemen gravitated to the Willamette Valley, which with its abundant game, mild climate, fertile soil, and lush grassland was gaining a reputation as the "garden of the Columbia."[48] Among the Astorians the valley was a "place notorious for gormandizing," with *chevreuil* (black-tailed deer) being particularly plentiful.[49] On his unpublished map of 1813-15 of the valley of the "Wilarmut" David Thompson noted: "This River flows through a very beautiful and rich country and happy Climate."[50] The district report of Fort George for 1824-25 echoed Thompson's view, calling the Willamette "a fine stream flowing through a rich Country."[51] Chief Trader John Work led a trading and trapping party of twelve men up the Willamette in the spring of 1834 and detailed the attractiveness of the valley at its lower end:

> The country, in getting out of the woods [on the west] has a beautiful appearance, it is a continuation of plains, (which commence here and continue on to the Southward,) separated by numerous strips of timber, bounded to the Eastward by the strips of wood land which occupy the banks of the Willamet, and to the westward by the woods which occupy the base of the Killymaux [Tillamook?] Mountains. The Soil is a rich blackish mould covered, (but not with a close thick sward,) with grass and other plants among which are considerable quantities of strawberry plants now well furnished with fine fruit. Not a stone and scarcely a shrub to interrupt the progress of the plough, which might be employed in many places with little more difficulty than in a stubble field. The Country here though termed plain from being clear of wood is not a dead flat but composed of portions of level land with gently rising grounds, portions of the flat land are springy, here the soil inclines to be clayey. The vegetation is not rank, yet it yields a great deal of pasture ... The open country here is of an irregular form, as parts of woods jut out into the plains from both sides. There can be no doubt but abundant crops of every kind of grain would amply reward the labours of the husbandman besides it being so well adapted for pasture both of Cattle & Sheep.[52]

Work's assessment was vindicated by the influx of retired traders in the 1810s, 1820s, and 1830s and overland migrants in the 1840s.

THE HBC ON THE COLUMBIA AND THE FRASER

Increasingly violent conflict between the NWC and its longtime and disliked rival, the HBC, which had successfully undertaken a reorganization of its own in the 1810s, led to an absorption of the NWC by the HBC in 1821 under pressure from the Colonial Office. The "new concern," which retained all of the trappings and workings of the old HBC, including its name, monopolized British involvement in the fur trade. Chief Factor John Stuart at Stuart's Lake was officially notified of the merger by letter: "after a long negociation between the Hudson's Bay Company, and the Gentlemen meeting in London for the North West Company, the differences between the Companies have been terminated by an arrangement for a coalition of their Interests in the Indian Trade, which accordingly is henceforward to be carried on by and in the name of the Governor and Company of adventurers of England trading into Hudson's Bay."[53] What the Indians called the "great company" was finally ensconced on both the Fraser and the Columbia, which now became separate districts, or departments (under the NWC, New Caledonia had been considered part of the Columbia District).

The HBC had tried, unsuccessfully, from 1818 through 1820 to establish itself in New Caledonia in particular, it being a "country according to all reports rich in furs and the natives perfectly independent."[54] The "lower country" (Columbia District), being subject to competition from American traders, was seen as a buffer for the "upper country" (New Caledonia), and its fur resources – especially those south of the Columbia River – were to be "scoured" (overhunted) in the event of the loss of the district to the United States under the terms of a future boundary agreement with Great Britain (until then it was open to "joint occupancy" by the two countries).[55] In early 1822 Beaver House (the London headquarters of the HBC, formally the "Governor and Committee") told the new governor of the Northern Department, George Simpson, that although it was their understanding that hitherto the trade of the Columbia had been unprofitable, and would likely continue to be unprofitable, nevertheless if the losses could be reduced, it might be "good policy" to retain the region "with the view of protecting the more valuable districts to the North of it." This opinion was shared by the Columbia District's officers, who later that year advised Simpson that "it would not be politic to withdraw from that Country as if it does not realize profits no loss is likely to be incurred thereby and it serves to check opposition from the Americans." Although the district's 1821-22 returns were "rather more flattering than hitherto, however large profits can scarcely be expected," wrote Simpson, and the trade "might support itself, provided always, that no formidable opposition from the Americans assail us, in that quarter" – in which case all competitors would likely lose money. All in all, it "might be premature" to abandon the trade of the Columbia quarter.[56]

Indeed, in 1823 Simpson was able to report that the district's returns had increased and its expenses decreased and that he was hopeful that its trade "will not only clear itself but yield moderate profits."[57] However, the beaver and otter skins taken on the west side of the mountains, particularly those of the Columbia District, were "far inferior" to those taken on the east side.[58] Their inferiority arose partly from the milder winters of the Pacific Slope, especially in the south, and partly from inadequate stretching, cleaning, and storing by natives and freemen.[59]

The HBC's hopes were much higher for New Caledonia, which was more distant from American mountain men and less depleted of fur bearers. It was the real prize of the corporate takeover. A longtime servant in New Caledonia, John Tod, recalled late in life that "it was the finest & richest part of the [Indian] Country for furs."[60] John Stuart was more temperate but still sanguine in his appraisal:

> This part of the country lies under many disadvantages, and its distance from any Port of entry, and the difficulty of getting the necessary supplies will continue to operate against it. The number of people required will be more than in proportion to the returns, and such as expect a rapid increase of returns will be disappointed, The nature of the Country cannot admit of it. Another matter not unworthy of consideration is the bad living in this quarter; It is no more to be compared to the East side of the Mountains than "*Tripe de Roche*" is to Turtle Soup, and unless an addition in this quarter is made to the usual quantity of Stores allowed in other places, no Gentleman however devoted to the Service will be willing or able long to remain, and it is only after a person acquires a Knowledge of the Country that he becomes of essential Service; It was customary with the North West Company to make a difference both in this quarter, and in MacKenzie's River, and a double share would not be too much.[61]

Stuart added that New Caledonia never abounded in beaver but that they were widespread, so that the trade could yield a gradual increase in returns, "unless too much is attempted."[62]

The merger produced another round of restructuring, including the firing of redundant servants and the closing of duplicate posts. Even before the coalition the NWC had grown fat in New Caledonia, John Stuart complaining that "not one of the rules and regulations [NWC reforms] laid down in Oct. 1815 were adhered too – unbounded extravagance crept in and no separate nor indeed any, accounts were kept for the different establishments but the whole was blended together in one block."[63] Right after the coalition Stuart was warned that "you may depend upon it things & times are now altered" and that "economy is the order of the day."[64] He acknowledged that "we are overloaded with men, which this year must remain a dead burden upon the Dept."[65] In 1823, "aeconomy being the order of the day," in Stuart's words, the summer complement of men at Stuart's Lake was only four men, and no goods were to be sold or given to the Indians until their debts were paid.[66]

Logistics were also affected, with the new HBC trying to determine the best way of supplying New Caledonia – via the Peace or via the Columbia. In fact, one year before the merger, the NWC made another attempt to bring at least part of its outfit from the Columbia, while at the same time sending its returns, as usual, via the Peace. Evidently this attempt marked the first time since 1814 that the Fraser-Columbia route had been used by the brigade. Clerk James McDougall described the brigade's departure from Stuart's Lake in the post journal:

> Thursday 1st [of June]. Fine Warm Weather, About 9 A.M. Mr. [Hugh] Faries took his departure for the Columbia with J. B. Boucher our only Interpreter & eleven Men in three Canoes light with the exception of a few sundry articles Mr. Faries has taken for trade and only three hundred [dried] Salmon for Provisions, as Mr. Laroque [of Thompson's River] promised to send a man to this end of the [Fraser-Thompson] Portage between his place & Fraser's River with Horses & provisions between the 4th & 6th Instant which will be about the time he will reach that place & by all accounts he will be at Okanagan where he will meet his Outfit from the Sea on or about the 20th, But there owing to the heighth of the Water [river] & want of Provisions they will have to remain untill the 25th of July at least so that we cannot well expect them here before the beginning of October, at which time we will be anxiously looking out for them and not without reason ... for our Shop is empty & we have not goods sufficient to answer the demands of half the natives that will come in this month.

McDougall added, somewhat plaintively, that "I remain for the Summer with two Men, 3 women & 2 children and only 500 odd very indifferent Salmon, therefore we now entirely depend upon kind Providence and the natives for our Subsistance untill [salmon] come up the River [in August]."[67] Chief Trader Faries returned on 20 October in one boat and two canoes with eighteen men and sixty-nine pieces – an "enormous outfit." On his outward voyage he had lost two men and a canoe in a whirlpool in the Fraser while running a "dangerous" rapid. They were supposed to have met the "Columbia Gentry" (commissioned gentlemen, i.e., chief factors and chief traders) at Fort Okanagan, but the latter had not been prepared to meet them, so that the brigade had been obliged to proceed to Fort Nez Percés, whence it made two trips to Fort George for the New Caledonia outfit.[68] The rest of the district's outfit – roughly a quarter of it – reached McLeod's Lake via the Peace on 14 October, when three canoes with five men and twenty-three pieces arrived from Fort William, which they had left on 1 July in a flotilla of eight canoes.[69]

Again in 1821 and in 1822, New Caledonia was outfitted from the Columbia without sending its returns there, although the 1820 brigade had suffered a fatal accident and returned very late.[70] Determined to overcome these problems, the NWC in 1821 especially reassigned the veteran John Stuart to New Caledonia to render the "communication between this place [Stuart's Lake] and the Columbia not only practicable but perfectly established."[71] Not having to convey returns, and not wanting to return late, Stuart made an early start at the end of February – well before spring break-up, meaning that he had to use sled dogs and pack horses until he reached Okanagan Lake or even the Columbia River. Again Chief Factor McDougall described the departure of the brigade in the post journal:

> After Breakfast Mr. Stuart and his servant man, took his final Departure for the Columbia agreeable to the Plans settled upon [last year] between Mr. Faries and the Columbia Gentlemen to get our supplies from that quarter, as those Gentlemen told Mr. Faries it would be impossible to follow the original plan adopted by the Agents [of the NWC] in 1819, however it will be more impossible for us to carry on these last measures unless we have a double set of men for that express purpose, which will create expences whereas when the Plan was suggested it was to save and not incur expences, besides as long as people leave this for the Columbia in Winter, we are deprived of the services of all those men at the very moment we most stand in need of them for our transporting [of returns to McLeod's Lake for dispatch via the Peace], this Year Mr. Stuart is obliged to take no less than eighteen from us [leaving twenty-one in New Caledonia], having eight of the Columbia men to replace or return & we remain with the exception of a few, with a parcel of invalids that can be little depended upon.[72]

Here McDougall reveals that the NWC's directive to outfit New Caledonia from the Columbia dated from 1819 and that the Columbia District, for want of supplies or servants, had been unable to comply fully. He also discloses a long-standing shortcoming of New Caledonia – its shortage of personnel, especially for transport. Another handicap was the scarcity of winter provisions, including provisions for brigades. Stuart took 1,050 dried salmon for the trip to the Columbia and back.[73] He departed Fort George on 7 June and returned to Stuart's Lake on 11 October with ninety pieces.[74]

The 1822 brigade, comprising sixteen men under Stuart, did not leave Stuart's Lake for the Columbia until 1 May – after spring break-up – in order not to deprive the district of sufficient servants for the transport of returns to McLeod's Lake at the close of the 1821-22 outfit year (the end of winter);[75] these returns, 103 packs (1 pack = 50-60 beaver pelts and 85-90 pounds) of furs and 6 kegs (1 keg = 45-50 pounds or 10 gallons) of castoreum, left McLeod's Lake via the Peace in four canoes on

6 May.[76] The Columbia brigade returned in five months on 1 or 2 October, "all safe" and "with an ample outfit."[77]

Although this was the fastest time yet made by a brigade, and it returned with a sufficient outfit and without accident, during the next three years New Caledonia was outfitted from the Peace, not the Columbia (the Columbia District, however, continued to receive its supplies and dispatch its returns via the annual "London ship"). That decision, taken in early 1822 by the HBC's Governor and Committee in London, almost certainly did not meet with John Stuart's approval. In the spring of 1822, just before his departure for the Columbia as the leader of the brigade, he wrote: "I am ignorant by what line of communication this quarter [New Caledonia] will continue to receive its supplies, but as far as I can judge, the Columbia is the only place that can ever effectively answer the purpose."[78] Earlier that year he explained his preference: "I believe that most things of what the New Cala. Gentln. require, can be had in the Columbia, and such as gave me memoa. [memoranda] last Spring had their orders completed, nor in estimating the expences attending getting supplies from that quarter ought the Freight from England to Fort George be taken into account being merely nominal, for the freight of the New Cala. outfit does not cost a single farthing of additional expences & while a Vessel is required for the Columbia, it will be immaterial for the Coy. whether she is light or loaded."[79] Later, when his opinion was apparently solicited by the Council (chief factors and chief traders) of the Northern Department (convened every summer at York Factory by Governor Simpson), Stuart was more equivocal. He replied that he did not presume to offer an opinion, but he did assert that if the Peace route were chosen, then the outfit would have to be brought at least as far as Cumberland House for the New Caledonians to fetch, since it was "absolutely impossible" for them to venture farther and return in time to distribute the outfit by canoe before freeze-up, the district not having half the requisite number of servants and dogs. "Either quarter [east side or west side of the Rockies] will be attended with difficulties and great expences," he concluded.[80]

At any rate, at the end of February 1822, Beaver House informed Governor Simpson at York Factory that "hitherto New Caledonia has been supplied with Goods by way of the Columbia, but from all the information which we are at present possessed of we consider that it will be better to outfit that Country from York [Factory] ... as well as bring out the returns by that route." This measure would ensure that the Columbia District, without the necessity of having to outfit New Caledonia, would have enough supplies in store by the summer of 1823 to last for three years, that is, until the summer of 1826.[81] Governor Simpson gave three reasons for the change: (1) the "saving in the number of men would be great and the labour not much more"; (2) it was "desirable" to close the route between New Caledonia and the Columbia District "as it is establishing a road for [American] opposition"; and (3) it was "good policy" that as many district representatives as possible attend the annual summer meeting, and it would be possible for the gentlemen of New Caledonia to do so if they led the brigade eastwards to York Factory but not if they led it southwards to Fort George.[82] The first reason was presumably the most cogent. Chief Trader William Brown, however, supposed that the "line of communication" between New Caledonia and the Columbia had been abandoned for political reasons, namely, the restitution of Fort George, the Columbia depot, to the United States under the terms of the 1818 agreement to draw the international boundary along the forty-ninth parallel westwards from Lake of the Woods to the crest of the Rockies.[83] Whatever the reasons, by the end of 1822 Brown was able to report to Simpson that "that line of communication is now abandoned."[84]

The change was bound to displease Stuart, as well as put more pressure on the Peace route. Clerk James McDougall wrote Simpson that "by Mr. Stewarts account of the Route to the Columbia it is Plain he will not like after so much trouble to open that communication to see it broken up at the moment it proves practicable and easy," adding that so many more New Caledonians would now be plying the Peace route with returns and supplies that at least five more canoes would be needed at the Rocky Mountain Portage.[85] Stuart expressed his reaction in two district reports – that for Stuart's Lake of 1822-23 and that for McLeod's Lake of 1824. In the Stuart's Lake report he declared that New Caledonia's returns had been

> of late years rather improving ... and as far as I can judge it has in a great measure altogether arisen from the facility of getting the Country supplied from the Columbia, which mode was adopted in 1820. From that quarter even the most distant establishments received their supplies by water, not later than the middle of October, leaving a sufficient time for collecting the provisions required for the winter, previous to the navigation being closed and affording the means of afterwards having the people, in exploring the Country and in Trading excursions to the distant Villages, thereby getting acquainted with the different Indians.

The chief factor added:

In my opinion the alteration that would prove most beneficial to New
Caledonia in the way of collecting returns and extending the Trade would be
to resort to the old channel of having the Country supplied from the Columbia.
It is said to be attended with great expences, but I cannot perceive it, the party
going to the Columbia for the goods would be fed chiefly on Salmon, the
natural production of New Caledonia and it would cost the District 500 per
cent less than their maintenance will cost on the East side of the Mountains
and it has been proved last summer [1822] that the New Caledonians of themselves without any assistance from the Columbians could go to and bring their
Outfit from Fort George, but that channel being as I conceive definitively
abandoned it will be unnecessary to advert to it.[86]

But Stuart did advert to the matter again in his 1824 district report,
using nearly the same words to make the very same points.[87] The HBC's
failure to follow Stuart's advice may have contributed to his feeling that
he had outlived his usefulness to the company. "It is now Seventeen years
since I first Established this place," he lamented from Stuart's Lake at
the beginning of 1823, "and next Spring, I shall have served the Hudsons
Bay Company two years in New Caledonia, but daily experience con-
vinces me more and more, that I am no longer fit for this quarter [because
of illness], and by the time every other Chief Factor have lived two years
on dry Salmon, I shall be in my grave."[88] Stuart felt that he enjoyed less
independence as a chief factor of the HBC than he had as a wintering
partner of the NWC, and that he lacked Governor Simpson's full confidence and therefore should retire.[89] He was transferred in 1824 but not
superannuated until 1839, long after seeing his opinion vindicated by the
company's decision of 1825 to revert to the Fraser-Columbia route.

CHAPTER 2

Linking the Oregon Country

*A diversity of opinion has been found to exist previous
to the [1821] Coalition, and even subsequently whether the
Profits of the Trade [of New Caledonia], and facilities [are]
greater by going to York Factory for the Outfits or immediately
to the Columbia River – both routes have been pursued and
since the Union it has been decided – the Returns shall be
taken to the Columbia – and as shipping comes out regularly
[from London to Fort Vancouver] – the Outfit for the Post
[Fort Alexandria] (and the District) are taken in.*

– CHIEF TRADER JOSEPH MCGILLIVRAY, 1828[1]

THE PEACE RIVER ROUTE

From the beginning, New Caledonia had always dispatched its returns, and usually received its supplies, via the Fraser-Peace-Athabasca-Churchill route. The returns of the district's several posts had to be pressed and packed and then delivered by sled dogs to the depot of Stuart's Lake by the middle of February for checking and then forwarding to the departure point of McLeod's Lake before spring break-up.[2] "The transportation of the Furs must if possible be accomplished before the warm weather sets in – as after that they cannot be carried without being damaged," wrote Chief Factor Stuart's successor, William Connolly, from Stuart's Lake in 1825.[3] So the occasional mild winter was disadvantageous. The thin river ice of the moderate winter of 1824-25 exposed the musher of the January shipment of furs from Fort Alexandria to Stuart's Lake, Clerk George McDougall, to the "greatest difficulty and dangers I ever experienced in this part of the Country."[4] New Caledonia's winter of 1821-22, reported John Stuart, was "uncommonly mild," and this fact "not a little retarded our progress in the way of collecting Furs and getting them conveyed to the place of embarkation [McLeod's Lake]." But of "most detriment," he added, was the "want of Dogs." "It is not too much to say that circumstanced as we are at present, one Dog would be of more essential service to the concern in New

Cala. than three men."[5] Later the same year Stuart stressed the same point: "But Dogs is the most necessary article that can be sent to New Cal. They are the tools with which we labour."[6]

Dogs, however, were not infrequently in short supply, dying of starvation in the long, cold winters following the periodic failure of the summer salmon run. "Some of the Company's Dogs I apprehend will starve to death and it is impossible for me to save them for want of Salmon," lamented Stuart a month before the August salmon run of 1820.[7] Dogs were also in danger of being eaten by starving natives or hungry whites. Brigaders not infrequently ate dog flesh and horse meat. Simon Fraser testified that dog was a "favourite dish" of Canadien voyageurs,[8] and Canadien boatmen on the Columbia considered it "choice food."[9] To them, dog flesh was "mutton," which they preferred boiled.[10] In New Caledonia fattened dogs were called "New Caledonia bears," and they were usually saved for special occasions, such as 25 December 1824 at Fort Alexandria: "this being Christmas Day, the Men did nothing & got a dram each with 2 Dogs as their Christmas Goose."[11]

Break-up normally occurred in late March, and the North canoes left McLeod's Lake for Fort Dunvegan on the middle Peace and Fort Chipewyan on Lake Athabasca with the returns (furs and castoreum) in late April or early May. The 1824 brigade left McLeod's Lake on 12 May, made the Rocky Mountain Portage on the 14th and left it on the 16th, reached Fort Chipewyan on 28 May and departed on 6 June, and arrived at York Factory on 29 June.[12] The 1825 brigade left McLeod's Lake on 5 May in five canoes with twenty-four packs of furs and one keg of castoreum, as well as 220 dried salmon per man.[13] The last brigade in 1826 of sixteen men also left on 5 May but with forty-four pieces of furs plus castoreum (and an additional four men went as far as the eastern end of the Rocky Mountain [Giscombe] Portage in order to "accelerate their passage" and to "add strength to the party in case of an attack from the Beaver Indians").[14] The 1826 brigade comprised only two canoes because the returns were supposed to have been shipped via the Columbia route, which, however, could not accommodate all of the returns in the wake of the death of most of the brigade's pack horses at Fort Alexandria during the very cold and snowy winter of 1825-26.

Shortly after leaving McLeod's Lake the brigades had to portage to the headwaters of the Peace system – "but eight hundred yards over a fine level Country," according to Stuart.[15] A couple of days took them to the Rocky Mountain Portage, which bypassed the Peace River Canyon, the foremost obstacle on the entire route. A westbound Simon Fraser found in 1806 that the navigation of the upper Peace "is very bad and dangerous," and at the portage "the road is amazing bad and the Portage is at least 14 or 15 miles long."[16] The chief difficulties were steep hills and fallen trees, which were so formidable that not infrequently canoes had to be kept at either end of the portage in order to avoid the necessity of carrying them. The portage was so crucial that a NWC post had been founded on its eastern end by James McDougall in 1804; the post was considered part of New Caledonia until 1813, when it was transferred to the Peace River District, only to be abandoned a year later (in 1820 it was ordered re-established, and it was intended to implement this order in the fall of 1823, but it was not done).[17]

William Connolly, who had crossed the portage more than once, recalled that "the difficulties which were experienced in carrying over this Portage, even when the Road was in its most favorable state, were at all times very great."[18] The "old track" across the portage was thirteen to fourteen miles long and "very ruggid," and it took a brigade of canoes at least a week to cross it.[19] In early 1822 Stuart complained to Faries that "the Portage you know to be in a bad state and I beg you will get the road cleared of fallen trees & in other respects improved as much as possible and ... I have no doubt that the distance might be shortened and many of the hills avoided."[20] It eventuated that Stuart had to do this work himself. Returning to New Caledonia at the head of the brigade in October of 1823, he measured the portage and found it "but very few yards short of twelve Miles from waters edge to waters edge." Stuart also improved the crossing by clearing the track of windfalls, shortening it, and rerouting part of it through less hilly terrain.[21] Connolly used the "new track" in the fall of 1824 and reported that it was thirteen miles long and still "much encumbered with fallen trees," as well as dotted with several hills; his westbound brigade took nine days to cross it.[22] Chief Trader Archibald McDonald crossed the portage with Governor Simpson at the beginning of September 1828 – three years after its abandonment by the brigade – and on the second day suffered "about a mile of the worst road in Christendom ... with unspeakable misery to the poor men ... no people having passed this way for the last three years, and, of course, no clearance made in a road that at best must be an infamous one."[23] Five years later Clerk John McLean was equally appalled: "... we reached the portage ... on the 10th [of October], the crossing of which took us eight days, being fully thirteen miles in length, and excessively bad road, leading sometimes through swamps and morasses, then ascending and descending steep hills, and for at least one-third of the distance so obstructed by fallen trees as to render it all but impassable. I consider the passage of this portage the most laborious duty the Company's servants have to perform in any part of the territory; and, as the voyageurs say, 'He that passes it with his share of a canoe's cargo may call himself a man.'"[24]

Indeed, the portage track was so difficult that in desperation a brigade would occasionally run the rapids rather than carry their canoes in order to save time and toil, but this expedient was risky, as James McDougall ruefully reported to Governor Simpson in the fall of 1823:

> Having nothing worthy [of] your notice to communicate I have postponed addressing you untill the present to inform you of our progress which I am sorry to say has neither been prosperous nor expeditious owing not only to the Lading of the Craft being heavy but also to my having unguardedly allowed two of the Canoes to come up by the Rapids of the Rocky Mountain Portage in hopes of their gaining time as the carrying place was realy bad for men to cross canoes – and crafts having already with heavier loads come up those Rapids safe and in a shorter time than I could expect them to take by the Portage, but contrary to my expectations they took nine days, broke a canoe and lost one Roll of Tobacco one Bale of Parchment Skins and the agres [equipment] of a canoe with the Provisions, which oblidged me upon hearing of the Misfortune to return to the east end of the Portage get a canoe Crossed & trade Provisions to enable us to reach this Place [Stuart's Lake] there being fortunately Indians on the spot, during which time the men got up with the Cargo they had coming up the Rapids and carelessly put their Cargo so nigh the water['s] Edge that the dogs rumaging during the night overturned two Bales of Leather [hides] & Babiche [thongs] into the River which notwithstanding our researches could not be found.[25]

Eight of Governor Simpson's 1828 entourage tried paddling instead of carrying the two canoes; one of them "had a most miraculous escape," coming "within an ace of going to perdition," the navigation being "excessively bad and hazardous."[26]

The journey from the portage to the depot (York Factory) was relatively uneventful, being downstream and unobstructed. The 1825 eastbound brigade reached Fort Dunvegan at the eastern end of the Rocky Mountain Portage on 16 May after leaving McLeod's Lake on 5 May, when it was discovered that "the coverings of the Canoes were extremely bad & by no means fit to secure the Loadings from damage" (such was the importance of "leather" for wrapping and covering freight); the brigade reached York Factory on 6 July.[27] Not surprisingly, the furs often reached the depot in defective condition. Governor Simpson estimated in 1825 that New Caledonia's returns were reduced in value by at least 25 percent by damage suffered in transit.[28]

Westbound brigades usually left the Bayside for New Caledonia in the middle of July and reached McLeod's Lake in late October – a long upstream journey of three to three and a half months. The 1823 brigade returned to McLeod's Lake on 25 October in seven canoes with thirty-six men, an "ample" outfit, and "a good supply of Dogs";[29] the 1824 brigade left York Factory on 27 July in four canoes with thirty men and ninety-nine pieces and made McLeod's Lake on 30 October;[30] the 1825 brigade departed the depot on 12 July in four canoes with four men and eighteen pieces each plus five other men to crew a fifth canoe at Split Lake, and the brigade arrived at McLeod's Lake on 31 October in six canoes with twenty-three pieces each.[31]

The westbound journey was lengthy and tiring but otherwise straightforward. The 1826 brigade's experience was unusual: owing to the "extraordinary height of the waters," the brigaders "experienced on their return, the utmost difficulty, and from the unexpected length of time they took suffered much from starvation."[32] Sometimes, too, personnel problems arose. In the fall of 1825 three men deserted Connolly's brigade at Portage de la Loche, and a fourth man was disabled by disease (probably venereal), so that the brigade's progress was "materially" slowed; the crews were reduced to four men per canoe by the western end of the Rocky Mountain Portage, and several of the men were "young hands unaccustomed to the Voyage and worn out with fatigue," so that McLeod's Lake was not reached until 31 October.[33] Connolly wrote an ambivalent assessment of the brigaders:

> The men are I believe the greatest Black guards in the [Indian] Country, and as much given to theft as the *Carriers* themselves – Their conduct on the voyage from the Depot [York Factory] last season [1824] was extremely bad. They stole a considerable quantity of Property such as Flour, sugar etc. During the winter [of 1824-25] they behaved well, for want of opportunities to do otherwise and performed their duty with alacrity, and so far I am satisfied with them – In General they are an active set of fellows – for a Country such as this [New Caledonia], where the labour is perpetual and the living very bad, none other can answer.[34]

Upon arrival at McLeod's Lake the outfit was unloaded, forwarded (with the exception of McLeod's Lake's portion) to the depot of Stuart's Lake, divided, and distributed to the remaining posts by pack horses before freeze-up. The undermanned 1825 brigade, which had reached McLeod's Lake on 31 October, was unable to forward the outfit to Stuart's Lake until 12 November, whereupon three days were spent dividing it, and not until the 16th were the different lots sent to their respective destinations.[35]

Upon the arrival of the 1824 outfit at McLeod's Lake, it was found by Connolly to be damaged and pilfered:

> Sunday 31st [October] Some of the Goods were unpacked & what was found wet was hung up in the Houses to dry – The outfit for this place was laid aside & consists of about 18 pieces, the charge of which & of the Fort, I gave to Mr. [John] Tod, who I have no doubt is adequate to the task of conducting the Business to advantage – Having so little Room, the work proceeds but slowly & I fear that some confusion will occur – The Goods are in general wet & otherwise in bad order, & the weather so bad its impossible to dry them out of doors – On examining the whole Pieces it appears that hardly a Keg of sugar or Keg of Flour has not been broke open – The men of course committed these thefts & ought of consequence to suffer, much blame also attaches to the Guide, [Charles?] Ross, who appears to be a sleepy blockhead – The property intended to be Transported immediately to Fort St. James was also laid aside – as much of which as can be dispensed with at the other Posts will be forwarded to Alexandria, which is by far the most remote & consequently the most difficult to be supplied.[36]

Then the track from McLeod's Lake to Stuart's Lake, being "hardly passable," had to be cleared for the pack horses by three men. It took a day to find the horses, which carried two pieces of forty-eight pounds each. Twenty-five pieces were sent to Stuart's Lake and twelve to Alexandria. Finally, Connolly reported, "the canoes being no longer required this season were buried in the ground to preserve them for the Spring in case circumstances should not permit us to procure new ones – Bark, I understand is scarce, and with such an indolent man as Ross I hardly expect any will be provided."[37]

John Stuart in particular bemoaned the logistical predicament of New Caledonia arising from its dependence upon the Peace route. He asserted in his report on the district for 1822-23 that its principal disadvantage was its remoteness from the York Factory depot:

> The greatest of many disadvantages New Caledonia lies under is the difficulty of access; more time and labour being required to convey the goods required, from Fort Chepewyan to the first Establishment, McLeods Lake, where the navigation terminates, than from Norway House to Fort Chepewyan, – from McLeods Lake to Saint James the next Establishment, the distance across land is not less than 100 Miles and the other Establishments is from 60 to about 350 Miles distant from Saint James, and as the navigation terminates at

McLeods Lake, the other establishments must receive their supplies from there across land in winter, an immense labour and when added to the burden of conveying the returns to the place of embarkation and collecting provisions, leaves not a moment to the people, in fact, so hard is the labour that when added to the bad living, scarcely any thing but dried Salmon of the worst quality, seldom any man, even the most robust, without destroying his constitution, can remain in New Caledonia more than two or three years.[38]

Governor Simpson rated the brigade system the "most tedious harrassing and expensive transport in the Indian Country."[39] Because of their harder labour, New Caledonia's boatmen [bowsmen and steersmen] and middlemen were paid, respectively, £27 and £22 annually in 1824, whereas those of the Columbia District were given £22 and £17 and those of the Athabasca District £22 and £19, respectively.[40] William Connolly also emphasized New Caledonia's logistical difficulties. In his report on the district for 1824-25 he declared that its two principal drawbacks were the "remoteness from the depot" and the onerous transport, which "occupies the whole of the people to the exclusion of all other duties – and leaves no time for any attempts at improvements."[41] He was determined to eliminate these two disadvantages by switching the supply route to the Columbia, thereby permitting the earlier dispatch of returns and the much earlier receipt of goods, and by relying more upon horses and less upon canoes. When the Council of the Northern Department approved the switch in 1825, he was delighted:

> The Greatest disadvantages under which the District [New Caledonia] laboured were its remoteness from the Depot [York Factory], and the difficulties attending the transportation of the outfit & returns to and from the different Establishments – by the former our outfits arrived so late in the Autumn that the Indians could not be supplied in time to take full advantage of that season for Hunting – And the latter occupied every individual in the District throughout the Winter to the exclusion of all other duties – These Bars are now happily removed by the change of system at present introduced of receiving our supplies from Fort Vancouver instead of York Factory – By this route our early arrival will enable the Indians to receive their supplies at a period to allow them time to add much to their usual Hunts – And so the respective establishments, (excepting McLeods Lake) will receive their outfits by water. The time therefore that was hitherto occupied in the transportation, will be more beneficially employed in improving the Trade.[42]

However, although both the New Caledonia and Columbia Districts, which were united to form the Columbia Department in 1826, used the

Fraser-Columbia route from that date for transporting their returns and supplies, they continued to receive two articles – "leather" and mail – from the "east side the mountains."[43]

THE LEATHER BRIGADE

"Leather" was dressed moose (especially), deer, elk, or bison hide, which was used mainly for the "carrying service" throughout the Columbia Department.[44] It was "scarce" west of the Rockies, however, so it was brought from the "east side," where it was abundant.[45] Leather was particularly indispensable in New Caledonia as *babiche* (thongs for making snares and nets), pack cords (for tying bales of furs and securing horse packs), sinews (for making snowshoes), and "parchment" (for making moccasins). The district's bourgeois, William Connolly, stressed leather's importance. "Leather is in universal demand," he reported in 1824, adding that "the trade of the Country cannot be carried on without leather, the natives prefer it to almost any other commodity."[46] Later the same year he reiterated that "leather is an indispensable article, it being not only the means of saving other property [in trade with the Indians], but is in many cases preferred [by the Indians] to any commodity we have." Connolly said that five hundred to six hundred moose skins could be sold to the Indians yearly.[47] In the 1827-28 outfit year, New Caledonia required five hundred dressed moose and red deer skins, thirty parchment skins, two thousand fathoms (twelve thousand feet) of pack cords, seventy pounds of babiche, and thirty pounds of sinews.[48]

Leather was one of the HBC's chief articles of trade with New Caledonia's natives because, as Governor Simpson reported, "large animals are very scarce throughout the District."[49] John Stuart confirmed that New Caledonia was "nearly altogether destitute of large animals,"[50] and another longtime servant, John Harriott, rated the district the "worst country for game he ever saw."[51] As a result, New Caledonia was obliged to import leather, as well as "grease" (tallow for pemmican, soap, and candles); for the same reason, it was obliged to depend heavily upon salmon. Simpson warned Beaver House in 1825 that the "principal difficulty" stemming from the shift of the brigade route from the Peace to the Columbia was the impossibility of getting leather in the Cordillera.[52] A year later he cautioned the chief factors of the Columbia Department's two districts, McLoughlin and Connolly, that henceforth York Factory would have neither the inventory nor the transport for supplying New Caledonia with anything other than leather, and that even leather could only be furnished "at very great inconvenience."

He added that he preferred that leather be obtained from the Columbia quarter.[53]

At the turn of the century, the elk (*biche*) of the Willamette Valley had been the source of the "leather war dresses" so highly prized by the Northwest Coast Indians, and during the 1810s the source of the "great quantity" of leather supplied to Fort George by the Willamette freemen.[54] But in 1821 most of the Willamette freemen left for the Snake Country,[55] probably because the valley had been overhunted and over-trapped.[56] In early 1823 Alexander Ross reported from Fort Nez Percés that the Snake Country "has of late become the General rendezvous for all worthless free men."[57] And in 1825 McLoughlin informed Beaver House that "formerly when there were many freemen in the Multnomah [Willamette] and not a sufficiency of Beaver to employ them they hunted animals [elk] and gave a great quantity of Leather, since they have diminished to the present number we never could get a sufficient quantity for the expenditure of the place [Fort George] and always took of the old Stock till it is all expended and this year are very short of that article for Shoes for the men."[58] Leather could be had within the "lower country," however, from the Blackfoot via the Flathead Post, whose summer 1830 returns included – besides 294 beaver – 100 *apichimons* (hide saddle blankets – usually made of buffalo-hide – and fur pack wrappings), 90 *parflèches* (hide wrappings for sacks), 80 ½ pack cords, 80 babiches, 60 pack saddles, 9 buffalo robes, and 4 leather tents.[59] But this amount was not enough for the New Caledonia District, too.

The deficiency was overcome by forwarding this "indispensable commodity" with the Columbia express canoe from Fort Assiniboine in the Saskatchewan District to Fort Okanagan via the Athabasca Pass and the Columbia River initially and to Tête Jaune Cache via the Yellowhead Pass and the Fraser River eventually.[60] Connolly believed that the Athabasca Pass to Fort Okanagan route would be the "cheapest safest and easiest method."[61] But in the fall of 1825, James McMillan had been ordered "to survey the track between Jaspers House and the head waters of this [Fraser] River, in order to ascertain the practicability of transporting the leather etc required for this District [New Caledonia] from the Sascatchewan to the latter place, from which it can be brought down & forwarded to every Post in the district."[62] McMillan found that the Yellowhead Pass would "admit of Horses travelling through it without much difficulty" and that the route "will be very practicable for Horses," so that Saskatchewan leather "can be easily introduced into this District [New Caledonia]."[63] He reported that "the Road by land [through the pass] is not so bad as the Columbia [Athabasca] Portage and I see no difficulty in supplying Western Caledonia with leather by that route as horses can pass with ease."[64]

The Yellowhead, which became known as the Leather Pass, was named after Tête Jaune, the *nom du pays* of an Iroquois or "halfbreed"[65] guide, Pierre Bostonais, who knew the route and the cache at its western end.[66] McMillan found, too, that the Fraser from the cache to the "Forks" (Fraser-Nechako junction at Fort George) was "interrupted only by one Portage and a few Rapids, which at low Water can be passed without any danger."[67] This route from Jasper's, or Rocky Mountain, House through the Yellowhead Pass and along the Fraser River to Fort George became known as the Leather Track. From 1826 it served the Columbia Department, with the exception of the period from 1830 through 1835, when the HBC sent leather to New Caledonia via the Peace route; in 1835, however, Chief Factor Peter Dease of Stuart's Lake successfully urged a return to the Yellowhead route because it would save time and enable the distribution of the leather to New Caledonia's scattered posts before freeze-up.[68]

The leather usually arrived at the "sources of Fraser's River" in late September from the "east side the mountains." So in late September or early October, two canoes and six to eight men, plus any passengers (usually ailing, resigning, or retiring servants), paddled from Stuart's Lake up the Fraser to Tête Jaune Cache, from which they hurriedly returned (minus passengers) before freeze-up with the "annual supply of leather," either receiving it from the Jasper's House men or, if late, retrieving it from the cache. Lateness or failure of the August salmon run delayed the leather brigade, as Connolly reported in 1827: "The voyage for the Leather [from Stuart's Lake] will occupy the greatest part of our men for upwards of a Month, and as they cannot be sent on this service until we can procure a Stock of dry Salmon, which I do not expect will be earlier than the middle of next Month, the fall will therefore be far advanced before they can return."[69]

In 1824 and in 1825, before the abandonment of the Peace route, there was a "scarcity" of leather in New Caledonia, and it was "injurious" to the trade."[70] In those two years the district received only half of the 500 to 600 moose skins that were required.[71] In the fall of 1825 only 300 moose skins were brought by the leather brigade, so that, Connolly wrote, "leather will be as scarce as last Year if not more so." "Of this number," he continued, "upwards of 70 will be required for the Gentlemen & Men, who no more than the Carriers can walk barefoot in the winter, there will of consequence remain no more than 230 to be divided amongst four Establishments."[72]

The year 1826 saw the first delivery of leather via the Yellowhead route. It did not arrive until 3 November but contained 475 dressed skins, 55 parchment skins, 360 pounds of pack cords, and 30 pounds of sinews, all "generally of a good quality, and well adapted to the taste of the Carriers."[73] The 1827 leather brigade, comprising three large canoes with ten servants, three Indians, and 1,140 dried salmon, was led by the veteran Waccan, or Wacca, the nickname of Jean Baptiste Boucher, a mixed blood who was rated by Connolly as "the best Interpreter in New Caledonia."[74] He departed Stuart's Lake on 22 September for Tête Jaune Cache, where one of the canoes was to be left for the conveyance of personnel expected from York Factory and the other two were to return with the leather. The New Caledonia brigade reached the cache around 14 October, several days before the Saskatchewan brigade, and returned with enough leather for more than a year – 703 dressed moose skins, 194 dressed buffalo skins, and 88 parchment skins – plus eight recruits. Upon arrival at Stuart's Lake, however, the leather was found to be "all wet & Frozen," and "many" of the skins were "very much damaged, and not a few perfectly rotten."[75] The 1828 leather brigade – two canoes with eight men – departed Stuart's Lake on 4 October and returned on 12 November, having reached Tête Jaune Cache on 27 October and found the leather "very carelessly laid up and ... unguarded." The 529 large and 92 small dressed moose skins, 87 full and 3 half buffalo skins, 35 parchment skins, 11 lodge skins, 191 pounds of pack cords, and 40 pounds of sinews were all of "good quality."[76] The 1829 leather brigade of two canoes and seven men (plus two outgoing invalids) left on 4 October and returned on 26 November after a "very long absence" with twenty-eight bales of leather and no pack cords, the Saskatchewan brigade having been delayed by early ice in the Athabasca River.[77] In 1830 the Council of the Northern Department ordered that 650 dressed moose skins, 100 pounds of babiche, 2,000 fathoms (12,000 feet) of pack cords, and 50 pieces of grease be sent to New Caledonia in the fall via the Peace route from Fort Dunvegan.[78] The full amount of leather, minus the grease, reached New Caledonia from Fort Chipewyan.[79] Five years later the leather brigade reverted permanently to the Yellowhead route.

THE ANNUAL EXPRESS

The overland express, or packet, was commenced by the NWC in order to expedite the conveyance to Fort William of the annual report on the Columbia District. The three-month trip was performed in a special light canoe that left Fort George at the beginning of April and reached Fort

William at the beginning of July; it then left the Lakehead in the middle of July and reached the mouth of the Columbia in the middle of October.[80] Under the HBC, the express – usually three boats, each with nine or ten men, plus a few passengers – took longer. The spring (York) express left Fort Vancouver in the middle of March with mail ("paper trunks," containing letters, reports, journals) and servants who had resigned or retired or who had been furloughed or relocated and made York Factory in late June or early July; it left Hudson Bay as the fall (Vancouver) express in late July with mail and recruits or veterans and made the lowermost Columbia in late October or early November.

The principal impediment was the Athabasca Portage, which stretched 120 miles through the Rockies between Jasper's House on the headwaters of the Athabasca River and the Boat Encampment on the "Big Bend" of the Columbia River, where a tributary, the Canoe River, was "celebrated among North Westers for the quality of the birch bark."[81] At the Boat Encampment, where the painter Paul Kane "found the senerey the most beautifull that I have aver seene in aney cuntrey,"[82] the Columbia boats were "hauled up" and a cache of supplies and equipment made; from there snowshoes and horses were used as far as Jasper's House, where boats were waiting. The portage impressed even the peripatetic Simpson in 1825: "The scenery here is wild and majestic beyond description, the track in many places nearly impassible; and it appears extraordinary how any human being should have stumbled on a pass through such a formidable barrier which nature seems to have placed here for the purpose of interdicting all communication between the East [and] West sides of the Continent."[83] Even the continental divide, however, did not slow the express much.[84]

The only faster HBC journeys were Governor Simpson's "flying visits" to the Indian Country. In the fall of 1841 he travelled from the Red River Settlement to Fort Colvile – a distance he estimated at nineteen hundred miles – in forty-seven days, spending eleven hours per day in the saddle and killing more than two hundred horses in the process,[85] prompting John Tod to quip that "he at least forms an exception from the general rule 'that great bodies move slow.'"[86] It was one of these speedy tours of inspection – that of 1824-25 to the Pacific Slope – that prompted the reorganization of HBC operations there, including the rerouting of New Caledonia's lifeline to the Columbia.

CHAPTER 3

Reforming the Oregon Country

The trade of this side the mountain if sufficiently extended
and properly managed I make bold to say can not only be
made to rival, but to yield double the profit that any other part
of North America does for the Amount of Capital employed
therein but in order to turn it to the best advantage New
Caledonia must be included and the Coasting trade must
be carried on in conjunction with the inland business.

— GOVERNOR GEORGE SIMPSON, 1825[1]

In early 1822, a year after his appointment as governor of the Northern Department, George Simpson was instructed by the Governor and Committee in London to appraise the Columbia District.[2] Its returns were "falling off," and among HBC servants there was a "general feeling against it" as a "bad, barren Country,"[3] probably owing to its inferior beaver pelts, more belligerent natives, more turbulent rivers, more monotonous diet, keener American competition, and rainy coast.[4] But the governor had to finish a tour of inspection of the Athabasca District first, and he was unable to cross the Rockies until 1824. From the autumn of that year until the spring of the next he investigated the Cordilleran region that the HBC had gained only three years earlier from the NWC. Simpson, whose twin idols were industry and economy, concluded that it was "expensive and unprofitable," so much so that a "total stranger to the Country and trade could not range more wide of the mark." "It is absolutely necessary that a radical change should take place in the whole system," he declared.[5] He wrote:

Everything appears to me on the Columbia on too extended a scale *except the Trade* and when I say that that is confined to Four permanent Establishments [Forts George, Nez Percés, Okanagan, and Spokane, Thompson's River and the Flathead Post being winter posts only] the returns of which do not amount to 20,000 Beaver & Otters altho the country has been occupied upwards of Fourteen Years I feel that a very Severe reflection is cast on those who have

had the management of the Business, as on looking at the prodigious expences
that have been incurred and the means at their command, I cannot help thinking that no economy has been observed, that little exertion has been used,
and that sound judgment has not been exercised but that mismanagement and
extravagance has been the order of the day.[6]

The Columbia District, Simpson continued, offered an "ample field" for
putting company business on an "improved footing,"[7] and he believed
that even with only "tolerable" management the district could become
"our most important and valuable Department."[8] The effort would be
worthwhile, he explained, because the Columbia quarter would not only
yield a "handsome recompense" but also enable the company to "recruit"
the "overwrought" trade of the east side of the mountains.[9]

The governor's self-styled "scheme for the remodelling of the business
of this side the mountain generally and for the extension of its trade"
was drafted during the winter of 1824-25 with the "assistance and advice
of some of the Commissioned Gentlemen."[10] The plan entailed a series
of measures designed to increase returns and decrease expenses.[11] Simpson envisioned a "fine field for extension of the trade" northwards and
coastwards in particular. The coast trade should be entered "with spirit
and without delay" in order to eliminate the American "coasters" (trading vessels) and terminate their tapping of land furs from the interior
through coastal native middlemen. New Caledonia and the Columbia
quarter should be merged into one department – the Columbia Department (1827) – because the coast trade would yield the HBC double the
profit on capital of any other part of the Indian Country only if the two
districts were united and the coasting trade were pursued in conjunction
with the inland trade.[12]

For a "variety of important reasons," the governor deemed it "highly
expedient" to transact all of the company's business on the west side
of the mountains from one depot. He recommended that Fort George
be abandoned and that the "principal Depot" be situated at the mouth
of the Fraser River, where it would be "more central for the general
business."[13] Accordingly, Fort Langley was founded near the Fraser's
mouth in 1827, but it did not become the depot. Fort George was not
vacated but simply replaced as the "grand depot" in 1824-25 by a new
post – Fort Vancouver – on a more arable site on the northern side of
the Columbia, which proved superior to the Fraser as a route to the
interior.

Simpson reduced expenses by cutting servants and supplies. The
number of servants was "nearly double what is necessary or that the trade

can afford." The complement of personnel in the Columbia District alone was reduced from 151 officers and men to 87 for an annual saving of £2,000 in wages alone. The number of brigaders was halved from forty to twenty. The governor was especially critical of transport; far too many manufactures, provisions, and passengers were being conveyed. He cautioned McLoughlin to examine requisitions closely in order to prevent the "prodigious" accumulation of unnecessary goods; otherwise, the "Columbia will continue the same expensive and unprofitable Department it has hitherto been." He instructed the chief factor to discontinue the brigade's use of "expensive" oil cloths, "as there is scarcely a Shower of Rain at the season the craft are on the voyage," and "to protect the Furs a few pieces of Leather" could be used (the trade goods needed no covering, he said). Sails and rigging were also "expensive unnecessary appendages," since the brigaders had an "abundance of time to perform the voyage and the exercise of paddling is conducive to health," and if they wanted "to relieve their arms they can make a shift with their Blankets when the wind favours." And provision bagging – "an expensive article" – was to be discarded in favour of wooden kegs, "which do not cost half so much." Even the "waste and extravagance" of tents were regarded as "really shameful" by him. "Every *Boy* in the Columbia must sport a Tent," he found, although all of the officers admitted that they were simply fashionable and really unnecessary. "I have continued to travel many thousand miles in this country without a Tent and I see no reason why our Clerks should be more fashionable than our Governors," he declared, adding that henceforth they "can in a few minutes with their Axes make a good comfortable Hut which is more secure than Russia sheeting and on the coast a mat 'Bear' [bear rug] is better than any Tent."

Furthermore, Simpson felt that too many of the servants had families "which are ruinous to the Trade as their consumption of Provisions reduces the Post[s] to starvation." He ordered McLoughlin to replace the culprits with single men; only officers and tradesmen were to be permitted to keep families at the posts. Also, no men were to be allowed to "take [native] women"; "if every man is allowed to take a woman at pleasure as heretofore," he wrote, a "great proportion of what otherwise would be gains must be consumed in providing them with imported provisions from the Coast." The governor was confident that if these steps were taken, "there will be no difficulty in maintaining the poorest establishment in the Columbia." Also, he forbade the brigades to hire "extra men" or to convey women to the coast (a practice "which has so long been a source of expense and trouble") and the hunting-trapping expeditions to include single women or families (an "inexhaustible source of trouble and vexation"), freemen, if possible ("even the very best of our Freemen are but bad and dangerous subjects"), or "luxuries" such as tents and grog.

Especially the heavy conveyance and consumption of "European Provisions" appalled Simpson. He learned in the autumn of 1824 that "for several years past" five or six boats and thirty to forty "extra men" had been used to take the district's outfit up the Columbia for the interior because of the heavy requisition of "eatable drinkable and *domestic concerns* [country families]," whereas two boats with eighty to one hundred pieces and sixteen men would have sufficed, provided the interior posts lived off the land. In the winter of 1824-25 he found that during the last three years (1822-24) an average of 645 pieces had been transported from Fort George to the interior annually, comprising 462 pieces of victuals and luxuries and only 183 pieces of goods, private orders, and equipment; this amount, he said, ought to be reduced to 200 pieces altogether in four boats with thirty-six men. Chief Factor Alexander Kennedy of the depot elaborated:

> The provisions sent annually from Fort George to the interior including that for the voyage forms more than half of the boats cargoes which is a considerable drawback on the profits and independent of the cost it requires a greater number of men to transport it. The following is a list of the provisions sent into the Interior [for Forts Nez Percés, Okanagan, and Spokane] summer 1824 including the expenditure on the voyage 772 lbs Beef 990 lbs Pork 244 lbs butter 10328 lbs Flour 92 lbs Rice 1258 lbs Sugar 1985 lbs tallow 57 Gallons Molasses 20 bushels Indian corn & Meal 20 bushels Beans 53 bushels Pease 69 lbs of Tea & 12 lbs Chocolate.[14]

Such heavy transport, Simpson found, had been excused by the fact "that the brigade must come up formidable on account of the Hostility of the Natives that a ship must come out annually and that therefore the provisions cost nothing beyond Invoice prices which are cheaper than dog or Horse flesh. But," he retorted, "from the best information I am able to collect 35 Officers and Men is a sufficient force to pass with safety from one end of the Columbia to the other, that that number is adequate to bring up all the Outfits and sufficient to establish all the Country above Fort George a few summer men excepted & further that a dog & Horse flesh is expensive food it need not be indulged in as the waters at little Cost and trouble can supply all Wants [i.e., fish] in that way." He told McLoughlin that for the upriver brigade four boats manned by eight men each, or – if the cargo were reduced by eight pieces in order to make the boats lighter for the portages – five boats manned by six men each would suffice.

The governor stressed that the servants could meet most of their food needs by catching fish, shooting game, picking berries, and digging roots, that is, by eating "country produce" – plentiful, tasty, and nutritious, as well as economical – in place of "imported provisions." Columbia salmon were esteemed for their large size and high quality – the largest in the entire department[15] and "perhaps as fine as any in the world," according to the Astorian and Nor'Wester Alexander Ross.[16] He added that the river's sturgeon were "tender and well flavoured," as well as "very abundant, and of uncommon size ... many of them weighing upwards of 700 pounds."[17] The Fraser was equally rich in fish.

But it was post farming, Simpson believed, that held the most promise.[18] It could yield enough grain and beef for the department itself (therefore lessening transport) and for profitable export. Then the only provisions that would have to be sent inland would be those for the use of the ingoing brigade, the outgoing being able to eat "country produce." "Every Post can and must provide for itself," he declared. With the expansion of the trade, he warned Beaver House, provisions would be "in greater demand than ever and if imported will cost the concern thousands of Pounds annually." Chief Factor McLoughlin implemented Simpson's policy, telling a confrere in the fall of 1827 that "at Every post as much Ground ought to [be] Cultivated as we can with the men of the place provided it can be done without interfering with the trade."[19] Already by then McLoughlin was able to report from Fort Vancouver, which opened the largest farm, that "our Crop at this place will afford us sufficient provisions to do our Business,"[20] and in 1832 the depot's farm produced enough grain and peas "to serve all our demands for 2 years."[21]

Moreover, farming would soon free the posts from their dependence upon "country produce," which the servants did not like as much as grain, beef, and the like and which – more importantly – were mostly traded from the natives. At Fort Colvile in the late 1820s, two-thirds of its expenses went for furs and one-third for "country produce" (mostly provisions), so that successful farming would reduce expenses and increase returns, the Indians having to trade more furs and less "country produce" for goods (and by 1830 the farm had rendered the post "nearly" independent of fresh and dried salmon, venison, roots, and berries).[22]

Finally, Simpson recommended that New Caledonia switch from the Peace route to the Columbia route as the channel for brigading both its returns and supplies (and at the same time he recommended the abandonment of the northern [English River-Beaver River] route in favour of the shorter and safer southern [North Saskatchewan River] route across the Western Interior at a saving of thirty-two men [forty-seven instead of seventy-nine] and £1,000 annually[23]). These measures marked the culmination of the governor's program of reform of the HBC's river transport system. At the time of the 1821 merger, according to Colin Robertson, the need for improvement of the system was a "general subject of conversation ... as it would be of no inconsiderable importance could any plan be devised whereby our means of transport could be made less expensive and more expeditious."[24] Simpson's solution came in 1822, when he recommended that "in all parts of the Country except New Caledonia," boats (York, or Inland, boats) be substituted for canoes (North canoes) because the former were cheaper and safer.[25] Boats, which were propelled by oars, sails, or towline and which carried fifty to sixty pieces and only six or seven crewmen, came into general use in 1824. "Much expense" was saved by using boats, since four of them could carry the cargo of ten canoes and hence require twenty-three fewer men.[26] It was estimated that the saving in wages would exceed one-third, and that the cargo would be less liable to damage.[27]

At the same time, the governor reported that, as crewmen, Canadiens – "active and indefatigable" – were preferable to Orkneymen – "of slow inanimate habits," although the latter were cheaper. Canadiens, in his opinion, were a "volatile inconsiderate race of people, but active, capable of undergoing great hardships and easily managed by those who are accustomed to deal with them," while Orkneymen were "slow and do not possess the same physical strength, and spirits necessary on trying occasions," as well as "obstinate to an extreme" and "guarded." Irish and Scots were also to be avoided, he added, "being quarrelsome, independent and inclined to form leagues and cabals."[28]

Although boats required only two-thirds as many men as canoes, they were heavier and hence drew more water and moved more slowly than canoes; consequently, the New Caledonia brigade had to be "always conducted by Canoes as the distance is so great that Boats cannot perform the Voyage in the short interval of Open Water."[29] A canoe, which was manned by middlemen (paddlers) and *boutes* (bowsmen and steersmen, i.e., both paddlers and pilots), still carried a lot of cargo, as John Stuart testified upon his departure from York Factory with New Caledonia's outfit in the summer of 1823:

> Being reappointed by the Governor & Council of the Northern Factory to the superintendancy of the Company's business in Western Caledonia, I this day in Company with Messrs. Samuel Black, and Donald McKenzie junior, took

my departure from the Factory in a North West Bark Canoe perhaps the most encumbered that ever left that or any other place. There being on board a crew of eight men exclusive of a Guide which with Messrs. Black, McKenzie, and myself make twelve persons; and a Bale of Goods, a Case of Soap, a Keg of Sugar a Roll of Tobacco, a case of Teas, a Manaron [?], a case of Sundries, a case of Saws for Outfit and Gentlemen's Orders, Six pieces Mr. Black's Baggage an equal number including the Paper Trunk belonging to myself, three Pieces belonging to Mr. McKenzie, Six pieces belonging to the rest of the Crew and four Bags Pemican, two Bags Flour a Keg of Sugar a Bag of Pork & Ham a Bag of Tongues a Bag of Biscuit and a Bag of Bread as provisions for the Voyage making in all forty pieces most of them weighty.[30]

The canoe continued to be used on the Fraser after 1825, but transport on the Columbia conformed with Simpson's reforms by using a special type of boat, the "batteau," which will be described later.

Simpson's reasons for rerouting New Caledonia's lifeline from the Peace to the Columbia were strictly economic. "The great advantage of outfitting New Caledonia from this [west] side instead of from York Factory," he told the Governor and Committee, "is that the business can be done with greater facility and less expense." At the outset of his tour the governor had found that brigading via the Peace route "is the most tedious harrassing and expensive transport in the Indian Country." He reported that "nearly the whole year round was occupied in transport, and the unceasing labours of the people added to the privations to which they were exposed from the poverty of the Country in the means of living rendered the service the most painful and harrassing in North America and operated as a check to enterprize and exertion."[31] New Caledonia produced about one hundred packs of furs annually but had been employing no fewer than sixty to eighty officers and men, whereas, under the new system, that complement would be reduced by nearly one-half to forty, and boats would be substituted for canoes (on the Columbia, at least), for a total saving of 25 percent of the value of the returns.[32]

The August 1825 meeting of the Council of the Northern Department "unanimously" agreed with Simpson that the trade of New Caledonia could not be extended as long as it was outfitted from York Factory, so that beginning in 1826 the district would send its returns to, and take its supplies from, Fort Vancouver via the Columbia.[33] The July 1825 meeting of the council had likewise concurred with the governor's opinion, and it had ordered Chief Factor Connolly of Stuart's Lake "to proceed to Fort Vancouver with his Returns next Spring and take his Outfit from thence accordingly."[34] "To effect this desirable object," Simpson told McLoughlin, "it will be necessary that a sufficient number of Horses (say about 80 to 100) be forwarded to Alexandria this Fall from Thompsons River with the requisite Pack Saddles Epishimeans [apichimons] etc."[35] The governor added that "I consider the whole west side of the mountain to be now on the footing of one entire District or Department."[36]

John Stuart would have been pleased with Simpson's change, but William Connolly, who had just succeeded Stuart as chief factor at Stuart's Lake, was unsure, at least at first. On 10 May 1825 on the Rocky Mountain Portage, which he was crossing while leading the eastbound brigade to York Factory, Connolly received two letters from the governor. "The subject of the second [dated 20 October 1824 at the western end of the portage]," he wrote, "is regarding a new route by which Mr. Simpson thinks the outfits of Western Caledonia & the returns etc might be Conveyed with less difficulty than is experienced by the road at present followed." The new chief factor, however, felt that his knowledge of the country followed by the proposed route was "not sufficiently extensive" to enable him to weigh its advantages and disadvantages, so he declined "giving any opinion on the subject for the present."[37] By summer's end Connolly was more receptive to the change, saying that "by enabling us (independent of many other advantages) to bring in our outfits at a much earlier Period," the deficiency of dry goods that had come via the Peace route the previous year would "not therefore be attended with much inconvenience, and I trust with no loss to the Trade; Evils which undoubtedly would have been felt had not this change been effected."[38] Finally, by the spring of 1826, on the eve of leaving Stuart's Lake at the head of his first Columbia brigade, Connolly was wholeheartedly in favour of the new route in a letter to Simpson:

> I have made out a rough estimate of the expences attending the voyage from hence to York factory and Fort Vancouver which is much in favor of the latter, but this in my opinion is but a small proportion of the advantages that will result to this district from its connection with the Columbia – the means it will afford of equipping the Natives at a much earlier period will enable them to take full advantage of the most favorable Season of hunting, which will no doubt add considerably to their success, and by having much time upon our hands, which heretofore has been devoted entirely to purposes altho' connected with the trade, that tended but little to its advancement[,] a facility will exist of acquiring a better knowledge of the Country and of attending to the improvement of the Trade.[39]

Connolly's southward and northward passage – the locales, routes, stopovers, brigaders, carriers, loads, problems, changes – is followed in the ensuing chapters.

PART 2

The Outgoing Brigade

*... an uninterrupted intercourse with the Columbia on
which the welfare of this district [New Caledonia] so much depends.*

– CHIEF FACTOR WILLIAM CONNOLLY
to the Governor and Council of the Northern Department,
1 May 1826, in HBCA, D.4/119, Governor George Simpson –
Correspondence Book Inwards, 1824-26

CHAPTER 4

Canoeing down the Fraser

From Stuart's Lake to Alexandria

New Caledonia, receives its supplies from Fort Vancouver the
Voyage out and home occupying about Four Months; the mode of
transport being from Fort Vancouver to Okanagan by Boats, from
Okanagan to Alexandria by Horses, from Alexandria to Stewarts
[Stuart's] Lake by North Canoes, and from Stewarts Lake to
the outposts by a variety of conveyances, vizt. large and small
canoes, Horses, Dog Sleds and Men's backs; in short, there is
not a District in the [Indian] country, where the Servants have
such harassing duties or where they undergo so many privations;
to compensate for which, they are allowed a small addition to the
Wages of other Districts.

– GOVERNOR GEORGE SIMPSON, 1828[1]

THE SIBERIA OF THE CANADIAN FUR TRADE

New Caledonia, from which the brigades departed with the returns
(furs and castoreum) in the middle of spring and to which they returned
with the outfit (supplies and trade goods) at the end of summer, was
valued by both the "Greys" of the NWC and the "Blues" of the HBC
for its beaver. The output of pelts was sizable and regular. Also, for the
servants personally the "principal inducement" was the "indulgence they
find among the females;"[2] their "country wives" and families sprang from
this "indulgence."[3] But nothing else in the district seemed to appeal to
the fur traders. Indeed, most of them seem to have had an aversion to
the entire Columbia Department, or Oregon Country, with the exception of the lush Willamette Valley.[4] The department was notorious for
being "prolific in misfortunes," in the words of John Harriott,[5] who joined
the HBC in 1809 as a twelve-year-old apprentice and spent the next
forty-six years of his life in its employ. These mishaps were associated
mostly with the treacherous bar at the mouth of the Columbia, the fero-
cious rapids at the Dalles, epidemic outbreaks of "intermittent fever"
(malaria) on the lowermost Columbia, periodic salmon failures in the
interior, and native reprisals throughout the department. All contributed

to what Chief Trader Archibald McDonald termed the "precious Bill of Mortality" of the quarter, which, he added, was "fertile in disasters."[6]

The Columbia River itself proved especially lethal from the very beginning. In March of 1811, eight Astorians and two boats from the *Tonquin* were lost at the river's mouth,[7] and three years later, in May of 1814, seven Nor'Westers, including Donald McTavish and Alexander Henry the Younger, were swamped and drowned at the same place while boating from Fort George to the *Isaac Todd*.[8] The Columbia Department's worst year was 1830, which took a "very great" toll of life – twenty-six HBC men.[9] This toll included nineteen drownings in the river: in late June or early July, Peter Skene Ogden's Snake Expedition lost nine men, a wife, and two children and 300 to 500 beaver skins "in running down the Rapids" of the Dalles,[10] and in late October while "running down a Rapid a few miles above [Fort] Okanagan" one of four boats "struck on a stone and upset," and seven men, including six *mangeurs du lard* ("pork eaters," i.e., greenhorns[11]), were drowned and all of the cargo save seven bags of flour were lost.[12] The ensuing winter brought more casualties. From the beginning of November 1830 until the end of February 1831, twenty-four more servants perished in the Columbia Department.[13] "What a dreadful mortality, particularly by accidents, in one season" for the Indian Country, exclaimed Chief Trader Francis Heron of Fort Colvile.[14] His successor as the post's bourgeois, Archibald McDonald, concluded that "Man's life now in the Columbia is become mere lottery."[15] Narcissa Whitman, the wife of the American missionary head of Waiilatpu near Fort Nez Percés, asserted at the end of 1836 that more than one hundred white lives had been lost at the Dalles alone.[16]

The Columbia exacted another heavy toll in 1838, when a dozen persons, including the English botanists Peter Banks and Robert Wallace and their wives (Banks's was Governor Simpson's daughter), were drowned when their boat capsized in the Dalles des Morts (Little Dalles) on the upper Columbia in October (two Catholic missionaries, Fathers François Blanchet and Modeste Demers, were spared).[17] And from the middle of 1838 to the middle of 1843, thirty persons were drowned in the lower Columbia and Willamette Rivers.[18] By the end of 1846 the Columbia had seen sixty-eight "Axedunce" (accidents) to whites, including twenty-six at the Grand Dalles and fifteen at the Little Dalles.[19] "No river on the globe, frequented as much," observed the Catholic missionary Father Pierre-Jean De Smet at this time, "could tell of more disastrous accidents."[20] He had also noted in 1842 that "of a hundred men who inhabit this country [Columbia Department], there are not ten who do not die by some or other fatal accident."[21]

Little wonder, then, that John Work, a "queer looking fellow" but a "Shrewd Sensible Man" who spent thirty-eight years (1823-61) in the HBC's service on the Pacific Slope,[22] wrote to a friend in 1838: "Would to God my means admitted of my quitting this wretched country of which I have so long tired."[23] In earlier letters to the same friend Work referred to the Columbia Department as a "barbarous country" and – more than once – as a "cursed country."[24] John Tod, who served a quarter of a century in the department, disdained it as "this vile Country." And Tod's Scottish compatriot, Archibald McDonald, acknowledged the common dislike of the region in a letter to a friend in 1843 on the eve of the boundary settlement: "I fear, little as was formerly thought of the Columbia, we shall all miss that department of our resources when it is no longer ours."[25]

It was New Caledonia, however, that was especially reviled by the Bay men, who hated what Tod called the "hard duties and still harder fare" of the district. In early 1828 Work wrote to an ex-servant, Edward Ermatinger, to tell him that he was "glad" to hear that his brother, Frank Ermatinger, had "escaped" New Caledonia, with its "eternal Solitude," through transfer.[26] In a later letter to Edward Ermatinger, Work noted that a mutual friend, William Todd, was returning to "Starvation & Solitude in N. C."[27] Archibald McDonald called the district a "land of privation & misery."[28] Those New Caledonia servants who did not desert their posts commonly quit the company rather than serve another term in the district, as Chief Factor McLoughlin informed Governor Simpson in 1827:

> The Men in this district having been placed in regard to wages on the same footing as those in the Columbia although the labour and mode of living between the two will bear no comparison is a circumstance which occasions much discontent and added to the small proportion of comforts they can procure at Fort Vancouver even en passant during the few days they remain there [as brigaders], has created such a revolution in our Mens minds that all those whose times expire in Spring 1827 have given notice of their intention of quitting the Department.[29]

Indeed, the living conditions of New Caledonia were so punitive that errant servants were deliberately posted there. In early 1829 Chief Factor Connolly wrote to the Governor and Council of the Northern Department to "beg it as a favour that no more Convicts be transported hither, we have outdoor Rogues enough to guard against without having any among ourselves."[30] And in the early 1840s, Chief Factor

Ogden complained that lately the "refuse of brothels and Gaols" in Canada had been recruited for his district.[31] According to John Tod, "New Caledonia was then looked on in the light of another Botany Bay (early penal colony), Australia, the men were in dread of being sent there."[32] No wonder that the district's servants were dubbed "exiles."

The principal deterrents were the extreme isolation, monotonous diet, debilitating diseases, wearisome labour, and violent death from accident or murder. New Caledonia was the HBC's most isolated district; the Columbia District and the Northwest Coast were as remote, or even more so, but they had more frequent communication with the "civilized" world via London ships and coasters. Especially the chief factors, chief traders, and clerks with their educated tastes felt the "dreadful solitude." So an infrequent visit from a colleague was relished as a social occasion, as Clerk John McDonnell of Fraser's Lake acknowledged in the post journal in the late spring of 1822: "I am today enjoying the greatest if not the only happiness that I can expect in this country: the company of an intelligent friend, – Mr. George McDougall having arrived here at 1 P.M. from Fort St. James."[33]

Killings and drownings also blackened New Caledonia's name. Perhaps the most notorious homicide occurred in August 1823, when the two men (Joseph Bagnoit and Belone Duplantes) left in charge of Fort George by the diminutive bourgeois, Clerk James Yale ("Little Yale"), during his visit to Stuart's Lake were murdered in their beds by a native and the post's property was pillaged; their bodies were subsequently ravaged by hungry dogs, and the fort was temporarily abandoned.[34] So in the fall John Stuart warned James McDougall at Stuart's Lake: "... circumstances are such this Year – that the utmost circumspection and caution, is required on the part of us all – and if no Blood is shed in Winter – I will consider the Business as well conducted and that every one has done his Duty – Furs is what brings us to the Country – But this Year must be a secondary consideration, and all I request of you is to be prudent – to Keep enough of people for the safety of the Post and no more."[35] In May 1829 the wife and child of Clerk William McGillivray, the mixed-blood bourgeois of McLeod's Lake, were drowned, and less than three years later, at the end of January 1832, McGillivray himself and another man were drowned in the Fraser River after drifting ice upset their canoe.[36] In 1841 Chief Factor Samuel Black, bourgeois of Thompson's River, was shot dead by a native, and in 1844 the bourgeois of McLeod's Lake, Clerk John McIntosh, was killed by two natives.

New Caledonia's unattractiveness resulted, too, from its morbidity, the health of the HBC servants being impaired by their spare diet and hard work. The provisions, declared William Connolly at the end of the winter of 1825-26, "I must confess are neither very wholesome nor palatiable," and he added that "it is not probable that any change in that particular will ever take place."[37] Connolly reported that in the summer of 1825 Chief Trader William Brown of Babine Lake had been in a "very bad state of Health," which had "confined him to his bed for the space of three months & totally incapacitated him from attempting the voyage of Discovery [towards the coast] upon which he was ordered, and for which every preparation was made in the spring, at an expense of £376 in wages to [eleven] extra servants."[38] From the autumn of the same year until the spring of the next, Clerk Pierre Pambrun (who was to be killed in 1841 by a fall from his horse at Fort Nez Percés) was so sick as to be unable to perform any duties; he was too ill to accompany Connolly with the first of the brigades to be rerouted from Hudson Bay to the Pacific Ocean, having to be replaced by James Douglas (Connolly's future son-in-law and first governor of British Columbia). Clerk Charles Ross of Connolly's Lake told a friend in 1831 that he had suffered from scurvy for two months at the end of the winter of 1829-30 and that a year later his health was still "not yet perfectly re-established and I fear will not so long as I continue a Salmon eater – How long oh L—d!"[39] Also, the licentiousness and promiscuity of the servants spread "Chinook lover fever" (venereal disease). It "unfortunately is too common amongst the New Caledonia people," admitted Chief Factor Connolly.[40] Their health was probably impaired, too, by alcoholism.[41] Even New Caledonia's blackflies, unlike its mosquitoes, could be more than a nuisance, as John Stuart reported in the summer of 1820: "The men busy as yesterday, but the flies are so numerous that they cannot stand it, and indeed I never yet saw so many flies yet, owing I suppose to the Dephth of the Waters which hardly lowers." On 3 August one of the men, Alexis Landrie, "choped and corded five cords of wood and was done early owing to the number of Flies that annoyed him."[42]

But it was the district's heavy duties and meagre rations that particularly galled the servants. Throughout the year, and especially during the long and cold winters,[43] they were kept constantly busy by a variety of tasks: trading furs, keeping journals and writing reports and letters, burning wood for ashes for soap making, cleaning post buildings, felling timber, squaring logs and sawing boards, burning wood for charcoal. But most onerous were the demands of transport. Trails had to be cleared of windfalls, "sledges" (sleds) and snowshoes made, fish stocked and fetched, firewood chopped and lugged, furs packed and hauled, bark "raised" (peeled) for canoes, which in turn had to be repaired and fashioned, and, most importantly, returns had to be delivered and supplies distributed. For example, in the summer of 1825 some men were ordered by William Brown, bourgeois of Babine Lake, "to clear the Track from Fraser's Lake to this [Stuart's Lake] & then to Ft. Simpson [McLeod's Lake], under the conduct of Mr. Yale ... a most necessary object, to facilitate our Transportation, both Summer & Winter for from whatever Quarter Western Caledonia gets its Outfits in future [York Factory or Fort Vancouver], much of work must go on through those Roads, that are now almost impossible from the Quantity of fallen wood."[44] Clear tracks were essential for the district's horses, ten of which had been brought from Fort Alexandria that summer, and this track was "so much obstructed with fallen trees as to be in many places almost impassable for loaded Horses," according to Chief Factor Connolly.[45] The clearing was not finished until the end of October.[46]

Canoes and horses were used in summer and dog sleds and snowshoes (*pas d'ours*, "bear's paws," snowshoes that were rounded at both ends) in winter.[47] After freeze-up in late November, pack horses were succeeded by sled dogs until break-up in early April. Dogs, as John Stuart reported in 1823, were "absolutely necessary" because "all hands are constantly employed throughout the winter either in quest of Furs, [or] in collecting provisions and conveying the goods to the different establishments and the returns to the place of embarkation."[48] This transport was especially burdensome and protracted, as Chief Factor Connolly took pains to explicate:

> The most important Duties and those which almost exclusively occupy the whole of the People in the District from their arrival in autumn to their departure in the spring [with the brigade] for the Depot, are the Transportation of the Property of all descriptions to and from every Post, which is performed throughout with Sledges & Dogs –
>
> The better to comprehend the difficulties arising from this mode of transportation, and the many evils it occasions, it is necessary that the distances from McLeods Lake, the point of disembarkation, to the different establishments be explained – From that Post to Stuarts Lake the distance is five days march – to the Babine Country ten days – To Frasers Lake eight days, and to Alexandria twenty days – These distances are calculated by the shortest route at the rate that loaded Sledges travel without however making any allowances for bad roads, unfavourable weather, or any accidents to which long voyages are liable – The outfits and returns are not the only property transported, exclusive of these in years of scarcity at Stuarts Lake, which frequently occur provisions must be procured from the Babines and Frasers Lake not only for the use of that establishment, and for the General transportation

to and from McLeods Lake, but also for the maintenance of the last mentioned place throughout the winter, for the support of the people whilst they
are all assembled there in the spring previous to their Departure for the Depot,
and for the voyage from there to Dunvegan – In performing these services the
winter is completely occupied, and in unfavourable seasons for travelling, such
as the present was, the spring must necessarily be far advanced before the
whole can be accomplished – Altho' every precaution was taken last autumn
[1824] to forward the business as much as possible, and hardly a moment lost
in prosecuting it throughout the winter, it was notwithstanding the 28th of
April when the last sledge loads reached McLeods Lake – long before which
period the roads were in such a state that nothing but the utmost necessity
could have obliged people to travel through them.[49]

However, Carrier Indian dogs, as John Stuart found, were unsuitable
for sled pulling (although suitable for eating): "what greatly increases the
disadvantages New Caledonia labours under is the want of Dogs fit for
the Train among the Natives, those are the tools with which in New
Caledonia we labour, and the Natives cannot supply them, nor have we
as yet been able to get a supply from the East side of the Mountains,
and it is no less a fact that there are not this day in New Caledonia Dogs
to move four good Sledges."[50] More dogs were soon brought from the
Athabasca District. In early September of 1823, just outside Fort Chipewyan, the westbound New Caledonia brigade under Stuart embarked
thirty-nine dogs (thirty-three of them fully grown) that had been bought
from the natives; the brigade reached McLeod's Lake with fifty-five sled
dogs altogether (including eight that had been "pupped" en route), and
not one had been lost or left since Fort Chipewyan.[51]
The harder duties in New Caledonia necessitated higher wages, as
Stuart reminded Governor Simpson at the beginning of 1823:

> I cannot suppose any one will remain [in New Caledonia] on the same terms
> allowed in other parts of the [Indian] Country, nor would it be fair in any one
> that know[s] the difference to ask them. The voyage from Fort Chipewyan
> alone is attended with more misery and requires more time than from York
> Factory to that place [twice the distance], while the winter labours is more
> than double what it is in any other part that I know & the living no more to
> be compared to what it is in other parts than roast beef is to *soupe maigre* [thin
> soup] and the terms allowed by the North West Company was never less than
> two hundred livers [livres] in addition to the Athabasca wages.[52]

The previous year Stuart had told the Governor and Council of the
Northern Department that "the personal labour every Class of people,

from the highest to the lowest have to undergo in this quarter is uncon-
ceiviable to those who never crossed the Rocky Mountains and was it
nothing else but the very living is so bad that no Gentleman however
devoted to the Service will be willing, or able long to remain ..."[53] So
demanding was service in New Caledonia that the NWC issued more
"stores" (provisions) to its men there than to those on the east side of
the mountains, and Stuart believed that the HBC should issue a
"double portion," as well as "higher Wages," to its New Caledonian
servants.[54] Such was the case by 1827, when the district's steersmen and
bowsmen, for instance, were annually paid £2 more (£24 and £19, respectively) than their counterparts in the Columbia District.[55]

The extra wages, however, did little to improve the diet of New
Caledonia, particularly after Governor Simpson's curtailment of provision imports from 1826.[56] It was primarily because of this monotonous
and unhealthful diet that in July 1824, at York Factory, the company was
able to recruit only thirty of the thirty-six men authorized for New
Caledonia, as Chief Factor Connolly attested: "The reluctance evinced
by the men to engage for Western Caledonia arises not so much from
the great distance that District is from the Depot, as from the bad quality of the provisions that Country produces and which can hardly support men who have such laborious duties to perform throughout the
Winter – The spirit of discontent was such that not one of the men
whose times were expired could be prevailed upon to renew their contracts, altho most of them willingly engaged for other parts of the
[Indian] Country."[57] The Columbia Department's extra rations simply
meant more of what Clerk Frank Ermatinger termed the "misery of
Damned Dried Salmon,"[58] the "New Caledonian staff of life."[59] Initially,
at least, a steady diet of salmon had the same effect on the bowels as a
laxative.[60] Clerk Thomas Dears of Thompson's River bemoaned this fact
in a letter of 1831 to Frank Ermatinger's brother, Edward, an ex-servant:

> and if your destination was to have been this way think it one of the most
> fortunate occurences of your life you did not return. You Know I am gener-
> ally a slender person what would you say if you saw my emaciated Body now
> I am every morning when dressing in danger of Slipping through my *Breeks*
> and falling into my Boots. many a night I go to bed hungry and craving some-
> thing better than this horrid dried Salmon we are obliged to live upon. it is
> quite *Medicinal* this very morning one of my men in attending on the calls of
> nature evacuated to the distance of six feet. this is a reall fact, and is almost
> incredibale and often are we trouble[d] this way. excuse me. these hardships
> are enough to drive me out of the [Indian] Country.[61]

Fish, in general, dominated the menu of the district's whites and natives. Salmon and sturgeon – "Albany beef" to the Bay men[62] – were caught in the rivers, and sturgeon, whitefish, trout, and carp in the lakes (hence Trout Lake north of McLeod's Lake, Carp Lake southwest of McLeod's Lake, and Sturgeon Lake, also known as Stuart's Lake). The sturgeon was especially tasty, at least to John McLean, who found that their "flesh was the most tender and delicious I had ever eaten, and would have been considered a delicacy by Apicius himself [Marcus Apicius, a Roman epicure]."[63] The sturgeon were also enormous, averaging some four hundred pounds each;[64] in the summer of 1831 a sturgeon measuring 14½ feet in length was caught at Fort George.[65] Indeed, the sturgeon were so large that not infrequently they broke the nets that were set to catch them, even though the nets were made of sturdy Holland twine.

The salmon were less tasty but more abundant. Fresh salmon, averaging ten pounds each, were "very palatable"; in order to keep, however, they had to be split and dried, and these *bardeaux* ("shingles") averaged one pound each and had "little more substance than a piece of rotten wood."[66] "The process observed in curing them," reported Chief Factor Connolly, "is merely by splitting and hanging them in the Sun to dry – after which they require only to be Kept from moisture to preserve them for two or three years."[67] Before being cooked, the hard strips had to be soaked for some time.[68]

The HBC servants themselves netted and dried salmon but seem to have traded most of their stock from the natives, apparently because the latter had more skill and more time. John Stuart reported that the drying of salmon at Stuart's Lake by his men was "always attended with much inconvenience & expenses besides the loss of labour of the men – and the Salmon so dried are far inferior in quality to those dried by the Natives at the [nearby] Village."[69] The Carrier village of Stullah, or Stillah, at the northern end of Fraser Lake was a major source of HBC salmon. It supplied the company with some 23,000 salmon in the middle of January 1824 and Fraser's Lake with 27,000 salmon at the end of December 1825.[70] Connolly was unhappy with the extent of the company's dependence upon the natives for fish. "From what little I have seen & heard," he wrote, "I am concerned that one third of the yearly Outfits are expended in purchasing salmon or other fish, & paying Indians for their services." He added: "It is no less singular that in a country such as this which abounds with fish, not one fisherman should be found at any of the Companies Establishments – Every article in the shape of Provisions is purchased, which may indeed be the easiest mode of procuring food – but certainly cannot be either the most sure or the cheapest."[71] The chief factor asserted that an "excellent fishery" for whitefish could be established by the Bay men in Stuart Lake, "an object not only worthy of attention, as it would not only lessen our dependence upon the natives, as well as the expenses perpetually incurred in purchasing food, but might also be the means of adding something to the returns by obliging them [the natives] to Hunt Furs in order to procure the means of purchasing such necessaries [leather and tobacco, for example] as they can now obtain for fish."[72] The company, however, lacked the necessary hands, if not the requisite skill as well, although the district's posts became somewhat more self-sufficient in the wake of Governor Simpson's reforms. The Indians used *vorveaux* (cylindrical weirs, "dams" to the whites), which were installed in the rivers in August and removed in early October; in 1829, for example, they had fourteen vorveaux set in the Fraser River in the vicinity of Fort Alexandria by 21 August.[73]

Sometimes the summer runs were prolific, so much so that the "Natives may in the space of a month [August-September] catch and dry a sufficient quantity to last them until that time the year following."[74] The year 1821, for instance, saw a "great abundance of Salmon," and by November there were at least 60,000 dried salmon "in store" at New Caledonia's five posts.[75] The salmon run was likewise "abundant" in 1825, 1829, 1833, 1837, 1841, and 1845. Babine Lake was especially productive; in 1825 the post procured 44,000 salmon but consumed only 26,000 of them, sending the rest to the other posts.[76] By the early 1840s two-thirds of New Caledonia's salmon requirement was supplied by Babine Lake.[77]

The company's servants ate a lot of fish. The daily fish ration was ten pounds of salmon (one fish), fifteen pounds of whitefish (twenty fish), or twenty pounds of carp;[78] the usual allowance of dried salmon was four per day but in winter seven to eight per day for one man and his two dogs.[79] The keeper of the post journal of Fort Alexandria was astonished by the servants' appetite for fish: "our Men are the greatest gormandizers that I have ever come across, yesterday Evening they got two of the largest Salmon Caught weighing without exaggeration 40 lbs Net and 12 dog Salmon which they devour'd without having a fish this Morning – this is between 3 Men 1 Woman & 2 Children."[80] Stuart's Lake alone consumed 36,450 salmon in 1824.[81]

In summer the monotonous salmon diet was relieved by fresh berries. "We now get Berries Dayly and a sufficiency which is a good thing for the men, who are really & not without reason disgusted with the Salmon – it is really bad," reads an entry in the post journal of Stuart's Lake for 24 July 1825.[82] Large quantities of other "country produce" were also eaten, particularly rabbits, which seemed to "increase in number as the salmon decrease, until they swarm all over the country."[83] Wildfowl, too, were not unimportant. "It saves Salmon," said the servants.[84] In 1836 the two officers, seven clerks, and fifty-two men at the seven posts of New Caledonia consumed an astonishing total of 67,318 dried and 30 fresh salmon, 781 sturgeon, 346 trout, and 11,941 other fish, plus 2,166 rabbits, 153 ducks, and 58 geese, as well as 226 kegs of potatoes and 153 kegs of turnips.[85]

Not infrequently, however, the salmon run of late summer was thin or late. Indeed, according to Daniel Harmon, who served the NWC in New Caledonia for the decade of the 1810s, "it is only every second year that they are numerous."[86] Even when the run was prolific, sunny weather was needed to dry the split salmon, but, as Chief Factor Connolly noted, "fine weather ... is at this Season of the year [first half of September] seldom experienced in this quarter."[87] Much more problematical, however, was the cyclical failure of salmon. In Connolly's words, "the entire failure of salmon at this place [Stuart's Lake] is an unfortunate tho' not uncommon occurrence."[88] Then both natives and whites starved and returns dropped.[89] "No salmon, no furs" was a saying on the west side of the mountains.[90] The month of August was, as Clerk George McDougall put it, "that critical Season, when our stock of Provisions must be made for the Ensuring 13 months."[91] Failure to do so spelled disaster, as John Stuart noted in 1823:

> whenever salmon fails, and they are never abundant two years following [consecutively], all fails, and both the Natives and Traders may be said rather to exist than to live, for so scarce are animals that excepting at the public feasts given in honour of the dead, nine tenths of the Natives do not taste meat perhaps not once in ten years and such miserable stuff is dried Salmon in that part of the [Indian] Country that it ruins the constitution of the *most robust* and the very best of our Men are every spring so much reduced that two of them cannot perform the ordinary labour of an ordinary man; nor is it better with the Officers, and no one that can avoid it will be disposed to remain in that quarter.[92]

The 1820 salmon run, which did not materialize until the end of the second week of September, was the latest since 1811, when the fish did not appear until 22 August. Owing to the lateness and lightness of the summer run, by 23 February of the following winter of 1820-21 the district had only enough provisions to last until 15 April, "so that," Stuart recorded, "we shall have to put the people on short allowances to get thru our work, otherways it will be impossible." By 1 March the daily dried salmon ration had been reduced to three per man; by then sled dogs ("giddees") were being eaten. Stuart cautioned Clerk James McDougall, his 1821 summer replacement during his absence with the brigade, that "though furs is the first object you will find Salmon to be of equal consequence too much cannot be traded & the sooner it is got the better."[93]

The year 1823 was another "year of scarcity" in New Caledonia. Both salmon and whitefish failed, and these twin calamities were followed by the coldest winter (1823-24) that John Stuart had yet experienced on the west side of the mountains.[94] "It is seldom we take a meal a day," he reported on 20 November 1823 from McLeod's Lake.[95]

The consecutive failures of 1826, 1827, and 1828 were disastrous. The magnitude of the 1827 failure was considered to be *"unprecedented."*[96] "Salmon is so scarce," noted the post journal of Fort Alexandria in late fall, "that the People are confined to ¾ Allowance and the Men distributed in equal proportions to the different Posts excepting this Place."[97] The "scarcity of provisions" forced Chief Factor Connolly to send six servants to Fort Vancouver for the winter to ensure their survival.[98] In the middle of August 1828, facing the likelihood of another failure of the salmon run, Connolly acknowledged that "... from that source it is that New Caledonia derives its principal means of subsistence, and the failure of it is necessarily productive of great trouble and no small degree of Privation to us, and of extreme misery to such of the natives (and those are not a few) who have no other dependence."[99] At the beginning of September he tried to console himself with the improbability of three consecutive failures: "Three successive years of scarcity were never known to have happened in New Caledonia. We have already experienced two such years [1826 and 1827]; surely the present year, fortune will be a little more kind, and tho' she should deny us every other gift will, I trust, at least, afford us the means of subsistence." Connolly had not lost all hope: "But as none other than the large salmon have as yet been taken, and the small kind, which are always much more numerous, generally succeed the former, I yet entertain hopes that a stock for the winter will be collected."[100] These hopes were dashed, however. Fortunately, berries were "very abundant," and the natives dried "great quantities" of them, and "these in the event of salmon being scarce, will be of material service to them," as well as to the whites.[101] The 1829 run did not fail, but the chief factor well knew that inevitably it would again: "The distress which the District has been in during the two last years [1827-28] has sufficiently proved that that resource [salmon] is not always to be depended upon. The only means therefore by which the miseries consequent on a failure can be averted is by collecting as large a stock as possible whenever providence lays the opportunity of doing so in our way."[102] As if to prove Connolly's perspicacity, the salmon run failed again in 1831, causing "great privations" among the whites and "much loss of life" among the natives.[103]

And so it went – a year of plenty followed by a couple of years of scarcity.[104] In order to offset salmon failures, as well as reduce grain imports from the Columbia District,[105] farming was attempted at New Caledonia's posts, especially from the middle 1820s, in accordance with Governor Simpson's determination to make them more self-sufficient and thereby reduce costly importation and transportation. Accordingly, some barley but mostly vegetables (potatoes, turnips, beets, carrots, radishes, onions, cabbage, and peas) were tried. Hay was made for horses,[106] but apparently the first cattle were not introduced until 1833, when some were driven from Fort Vancouver to Stuart's Lake and Fraser's Lake via the brigade route.[107]

These agricultural efforts were not very successful, however. As Connolly reported in 1825, "all the establishments except the Babines have a garden attached to them in which Potatoes, Barley & Turnips are grown, none of them however, excepting McLeods Lake produces crops proportioned to the seed put into the ground."[108] The primary obstacle was the shortness of the frost-free season. There was some predation – at Fraser's Lake "striped squirrels" (chipmunks) and mice often ate the barley and peas before they could ripen[109] – but the greatest damage was done by early and late frosts (which sometimes occurred so close together that it was impossible to distinguish one from the other). The soil was covered with snow from mid-November until mid-May, and, as Daniel Harmon observed, "in every month in the year, there are frosts."[110] Consequently, as John Tod recollected, "it was mostly too cold for gardens."[111]

The fragmentary record supports Tod's summation. At Stuart's Lake in 1820 one keg (nine gallons, or three bushels) of barley was planted and seven and one-half were reaped – a "poor crop" – and five kegs of potatoes were sown and six and one-half harvested (two kegs of turnips and half a keg of beets were also harvested). "This has been an unfortunate year for the gardens," understated the post journal. It noted the reason on 11 August: "The Tops of our Potatoes froze last night a little for the first time this season."[112]

A "tolerable" crop of seventy bushels of potatoes was produced from five of seed in 1828, but only twenty-six bushels from nine of seed in 1829.[113] In 1831 early frost again lowered yields, as the post journal recorded on 23 September: "Had some frost last night. A fine clear day, got what Barley we have thrashed, but scarcely the seed returned & that has been blighted by the frost in the forepart of the Summer, our Potatoes are not much better, the Cabbages are tolerable large but not headed, we have however a crop of very fine turnips, one of which without the leaves weighed 8 ½ lbs." Finally, and again typically, in 1841 "in the course of two hours our crops were collected there not being three Kegs Turnips and scarcely two of Potatoes such a complete failure was never known here before ... frost and [the] dry season are the causes assigned."[114] Thus, only enough potatoes and turnips were produced for sparing use as a holiday treat or as a salmon supplement. Thus, too, were dashed John McLean's hopes that "pancakes and hot rolls were thenceforward to be the order of the day" and "Babine salmon and dog's flesh were to be sent – 'to Coventry!'"[115]

Gardening was more successful at Fort Alexandria, "so that," boasted McLean, "our fare was far superior to that of the other *exiles* in the district."[116] The post produced 90 bushels of potatoes in 1824 and 70 in 1825 (1 bushel = ⁴/₅ of a keg), 56 kegs of potatoes in 1827 (30 from the western and 26 from the eastern side of the Fraser), 136 kegs of potatoes and 354 of turnips in 1837 (plus 1,646 bundles of hay for the brigade horses), 643 kegs of potatoes in 1842 and 660 in 1843, 420 kegs of potatoes and 200 of turnips in 1844, 632 kegs of potatoes and 150 of turnips in 1845 (as well as 1 ½ bushels of onions and one-half of a cart-load of carrots), 90 kegs of potatoes and about 100 of turnips in 1846, and 600 kegs of potatoes and 23 of turnips in 1847.[117] But Fort Alexandria's gardens also suffered, if less so, from the vagaries of weather and the ravages of pests, as in 1824. On 29 May of that year the keeper of the post journal reported that "the drought plays the devil with us"; "I believe it Seldom rains here in Summer," he added; "this drought is much against *Vegetation*." On 5 July he noted that "the Confounded Grasshoppers of which there are swarms Infesting this Place, begin to destroy our Turnips," and the next day they attacked the carrots. And on 22 July he wrote that "the Squirrels & Grasshoppers play the Devil with our Pease & Barley."[118]

With the introduction into New Caledonia of cattle in the early 1830s and of swine and poultry in the early 1840s, at least some beef, pork, milk, butter, and eggs became available. Clerk Archibald McKinlay reported from Stuart's Lake in 1837 that "as regards food the district has much improved of late years, Cattle are now getting numerous at all the Posts except one (Connollys Lake) so that we have milk and butter in abundance, that with plenty vegetables make the salmon very palatable."[119] But salmon remained the staple, and the diet had improved only moderately over that which Governor Simpson had decried five years earlier:

New Caledonia is, without exception, the poorest District as regards the means of living in the Indian country; the lakes are so near the height of land that they produce little or no fish; of large animals there are very few; the soil is so poor & barren and the climate so cold & inhospitable, that the labour bestowed on the gardens is frequently lost, and in the most favorable seasons they only produce a very few potatoes of bad quality; in short the main, and I may add the sole, dependence of the establishments and natives is on the salmon, which come up from the coast at the spawning season, when they are likewise of bad quality.[120]

Occasionally all of New Caledonia's shortcomings were felt in the same year. Two of the worst years were 1823 and 1828. In 1823 not only did the salmon fail but also two men were killed by natives at Fort George, the post of McLeod's Lake was destroyed by flooding, and the district's returns dropped to only half of those of 1822. By the end of the year John Stuart feared that "if there are others [disasters] of a similar nature to add to them Western Caledonia is lost." To make matters worse, January 1824 brought the coldest weather that Stuart "had ever witnessed before, not only on this, but on the other side of the Mountains also." (An additional problem, he confided, was the "prevalent custom lately introduced into Western Caledonia ... of taking Native Women into keeping" and the "admission of Native Women into their [HBC's] Forts." He wrote that "it is long since I apprehended that too free [an] Intercourse with the Carrier Women would be the ruin of the Company's affairs in this quarter," and he recommended that only married men be posted to the district.[121]) The year 1828 was nearly as disastrous. The failure of the salmon run for the second consecutive year and the death of five of his men prompted William Connolly to brand it a "year of misfortunes" and the "most unhappy year of my life."[122]

Not surprisingly, such conditions bred dissension. The 1 July 1824 meeting of the Council of the Northern Department at York Factory noted "serious differences and insubordination" among the gentlemen of New Caledonia and urged that either these "evils" be suppressed or the culprits removed.[123] The dissension, in turn, generated desertion. From 1825 through 1828, thirty-eight employees deserted the district.[124] The desertions, coupled with New Caledonia's repellents, meant that it was usually shorthanded.[125] John Stuart bemoaned the shortage of servants at the beginning of the summer of 1820, when someone had to be sent to investigate the killing of a native woman: "... had it been possible I would have gone myself but I cannot [leave] the place [Stuart's Lake] with so many Indians about it, It is certainly shameful to see the Establishments so bare as they are, owing to want of Gentlemen to take charge of Posts, if any misfortune was to happen [to] any of the Posts it is out of my power to give any assistance, It is not only risking the Company's Property but the lives of all the people in this Quarter for there is no dependence upon the Indians about the places, they are perfect *Brutes*."[126] The undermanned company was at the mercy of the natives. "In no part of the Indian Country," reported Stuart from McLeod's Lake in 1823, "are the whites a match for those Natives who know the advantages they possess and in no part of it with which we are acquainted, less so than this quarter."[127]

There were so few servants that the rebuilding of the post of Stuart's Lake, commenced in 1822, was not finished until the autumn of 1825 (just in time for its new role as New Caledonia's depot). And the district was already shorthanded in the late summer of 1828 – its "complement of men" was "very reduced" – when the imperious Governor Simpson and his retinue of twenty-two reached McLeod's Lake on 11 September and requisitioned two of Chief Factor Connolly's canoes and four of his best men, including his sole interpreter. "The demands," complained Connolly, "... will not only greatly obstruct our operations, but may also involve us in difficulties out of which we will probably not be able to extricate ourselves." He added that "the Establishment of the District in consequence of deaths, sickness & desertion, is already seven hands short of the number absolutely required for its immediate duties, and adding to this deficiency the four men the Governor is determined upon taking with him, leaves us precisely sixteen men." On 4 September Connolly had had twenty-one men, and one of these had deserted on 6 September en route from Fort Alexandria to Stuart's Lake with the brigade. These losses occurred at a time when the natives were, in Connolly's words, "by no means in a tranquil state." "At such a momentous crisis," he warned, "a stronger force than usual would be absolutely necessary, but instead of this, the existing deficiency in our establishment is not only further reduced, but the only Interpreter we have, whose services would be indisposably required to restore order amongst the natives, is taken from us."[128]

Because there were not enough employees, they were assigned a variety of tasks, and they did not prove equal to all of them, as the following entry from the post journal of Stuart's Lake attests: "The smith commenced working, but his Knowledge of the Trade he follows is so very limited, that he generally spoils every thing which he takes in hand – With regard to Guns & Traps he can repair neither, unless their damages are very slight indeed."[129] This unskilfulness was compounded by the fact that particularly able-bodied and able-minded men were reluctant to serve in New Caledonia (as well as, it seems, in the company's employ generally after the coalition). An explication of this problem by William Connolly was prompted by his dissatisfaction with the "disservice" of John Harriott at Fraser's Lake:

> I will use the freedom [take the liberty] of observing that forming the establishment of clerks in this District with so many old hands as have lately been sent to it, was not the best expedient which could have been recoursed to for supplying it with servants of that class. Most of those gentlemen having been accustomed to a mode of live very different from that which they lead here, they therefore find their situation disagreeable and before they have acquired a sufficient knowledge of the district to render them useful, they are anxious to quit it. Another disadvantage attending people of this description is the difficulty which even those who make the attempt, find to acquire the language of the natives, which of itself is a matter of much importance, particularly on account of the great scarcity of Interpreters. These inconveniences would not have existed had a proportion of those gentlemen consisted of able young men, but of these only two have been sent in, and one of them, M. [James] Douglas, is at present the most efficient man we have. The other Mr. Wm. McGillivray has been here but a short time, and I am persuaded that he will in a short time be qualified to render most essential service.[130]

Not surprisingly, the problem seems to have become more acute towards the end (1846) of the period of "free and open" access to the Oregon Country by both British subjects and American citizens. As the fur trade waned, able young men sought their fortunes in more promising fields. John McLoughlin complained to Governor Simpson in 1843 that "indeed from year to year our men are falling off so much that out of those come these last four years [1839-42] we have been able to get only one to make a Boute [bowsman or steersman] and yet he is a poor one."[131] Simpson's reply was revealing:

> With reference to the 1st par. of yours of 20th March, in which you complain of the inefficiency of the recruits, I have only to say that I am informed they were a fair specimen of those who presented themselves for engagement to the Company's Agent; and that, with regard to Boutes, it is quite impossible to get such now in Canada, as Canoes have long fallen into disuse there. The Columbia and New Caledonia being the parts, where such crafts are now principally in use, they must in future depend for people of that capacity on those reared on the West side the Mountains, which is now the great nursery for Canoemen. Before concluding this subject I am sorry to be under the necessity of saying that the Service of the West side the Mountains is become so unpopular with Canadians, Orkneymen and Halfbreeds, that it is a most

difficult matter to get men for that part of the country. This unpopularity appears to arise from loud complaints, industriously circulated, of extreme ill-usage, being, as they say, starved, beaten and maimed by the Company's Officers in the Columbia.[132]

Later the same year the HBC's Governor and Committee acknowledged that "there is an insurmountable reluctance on the part of respectable laborers to accept employment on the West side the Mountains occasioned by the reports circulated by those who have returned from that quarter."[133]

THE OUTGOING BRIGADE

Thus, with the arrival of spring break-up in New Caledonia the brigaders were undoubtedly eager to leave in expectation of a change of scene and the social and material benefits of the Columbian depot, even though the journey would not be easy. But first the returns and the servants had to be assembled from each of the posts. The castoreum was transported in kegs; the furs were compressed by a screw press, tied with cords into packs, and wrapped with apichimons (or epichimons). "And as the security of the Furs depends greatly upon the mode of packing them," noted the post journal of Stuart's Lake on 1 April 1828, "every possible attention is therefore paid to that object. Five men are employed in this duty."[134] Within four days these five men made fifty packs.[135] Each pack weighed from eighty-five to ninety pounds.

Canoes and flat-bottomed "boats" (batteaux) also had to be made for the river passage to Fort Alexandria. The three essential materials for canoes were bark (usually birch but sometimes pine), gum (pine or spruce pitch [resin], boiled and thinned with salmon oil), and *watap* (spruce-root withies). Bark could be "raised" throughout the year but especially in May, June, July, and August.[136] In New Caledonia, April-May was the busiest barking period. Suitable bark was not abundant, however, as John Stuart observed in the spring of 1820: "Martenian [Martineau] and the rest of the men busy working at the Canoe but I am sorry to say he makes poor progress & still worse Work, he is apprehensive of wanting Bark for the third Canoe and tho we sent two men yesterday in search of some they came back today unsuccessful therefore we will have to make use of the Bad [bark] after all."[137] In the spring of 1826 William Connolly reported from Stuart's Lake that "the uncommon backwardness of the season rendered the procuring of Bark and other materials required to build Canoes extremely tedious and difficult."[138] "It was late in April," he wrote, "before the bark was provided, and we hand [had] to send for it at the distance of about 150 miles from hence."[139] He added:

> And those [men] who were sent to raise Bark also arrived after an absence of 32 days – The severity of the weather would not permit them to raise the Bark until the latter end of last month [March], and after accomplishing which, the distance would not admit of their returning sooner – They brought a sufficiency of Bottom Bark for six Canoes and of side for three ... The remainder can be easily procured here ... In providing every thing requisite to build Canoes the only difficulty will now be to procure roots for making wattapps to sew them with – And these cannot be dug up until the ground is clear of snow & in some measure thawed.[140]

Natives were hired to collect canoe gum at the rate of two beaver skins for one keg of gum.[141] Four "excellent" canoes were finally readied.[142]

In April of 1827 bark was raised for making four new canoes, and three old canoes were repaired, while clear gum was collected for sealing the interior seam, and wood was gathered for making paddles.[143] Canoes were equipped with paddles and poles, and boats with oars and poles. In 1828 the outgoing brigade stopped at Birch Point, just below Fort George, and raised forty-two fathoms (252 feet) of birch bark "of a tolerable good quality, which we put *en cache* [until the brigade's return in late summer]."[144] Once enough suitable bark had been obtained, it was sewn and gummed into canoes on stocks in the canoe yard; boats were nailed and gummed. The scarcity of bark in New Caledonia prompted the use of wooden canoes from the 1820s.

At first, when the brigade followed the Peace River route, the "place of embarkation" was the district's oldest post – McLeod's Lake, or Fort Simpson, as it was called during the middle 1820s.[145] In 1823 disaster struck. Chief Factor John Stuart reported that "the whole of the buildings a snug little Fort were carried away in summer by an uncommon high flood."[146] James McDougall of Stuart's Lake provided details of the disaster:

> I received a few lines from Mr. Fleming [the clerk at McLeod's Lake] who informs me that he is well, tho he is without a house Store of [or] Fort having been swept away by the waters on the 30th Inst. [of June] in consequence of the small river back of the fort having almost overflowed its Banks and upon the Waters subsiding the Bank gave way so rapidly that ere they could take measures to save the Timber part of the fort fell in and they had just

time to save the Property out of the House and Store when the whole of
the Building and Stockades went adrift except the flooring of the Big House
which was also saved – so that he is now encamped upon the point between
the Hill and the place where the fort stood – but as that part will soon give
way also he wishes me to give him directions where to build But I do not like
to interfere.[147]

All of the property was saved, but all of the wooden buildings – even
the pickets – were washed into the lake.[148] The post was rebuilt, but as
a depot it was still found wanting by Stuart's successor, William Connolly, in the fall of 1824:

The accommodation[s] are very bad, and the worst of it is the want of a place
to secure the Goods – A large Building intended for this purpose was erected
in [the] course of the summer but being covered with a single layer of Pine
Bark, is therefore not fit for use not being able to resist a drop of rain – I am
at a loss where to examine the Goods after they are here which it would be
necessary to do after the series of wet weather we have had – For securing
them afterwards the store may answer by using the oil cloths as coverings –
But where the Furs will be put after the transportation commences, is a
question I am not prepared to answer.[149]

McLeod's Lake supplied itself with whitefish, trout, and carp for half
of the year and relied upon the district's other posts for salmon for the
other half.[150] In Governor Simpson's opinion, "in regard to the means of
living, McLeods Lake is the most wretched place in the Indian Country; it possesses few or no resources within itself."[151] Five years later, in
1833, John McLean was struck by the forlornness of the post: "A More
dreary situation can scarcely be imagined, surrounded by towering mountains that almost exclude the light of day, and snow storms not seldom
occurring, so violent and long continued as to bury the establishment. I
believe there are few situations in the country that present such local
disadvantages; but there is the same miserable solitude everywhere."[152]

By 1826 McLeod's Lake had been supplanted by Stuart's Lake as the
brigade's terminus and the district's depot. The new headquarters was
located one hundred miles southwest of McLeod's Lake on Stuart's, or
Nakazleh, Lake, also known as Sturgeon Lake after its very large and
"most excellent" sturgeon.[153] In 1823 or 1824 the old post was moved to
a "more convenient spot," but John Stuart still rated it the "most difficult [post] in Western Caledonia."[154] The complement (1823-24) comprised 1 officer and 3 labourers in summer and 1 officer and 6 labourers

in winter, plus (1826) 114 native men.[155] Its average yearly returns were twenty-one or twenty-two packs of furs, mostly beaver and marten.[156]

In 1824 William Connolly succeeded John Stuart as New Caledonia's *homme d'affaires* and selected Stuart's Lake as his headquarters because, although "not the most important in point of Trade," its location was the "most convenient," being "in General conducive [accessible] from all quarters."[157] The post's staple was salmon, plus some whitefish, trout, carp, and roe, but the "almost entire failure of Salmon three Years out of four" resulted in increased expenses (for salmon purchases from the natives), decreased returns (from the dispersed and distracted natives), and overworked servants, who "must be constantly Kept on the go, which is attended with much expense and is the cause of our having such a number of Invalids every winter" (particularly when having to use Carrier dogs, a "dwarf Kind simply calculated for the chace," instead of imported Huskies).[158] So salmon had to be hauled to both Stuart's Lake and McLeod's Lake from Fraser's Lake (and sometimes Babine Lake) "over a mountainous Country distance fifty miles from hence, and for which hard labour Dogs are absolutely required to enable the men to perform their Duty."[159] More provisions were expended at Stuart's Lake than at any other post in New Caledonia, it being a "centrical [central] Post where the people pass and sometimes rest"; in 1823, 1,000 fresh and 6,500 dried salmon, 2,800 whitefish, 2,000 fresh and 3,000 dried carp, 7 sturgeon, and 4 kegs of roe were consumed by the post itself and 8,600 dried salmon by winter travellers.[160] To make matters worse, the soil around Stuart's Lake was shallow (no more than six inches deep) and infertile (clayey and stony), and summers were warm and dry, so that vegetables did not flourish, potatoes sometimes not even yielding the seed.[161] The gardens were especially vulnerable to the "cold and frosty nights we have in the summer months."[162]

The brigade could not depart until the rivers were free of ice. The "navigation" normally opened by the end of April and closed by the end of November.[163] The season was short enough, and the journey long enough, that the brigaders could afford to lose little time in leaving. In the words of Clerk George McDougall, "... in this Part of the [Indian] Country we must be ready for the Season as the Season for Embarkation will not wait for us."[164] Nevertheless, the brigade could not normally leave on a Friday, as Clerk William McBean of Stuart's Lake explained in 1843: "It was my intention to go off the day after tomorrow [Friday]; but, the Canadians have a superstitious reluctance to starting on a Friday, which it is customary & prudent to honour, when there is no probability of eradicating it."[165]

It was likewise essential that the brigade time its departure to coincide with the availability of provisions (fish) en route. This point was stressed by Chief Factor Connolly upon his return with the brigade from the Columbia in the summer of 1827:

> The former [a letter to John McLoughlin at Fort Vancouver] relates to the Period appointed for our Meeting in the spring at Okanagan (1st June) which, without being attended with any particular advantages, deprives us of the resources in provisions which a later date would afford both in the Columbia & Frasers River. In our return this year what I have past stated was very sensibly felt, the Columbia gave us but little, & in Frasers River we could not procure a single salmon. Ten or twelve days later both those rivers could supply us with a sufficiency not only to enable us to save much provisions, and the inconvenience of their being carried such a distance but would also remove all danger of being exposed to privation. Our arriving in the District [New Caledonia] ten or fifteen days later than we did this year, could not be of any disadvantage to the Trade. And if no objection on the parts of the Columbia Gentlemen should be made, I propose to Mr. McLoughlin that the period of meeting at Okanagan should be put back to the 10th June.

Subsequently, however, the scarcity of provisions for the winter of 1827-28 forced Connolly to reverse his request and to leave earlier and meet at Fort Okanagan on 24 May instead of 10 June 1828.[166]

Most of New Caledonia's servants were boatmen, so they constituted most of the brigade, although some brigaders were added en route at the various posts. In 1822 the district contained eight gentlemen and thirty-two men, of whom three gentlemen and twenty-one men (three-fifths of the servants) took the returns to Fort George.[167] In 1823-24 there were fifty-nine servants in the district, including thirty-two middlemen, six steersmen, and six bowsmen;[168] however, at that time the Peace River route was being used, and it required a larger complement and a larger proportion of boatmen than the Fraser-Columbia route. Similarly, in 1824-25 New Caledonia's complement numbered sixty servants, thirty-one of whom were "employed in the voyage to & from the Depot [York Factory]."[169] The rerouting of the brigade to the Fraser-Columbia decreased the district's personnel in 1825-26 to eight gentlemen and forty-one men, of whom one gentleman and twenty-five men formed the brigade.[170] Twenty-four manned the brigade and thirteen stayed inland in 1826, and twenty-four and fifteen, respectively, in 1827.[171] At the end of the winter of 1826-27, McLoughlin reported from Fort Vancouver that he had ninety-four men in the department: thirty for the brigade, twenty-one for Fort Langley, twenty for Fort Vancouver, sixteen for the coast trade, and seven for the express; he added that he needed fifty-two men for the brigade alone, now that it served both districts.[172] In 1828 the outgoing brigade employed fifty-four servants altogether: twenty-five from New Caledonia, nine from Thompson's River, twelve from Fort Colvile, and eight (including the Columbia River guide) from Fort Vancouver.[173] And in 1829, when New Caledonia's employees numbered thirty-nine, twenty-three of them manned the brigade; they were joined by two in the Columbia District.[174]

Both canoes and boats were used on the Stuart's Lake-Fort Alexandria run. Boats were introduced in 1825 in accordance with Governor Simpson's policy of replacing North canoes with more efficient York boats. William Connolly described New Caledonia's boats as "wooden machines made somewhat in the form of a Canoe."[175] But he preferred them to canoes:

> This [Stuart's Lake] as well as many other Posts in the [Indian] Country, being intirely unprovided with any Kind of Craft, except wretched wooden canoes which are almost unmanageable; I have conceived the idea of Building a Batteau at this place, & if I can succeed it will be no difficult matter to get others built at the Babines & Fraser's Lake, – They will cost nothing but the nails required to join the materials together, & one of them will perform as much service as ten of the vile Craft [canoes] now in use, and that too with much more safety and expedition – As a beginning I got the stumps of Small Trees dug up for the purpose of making Knees.[176]

So at Stuart's Lake in the middle of March 1825, the sawyer was busy sawing boards and planks and the blacksmith making nails for two batteaux.[177] The shortage of *boutes* (bowsmen and steersmen) following the general disuse of freight canoes in the Northern Department in the 1820s, as well as the smaller capacity of canoes, reinforced the use of boats on the upper Fraser in the 1830s.[178] By the 1840s usually five craft – boats and canoes – left with the returns.

Before they did so, the brigaders and their vessels made a pact. The Astorian, Nor'Wester, and Red River settler Alexander Ross wrote that "on all such occasions there is a kind of mutual understanding between both parties, that is, between the canoe men and the canoe, the former undertaking to carry the latter over the land part of the journey, while the latter is bound to carry the others safe over water."[179] And as soon as the brigaders set out, they "at once struck up one of their boat-songs ... each voyageur in succession took up the song, and all joined in the chorus," observed Lieutenant Wilkes on the lower Columbia.[180] They sang, of course, in Canadien French, the working language at the company's posts, including Fort Vancouver, where Wilkes found that "even those who come out from England after a while adopt it, and it is not a little amusing to hear the words they use, and the manner in which they pronounce them."[181]

The brigade left Stuart's Lake and went down the Stuart River and through the Chinlac Rapids just above the Stuart's junction with the Nechako River at the "Small Forks" (see Map 1); here the returns from Fraser's Lake were added. The Nechako was followed to the "Big Forks," or simply the "Forks," the confluence of the Nechako and Fraser Rivers and the site of Fort George, whose returns were added at that point. Fort George had been established in June 1821 and temporarily abandoned in 1824. John McLean recalled that "the situation of the post is exceedingly dreary, standing on the right bank of Frazer's River, having in front a high hill that shades the sun until late in the morning, and in the midst of 'woods and wilds, whose melancholy gloom' [Walter Scott?] is saddening enough."[182] Descending the Fraser, the brigade ran the Grand, or Great, or Big Rapids of the Fort George Canyon just below Fort George and then the Clayey Rapids of the Cottonwood Canyon just above Fort Alexandria near the mouth of the Rivière de Liards (Cottonwood River).

The downstream passage from Stuart's Lake to Fort Alexandria was perhaps the most uneventful and expeditious stretch of the entire brigade route, with the possible exception of the downriver run from Fort Okanagan to Fort Nez Percés. The spring run-off made the Fraser deep and fast, and the craft went with the current and faced no major rapids. However, the 1826 brigade – the first to follow the Fraser-Columbia route following the final abandonment of the Peace route – encountered low water, the long, cold winter of 1825-26 having delayed the spring freshet. "The water is very low," reported brigade leader Connolly, "none of the snow in the mountains being yet dissolved, and the current is therefore not strong, and our progress, altho we have a crew of nine men, is not as great as might be expected."[183] The three canoes with eleven men took six days (3-8 May) to make the run.

The 1827 brigade, which left on 1 May, was more typical. Connolly wrote: "The people carried the packs & Canoes over the Ice [of Stuart's Lake] to the entrance of the [Stuart] River, where they embarked about sunrise to proceed on their voyage," and, assisted by the Fraser's "very strong" current, they reached Fort Alexandria on 4 May with "every thing safe and in good order."[184]

The 1828 brigade embarked on 30 April in two canoes, one with

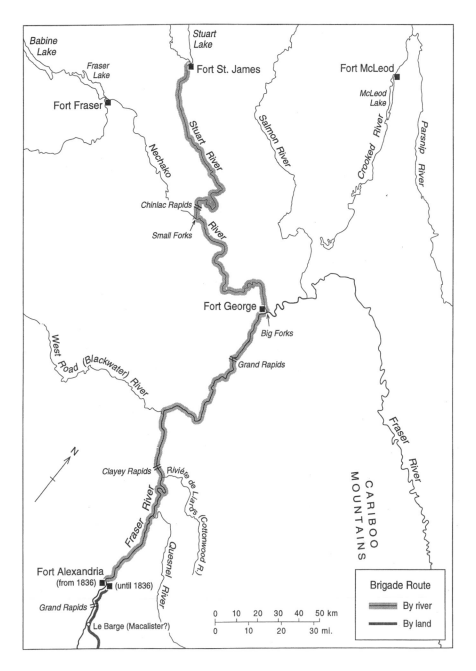

MAP 1 From Fort St. James to Fort Alexandria

twenty-seven pieces and the other with twenty-two. A third canoe with seven men (including the chief factor) and eighteen pieces departed on 1 May and overtook the others at the foot of the Chinlac Rapids, where they were joined the next day by a fourth canoe from Fraser's Lake with thirty-four packs. The ladings of the four canoes were equalized and the brigade proceeded, camping on 4 May just above the Grand Rapids, "which is too strong and dangerous a place to be passed in the Night." Fort Alexandria was reached on the 5th.[185]

The 1829 brigade departed on 2 May in two canoes and one boat with seventy-eight packs of furs and six kegs of castoreum, plus provisions (dried salmon) for the "march" (any journey on foot, horse, or boat) and Fort Alexandria, and four bales of leather and *sifflux* ("buffalo robes" – bison hides, dressed on one side and haired on the other, used as blankets) for Chilcotin's Lake, which had been established the previous year. At the Chinlac Rapids it received the returns of Fraser's Lake – thirty-three packs and two kegs – and two passengers, John Harriott, bourgeois of Fraser's Lake, and his sick wife. The boat was damaged in the rapids and had to be unloaded, "hauled up," and repaired. On 5 May the whole day was spent seeking canoe bark, but only thirty fathoms (180 feet) were raised. On the 6th at the Grand Rapids "from the height of the waters it would have been a great danger to attempt shooting it with full loads," so each of the craft made two trips with half loads. The same day the brigade made Fort Alexandria and added its returns of twenty-two packs and one keg. The canoes were "carefully laid up" on the 7th in a shed that had finally been built for that purpose.[186]

This run was one of the safest legs of the brigade route. One of the very few accidents occurred in 1831, when the brigade was later than usual in leaving Stuart's Lake on 7 May under Peter Warren Dease; 124 packs of furs and 8 kegs of castoreum were loaded in five canoes with four men each and one boat with five men. Tragedy struck four days out:

> This morning [Wednesday, 11 May] at 9 A M got to the Big Rapid which L[oui]s. Paul who was leader of the Brigade was sent to Examine previous to going down the Water being in a fine state he led the way with the Batteau, the Canoes following each other at a moderate distance. Ls. Paul after having got down safe with his batteau observed in looking back one of the Canoes taking the Eddy Current too soon, fearing it would be driven against the Rocks turned round to warn them to take care, when the Sweep oar fixing in the water threw him over the Boat after a short Struggle the poor man sunk to rise no more. By this melancholy event I have to regret the Loss of the Best Boute in the District, which cannot easily be replaced.

Later the same day the brigade reached Fort Alexandria, where another thirty-eight packs and three kegs were received.[187] In an upset in the same rapids on the same date in 1833, a steersman was drowned and two kegs of castoreum were lost.[188]

Such occurrences were unusual, however. Year after year the brigades arrived at Fort Alexandria without loss of life, cargo, or time, as Governor Simpson himself experienced in 1828: "... I resumed my Voyage, leaving Stuarts Lake, on the 24th September, and descending Frazers River about 300 miles got to Alexandria on the 27th; found that part of the navigation safe and tolerably good, the current Strong and abundance of Water, with many short rapids, but none of them dangerous."[189]

CHAPTER 5

Packhorsing over
the Mountain

From Alexandria to Thompson's River

*At Alexandria we only remained a few hours, and continued our
route on the 27th Septemr. [1828], our road leading a short distance
along the Banks of the [Fraser] River, and then taking a Southerly
direction through an open Country, intersected by Small Rivers and
Lakes, amidst beautiful Valleys, over high Hills, across the faces of
precipices many Hundred feet high (where a false step in our broken
track rarely 12 Inches wide would have proved fatal) occasionally
over points of Wood, and at times through deep Swamps; in
short, we had a ride occupying Eight Days, and possessing all
the agreeable and disagreeable varieties of Scenery & Road,
which the most ardent admirer of the Wilds could desire.*

– GOVERNOR GEORGE SIMPSON, 1828[1]

ALEXANDRIA

At Fort Alexandria the outward brigade left the Fraser River proper for
the six-week "transit" by pack horses to the Columbia River proper at
Fort Okanagan. Alexandria, as it was commonly called, was named in
honour of the NWC explorer Alexander Mackenzie, who, upon the
advice of the local natives, halted his journey down the Fraser just upriver
from its site and took instead the shorter and easier West Road (Blackwater) River route to the sea.[2] It was founded upon John Stuart's return
with the Columbia brigade in September of 1821,[3] presumably in order
to exploit the Atna territory and to launch forays into the Chilcotin
Country. And from 1825, of course, it gained additional importance as a
station on the brigade route, as Chief Factor Connolly noted: "The situation of this establishment is perfectly adapted for a Depot, which is
required from the route we are hereafter to follow – It being from here
that the land carriage to the Columbia commences, and here of course
where the Horses & appointments must be left, as well as the Canoes
required for the navigation of Fraser's River."[4] The post's own bourgeois,

Chief Trader Joseph McGillivray, likewise stressed that "it is absolutely necessary of having a station for the support of the Horses, for the better transport of the Returns of the District and bringing in the Outfit from Columbia River," as farther north "subsistence for these Animals is not [to] be had for such a large number."[5] In other words, Alexandria was the northernmost post with sufficient pasture for the brigade's pack horses, the mountainous and forested terrain upriver being unsuitable for the maintenance of "such a large number" of horses.[6]

The establishment was apparently the most attractive and the most congenial of New Caledonia's posts. "Without any pretention to elegance," observed Connolly on a visit at the end of the winter of 1824-25, "the Fort is good & solid, & sufficiently convenient to answer every necessary purpose."[7] In early 1826 a storehouse was built to house the returns and outfits of the new brigade route. By the summer of 1827 a new two-storey house was under construction, although the fort itself was "much decayed."[8] The post's setting was extolled by Chief Trader McGillivray: "The front of the Fort faces Frasers River – and both sides of the Country presents a very beautiful and romantic appearance – the Banks of the river are succeeded by an inclined plane, and extends in gently rising steps – these are diversified with Groves of Fir and Poplar."[9] John McLean, who became bourgeois of the post in March 1834, two years before it was moved across the river, was even more effusive: "Fort Alexandria ... is agreeably situated on the banks of Frazer's River, on the outskirts of the great prairies. The surrounding country is beautifully diversified by hill and dale, grove and plain; the soil is rich, yielding abundant successive crops of grain and vegetable, unmanured." "The charming locality, the friendly disposition of the Indians, and better fare," he added, "rendered this post one of the most agreeable situations in the Indian country."[10]

McLean may have exaggerated the post's arcadian locale and agricultural productivity but not its advantages. The salmon fishery, which afforded the main food, lasted from the middle of July until October.[11] The run never failed completely here, so there was seldom any shortage.[12] The post had 6,204 dried salmon in store at the end of 1823 and 7,423 at the end of 1824,[13] whereas Stuart's Lake and McLeod's Lake, at least, would by then have to be hauling salmon from Fraser's Lake or Babine Lake. In the summer of 1825, some 26,000 salmon were taken at Alexandria.[14] Trout of a "most exquisite flavour" and weighing from ten to thirty-five pounds each were caught in October.[15] Even marmot afforded an "exquisite repast," and Indian dogs (curly tails, small ears, pointed noses) were "eagerly purchased" by the whites for their "Holiday meals."[16] Berries were abundant. "The natives have large quantities of dry berries (which this season has produced in great abundance)," noted Connolly in the late summer of 1826, "And as they are disposed to part with them at a moderate price, I have directed Mr. Yale to purchase all they have to spare."[17] And Alexandria was the district's most successful agricultural post. So its provisions were more plentiful and more diverse. In 1827 the post's seven men, four children, and two women (plus another five children and two women from February through August) consumed a total of 8,573 dried salmon, 1,454 fresh salmon, 154 rabbits, 9 dogs, 3 horses, 3 beaver, 135 pounds of pemmican, 283 berry cakes, 56 kegs of potatoes, and 100 suckers.[18] At the beginning of the autumn of 1842 Alexandria was even able to send thirty-eight horse loads of provisions (and one of private property) to Thompson's River (as well as twenty-five "choice" horses for forwarding to Fort Colvile for the York Factory express).[19]

The post, however, "claimed [the] particular attention" of the district's *homme d'affaires* because of its "remote location [from the depot] and the deranged state of the Natives." Particularly the Indian warfare was "productive of the most serious and injurious results,"[20] that is, less peltry and less salmon. Hostilities between the Atnas and the Chilcotins in the summer of 1826, for example, reduced Alexandria's returns by three-fourths (three packs that summer instead of the usual dozen);[21] its returns totalled fifteen and one-half packs in 1826-27, compared with thirty-four in 1825-26.[22] Also, the natives were numerous, especially outnumbering the whites in summer. As John Stuart reported, "it is a place attended with more danger in Summer than in winter, the Indians being there flocking to it from every direction, and *faux pas* might ruin all."[23] This congestion was noted by the keeper of the post journal on 23 June 1824: "Almost all the Indians of this Place have now arrived from their respective fishing Lakes & Root Grounds – this Fort has been like a thoroughfare all Day, for I believe every Man, Woman & Child of the Place ... were here. We have Spent nearly a foot [of] Tobacco to give them to Smoke. I mean the principal men."[24]

THE PACK HORSES

At Alexandria, New Caledonia's returns were switched from canoes and boats to horses for packing across the lengthy "portage" (interfluve) between the Fraser and Columbia systems. Horses were brought from the Columbia District in 1825, when they were reintroduced in order not only to facilitate the brigade but also to accelerate transport within New

Caledonia.[25] William Connolly believed that it would not be possible to distribute the district's outfit before the onset of winter and to expand its trade until sled dogs were supplemented by pack horses:

Under such circumstances no idea of improving the trade either by extending the establishments, or by any other means can possibly be entertained – Before any attempts of this nature can be made, or any reforms introduced the existing system must be abandoned and a new one adopted, in the establishing of which no difficulty appears to me to exist, as the following facts will prove – As I have before observed the point of disembarkation is McLeods Lake from whence to Stuarts Lake no water communications exists, and the journey must therefore be performed by land – The distance by the summer road between both places for loaded men on Horses is from seven to eight days; from the last mentioned places to the Babines and Alexandria there is a communication by water without any obstruction, excepting one Portage of ten or twelve miles, which divides the Babine from Stuarts Lake – To Alexandria which is the most remote, and from the nature of the Country the most difficult of access, the navigation is without any obstruction and with proper craft is perfectly safe – The only real obstruction which exists, and from which so many evils arise, is the portage between McLeods & Stuarts Lakes – a difficulty which could be removed with little expense as thirty Horses would be sufficient to carry over the outfit from the former to the latter place, from whence the different posts would receive their supplies for the whole year immediately in the Fall – Those for the Babines & Alexandria would as above stated be forwarded by water, and those for Frasers Lake would be conveyed by the Horses – By the same means the supplies of salmon for McLeods Lake, as well as the Furs which might at that period be collected at Frasers & Stuarts Lakes could be forwarded to the former place – Thus before the closure of the navigation as much work would be accomplished as now occupies the greatest part of the winter, which would leave a sufficient number of hands, and of time at our disposal to explore the Country, extend the trade as far as practicable, or to make trading excursions to such parts as will not admit of being established.

Many other advantages would naturally result from the adoption of this plan, amongst which the benefit every post would derive from receiving at once in the Fall a complete assorted outfit, instead of being supplied as is now the case by piece meal, is obvious – much confusion would be avoided and every one being aware of the quantity of Goods at his disposal, would manage them in such a manner as to make them hold out until the succeeding outfit should arrive – It might perhaps also act as a stimulus to the exertions of the Indians, and encourage many of those who inhabit distant parts to frequent the establishments, which the uncertainty of being able to procure the articles they require, prevent them often now from doing.[26]

The earlier return of the brigade via the new route would also, of course, serve the chief factor's purpose of expediting the distribution of the outfit. To help the prospective horses accommodate this earlier distribution he had two batteaux built at Stuart's Lake, one at Fraser's Lake, and one at Babine Lake.[27]

In the autumn of 1824 Connolly, because of "the important advantages which appear to me would result from having the whole outfit transported hither [Stuart's Lake] from Fort Simpson [McLeod's Lake] immediately in the Fall, from whence the other establishments could be supplied with their yearly outfits before the setting in of the winter," ordered from twenty to twenty-five pack horses from Thompson's River for Stuart's Lake, to "be ready to assist in the transportation the ensuing Fall [of 1825]." In the spring of 1825 the chief factor sent James Yale with three other men, including a Thompson's River native interpreter and guide, to Fort Okanagan for horses. "The very important advantages which would result from having Horses for transporting the property in the Fall, are so evident," wrote Connolly, "that we have resolved upon embracing Mr. McLeod's [the Thompson's River bourgeois's] offer, by sending to Okanagan for those he has offered to deliver at that place." Yale returned to Stuart's Lake on 10 May but with only four horses, two from Fort Okanagan and two from Fort Alexandria, "circumstances not admitting" a larger procurement. "Horses will only be wanted much this ensuing Fall," noted Connolly, "as it is in contemplation for the future, to supply this District again from the Columbia, by which Route also I understand the Returns are to be taken to Market."[28]

So a large stock of horses had to be procured during the summer of 1825 for the brigade and forwarded to Alexandria before the winter. The nearest and cheapest source was the Columbia District, where the Nez Percé Indians in the vicinity of Fort Walla Walla kept large herds derived from Spanish stock. Governor Simpson estimated that about one hundred horses would be needed "for the business of next season [1826]," including seventy for Alexandria and twenty for Thompson's River (and the rest presumably for breeding).[29] This estimate, however, did not include the animals required by the Snake and Umpqua (or Southern) trapping expeditions – after the brigade, the company's heaviest users of horses in the department. So when Simpson wrote to McLoughlin on the subject in the spring, he stated that "there will be a very great demand for Horses next year" – up to 150 for New Caledonia and the two expeditions; seventy of these were to be forwarded in the fall to Alexandria for the 1826 brigade.[30]

In July McLoughlin was ordered to acquire a "large Band" during the summer, as they were "absolutely necessary" for the brigade and the Snake and Umpqua expeditions, as well as another expedition to the mouth of the Fraser (where it was intended to establish the department's new depot in place of Fort George). Now from 80 to 100 horses with "appointments" (gear) were to be sent to Alexandria.[31] Meanwhile, Chief Factor McLoughlin had instructed John Warren Dease, bourgeois of Walla Walla, to buy up to 200 Indian horses, including 70 for Alexandria, 20 for Thompson's River, and the rest for the trapping expeditions.[32] During the first half of July a party of thirty-one men in two canoes under John Work was absent nineteen days from Walla Walla buying 112-13 horses (6 of which later died) at the Snake River "Forks" (Snake-Salmon junction?). They were traded for ammunition, tobacco, and blankets, and the Bay men had to pay "much more than usual" because they were in a hurry. The "whole band" was driven to Fort Okanagan.[33] Towards the end of summer, McLoughlin instructed Dease to buy "as many Horses especially mares as you can conveniently."[34] Altogether that summer Dease managed to acquire 250 horses.[35]

But the animals still had to be driven several hundred difficult miles to New Caledonia. At the end of August, twenty horses were dispatched from Walla Walla to Fort Spokane and seventy-three to Fort Okanagan for forwarding to Thompson's River; seventy-one of these were forwarded but only sixty-seven survived, one straying en route and three dying at Thompson's River (undoubtedly from the hardships of the journey), and five of the survivors were kept at Thompson's River by bourgeois John McLeod in order subsequently to convey the "appointments" to Alexandria that were expected from Fort Okanagan.[36] The remaining sixty-two animals were sent to Alexandria, but of these two died en route and four after their arrival, and one or two were given to native guides, leaving fifty-five or fifty-six, all in "excellent order" and all, save one, "healthy" and "most of them young Animals, which with proper care promise to last several years," according to Connolly. However, he added, this was "a number quite disproportioned to the quantity of Property we will have to transport."[37] From eighty to one hundred horses were supposed to have been provided, and a minimum of seventy-five would be required to haul New Caledonia's returns from Alexandria to Fort Okanagan in the spring of 1826, or even as many as eighty, allowing for five losses en route. Moreover, there were only thirty pack saddles at Alexandria. Connolly even suggested to Clerk McDonnell of Thompson's River that "from the badness of the Roads around Okanagan Lake, it would be a material object to have outfits to transport part of the Property by water; but from the reduced establishment of your Post, I do not suppose that

you will have any men to spare for the purpose of constructing machines
[craft] fit to cross the lake."[38] Furthermore, complained Connolly to
McDonnell, "a considerable proportion of the horses sent here not being
broke in, and as they appear to be naturally very wild I have reason to
conclude that we will have much difficulty to set them a going particularly as none of our men understand much of horsemanship."[39]

Because the number of horses at Alexandria was "far short of what
were indispensably required," Connolly dispatched four men under the
mixed-blood interpreter William McBean to Thompson's River to get
twenty-two additional horses in order "to complete the number of 80
which were required, and appointments for 75."[40] In the third week of
December McBean left Thompson's River with the twenty-two horses
and appointments for seventy-five and reached Alexandria on 2 January
1826 with "the number of Horses required and a large proportion of agres
[*agrès*, "gear" for pack horses or river boats]." But the animals were in
such "poor" condition when they left Thompson's River (from autumn
work) and were so "much reduced" by the trip over the snow-bound
"Mountain" (the height of land – the Thompson Plateau – between the
North Thompson and Fraser Rivers) that they made Alexandria with
"much difficulty," and one soon died "after such a fatiguing march."[41]

The chief factor was greatly relieved because the Northern Department's Council had ordered him to take his returns to, and fetch his
supplies from, the Columbia in the spring, and no arrangements had
been made to enable him to go to York Factory instead.[42] But the worst
was still to come, and very soon. In January it snowed "almost continually," resulting in three to four feet of snow cover, and February and
March saw "frequent and heavy" snowfalls to the extent of another three
to four feet, as well as "intense cold" (with disastrous consequences for
not only horse keeping but hunting, too).[43] The horses experienced "difficulties in procuring food" in the "great depth of snow" around Alexandria. In addition, there were not enough apichimons (saddle blankets and
fur wrappers), which, Connolly wrote, "we will endeavour to supply with
Dog skins, of which, some of our Gentlemen are from their partiality to
the flesh of that animal, able to furnish a good stock."[44]

By the end of January from thirteen to seventeen horses, including all
of the December drove, were dead, having "suffered too much getting
here to stand the severe weather we have had ever since," reported bourgeois George McDougall from Alexandria. He added that the "very hard
and thick crust" on the snow hampered their grazing, especially on the
part of the weaker animals. Once the ice on the Fraser was thick enough
(by the end of March), the horses would be crossed to the western bank,

where, he reported, "there is much better feeding for them." McDougall believed that no more than fifty-four or fifty-six horses would be left for the spring brigade, plus perhaps eight or ten to be hired from the natives, but even then the number would be ten or twelve short of the seventy-five "absolutely required."[45]

Then the October drove also began to succumb to the "great difficulty" of feeding and the "long continuation" of severe cold.[46] Neither Connolly nor McDougall expected any of them to survive the winter, "as the weather has been so inclement, and the snow of such uncommon depth that hardly a possibility existed of their being saved." At Stuart's Lake the temperature fell to -36°F on 5 and 6 March, and all but two of its horses died. Connolly explained: "ever since the commencement of January East and North East winds have constantly prevailed, which will account for the Cold."[47] By the end of February fifteen more of Alexandria's band were dead, leaving forty-nine, and to McDougall there was a "certainty" that twenty-two more would not survive the winter.[48] The chief factor was aghast:

> Thus no more than twenty seven or twenty eight can be depended upon for the spring transport – a number so far short of what is required, that it will be impossible for the Columbia Gentlemen to make up the deficiency – Under these Circumstances the only alternative which holds out any prospect of getting out our returns, is to send as large a proportion to York Factory as the people to be discharged this spring are able to convey – And to endeavour to procure a competent [sufficient] number of Horses, in addition to those we still have, to transport the remainder to the Columbia – The returns will amount I presume to about 145 pieces, of which number no more than 45 can be taken to York, as the discharged servants will suffice merely to man two Canoes – And the above will form sufficient ladings, including the passengers, say four Gentlemen and their Baggage – One hundred pieces will then remain to be transported to the Columbia, to effect which, at the lowest calculation, 50 Horses will be required – And these must if possible be provided.

Connolly really had little choice but to rely upon the Columbia route, "no Outfit having been provided at York [Factory], nor any precautions taken along the Communication [Peace route] in procuring Craft, Provisions etc etc for the Out & ingoing," so that to send the returns to York Factory would wreak "certain destruction on the Trade of this District for the ensuing year" and "be attended with the loss of thousands of Pounds."[49] The "only expedient" open to him was to send "as large a proportion" of the returns to York Factory as the outgoing canoes could take and try to get "fresh" horses from the Columbia.[50] The unacceptable alternative was to leave most of the furs inland and thereby defer their sale by a year.

By the end of the winter the "frequent and heavy falls of Snow" and the "intense cold" had caused the death of "about 70" horses at Alexandria, or at least three-quarters of its herd.[51] So more horses simply had to be obtained from the Columbia. On 22 March McDougall stated that a minimum of thirty-four additional "able horses fit for service" were required.[52] Bourgeois Archibald McDonald of Fort Okanagan had taken twelve horses to Thompson's River for the brigade in the middle of March and had sent another twelve in the middle of April after learning of the winter toll.[53] It was not easy to get horses from the Nez Percés because lately they had exhibited a "great reluctance in parting with animals so much in admiration among themselves."[54] Nevertheless, McDonald intended to send another thirty horses to Thompson's River at the beginning of May.[55] Up to forty-five animals were to be forwarded to Alexandria in the middle of April, although from ten to fifteen of them were so "*very weak*" that they would be able to carry only light packs.[56] On 1 May McDougall arrived at Stuart's Lake to report in person to Connolly, who was "relieved from all uneasiness in regards to the transportation of our returns over land, being informed by Messrs. F. Ermatinger [bourgeois of Thompson's River] & Yale that forty five Horses can be furnished, which in addition to those we have still remaining will suffice for that purpose."[57]

On the same day that McDougall reached Stuart's Lake, Clerk Yale reached Alexandria with forty-nine horses (comprising twenty-nine taken from Thompson's River and twenty hired from Indians at the rate of eight beaver skins each), which were added to the fourteen already there that had escaped the "general destruction" of the winter and five others that had been hired from local natives, making a total of sixty-eight, "which number," Connolly wrote, "will just answer to carry out the Returns, and Provisions requisite for our support from hence to Kamloops." "Most of these Animals are extremely low," he added, "however with proper attention, and slow marching, I hope they will be able to carry out their respective loads, which are made up into packages to suit their strength, from 45[lbs] to 80[lbs] weight."[58]

Two canoe loads of New Caledonia's returns were sent via the Peace route with departing servants and the rest by pack horses to the Columbia.[59] Governor Simpson informed Beaver House that this strategy caused "considerable trouble and inconvenience" but "no serious loss."[60] However, he told Connolly that the "great mortality" among

Alexandria's horses during the winter of 1825-26 was "much to be regretted" because it had caused "serious Loss and inconvenience." Moreover, he said, "Horses are now getting scarce in the Columbia and the natives part with them unwillingly even for very high prices," so that they must be carefully tended at the posts. Otherwise the company's business in New Caledonia would be "brought to a stand," it being "entirely dependant on the services of these useful animals," at least until a water route was opened via the Fraser River to the proposed new depot at its mouth[61] – a route that did not materialize.

Chief Factor Connolly estimated that one hundred horses would be needed "to answer all our purposes" in 1827, including the brigade.[62] So more had to be obtained from the Columbia District. But it had also been affected by the cold, snowy winter of 1825-26, with the Indians losing "many" of their horses, so that in the spring of 1826 they had "few or any" to sell. In July Work led a party of thirty-three men in two canoes up the Snake to its junction with the Salmon River and succeeded in buying eighty horses from the Nez Percés (whom he called "Real free Booters in their Hearts"). Of these, twenty went to Fort Colvile and sixty to Fort Okanagan for New Caledonia (including fifteen for Thompson's River) to join seventy-five already there, so that Connolly was able to choose from a band of 120 (75 plus 45) "Excellent" horses at Fort Okanagan in the middle of August, when he left at the head of the brigade for New Caledonia.[63]

The animals were again wintered at Alexandria. They would have been "less exposed" to killing by starving natives at Thompson's River, but they would also have been subject to "the difficulty of getting them across [the Mountain] in the spring [to Alexandria] and the uncertainty of their being properly attended to [at weakly manned Thompson's River]."[64] Connolly was determined to avoid a repetition of the previous winter's toll. "To avoid similar misfortunes in future," he wrote, "and to ensure an uninterrupted intercourse with the Columbia on which the welfare of this district so much depends, it would be requisite that large quantities of hay be collected for the support of such of the horses as might not be able to live without it."[65] He implemented this measure at Stuart's Lake in late summer: "To avoid as far as lays in our power similar disasters to those of last year, Mr. Yale is directed to provide as much Hay as possible for the support of such of the Horses as may require it. The grass in this neighbourhood is far more luxuriant than last year. And as the season [winter] can hardly be expected to be as severe [as the winter of 1825-26], I have sanguine expectations that our Horses will pass it in safety. It behooves us nevertheless, to take every possible precaution by which their preservation may be ensured."[66] In October the only two scythes in New Caledonia were sent to Alexandria for cutting hay.[67] In early November Connolly learned that all of its horses, except two, were "in excellent health and in good order."[68] And on 7 January 1827 he was informed by Clerk William McGillivray that Alexandria's horses were, with one exception, all "in health" and "in excellent order" and had an "abundance" of feed. Connolly was alarmed, however, to hear that McGillivray had already killed and eaten one old horse, and he feared that others would also be "condemned to the kettle"; in the spring of the previous year the chief factor had found not that the brigade horses were too old but rather that some of them were "too young, and weak, for such a long voyage," so that "in the present scarcity of Horses, killing any to eat cannot be too much condemned."[69]

The disastrous winter of 1825-26 does not seem to have been repeated, sufficient hay usually being made to sustain the animals between autumn and spring. In August 1833, for example, three hundred bundles were made at Alexandria.[70] Occasionally summer drought reduced the hay crop, as in 1829, when by late August the grass in the neighbourhood of the post was "very thin & short" because of the "excessive heat & uncommon dryness of the summer," making it likely that the horses would suffer "much" during the coming winter.[71] The importance of haymaking at the post was stressed by its bourgeois, Chief Trader Alexander Anderson, in instructions to his deputy in the spring of 1848: "Hay must be made in as large a quantity as possible; about the 1st of July it may be begun – from *80 to 100 loads* (*full* loads) must be made."[72]

The only other threats to Alexandria's horses came from thieving and starving natives, starving servants, and hungry wolves. During the fall of 1827 and the winter of 1827-28, nine head either died or were killed, principally by Indians for their meat. Salmon was very scarce, and by the spring of 1828 the Indians around the post were "reduced to the utmost extremity of distress" by starvation. The severity of the famine was noted by the outgoing brigade when it stopped at Fort George on 3 May to embark the returns of its natives: "They have just returned from performing the melancholy duty of collecting the remains of a whole Family of their relatives who perished through want in [the] course of the winter. The accounts they give of their own sufferings are dreadful, and by the appearance they exhibit it is evident that in the recital of their misfortunes there is no exaggeration."[73]

Similarly, a shortage of provisions at Alexandria could force its servants to resort to eating the brigade horses.[74] In March 1829 the post's horses were reported "all healthy, and all danger of their suffering from

the weather is over for the season." However, because some of Alexandria's provisions (and two men) were lost in a rafting accident on the
Fraser, "some of those useful Animals will necessarily have to be sacrificed for its maintenance," warned the bourgeois.[75]

Wolves were an occasional nuisance. The post's journal recorded on
5 August 1824 that the vicinity "now Swarms" with wolves.[76] And on
9 May 1827 it noted: "last Night the Wolves Attack'd 3 Colts they were
wounded but not dangerously, put Bells about their Necks."[77]

THE HORSE BRIGADE

At Alexandria the canoes and boats were stored "in such a manner as
will secure them as much as possible from the injury they would unavoidably receive from exposure to the weather."[78] In 1829 the craft were
"carefully laid up" in a shed that had finally been built for that purpose.[79]
Then the horses were collected and fettered "that they may not stray."[80]
The horse appointments had already been repaired. Alexandria's returns
were received (after its furs had been pressed into packs and marked); in
1829 they amounted to 22 packs of furs and 1 keg of castoreum, making
a total of 133 packs and 9 kegs for the brigade.[81] At 2 packs, or pieces,
per horse, this total necessitated at least seventy-one pack horses, plus
"light" (spare) horses to relieve exhausted or injured animals and riding
horses for the brigaders themselves – say, up to one hundred head. A
pack horse's load comprised two pieces, or bales, of eighty-five to ninety
pounds each.

Each caravan was divided into several "brigades" (strings) of so many
horses and so many men each, and each string (and each horse) had its
own name, commonly French. For packing, the brigaders usually used
geldings, which were more tractable than stallions; mares were saved for
foaling. The animals were mustered and loaded at dawn and unloaded
and loosed (and hobbled) at dusk. The aim was, in Duncan Finlayson's
words, "to start every morning about day Light [that is, as soon as the
brigaders could see] & encamp with sufft. light to make a good Encampment."[82] The brigades left very early in the day – usually by 4 a.m. – but
not too early in the season, since the spring freshet made streams harder
to ford and pieces easier to wet. Once or twice during the day the horses
were "baited" – halted to feed and drink. They generally packed some
twenty miles each day. A day's march was termed a "hitching," according to Father Modeste Demers, because the horses were hitched and
unhitched only once each day.[83]

The brigades departed between the end of April and the middle of

May following the arrival of the "inland boats" from the "upper posts." Only a couple of days were spent at Alexandria. The 1826 brigade arrived on 8 May and departed on 10 May, when the horses were "mustered" and their loads were "adjusted" after the "horse appointments were examined and found in good order," reported Chief Factor Connolly. It consisted of twenty-seven men and sixty-eight horses with eighty-three packs of furs and six kegs of castoreum and fifteen bales of dried salmon, "besides our voyaging apparatus." For the "greater convenience of travelling" the brigade was divided into twelve strings of two men and five to six horses each. "By this arrangement," observed Connolly, "much confusion will not only be avoided, but if any of the Horses are injured the offenders will be easily discovered." He added that "some of the Horses having never before carried a load did not much like their Burthens which they contrived by kicking to throw them off their backs," so that progress was slow.[84]

The 1827 brigade made Alexandria on 4 May and left two days later. It comprised eighty-four horses divided into twelve strings of two men and seven horses each. There were twenty-six brigaders, plus Clerk Pierre Pambrun as far as the Mountain because the route until that point was "infested with Horse thieves," making it necessary "to watch every night to save the Horses from those vagabonds." Most of the brigaders rode their own horses, except those new hands who had arrived in February and those who had eaten their mounts during the winter. Connolly reported that "these last I shall take care will pay for their folly, by making them walk the whole of the voyage." The horses, he noted, were "all in fine order, and its a pleasing, tho' singular occurrence, that out of such a number, not one should have been lost or died through accident or disease." For breeding purposes one stallion and seven mares (four of which had already foaled) were left at Alexandria. Connolly added that "the Horse appointments are also in excellent order, having undergone thorough repairs."[85]

Twenty-seven men, plus the guide Baptiste Lolo (later known as Captain St. Paul) as far as Thompson's River, with 133 packs of furs, 8 kegs of castoreum, provisions, and the chief factor's baggage, formed the 1828 brigade. The horses, "all in very good travelling order," numbered eighty, divided into ten strings of seven horses with two men each and one string (the chief factor's) of ten horses with five men. "They [the horses] were all as orderly as I could have wished," wrote Connolly, "and much more so than I could have expected, considering that three fourths of them have not been made any use of since the month of July last." The brigade left on 7 May.[86]

The 1829 brigade arrived on 6 May and departed three days later. It comprised eighty-one loaded horses conducted by twenty men but with thirty persons altogether. It made, said Connolly, a "formidable appearance but in appearance only" because only twenty-two of the thirty persons were "effective hands." There were twenty "effective" and two "infirm" men, plus Connolly and four passengers (John Tod, John Harriott and his sick wife, and James McDougall), as well as one hired native to assist the "helpless" McDougall; one man was to be added at Thompson's River and another at Walla Walla. The horses were, in Connolly's opinion, in "excellent order, but their number is rather too limited and will barely suffice." The horse band had decreased since the fall by twelve head, partly through accidents but "more through the necessity which existed of killing several of them for the maintenance of the establishment," and even more would have been butchered that spring if it had not been for the "unusual success" of native fishermen in the nearby lakes.[87]

The 1831 brigade left on 14 May with 180 pieces for ten strings of nine horses and two men each, plus another string of two horses and one man, and still another of six horses and two men. There were twenty-four men altogether, including three who were "so wretched" as to be ineffective, according to Chief Factor Peter Warren Dease. The brigade was six horses short of affording a mount for each brigader, "as they cannot otherwise attach to their Brigades." The horses, Dease reported, were found "all in Excellent order and none lost during the [winter] season." But, he added, "much difficulty Existed in putting loads upon some of the Young Horses not yet broken in."[88]

The 1834 brigade was early. It reached Alexandria on 15 May in six canoes with twenty-five men and departed three days later on ninety-nine horses (eleven strings of nine horses each) with 163 packs of furs and 15 kegs of castoreum.[89] By contrast, the brigades of 1838, 1839, 1843, and 1844 were early, arriving "from above" on 28 April, 25 April, 25 April, and 25 April, respectively, and leaving on 2 May, 28 April, 1 May, and 29 April.[90]

From Alexandria the horse trail followed the left bank of the Fraser (and approximately the route of the present-day Cariboo Highway – Highway 97), passed the Grand Rapids, and left the river at Le Barge (present-day Macalister?) to skirt White Earth Lake (now McLeese Lake) and cross the Current River, or Rivière à Joseph (Soda Creek?), which entered the Fraser at the Atnah Rapids, or Head of Rapids (see Map 2). From there the pack trail again left the Fraser for First, or Fish, Lake (Williams Lake) and followed the San Jose River to Lac en Long

(Lac la Hache) and then the Salmon River (Watson Creek?) and Beaver River (Bridge Creek?) to Drowned Horse Lake, or Lac des Chevaux (Horse Lake). From there the track more or less followed the route of present-day Highway 24, skirting Salt Lake (Sheridan Lake?), Lac Tranquil (Bridge Lake?), and Lac du Rocher, or Lac des Rochers (Lac des Roches), to the Grand Muskeg (a "Large Swamp," at the southern end of Phinetta Lake?) at the foot of the Mountain (Thompson Plateau), which was crossed to the Traverse, or Crossing Plains (Little Fort), of the North River (North Thompson) forty-five miles upstream from its junction with the South Thompson River at Fort Kamloops. From the Traverse the trail veered southwards along the left bank of the North River and roughly followed the route of the present-day CNR to Barrière at the mouth of the Barrière River, Les Pineux (McLure?), the Stockades (Heffley Creek?), and Thompson's River (North Kamloops).

In the early 1840s the last half of this route seems to have been shifted, although there is very little direct documentary evidence of the change. The trail was apparently rerouted from Bridge Lake southwards, perhaps via the Bonaparte and Deadman Rivers, to Kamloops Lake, and then along the northern side of the Thompson River to the new site of Fort Kamloops on the northwestern instead of the northeastern corner of the North Thompson-South Thompson junction. John Tod, who took charge of the post in 1841 after the murder of Samuel Black, implied that this new leg was used as early as the summer of 1841.[91] He also intimated that the old fort was abandoned at least partly because Black had been killed there.[92] Whatever the reason, the new site meant that the risky Traverse of the North Thompson and the narrow valley of the river could be avoided, and the rugged Mountain, too, by turning south from Bridge Lake.

The "march" from Alexandria to Thompson's River took up to a fortnight. Progress was slowed by the rugged terrain, particularly during the spring thaw. As Chief Trader Joseph McGillivray of Alexandria wrote in 1828, "a ridge of Mountains ... makes the Country about Alexandria Mountainous and Hilly, and in whatever direction you may travel you encounter very bad roads, intersected by innumerable small Lakes, Rivers, and marshes."[93] Particularly the Mountain (also apparently called the "Big Hill") was "very rugged & Rocky."[94] In spring it could also be boggy and snowy. Connolly's 1826 brigade reached it on 18 May, when "it snowed considerably," and spent the next two days crossing it: "Our Route was through Marshes & very deep snow – in the former of which the Horses sunk in many places up to their bellies & were with difficulty extricated. This is the most fatiguing march they have yet performed, and they were

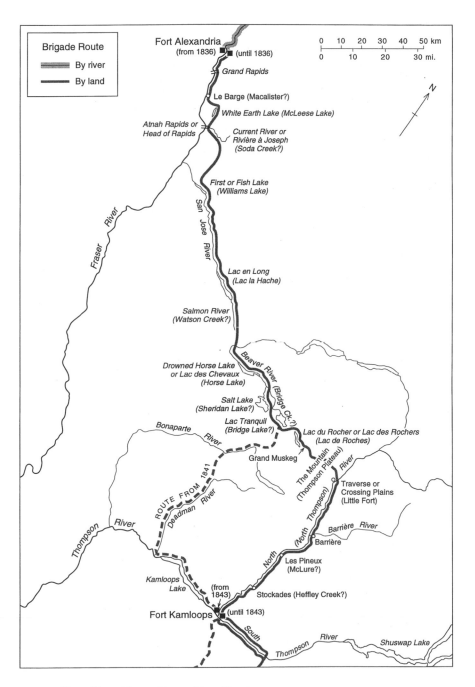

MAP 2 From Fort Alexandria to Fort Kamloops

entirely exhausted when they reached the swamp [at the summit], which unfortunately afforded but very poor means of recruiting their strength. One of the poor animals was left along the way, being unable to proceed any farther – In such cases it was impossible to avoid wetting some of the Packs, but none of them are sufficiently so to injure the Furs."[95]

The track along the left bank of the North Thompson River, which has cut deeply into the Shuswap Highland, was "the worst in the whole route from Frasers River to the Columbia [River]," in Connolly's opinion.[96] He found the bank "extremely rugged and fatiguing to the Horses."[97] Here in 1831 "part of the way being very bad along the River, going over a Point of Rocks which is dangerous on account of broken stones ascending and descending on each side of the Rocks very steep, one of the horses with his load of Packs rolled down from a height of about 80 feet & fell in the River, fortunately received but little hurt by the fall and swam down to an Eddy where the Packs were taken off safe and the animal got ashore."[98]

Some delay was also occasioned by the necessity of carefully guarding the horses against rustling by natives en route. This danger was noted by the bourgeois of Alexandria in the spring of 1844:

> In the evening Mr. William Todd arrived from Kamloops with a letter from Mr. [John] Tod Sen[r]. It appears that in consequence of a rumour among the natives that the natives about Lac Vert meditated molesting us, he had thought it expedient to send a reinforcement consisting of Mr. T & 4 men, to assist the brigade – I am of course obliged to Mr. Tod for this act of attention; but at the same time conceive that nothing in the present circumstances calls for any precautions beyond those usually adopted and always necessary. The Indians are, I fancy, neither better nor worse than usual; and if all their babbling rumours were to [be] received implicitly, we should have our hands full of imaginary troubles – However, it was recommended to Mr. [Donald] McLean [the brigade leader] before his departure, to adopt every precaution, and to guard his horses as soon as he arrived in the parts where depredations are to be apprehended.[99]

Along the way, roots and fresh trout and carp were traded from natives who were fishing the lakes, but because they were "Notorious Horse Thieves" a night watch was kept.[100] But nighttime guarding of the horses was soon discontinued. Connolly explained in 1828 that "having in our preceding voyages found that watching them at night was injurious to them, as it prevented them from feeding, it was therefore only on two or three occasions when the danger of their being stolen was too imminent, that this precaution was observed."[101]

Additional perils and delays were caused by the elements and accidents. In 1826 there were "frequent showers of rain, but none of sufficient violence to retard our march or injure the Furs," reported Connolly.[102] In 1827, however, on the first day out of Alexandria it rained so hard that the brigade had to encamp for fear of damaging the furs, but the camp was so close to the post that during the night some of the horses tried to return, and they strayed so far (despite being hobbled) that the next morning was "far advanced" before they had been collected. The trip to Thompson's River took twelve days, compared with fourteen in 1826, when, however, the horses were "very poor" and the men "so awkward" that "much" time was lost.[103]

In 1828 fine weather and low water permitted a smooth passage to Thompson's River. In 1829, however, on the second day out of Alexandria, rain prevented the brigade from starting until noon. At the Traverse over the North Thompson the high water level made the crossing "very dangerous" (although all of the horses were crossed safely); downstream the tributary Barrière River was so "exceedingly high" that it could not be forded by the horses with their loads, and a bridge that had been made of driftwood the previous year had been "washed away," so that canoes had to be used to cross the property.[104] By contrast, in 1831 Chief Factor Dease found "the weather fine & Warm & the Rivers not being in a high state, is a great advantage, having numerous Streams to ford which at high Water causes much difficulty & Delay besides the risk of Wetting the Packs." It took two days to cross the North Thompson River, where 169 dried salmon were retrieved from a left-bank cache of 200, and one day to cross the "very swift" Barrière River in a canoe, which could hold only seven pieces and two men at a time.[105]

Occasionally horses and brigaders suffered accidents, usually falls. In 1826, on the second day out of Alexandria at the head of the Grand Rapids, a young horse with two packs took fright and fell into the Fraser, only to be carried downriver through the rapids for four miles and deposited safely on the opposite bank with its load intact.[106] In 1827, again on the second day out of Alexandria, a horse fell over a cliff and into the Fraser; it saved itself but lost its two bales of dried salmon, and it was disabled "for some time to come" by its bruises.[107] Lac des Chevaux (Horse Lake) was so called because "some years" prior to 1831 eighteen horses had fallen through its thin ice cover and drowned.[108] In 1831, yet again on the second day out of Alexandria, a man was "seriously lamed" and incapacitated for the entire trip by a kick from a horse.[109]

Pasture for the pack horses was usually sufficient. Spring normally arrived earlier in the central interior between Alexandria and Thompson's

River than in the northern interior; by the time the pack horses began their trek in early May, the grass was no longer covered with snow or too "young" (short). In Connolly's words, "the climate is far more favourable than above" and the vegetation "pretty far advanced," thereby affording the horses "tolerable good feeding along the way." At the Atnah Rapids, where camp was often made at the end of the first day out of Alexandria, there was an "abundance of excellent feeding for the Horses." After leaving the bank of the Fraser here and striking inland, he continued, "the country we passed through is beautiful, the roads level & unobstructed, and food for our Horses plentiful, which enabled us to perform excellent marches." However, the vegetation became scantier as the brigade approached the Mountain, where "the Horses now feed for the most part either upon very young grass, or the stubble of last year, which does not afford much nourishment." On the other side of the Mountain at the North Thompson, the climate was "much more moderate" and the vegetation "farther advanced."[110]

According to Connolly, it was "expedient to allow the Horses a few Hours rest each day, by which means they are never exhausted ... soon refreshed and enabled to perform longer days journey with less fatigue than they possibly could by going from one Encampment to the next without Halting."[111] Dease found that resting/feeding stops of up to three hours made the animals "less liable in warm Weather to get their backs injured by the loads."[112]

River crossings could be hazardous, especially in high water. Loaded horses could ford rivers, provided they were shallow enough not to dampen the packs. Deep rivers could not be forded and had to be bridged with driftwood (if not too wide) or swum by horses without their packs, which were carried across by the brigaders on the makeshift bridges.

The North Thompson at the Traverse was the most dangerous crossing. Here in the spring of 1826, following that disastrous winter for Alexandria's horses, the brigade was met by three servants and two natives from Thompson's River with two canoes (faster and safer than rafts) for crossing the returns and ten fresh horses "to relieve such of our own as most required it" (here, too, Connolly was relieved to learn that twenty fresh horses for the brigade had arrived at Thompson's River from the Columbia). By sundown the property had been crossed, but the "much fatigued" horses were given the night's rest before crossing. In the morning the animals were "roped" across. Twelve pieces and two men were embarked in each of the two canoes, which would reach Thompson's River in a day, the North Thompson's current being "very strong." "The weakest [horses] were therefore not loaded," wrote Connolly, "and will be allowed to go light until they recover strength, & in their turn will occasionally relieve others who may fail along the way." That day an early stop was made to rest the horses, examine the packs, and dry any wet furs. Two days later the brigade reached Thompson's River and found the fresh Columbian horses "fat, but from bad usage on their way from Okanagan to this place, they have very sore backs, which is even worse than being low in flesh." The horses that had been rented from the natives at Alexandria were returned and their owners paid, the cost amounting to at least half of what it would have cost to buy them – an expense which, Connolly said, "will I trust not again occur."[113]

Late the following winter (the end of February 1827), a wooden canoe thirty-five feet long and two and one-half feet wide was built at Thompson's River. It was "just the thing for going up [the] North [Thompson] river in the Spring to cross the New Caledonia property at the *traverse*."[114]

CHAPTER 6

Packhorsing between the Fraser and the Columbia

From Thompson's River to Okanagan

*The Post of Kamloops, or Thompsons River, is a very
unprofitable Establishment, and the principal cause of its being
kept up as the people could be employed to more advantage elsewhere, is the danger to which the New Caledonia outfits and
returns would be exposed, from the Natives of Thompsons River in
passing to and from Vancouver, if we were to withdraw from their
country. The outfits of this Post are brought from Vancouver to
Okanagan by Boat, and from Okanagan to the Establishment which
is situated on the Banks of Thompsons River a distance of about 300
miles, by Horses. The Natives are upon the whole well disposed
towards the Whites, but being numerous, it is considered advisable
to keep a larger complement of people than the Trade can well
afford to guard against accident. Its present strength is two
Clerks and Eleven Men ...*

– GOVERNOR GEORGE SIMPSON, 1828[1]

"KAMELOOPS HOUSE"

Thompson's River, or Fort Kamloops, had been founded in 1812 by the
PFC as Alexander Ross's Fort She-whap [Shuswap] and quickly duplicated by the NWC's Fort Cumcloups. Owing to the vicinity's paucity of
beaver, as well as the hostility of the natives, the post was vacated every
spring and reoccupied every autumn until 1827, when it was "kept up"
over the summer by up to four men.[2] Otherwise, as Clerk Archibald
McDonald had warned in 1826, everything "must be left to the mercy of
the Indians if a couple of men as I have already hinted are not to remain
for the Summer." Indeed, in late 1824 Thompson's River was threatened
with permanent abandonment because its returns had decreased and its
expenses increased; the 1823-24 take of 1,700 beaver did "little more
than cover the interest on the capital employed."[3] The post was reprieved
by the rerouting of the brigade from the Peace to the Columbia, as well
as by Governor Simpson's economy measures. Although returns at

Thompson's River and Fort Okanagan together had risen from 1,600 beaver in 1817 to 2,950 in 1822 but fallen to 1,000 in 1826, both were retained because they were "necessary for the Communication," in the words of Archibald McDonald, who served as bourgeois at the former.[4] In 1825-26 the fort measured 110 feet square and housed eleven men.[5] Its population comprised fifteen men, eleven women, and seventeen children in 1827.[6] By the summer of 1843 its complement was down to nine men, having returned only ten packs of furs in 1842-43.[7]

Thompson's River was located on the left bank of the North Thompson, or North River as it was more commonly known, and the right bank of the South Thompson at the junction of the two waterways. The site was subject to occasional flooding, as in 1826 when the fort was "generally overflowed during the Summer flush."[8] Following the murder of bourgeois Black in early 1841, the post was moved to the western from the eastern side of the North Thompson. When Black's successor, John Tod, arrived in the summer of that year, he found the fort in a sorry state.[9] In the fall of 1841 and the winter of 1841-42, the men of the post were busy up both the North and South Thompson, cutting and squaring wood for a new fort, which was erected on the new site between the fall of 1842 and the fall of 1843, finally being occupied on 11 October 1843.[10]

Thompson's River was not an easy posting. According to the son of John McLeod, bourgeois of the post from 1822 to 1826, it was "a troublesome and most arduous, as well as perilous charge."[11] Not surprisingly, the interlopers found the local natives sometimes hostile (one was to kill bourgeois Black), as well as pesky. Particularly, their demand for tobacco seemed insatiable. "Nothing can exceed their fancy for Tobacco," reported McDonald.[12] They smoked so ardently that McLeod referred to their habit as a "smoking match."

Provisions were problematical, too. The servants ate mostly salmon (fresh and dried), a little venison, some horse and dog flesh, a few geese, some potatoes, and a bit of "corn" (grain). A potato yield of up to twenty-fold the seed was not uncommon,[13] and by 1841 some of the local Indians, including Chief Nicola, were growing potatoes. But salmon was the staple. "Here," reported McLeod, "we have nothing else to depend on but dried Salmon, God help him that passes many years on such poor stuff."[14] Thompson's River's servants spent much of their time procuring this staple. As McLeod's successor, McDonald, noted on 3 December 1826: "As usual we are hammering about [striving] after Salmon."[15] He added that "Dried Salmon is the Staff of life and fortunately seldom fails."[16] But, when that happened, wrote Governor Simpson, "they contrive to maintain themselves on Roots & dried berries, a species of living, closely allied to Starvation."[17] The daily allowance of dried salmon in 1827 was three per man, two per woman, and one per child, and in 1826, 18,411 were consumed at the post.[18] The salmon fare was seldom augmented, as on 25 December 1826 when McDonald reported: "This being Christmas day the two men at home with me were regaled with a good fat Dog & then three dried salmon each."[19]

Most of the salmon was traded from natives at the "Forks," the confluence of the Fraser and Thompson Rivers. Every autumn and winter four or five trips (each lasting from twelve to fifteen days) had to be made there for Fraser salmon, which, although smaller than Columbia salmon, still weighed one pound each when dried, split, and filleted.[20] The dried salmon were packed in bundles of one hundred each, and two such bundles formed one horse load. For example, on 11 October 1826 a party of seven men with twenty-seven horses returned from a two-week trip to the Forks with 6,000 dried salmon, and on 27 November another party returned from a twelve-day trip with 4,000 dried salmon (instead of the expected 6,000).[21] And sometimes Thompson's River had to supply Fort Okanagan with salmon. On 17 October 1826 two men with eight horses and 1,600 dried salmon left the former for the latter (and 500 of these fish were subsequently forwarded from Fort Okanagan to Fort Nez Percés), and on 4 December another 2,800 dried salmon left Thompson's River by horse for Fort Okanagan.[22] Again, in early December of 1841, 6,000 dried salmon were brought from Alexandria, and 2,000 of them were dispatched to Fort Okanagan.[23]

Being located at the midpoint of the horse trail between the Fraser and Columbia Rivers, Thompson's River also supplied fresh horses for the brigade. The post's servants included "horse keepers" and a "horse guard" (of usually two men in 1822-23), and the facilities, a "horse park" (corral). In the middle of December 1822 (the last year that the brigade plied the Columbia route before switching to the Peace route for the next three years) there were eighty-six horses and fifteen colts at Thompson's River, for which 200 "bundles" of "excellent" hay had been cut in the middle of August for the ensuing winter, which proved to be the coldest since 1810-11.[24] Consequently, starving local natives were tempted to raid the horses on the open range. Bourgeois McLeod complained that "we are not entirely independent, we have [a] great many Horses at their [the natives'] mercy in the plains." Later in the winter he added that "I am much in dread that the unusual number of OK [Okanagan] Indians who are now gathered here without any thing to subsist upon, will attempt to steal some of our Horses and consequently, unavoidably, breed a serious quarrel, they have been rather impartnent [impertinent] to our Horse Keepers for some days past." When on 22 January a local chief demanded the return of a horse that his late father had exchanged with one of the servants, McLeod "prevailed on the man to give it up, as this same Indian had on several occasions resqued many of the Company's Horses from the hands [of] other Indians."[25] Occasionally the servants slaughtered an injured horse for food, as McLeod reported on 8 January 1823: "Killed a mare that had a broken leg, we were keeping her for [a] time back in the Stable, but as she was only getting worse instead of better I ordered to Kill her whilst eatable."[26]

When the brigade was rerouted to the Columbia from the Peace in 1826, more horses were again kept at Thompson's River, although the number is uncertain. Besides the brigade animals, each man at the post had two horses for performing his duties, and each married man had one or two extra horses for gathering provisions for his family.[27] The horses continued to suffer, as the post journal for 1826-27 reveals. Overworked mares miscarried. "It is to be regretted," wrote McDonald to McLoughlin in the late summer of 1826, "that the Mares cannot be more moderatly used at Thompsons River – they are now by far the Greatest portion of our Horses – last fall 21 took the Stud but this Summer we have only the prospect of half a Dozen Colts." Sore throats (strangles, an infectious, febrile disease of young horses in particular), sore backs, and sore hooves were the main afflictions. In the middle of October the horse keeper, Antoine Bomdignon, moved his charges ten miles up the North Thompson to a more sheltered location because "many of them begin to get a bad Cough & swelled throats resembling the Strangles." "Several of them still much affected with the *Strangles*," recorded McDonald in the middle of November, "but a constant change to clean grass [to escape the bacterium] is the best Doctor they can have." At the beginning of December, however, he added: "Many of them unfortunately are affected with a dirty disease resembling the *Strangles*."

Their sore backs were caused by packing heavy loads over long distances without enough food or rest. Occasionally their backs were washed with a potash solution to ease the soreness, as on 17 September and 10 November. On 4 January 1827, following the return of a fish trading expedition of eight men and sixteen horses that had left on 23 December, McDonald noted: "The horses much harased after the trip, they suffer greatly from the wearing away of their hooves." On 29 January he added: "coming back [from another such expedition] the poor horses suffered much, tumbling in the hills head over heels like as many wool sacks" on account of their sore feet, being unshod. And on 14 February he wrote:

"Four more of our horses died within these three days – the effects of the misery they suffered on [the] last trip for the Salmon." Native rustling remained a threat, too, especially in winter, as McDonald reported on 2 February: "The last Brigade of horses taken up the North [Thompson] river with the rest, where two men will constantly attend them for the future, as now is the Season the Natives are more liable to stroll about & less scrupulous about helping themselves."[28] In the spring colts were "stamped" (branded) and gelded, and sometimes they died after being cut. And occasionally "marons" (or "marrons") – unbroken horses – were injured in the process of breaking.

THE HORSE BRIGADE

The horse trail from Thompson's River to Fort Okanagan (see Map 3) was well worn by 1826, since the former had always been served by the Columbia route and never by the Peace. The trail crossed the Thompson River right outside the fort and followed the route of the Trans-Canada Highway along the left bank of the South Thompson (and sometimes the right bank) as far as the Monté (Monte Creek), where it turned south to ascend the Thompson Plateau, approximating the routes of Highway 97 and the CNR. The trail followed the course of Monte Creek to Campement du Poulin (Monte Lake?), skirted the lake itself, and crossed the Birch River (Pringle Creek?) to Grande Prairie, the grassy valley of the Salmon River between present-day Westwold and Falkland. From there the northern side of the valley was followed through the Hills (plateau highlands) until the river turned northwards, whereupon the horse track veered southwards past Lac Ronde (Round Lake), crossed the drainage divide between the Fraser and Columbia basins, and descended to the northern end of Big Okanagan Lake (Okanagan Lake).[29] Taking approximately the route of Westside Road along the lake's western shore, it crossed the Rivière de Talle d'Épinette, or Red Deers River (Equesis Creek?), the Rivière de Borgnes (Naswhito Creek?), the Rivière de Aguires (Whiteman Creek?), and the Rivière au Paquets (Shorts Creek?), passed the steep, rocky cliffs of Mauvais Rocher just north of present-day Nahun, crossed the Rivière la Biche (Lambly Creek?), and reached L'Anse au Sable (Westbank). There it rejoined the route of Highway 97, crossed the Rivière d'Ours (Powers Creek?), the Rivière à Jacques et du Borgne (Trépanier Creek), and the Rivière à Trépanier (Peachland Creek?), passed L'Arbre Seul, or the Tree along the Lake, just north of Antlers Saddle on Highway 97, crossed the Rivière Prairie de Nicholas (Eneas Creek), and reached Prairie de Nicholas (Nicola Prairie, the site of Summerland).

South of here the track split into an upper (inland) trail and a lower (lakeside) trail. The upper variant crossed the Rivière de la Fruite (Trout Creek), the Rivière du Poulin, or Beaver River (Shingle Creek above its junction with Shatford Creek?), the Rivière la Cendri (Shatford Creek?), the Rivière aux Serpens (Marron River?), and the middle course of Park Rill (from *parc*, "corral") to Fourche de Chemin, just south of White Lake. There it reunited with the lower variant, which had followed the western shore of Okanagan Lake, crossed the Rivière aux Serpens, and skirted Lac du Chien (Skaha Lake). The horse trail then took Park Rill to Bute de Sable, or Côte de Sable, where the stream joins the Okanagan River, and followed its right bank across Rivière au Thé (Testalinden Creek) to the Narrows (Osoyoos) of Little Lake Okanagan (Osoyoos Lake). Sometimes the brigaders crossed the Narrows and skirted the lake's eastern shore, and sometimes they stayed on the western side. At its southern end the trail crossed the Okanogan River at its entrance, the Barrière, passed the forks (Oroville) of the Okanogan and Chemilcommen (Similkameen) Rivers, and followed the left bank of the Okanogan past the Little Chutes to its junction with the Columbia at Fort Okanagan.[30]

The pack train, after stopping overnight at Thompson's River, took just over a week to reach Fort Okanagan, usually arriving at the end of May or the beginning of June (so that the pack horses took three weeks altogether to go from the Fraser to the Columbia, and another three weeks in the summer to return). However, whenever New Caledonia was not served by the Columbia route – 1805-20 (generally) and 1823-25 – the brigade left Thompson's River much earlier than the middle of May, since it was not necessary to await the arrival of New Caledonia's returns via Alexandria. It was also not necessary to await spring break-up, since boats and canoes were not used on this leg. The 1823 brigade, for example, left Thompson's River on 1 March with thirty-four packs of furs (each pack weighing 90 pounds for a total of 3,060 pounds), three bales of "sundry" goods, and 4,600 dried salmon, plus 960 dried salmon for the trip, on ninety-one horses and fourteen colts (yearlings). Of the salmon, 1,500-2,000 were intended for Fort Okanagan and the rest for "the maintenance of all hands till the embarkation for Fort George." The keys to Thompson's River were left with Chief "Shewshapp" (Shuswap), "who is to take care of it all summer, as he has done for some years back," wrote bourgeois McLeod. The brigade reached Fort Okanagan on 18 March "with all goods and Chattles safe and sound without sustaining any other lose [loss] than that of one horse that was accidentally killed our third day from Thompsons River." En route one mare and one colt were sold for twenty-seven beaver and three otter skins, and another

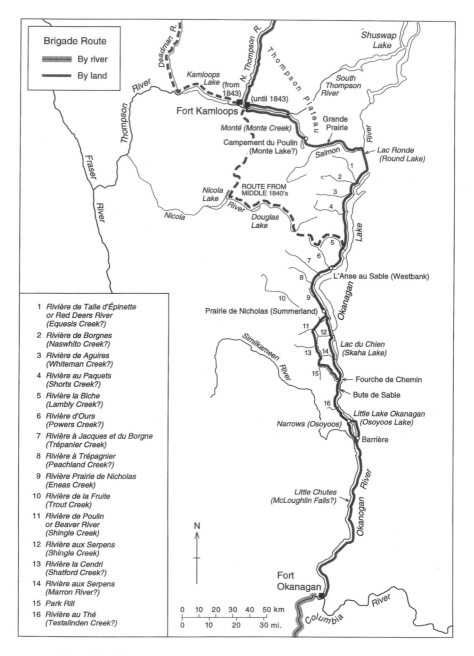

Brigade Route

⬜⬜⬜ By river
▬▬▬ By land

Shuswap Lake

Deadman R.

N. Thompson R.

Thompson Plateau

Kamloops Lake (from 1843)

South Thompson River

(until 1843)

Fort Kamloops

Grande Prairie

Monté (Monte Creek)

Salmon River

Lac Ronde (Round Lake)

Campement du Poulin (Monte Lake?)

Thompson River

Fraser River

1

2

ROUTE FROM MIDDLE 1840's

3

Nicola Lake

4

Nicola River

Douglas Lake

Lake

5

Nicola

6

7

8   L'Anse au Sable (Westbank)

10   9

Okanagan Lake

Prairie de Nicholas (Summerland)

11

12

Similkameen River

13   14   Lac du Chien (Skaha Lake)

15   Fourche de Chemin

Bute de Sable

16   Little Lake Okanagan (Osoyoos Lake)

Narrows (Osoyoos)

Barrière

Little Chutes (McLoughlin Falls?)

Okanogan River

Fort Okanagan

Columbia River

1   *Rivière de Talle d'Épinette or Red Deers River (Equesis Creek?)*

2   *Rivière de Borgnes (Naswhito Creek?)*

3   *Rivière de Aguires (Whiteman Creek?)*

4   *Rivière au Paquets (Shorts Creek?)*

5   *Rivière la Biche (Lambly Creek?)*

6   *Rivière d'Ours (Powers Creek?)*

7   *Rivière à Jacques et du Borgne (Trépanier Creek?)*

8   *Rivière à Trépagnier (Peachland Creek?)*

9   *Rivière Prairie de Nicholas (Eneas Creek)*

10   *Rivière de la Fruite (Trout Creek)*

11   *Rivière de Poulin or Beaver River (Shingle Creek)*

12   *Rivière aux Serpens (Shingle Creek)*

13   *Rivière la Cendri (Shatford Creek?)*

14   *Rivière aux Serpens (Marron River?)*

15   *Park Rill*

16   *Rivière au Thé (Testalinden Creek?)*

N

0   10   20   30   40   50 km
0   10   20   30 mi.

MAP 3 From Fort Kamloops to Fort Okanagan

fifty-three beaver skins were traded. Also, reported McLeod, "along the Route Several attempts were made to steal our horses by the Okanagan Indians but all in vain, we had a Guard of Six men every night keeping watch." Altogether, eighty-nine horses, thirteen colts, thirty-four packs of beaver at 90 pounds and one pack at 80 pounds (for a total of 3,140 pounds), and 4,600 dried salmon were delivered to Fort Okanagan. Between 18 March and 31 March all of Fort Okanagan's furs were pressed and packed, and all of McLeod's brigaders with two boats and thirty horses were sent to Spokane House to help bring its returns to Fort Okanagan.[31]

But from 1826 the brigades did not leave Thompson's River until the middle of May, when, incidentally, there was more grass for the horses and more fish and game for the brigaders en route. The 1826 brigade departed on 25 May, the horses having been "caught, tackled & loaded" after being crossed to the left bank of the "South Branch" (South Thompson River) the previous day. About 1,100 dried salmon had to be left at Thompson's River "for want of Cords to tie them with." The pack train made Fort Okanagan under Connolly on 3 June with the property – eighty-five packs of furs and six kegs of castoreum – "all in excellent order" and the horses "as well as can be expected." Fifty-seven horses remained, including five belonging to the natives of Alexandria; one hundred would be needed for the return trip.[32]

The 1827 brigade left Thompson's River earlier and reached Fort Okanagan faster, the horses being in better shape upon their departure, not having had to endure as severe a winter at Alexandria as that of 1825-26. They departed on 18 May and arrived at Fort Okanagan, after only eight days, on the 26th with "all the property in excellent condition" and the horses in "fair order."[33] Similarly, the 1828 brigade left Thompson's River on 19 May and reached Fort Okanagan eight days later, on the 27th, with the property in "good condition" and the horses in "excellent order"; the "voyaging agrés" were then dried and the boat ladings for the Columbia "given out."[34] The 1829 brigade left Thompson's River on 21 May, reinforced by the five servants of that post, "it being found inexpeditious to keep up that establishment during the summer." It made Fort Okanagan on the 29th – again, after eight days – with the property "safe and in good condition" and the horses in "as good condition as can be expected after such a long voyage"; it had been preceded on the 23rd by the Fort Colvile brigade with that post's returns.[35] And the 1831 brigade left Thompson's River on 26 May with two additional horses hired from the local natives (at a cost of ten made beaver each), as well as 1,018 dried salmon as provisions for the trip; it arrived at Fort Okanagan on 3 June – yet again, after eight days – with the packs "all safe and in good order & the horses in Excellent Condition considering the long voyage they have performed."[36]

Fewer delays were encountered on the Thompson's River-Fort Okanagan than on the Alexandria-Thompson's River stretch. The weather was warmer, the grass was higher, and the natives seem to have been less thievish. Spring here did tend to be rainy, however. The 1826 brigade leader, Chief Factor Connolly, reported that rain "retarded us much" on 29 May along the western shore of Okanagan Lake, and early in the morning of 1 June, probably between Deadman Lake and Osoyoos Lake, "much delay occurred in passing through a long miry Prairie in which the Horses sunk to their Bellies, and many of them could not be extricated without being unloaded."[37] Rain halted the 1829 brigade for half a day on 26 May and another half day on the 27th.[38] And the 1831 brigade had a late start on 30 May so "that the water may fall from the trees," it having "rained most part of the night."[39]

Provisions were sometimes scarce, too. The 1828 brigade sent two men ahead from the halfway point on 22 May to Fort Okanagan "in order that the [Columbia] Boats may be held in readiness against our arrival there," since the scarcity of provisions at that post "will not admit of our making any long stay." And when the brigade reached Fort Okanagan, two horses were slaughtered for food.[40]

But the worst obstacle was the rough terrain surrounding Okanagan Lake. The brigade trail along the western shore was, in Connolly's words, "rugged & fatiguing to the Horses."[41] To relieve their sore backs and sore feet they were "baited" once or twice daily, and occasionally, as on 24 May 1829, a man was sent ahead to Fort Okanagan to get a few fresh horses for "relieving such of our own as are beginning to fag, and to lend to some of our men whose feet are so sore" (these met the brigade on the 26th).[42] Usually half a dozen or more horses perished each trip. The survivors sorely needed the two-month rest at Fort Okanagan before returning to Thompson's River and Alexandria with the outfit at the beginning of August.

In addition, of course, there were the usual minor delays caused by straying horses. On 2 June, one day from Fort Okanagan, the 1826 brigade missed four colts, and Gregoire, the horse keeper, and a native were sent to find them.[43] And on 22 May, the second day from Thompson's River, the 1829 brigade made a late start because some of the horses had strayed "a considerable distance" during the night; consequently, the brigaders had to "force the march," not stopping until later than usual that day in order to regain the lost time.[44]

Upon reaching Fort Okanagan, the brigaders unloaded and pastured the horses and dried and stored the *agrès*. Usually only a couple of days were spent there readying the boats for the downriver dash to the sea, unless they had to await the arrival of boats from Fort Colvile with its returns.

CHAPTER 7

Boating down the Columbia

The Easy Leg
from Okanagan to Walla Walla

Amongst the innumerable rivers that traverse the American continent, and afford means of communication between its most distant portions, the Columbia river is one of the most remarkable, not only on account of its great importance, west of the mountains, but also from the dangers that attend its navigation.

— FATHER PIERRE-JEAN DE SMET, 1842[1]

FORTS OKANAGAN AND COLVILE

Fort Okanagan, like Alexandria, was a major transshipment point for the brigade system. Here the returns were transferred from pack horses to river boats and, conversely, the outfit from boats to horses. The establishment was founded in early September 1811 by the Astorians as Oakinacken Post (whence a party under Alexander Stuart probed as far north as the South Thompson, founded a post at its junction with the North Thompson, and wintered among the Shuswaps before returning in the spring).[2] The post, in 1841, was located on a flat, sandy neck on the right bank of the Columbia River, two miles above the Okanogan forks and sixty yards from the Columbia itself.[3] Earlier it seems to have been found on the left bank of the Okanogan just above the Columbia forks. In 1825-26 it measured 80 feet by 100 feet and contained two houses, one storehouse, and one Indian shop; the complement was only three men, for the local natives were "remarkable for their quiet and peaceable conduct."[4]

Archibald McDonald was very familiar with what he called "Okanokan, where a Gentl^n & two men are usually kept for the whole Year, & whose principal duty in the Summer is the Care of the Horses & the little that Can be done in the way of Gardening."[5] He added elsewhere that "like Kameloops it is necessary for the Communication."[6]

Governor Simpson noted in 1828 that the post yielded "few" furs and was retained "almost entirely … for the purpose of Watching Boats, Horses, Provisions &c."[7] Dried salmon was, according to McDonald, the "Staff of life."[8] But Lieutenant Amelius Simpson, R.N., the governor's uncle-in-law who visited Fort Okanagan on his way to Fort Vancouver to take charge of the company's "marine department" on the coast, found that potatoes of an "excellent quality" were grown and eaten, too, and that they tended "to render the Salmon, which forms the chief article of food, a far more palatable and healthy diet."[9] Lieutenant Henry Warre, a British army officer on an inspection tour of the Columbia District, described the post in the summer of 1845: "The Fort or rather the Buildings are enclosed by Palisades about 12 feet high, and without any other pretension to defence, being merely used as a Depot. It is situated on a small Plain on the North Shore & the River banks afford some Pasturage for the horses and Cattle belonging to the Company; On the South bank, opposite the Fort is a large Plain, but the greater part is flooded every spring. It however as soon as the Water recedes affords pasturage for Cattle after the grass of the Hills surrounding, is quite burnt up."[10] At Fort Okanagan the brigade added not only its returns but also those of Fort Colvile, which in turn included those from the Kootenay and Flathead Posts (temporary winter establishments, sometimes combined into one[11]).

Fort Colvile was founded in 1825 just above Kettle (Chaudière or Swahniquet) Falls, the highest on the Columbia at twenty-eight feet (they were the only falls on the entire river that were never run by the Bay men) and a popular native fishing spot. Lieutenant Wilkes rated the falls "one of the greatest curiosities in this part of the country"; here, he wrote, "the river forces its way over a rocky bed until it reaches the main fall, where the water is thrown into every variety of shape and form, resembling the boiling of a kettle."[12] The post replaced Spokane House (abandoned in 1826) because of, Governor Simpson reported, the "most serious expense and inconvenience" of transport between that post and the forks of the Columbia and Spokane Rivers (goods had to be hauled on horseback for two or three days).[13] Moreover, he added, Fort Colvile was a "more desirable situation in regard to Farming, Fish, provisions generally as also in respect to Trade."[14] Crop growing, stock rearing, horse trading, boat building, transporting (brigade and express), and outfitting (Flathead and Kootenay Posts), as well as fur trading, became the post's foremost functions. Already in 1830, when it contained 26 men, 13 women, and 28 children, the harvest comprised 751 bushels of wheat, 430 of corn, 168 of peas, 130 of oats, and 103 of barley, and 5,006 kegs of potatoes (twentyfold yield).[15] Farming was so successful that Fort Colvile became, as Governor Simpson reported in 1834, "the granary or provision Depôt of the interior," in spite of the occasional flood and severe winter. High water normally lasted from mid-May to mid-June, but in July 1830 "much" of the cropland was inundated by the Columbia, which on 12 July stood "higher than ever seen here before by our people"; in the winter of 1830-31 the horses were reduced to "mere skelitons" and many of them died (the surrounding natives lost "immense numbers" of theirs), and in the winter of 1846-47 it was "so coald in oragon" that 317 of the post's 320 horses perished (the local natives' horses also "suffered grately").[16] In 1841 Lieutenant Wilkes found that crop growing was Fort Colvile's "principal object of attention," enabling it to provision all of the northern posts.[17] When that year's incoming brigade reached Fort Okanagan, it was met by forty horses loaded with provisions from Fort Colvile destined for New Caledonia.[18] By the middle 1840s the thirty servants of Fort Colvile were reaping about 1,000 bushels of wheat from 118 acres and tending 300-400 horses, up to 100 cattle, and some 75 pigs.[19]

For the brigade system, however, boat building and boat handling were the crucial activities. Each loomed large in the 1830-31 round, for example, when vessels were built at the boathouse for both the brigade and the express: 12 April 1830, "Today [Pierre] La Course, the builder, with another man were employed at laying a boat on the stocks"; 23 April, four men were building boats, and another four were making rafting poles; 24 April, one boat was completed; 28 April, a second boat was finished and a third started; 4 May, a third boat was completed; 7 May, a fourth (and last) boat was completed; 10 May, "La Course & big Charles have gone off to the cedars to complete the Boats"; 21 May, six men were gumming the boats; 15 and 19 November, two men "raised" timbers for six new boats; 22 through 24 November, the boatbuilder fetched stem and stern posts for the new boats; during the winter of 1830-31 the logs for the new boats were sawn by a pit saw and then planed; and in the spring of 1831 the new boats were assembled.[20]

The post's boat handlers were equally busy: 20 April 1830, the eastbound spring express left for York Factory in one boat with eight crewmen and ten passengers; 24 May, Fort Colvile's returns of 173 pieces, including sixty-seven of furs, left for Fort Okanagan in five boats (four of them new) with twenty men, each of whom was given a regale (an issue of food and drink upon departure) of one loaf of bread and one pound of pork; 14 July, six men and fifteen horses were sent to Fort Okanagan to "relieve" the brigade boats bound for Fort Colvile with its outfit (they were being slowed by high water); 25 July, a horse party returned with thirty pieces; 27 July, another party of three men with fifteen horses was sent to relieve the boats; 31 July, the brigade of three boats arrived, and the second horse party returned with thirty pieces (and "Indians of all the different tribes begin to pour in to trade, so that we have our hands full"); 3 August, four Fort Okanagan men who had assisted the boat brigade were sent back; 25 September, the eastbound fall express of two boats with fourteen crewmen and eighteen passengers plus eighty pieces left "for the mountain" (Boat Encampment) to meet the westbound express; 21 October, the westbound fall express arrived in three boats and one canoe with fifty-four men and 108 pieces; and 23 October, the express left for Fort Vancouver in four boats with forty-one men.[21]

Usually up to half a dozen boats, as in 1828, plied the 140 miles from Fort Colvile to Fort Okanagan in late May to join the brigade, carrying provisions and leather for Forts Okanagan, Kamloops, and Nez Percés, as well as furs for Fort Vancouver.[22] Sometimes the horse brigade preceded Fort Colvile's boats at Fort Okanagan, as in 1826, when two boats with thirteen men did not arrive until 6 June, three days after the horse brigade.[23] Sometimes the boat brigaders arrived first, as in 1828, when they reached Fort Okanagan by 23 May, four days before the horse brigaders, and they spent the next three days repairing the old boats, which were in "very bad order" from exposure to "all weathers."[24] Peter Skene Ogden, bourgeois of New Caledonia from 1835 to 1845, usually left Stuart's Lake around 22 April in order to make Fort Okanagan in time to send his men to Fort Colvile "to assist in bringing down the Boats ... as with strong crews [they] are less liable to accidents in that most dangerous part of the river and with our weak bowmen for the safety of life and property too many precautions cannot be taken."[25]

The "Brigade of Boats"

The Fort Okanagan-Fort Vancouver stretch of the brigade route was called des porteurs, for in places, such as portages, the brigaders had to carry the property on their own backs.[26] Otherwise, of course, it was carried in boats, not canoes, which were too flimsy to bear the precious returns in safety in the turbulent waters of the Cordilleran rivers. Columbia boats, or batteaux, were clinker-built, flat-bottomed, shallow-draught boats similar in length (thirty feet) to York boats but narrower in the beam (five and one-half feet versus seven to eight feet) and smaller in capacity (fifty pieces versus seventy pieces); their lighter weight was more suited to the longer and steeper portages of the Columbia

Department.[27] Batteaus were described by Chief Factor Alexander Kennedy of Fort George in his district report for 1824-25: "Of a peculiar construction, they are made in imitation of bark canoes, & have been much improved upon since the first invention by Mr. David Thompson. The boats now carry from 40 to 50 pieces, and are navigated by 8 men each. They are wrought by paddles instead of oars, and are carried over the portages on men's shoulders, but it requires the crews of two boats to carry one."[28]

The vessels were made at Fort Colvile (previously at Spokane House) from quarter-inch yellow pine or red cedar boards, 30-32 feet long and 5½-6½ feet wide at the beam, pointed at both ends, large enough to transport up to fifty pieces (or up to 500 bushels of wheat) and light enough to be navigated and shouldered by eight to ten men. In the fall of 1825 at Spokane House, sawyers in fifteen days finished cutting enough wood for three boats: seventy-three boards 6 inches wide and 40 feet long for sideboards, three pieces 14 inches wide and 40 feet long for keels, and six pieces 2 inches wide and 40 feet long for gunwales,[29] so each vessel comprised twenty-four 40-foot boards, twelve per side, making each about 3½ feet high (allowing 1½ inches for overlap and 1 inch for curvature) and about 35 feet long (allowing 5 feet for curvature). Batteaus varied somewhat in their dimensions, depending upon where and when they were made, perhaps as well as by whom. The number of crewmen likewise varied – from seven to ten – in accordance with the amount of cargo, the state of the river, and even the condition of the boatmen.

Batteaux were, in fact, both rowed and paddled, depending upon the situation. With oars the boatmen could "do more work with greater ease";[30] in other words, they were more efficient. Oars were used, according to Wilkes, "after the French or Spanish fashion, adding the whole weight of the body to the strength of the arm."[31] Usually, however, oars were replaced by paddles, the reason being, in Kennedy's words, "that the current is very strong in some parts of the River where these craft by the means of paddles are enabled to Keep close in shore where the current is less felt than they could do if oars were used instead of paddles."[32]

Batteaux were nailed and pitched (gummed), not caulked, with a mixture of sawpit resin and tallow.[33] En route they had to be beached and gummed frequently because the sun's rays melted above-water gum and the seams opened.[34] Lieutenant Wilkes described the gumming operation:

> On landing the goods, the boats are tracked up and turned bottom up, when they are suffered to dry; two flat-sided pieces of fire-wood, about two feet

long, are then laid together, and put into the fire, until both are well lighted, and the wood burns readily at one end and in the space between; they then draw the lighted end slowly along the gummed seam, blowing at the same time between the sticks: this melts the gum, and a small spatula is used to smooth it off and render the seam quite tight. The common gum of the pine or hemlock is that used; and a supply is always carried with them.[35]

The origin of batteaux is likely traceable to David Thompson, who in 1811 named the Canoe River (the Columbia tributary that debouched at the Boat Encampment) after the wooden canoes that he built there for descending the Columbia.[36] Upon crossing the Rockies via Athabasca Pass at the end of 1810, Thompson had found "forest Trees [cedar and fir] of enormous size." He exclaimed: "on the east side of the Mountains the Trees were small, a stunted growth with branches to the ground; there we were Men, but on the west side we were pigmies."[37] Then Thompson found it necessary to build wooden instead of bark canoes:

> Having now [March 1811] examined the White Birch in every quarter, for Birch Rind [bark] wherewith to make a Canoe for our voyage to the Pacific Ocean, without finding any even thick enough to make a dish; such is the influence of a mild climate on the rind of the Birch Tree. We had to turn our thoughts to some other material, and Cedar wood being the lightest and most pliable for a Canoe, we split out thin boards of Cedar wood of about six inches in breadth and built a Canoe of twenty five feet in length by fifty inches in breadth, of the same form of a common Canoe, using cedar boards instead of Birch Rind, which proved to be equally light and much stronger than Birch Rind, the greatest difficulty we had was sewing the boards to each round the timbers. As we had no nails we had to make use of the fine Roots of the Pine [fir] which we split.[38]

After descending the Columbia as far as Kettle Falls in June, Thompson was unable to find any "good clean Cedar and White Birch" in the vicinity for making wooden or bark canoes.[39]

In 1812 Robert Stuart of the PFC observed what he called the "canoes" used by the NWC west of the Rockies. They were made of cedar boards, ¼ inch thick, which were secured by sturgeon twine to cedar braces, or knees, 3/8 inch thick, and were chinked with gum. He noted that they were "excellent in shallow water, long and bad portages, and may do tolerably well in small and insignificant rapids" and that they were the equal of bark canoes in terms of "facility of transportation."[40] Nevertheless, according to Astorian Alexander Ross, among the Nor'Westers "a great partiality subsisted in favour of the good old bark canoes of Northern reputation [North canoes]," so that the Columbia "country was ransacked for prime birch bark more frequently than for prime furs," and a stock was even shipped from Montreal to London and thence to Fort George via the Horn "to guard against a failure in this fanciful article." He added that on the Columbia, however, the PFC itself used craft that "consisted of split or sawed cedar boats, strong, light and durable, and in every possible way safer and better adapted for rough water than the birch rind canoes in general use on the east side of the mountains." They could carry some 3,000 pounds, yet were "nimbly handled" and "easily carried" over portages.[41]

En route to inspect the Oregon Country in 1824, Governor Simpson embarked at the Boat Encampment in Columbia batteaux, which he described with a view – as usual – to more economy:

> The Craft used on the Columbia are of a different construction to those on the east side of the mountain; they are called Boats but are more properly speaking Batteaux & wrought by Paddles instead of Oars, intended to carry 50 pieces Trading Goods besides Provisions for the Crew of Eight Men but they have of late reduced the size altho' they have not reduced the number of the Crew so that Eight Men are employed in the transport of about 35 pieces; I do not know whether this innovation is meant as an indulgence to the Masters or the Men, but suspect it is agreeable to both altho' injurious to the Comp[y] as thereby one third more people are employed in transport than necessary. I shall however take care that this evil is remedied before my departure and endeavour to improve on the original plan Seven Men being in my opinion quite sufficient to Navigate a Boat containing Fifty pieces Cargo and the Crews of two Boats equal to the transport of One across the Portages.[42]

One way in which the Columbia batteaux were "different" from those on the other side of the Rockies was their lighter weight. In early 1828, when Chief Factor Connolly of New Caledonia gave his "opinion in regard to the influence the change of [brigade] route [from the Peace to the Columbia] may have upon the affairs of this district," he said that "for the navigation boats will unquestionably be better adapted than bark canoes and from their superior lightness as they will have to be carried such as are used in the Columbia ought in my opinion to have the preference."[43] The relative lightness of the Columbia batteaux eased the long portages at the Dalles and the Cascades on the lower course of the river, as well as at Kettle Falls on the middle course.

Their lightness and sturdiness impressed Peter Burnett, an American settler who arrived on the lower Columbia with the "great migration" of

1843 (and later became the first governor of the State of California). He encountered batteaux at the junction of the Oregon Trail and the Columbia River near Fort Nez Percés:

> These boats are very light, yet strong. They are open, about forty feet long, five feet wide, and three feet deep, made of light, tough materials, and clinker-built. They are made in this manner so that they may be carried around the falls [Dalles] of the Columbia, and let down over the Cascades. When taken out of the water and carried over the portage, it requires the united exertions of forty or fifty Indians, who take the vessel on their shoulders, amid shouts and hurras, and thus carry it sometimes three fourths of a mile, without once letting it down. At the Cascades it is let down by means of ropes in the hands of the Canadian boatmen.[44]

Lieutenants Henry Warre and Mervyn Vavasour, the British military officers who inspected the Columbia District for Her Majesty's Government in 1845, reported that this "large Boat, made of Cedar," which could carry from fifteen to twenty men, had been found "after repeated trials to be the best adapted for the intricate River navigation."[45] Perhaps the best description of the Columbia batteau was provided by Lieutenant Wilkes, who as a navigator and explorer was a knowledgeable boatman. He wrote: "The boat was somewhat of the model of our whale-boats, only much larger, and of the kind built expressly to accommodate the trade: they are provided yearly at Okonagan, and are constructed in a few days: they are clinker-built, and all the timbers are flat. These boats are so light that they are easily carried across the portages. They use the gum of the pine to cover them instead of pitch."[46] Later he gave more details, noting in particular the lack of nails:

> The shape of these boats has been before described: they have great strength and buoyancy, carry three tons weight, and have a crew of eight men, besides a padroon [commander]: they are thirty feet long and five and a half feet [at the] beam, sharp [pointed] at both ends, clinker-built, and have no knees. In building them, flat timbers of oak are bent to the requisite shape by steaming; they are bolted to a flat keel, at distances of a foot from each other: the planks are of cedar, and generally extend the whole length of the boat. The gunwale is of the same kind of wood, but the rowlocks are of birch. The peculiarity in the construction of these boats is, that they are only riveted at each end with a strong rivet, and being well gummed, they have no occasion for nailing. They answer, and indeed are admirably adapted to, all the purposes for which they are intended; are so light as to be easily transported over the portages by their crews, and in case of accident are easily repaired.[47]

Up to a dozen batteaux plied the Columbia. For the 1827 outfit, nine boats manned by fifty-four brigaders were needed to take it upriver from Fort Vancouver.[48] In anticipation, the boatbuilder Pierre La Course was posted to Fort Colvile from Thompson's River in the fall of 1826 to build three new boats, for nine would be required in 1827, and two of the eight old boats were "very Bad."[49] In 1828 twelve to thirteen batteaux were required for the "River Communication," including two for the Snake Expedition, and the rest, presumably, for the brigade and express.[50] Ten craft were needed at Fort Okanagan for the downriver brigade in 1836, and nine in 1837.[51]

The brigade was commonly augmented by both goods and hands at Fort Okanagan – goods from Forts Colvile and Okanagan for Forts Nez Percés and Vancouver and hands for the batteaux, which required more manpower than horses. Ogden's 1837 brigade, for example, was ordered to embark twelve kegs of gum from Fort Okanagan and as much flour and grain as Fort Colvile could afford for Walla Walla.[52] Approximately one-half of the boat crews was provided by the lower posts. The 1827 brigade left Fort Okanagan in eight boats with forty-three hands – twenty-four from New Caledonia, twelve from Fort Colvile, and seven from Fort Okanagan itself.[53] The 1837 brigade of nine boats required at least fifty-four men – twenty-four furnished by Forts Colvile and Nez Percés and eight by Fort Vancouver, in addition to the twenty-four brought from New Caledonia.[54] And the nine boats of the 1838 brigade were crewed by fifteen men from Fort Colvile, ten from Thompson's River, and four from Fort Vancouver, as well as twenty-four from New Caledonia.[55]

A batteau's crew comprised a guide (pilot), *boutes* (bowsmen, or oars-men, and steersmen), and middlemen. Warre and Vavasour counted "6 Men as Rowers and a Bows Man & Stears man who guides the Boat through the Rapids with very large Paddles. The Bows Man is the responsible Guide and it is the duty of the Stears Man to follow his directions."[56] Their relative importance was reflected in their salary differential (for non-natives) in the early 1820s: £30 for guides, £24 for steers-men, £20 for bowsmen, and £17 for middlemen.[57] All were highly skilled boatmen. Their skill in Thompson's Rapids between Forts Colvile and Okanagan impressed David Douglas in 1826. "No language," he asserted, "can convey an adequate idea of the dexterity shown by the Canadian boatmen: they pass through rapids, whirlpools, and narrow channels where, by the strength of such an immense body of water forcing its way, it is risen in the middle to a perfect convexity." "In such places," he added, "where you think the next moment you are to be dashed to pieces against the steep rocks, they approach and pass with an indescribable coolness, leaving it behind cheering themselves with an exulting boat-song."[58] Lieutenant Wilkes was equally impressed, as well as more specific about their different roles and particular skills: "The management of the boats in the rapids is dexterous and full of excitement, as well to the passengers as to the voyageurs themselves. The bowman is the most important man, giving all the directions, and is held responsible for the safety of the boat; and his keen eye and quick hand in the use of his paddle, delights and inspires a confidence in him in moments of danger that is given without stint."[59] He continued on the basis of information supplied by Chief Factor Ogden, probably the most experienced and knowledgeable brigader of all, since he conducted it for a decade between the middle 1830s and the middle 1840s:

> Mr. Ogden informed me, that the most experienced voyageur is taken as a pilot for the brigade, and he is the bowman of the leading boat; which is looked upon as a station of great trust and honour. Each boat has also its bowman, who is considered the first officer and responsible man; the safety of the boat, in descending rapids particularly, depends upon him and the padroon, who steers the boat. They both use long and large blade-paddles; and it is surprising how much power the two can exert over the direction of the boat. These men, from long training, become very expert, and acquire a coolness and disregard of danger that claim admiration, and astonishes those who are unused to such scenes.[60]

The boutes were usually Iroquois;[61] the others were Canadiens and Hawaiians. Iroquois had been introduced by the NWC in the double capacity of canoeists and trappers, eventually forming nearly a third of the Nor'Westers on the Columbia.[62] Alexander Ross rated them "expert voyageurs but especially so in the rapids and dangerous runs in the inland waters, which they either stem [advance against] or shoot with the utmost skill" (he also, incidentally, described them as indolent, cowardly, treacherous, deceitful, and sullen!).[63]

Following the example of the coast trade, the NWC (and the PFC) likewise hired Hawaiians ("Kanakas") to offset the shortage of Canadiens. Again according to Ross, they were obedient, honest, trustworthy, and fairly industrious, although awkward, but – most importantly to him – they were particularly courageous towards the Indians, whom they allegedly held in contempt, so that "the principal purpose for which they were useful on [the] Columbia was as an array of numbers in the view of the natives especially in the frequent voyages up and down the communication." Also, Hawaiians were much cheaper than Canadiens, being hired "for almost their bare victuals and clothing." Furthermore, they were "such expert swimmers that little of our effects are lost beyond recovery which accident now and then consigns to the bottom of the waters in our perilous navigations: and it is next to impossible for a person to get drowned if one or more of them are near at hand."[64] The NWC employed a score of Hawaiians in the 1810s, the *Tonquin* having brought a dozen and the *Beaver* another dozen to Astoria for the PFC.[65]

The lot of the boatmen was not an easy one. They rose early, worked long and hard under hazardous conditions and severe discipline for low pay, and ate plainly. Lieutenant Wilkes described their unenviable situation:

> To all appearance, there is seldom to be found a more laborious set of men; nor one so willing, particularly when their remuneration of no more than seventeen pounds sterling a year, and the fare they receive, are considered. The latter would be considered with us [Americans] incapable of supporting any human being. It consists of coarse unbolted [unsifted] bread, dried salmon, fat (tallow [grease]), and dried peas. I am satisfied that no American would submit to such food: the Canadian and Iroquois Indians use it without murmuring, except to strangers, to whom they complain much of their scanty pay and food. The discipline is strict, and of an arbitrary kind; yet they do not find fault with it.[66]

Culprits were treated harshly. Paul Kane observed that for insubordination or desertion "the punishment consisted in simply knocking the men down, kicking them until they got up, and knocking them down again until they could not get up any more, when they finished them off with a few more kicks."[67] Their diet was likewise severe: four dried salmon or ten pounds of fresh salmon or fifteen pounds of whitefish or twenty pounds of carp or three pounds of pemmican per day in the late 1820s.[68] Their heavy labour necessitated frequent rest stops – "pipes" (smoke breaks) – of several minutes' duration. Despite their circumstances, the brigaders exhibited a cheerfulness that was noted by most observers, such as Wilkes, who remarked that "the voyageurs have a lot of toil and deprivation, yet few men are to be found so cheerful." They were "as peculiar in their way as sailors," he added. "I was struck with their studious politeness and attention to each other, and their constant cheerfulness." And as soon as they shoved off, they "at once struck up one of their boat-songs ... each voyageur in succession took up the song, and all joined in the chorus."[69]

From Fort Okanagan to tidewater ("to the sea," as the Bay men put it) the brigade navigated the lower half of the "Great Columbia River" of Lewis and Clark (see Map 4). The stretch from Fort Okanagan to Fort Nez Percés ran some 200 miles in a north-south direction, turning southwards where Clearwater Creek (the Chelan River) entered the Columbia, passing the mouth of the Piscouhoose River (Wenatchee River) on the right bank, Les Terres Jaunes (Marle Banks) on the left bank, the entrance of the Yakima River on the right side, and the "great forks" of the main river (the so-called north branch), and the "Lewis and Clark River," or simply "Lewis's River" (the Snake River, the so-called south branch), on the left side, and bending westwards just after the mouth of the "Nez Percés River" (Walla Walla River) on the left bank.

The landscape changed markedly south of Fort Okanagan, becoming drier, sandier, and browner in the rain shadow of the Cascade Range to the west, the mountains rising higher here than they did farther north. Here along the western margin of what Donald Meinig has called the Great Columbia Plain the river cut deeply into the volcanic plateau, creating falls and rapids wherever it reached the basement rock, and here and there extensive "coulees" (glacial spillways) met the river. Vegetation was sparse and wildlife scarce (rattlesnakes excepted). Travellers were invariably impressed, often unfavourably. Warre and Vavasour, for instance, remarked that "the Country is desolate in the extreme, [with] interminable sandy deserts, extending on either side of the river intersected by ranges of high sandy Mountains, surmounted by rugged Basaltic rocks."[70] On their way downriver they elaborated: "For some distance above this point [Grand Rapids, just above Fort Okanagan] all appearance of Trees cease & the country is one boundless extent of barren Rocks and immense Sand Hills thrown together in the greatest confusion & evidently having been subject to the action of Volcanic eruptions & of Water." They then added:

> The appearance of the country is now [at Priest's Rapids] more desolate & volcanic action is more obvious. In some places the basaltic Rock rises in perpendicular columns in others they are horizontal. Their appearance is very singular, standing like immense Chimneys far above the loose soil which gradually crumbling away covers their base. Below the Priests Rapid the Country becomes more undulating & the hills often present the appearance of moving clouds of Sand. A very scattered kind of tufted Grass, which soon loses its green Spring tints, mixed with Artemisia or Worm Wood, small Cactus, and wild Onions are the only Vegetation visible in this desolate region.[71]

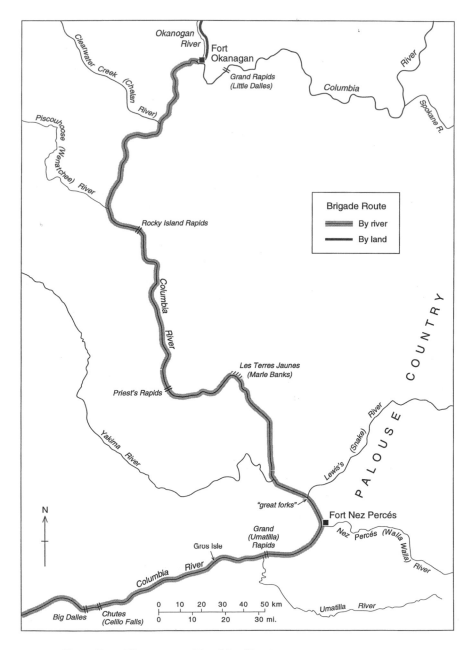

MAP 4 From Fort Okanagan to Fort Nez Percés

The landscape around Fort Nez Percés offered no relief. "The country is generally level and but few hills," observed John Work in 1824, "but still has a sandy barren appearance, and covered with great quantities of wormwood, but scarcely a tree to be seen."[72]

Fortunately for those brigaders who disliked this landscape, the voyage from Fort Okanagan to Fort Nez Percés was rapid – usually no more than a couple of days – because it went with the current during the freshet. Before 1826, however, the boat brigade missed the highest water by leaving Fort Okanagan earlier, since there was usually no horse brigade from New Caledonia to await. In 1824 it left on 1 May in seven boats with sixty-three men. "The banks of the river this day were hilly, & in many places high and abrupt," wrote John Work, "with in general a baren aspect with a few scatered trees to be seen here and there." Despite the early start, "the current was strong and many strong rapids" and "the river in many places very narrow and contracted." Another boat was added at Fort Nez Percés on 4 May.[73] Even in 1820, when New Caledonia did use the Columbia route, the horse brigade did not leave Stuart's Lake until 1 June and did not reach Fort Okanagan until about three weeks later. There it met the boat brigade, which had already gone downriver and back, and got its outfit.[74]

This schedule changed, of course, in 1826 with the shifting of the New Caledonia brigade route from the Peace to the Columbia. That year Connolly's brigade reached Fort Okanagan on sixty horses on 3 June and, following the arrival of two boats with thirteen men from Fort Colvile on 6 June, left for Fort Vancouver the next day in six boats, each handled by seven men and loaded with thirty-five pieces and four passengers, all under the guidance of the "experienced" Pierre L'Étang. The boat brigade proceeded "with much rapidity ... the Current being proportionate to the unusual height of the waters," wrote Connolly. John Work likewise noted that "the Current is very strong & the water high." At the first night's camp some of the boats, being "very leaky," had to be pitched. Fort Nez Percés was reached on the evening of the second day. There two boats were added to convey its returns (forty-five packs), as well as gum, to Fort Vancouver. But bourgeois Samuel Black could spare no men, so each boat's crew was reduced to six men. There, too, Black told Connolly that the requisite horses for his return brigade could likely be provided without having to trade them from the Nez Percé camps up the Snake River – a venture that would take from fifteen to eighteen days.[75]

When the 1827 horse brigade under Connolly arrived at Fort Okanagan on 25 May, he found five boats, two of which had been built the previous year and the others even earlier and all of which were "much" in need of repair "as they have not been touched since they were drawn out of the water last summer" and consequently were "hardly fit to take down Cargoes." Nine boats were required to descend and ascend the river, and only two new craft were under construction by bourgeois John Warren Dease at Fort Colvile, while only one of those left at Fort Nez Percés was usable. From 26 May to 31 May the brigaders were busy repairing the boats at Fort Okanagan. On 31 May two boats arrived from Fort Colvile with its returns, and at sundown of that day the brigade departed down-river in six boats with forty-five men plus five passengers (one boat was to be added at Walla Walla). Gregoire, the horse keeper, was left at Fort Okanagan to tend the horses. The brigade "drifted with the Current ... with little assistance from the Paddles" to Fort Nez Percés, which was reached on 2 June at 4:00 a.m. There the brigade overtook the seasoned pilot, Pierre L'Étang, who would guide it to Fort Vancouver.[76]

In 1828, four boats with twenty-four men and ninety-six pieces (including seventy packs of furs, twelve bales of leather, eight bales of apichimons, and two kegs of castoreum) left Fort Colvile to meet the horse brigade at Fort Okanagan. "Instead of paddles," recorded Work, "the people use oars by which they do more work with less labour." He added: "The current is very strong and swept us along at a rapid rate, but the water is not so high as last year, it is however in a good state, and none of the rapids dangerous ... The dalls [sluices] were found good and the boats shot down them with out stopping." The boat brigade reached Fort Okanagan on 22 May and had to wait five days before the horse brigade arrived. In the interval, Work's detachment was kept busy:

> Had three of the men employed making oars, all the others gumming three boats that were here to be in readiness when the N.C. people arrive. One of the boats was in the water and does not require much repairs, but the other two being exposed to the sun the gum was melted off them and the wood rent & seams opened so that it takes a considerable deal of labour to put them in order. There are two other boats here but they are so old & out of order and the wood so much deranged that it is considered impracticable to repair them so that they could be brought up the river again with any safety.

Following the arrival of the horse brigade on the 27th, "two horses were killed and given to the people with some barley for a regale." The next day the combined brigade left in nine boats, each carrying five to six men and 33 to 36 pieces (including 228 packs of furs, 70 of which were from Fort Colvile, 16 pieces of gum, 11 kegs of castoreum, 8 pieces of saddles, 7 bales of leather, 6 pieces of lodges, 1 piece of books, and baggage), plus four passengers. "The men," reported Work, "used oars in preference to paddles and had as many as could be worked in each boat ... The oars are far superior to paddles, the men do more work with greater ease." Nevertheless, the brigade's progress was so much impeded the first day by a strong headwind that camp had to be made before the Priest's Rapids were reached. On 29 May the boats arrived at Fort Nez Percés, where bourgeois Black, according to Work, was not very helpful: "Notwithstanding the want the men were in of refreshment, Mr Black is of such an unaccomodating disposition that he would not give them a horse [to eat], after a great many evasions he offered a colt that it was so small that it would not have furnished a meal for the people, & would not be accepted, however he gave us three bags of corn & pease & a little grease."[77]

In 1829 the horse brigade reached Fort Okanagan on 29 May, and the 30th was spent drying and storing the horse gear, appointing the boat crews, and distributing the cargo. It was difficult to appoint crews because of the shortage of boutes, making it necessary to use several of the best middlemen as boutes – an expedient that would answer as far as Walla Walla but perhaps not thereafter. The provisions comprised coarse wheat flour, which was "more convenient and palatable" than unhulled Indian corn, but there was no "grease to lard it with," so that one or two horses had to be slaughtered for that purpose. The boat brigade numbered eleven vessels (two of which would be left at Walla Walla for the returns of the Snake Expedition), which embarked on the 31st with "moderate" ladings: 200 packs of furs altogether, 10 kegs of castoreum, a few bales of saddles and apichimons, and a few kegs of gum. There were four to five men per boat and eight passengers; Gregoire was "as usual" left at Fort Okanagan to mind the horses. Downriver progress was slower "than is usually the case," owing to the Columbia's lower level and slower current. But the boats still took only two days to make Walla Walla, where some of them had to be gummed and two of them were "laid up in a cellar" for the Snake party.[78]

In 1831, following the arrival of the horse brigade at Fort Okanagan on 3 June, the boat brigade left on 5 June in nine vessels, the crews having been appointed to the different boats on the 3rd and the boats themselves gummed and loaded on the 4th. "The State of the Water in the Columbia River is fine," reported Chief Factor Dease, "and we have every reason for a Good passage hence to Vancouver." On 6 June they reached Fort Nez Percés, where its returns were added and provisions from Fort Colvile for the Snake Expedition were left.[79]

Clearly, a boat hauled more and moved faster (even upriver) than a pack horse and, moreover, did not have to be bought, fed, or rested. But the river route was much less flexible (indeed, absolutely fixed) and more perilous. The Fort George district report of 1824-25 noted that the Columbia was a "noble River," navigable from the sea almost to its source in boats carrying from fifty to seventy pieces of ninety pounds each. There were, however, four "great portages" where boats and their cargoes had to be transshipped: the Cascades, the Dalles, and the Chutes between Fort Vancouver and Fort Nez Percés and Kettle Falls just above Fort Colvile. The Dalles portage was the longest (nearly one mile) and the most rugged.[80] In addition to portages (where boats and their cargoes were carried), there were "several strong places" where part or all of the cargoes had to be carried and the boats towed. These riverbank bypasses of unnavigable stretches at low water were termed *décharges*; the *bordage* was the strand of the river along which the boatmen walked and packed the freight. Furthermore, the Columbia contained some "strong eddies & whirlpools," what Lewis and Clark called "sucks." Deadheads, or planters – *chicots* to the Canadiens[81] – were yet another hazard. Despite these dangers, stated the district report, "to skillful boatmen after a little experience the Navigation is easy and safe."[82]

Nevertheless, the boatmen were not always "skillful" and the river's state was not always normal, so accidents did occur. The Columbia's level fluctuated seasonally, of course, being raised to its highest point in late spring by meltwater (especially) and rainfall in its watershed. At Fort Vancouver in 1845 the river rose nineteen feet during the early June freshet,[83] and spring flooding occasionally submerged low-lying cropland at the post and created stagnant breeding grounds for malarial mosquitoes, particularly during the early 1830s.

Downstream travel was much faster, of course, than upstream travel. Paul Kane took only two weeks to descend the Columbia from the Boat Encampment to Fort Vancouver in the fall of 1846 but four months – eight times as long – to ascend the same stretch in the same season a year later.[84] Regardless of direction, lower water, even though it exposed some outcrops, was generally safer than higher water, whose stronger current carried the boats too rapidly. As Archibald McDonald, in the role of chief factor at Fort Colvile, told Simpson in the spring of 1842, "the Columbia this Season is likely to be exceedingly high, & the navigation of it of Consequence extremely dangerous & difficult."[85] At a lower level the river's current was less forceful and its rapids less hazardous. So, as Alexander Henry said, "the summer is the only season that furs can be conveyed from the interior country to this place [Fort

George on the Columbia] with any safety"[86] because then it was not cold in the interior and not damp on the coast, and the Columbia River was not too high.

Unfortunately for the outgoing brigade, however, when it reached Fort Okanagan at the end of May or the beginning of June the river might still be cresting, owing to a longer, colder winter and shorter, cooler spring in its upper reaches. Then the brigade had to wait until the high water subsided or, if that wait were too long, take the risk of proceeding. But even with lower water the voyage was risky. As Warre and Vavasour reported:

> The danger of the navigation of the Columbia River consists entirely in the strength of the Water, its bed being, in all most every case, of such depth as to prevent the possibility of the Boats foundering. At high Water the force of the Current is so great, that immense Whirlpools are constantly forming into which the Boats are drawn and being whirled round & round with great rapidity at length fill and sink involving all the Passengers in the Vortex. At low Water the Rapids are more formidable, so that the navigation may be said to be extremely dangerous without great care and many precautions are taken, at any season of the year.[87]

Father De Smet, who also travelled the Columbia, agreed, writing that "great care and attention are to be had in its navigation, for it presents a constant succession of rapids, falls, cascades, and dalles."[88] The river presented a series of such obstacles from its source to its mouth, ending in the notorious bar. The worst on the upper course was the Dalles du Mort, Kane's "rapped of deth,"[89] just below the Boat Encampment. It was usually run by the boatmen. Kettle Falls just below Fort Colvile was bypassed, but the Grand Rapids just above Fort Okanagan were not. Between Fort Okanagan and Fort Nez Percés, the Columbia was "obstructed by a number of rapids, some strong and dangerous," especially the Rocky Island (or simply Island) Rapids (also known as the Isles des Pierres) and the Priest's Rapids. The former sometimes entailed a portage of half a mile on the left bank; the latter was a "long shoot" of some ten miles where the river, dropping seventy feet, ran "with great violence."[90] The Priest's Rapids were so named in 1811 by David Stuart of the PFC after a local "medicine man" (native shaman) whom he saw performing there in the manner of a Catholic priest.[91] The Astorian Alexander Ross deemed it "a dangerous and intricate part of the navigation."[92] Here the river was divided into two channels by a small, rocky island, which was cut obliquely by a narrow dalle. The rapids were "considered one of the most dangerous parts of the whole river," according to David Douglas, the botanist.[93]

Falls had to be portaged, but rapids could be navigated, or at least cordelled. As Lieutenant Amelius Simpson observed just below the Columbia-Spokane forks in 1826, however, "the running of rapids is an operation that requires great skill and coolness."[94] Unfortunately, sometimes these requisites were absent, or the rapids were simply too formidable, and accidents resulted, causing at the most the loss of life and cargo and at the least delays while boats were fixed and pieces dried. As Father De Smet lamented in 1846, "no river probably on the globe, frequented as much, could tell of more disastrous accidents."[95] Their locations were memorialized by crosses. Duncan Finlayson noted in 1831 that "here & there along this River a monumental cross marks the spot of some fatal catastrophe."[96] The loss of the Banks-Wallace party in the Dalles du Mort in the fall of 1838 was, in Chief Factor James Douglas's words, but "one of those dreadful accidents, that imparts so fearful a character to the navigation of this River."[97] "Deeply" lamenting the loss of the twelve lives in the Dalles du Mort, the Governor and Committee blamed the negligence of the party's leader, Chief Trader John Tod, and added: "The Gentleman in charge of the Brigade should never be allowed to absent himself from such a charge, until delivered at the Depot, and in order to guard against hazardous running, in which the guides and boutes frequently indulge, sometimes in order to save themselves the trouble of carrying, and at others to make a display of their own address [skill]: a list should be made of the rapids, where to carry craft and cargo or to run light or half laden, according to the season of the year whatever the state of the water may be, as from experience we find it is not safe to allow the guides to exercise their own discretion in that respect."[98] Despite such urgings, the accidents and drownings continued.

The well-travelled stretch between Forts Colvile and Okanagan was especially fruitful in mishaps, as Lieutenant Warre reported in 1845: "We descended the Spokane Rapids at the Mouth of the River of the same name, the Rapids de Gingras, d'Puras, des Gropes Roches, Dominigue all of which have been named from some disastrous and often fatal occurrence. Hardly one of these Rapids are without their story of persons drowned or Boats upset & the name of the Guide or of the person drowned is then given to the particular Chûte."[99] In the fall of 1830, in rapids just above Fort Okanagan, a boat "struck on a stone and upset"; the boat, most of its cargo, and seven crewmen were lost.[100] In 1842 in the Little Dalles, in this same stretch, a boat was swamped and five men were drowned, including the guide, Canote Umphreville, a veteran of thirty-one years' service in the Oregon Country.[101]

Below Fort Okanagan and above Fort Nez Percés the Priest's Rapids was the most dangerous passage. The worst accident here occurred at the end of May 1828, when a boat in the downriver brigade struck a rock at the foot of the rapids and upset. The boat was wrecked and three of its seven crewmen were drowned; twenty-six packs of furs and some leather were saved, but one keg of castoreum, one bale of leather, and three kegs of gum were lost. The furs were "much damaged" by their soaking, particularly the small furs, which formed a "considerable proportion of the whole." The rescue of the survivors and the recovery of the property was made possible by the local natives.[102] The brigade's leader, Chief Factor Connolly, described the mishap in detail nearly two years after its occurrence:

On the morning of May 29th the Brigade consisting of nine Boats left the Encampment about 15 miles above the Priests Rapid – a short distance above the Rapid I ordered my Boat and those that were with me ashore, in order to assemble the whole before descending it. In the course of a few minutes they all arrived – and having previously observed that one of them went badly by which some loss of time had already been occasioned, in order to accelerate her progress by adding one hand to her crew, and to see that they did their duty, the Guide Le tang [L'Étang], who had so far come down with me was ordered to embark in her – after making this arrangement and directing that the Boats should keep at proper distances from each other – My Boat took the lead and followed by the rest in succession, proceeded down the Rapid – this place presents so little danger or at least what danger exists can be so easily avoided that the foreman of my Boat did not even rise from his seat through its whole course – at the foot of the Rapid no stop was made, and we proceeded on to the end of the *pipi* or spell which continued for about half an hour – It was then only that we perceived that one of the Boats was absent. However being quite unapprehensive that this was occasioned by accident, the Guide being on board of his, and she being old and leaky, my belief was that the guide had put ashore at the foot of the Rapid to gum her after drifting down with the current for some time in expectation of seeing her cast up, but finding that she did not make her appearance confirmed this belief – and I therefore determined to proceed on to Walla Walla which I was anxious to reach that day in time to complete the necessary arrangements so as to be able to leave that place on the following morning – this was the more necessary as we were not supplied with provisions for more than two thirds of our voyage to Fort Vancouver – In the afternoon I reached Walla Walla with eight boats – And two or three hours afterwards Le tang, the Guide, arrived when I was made acquainted with the melancholy occurence. By this mans account it appeared that the Boat was the last that left the shore when the order for shooting the Rapid was given, which was done immediately after the one which preceded it had got to a sufficient distance to prevent them from coming in contact with each other and that through the obstinacy of the foreman the boat was drawn towards the rock upon which she was wrecked. The necessary measures were instantly taken to secure the property which had been rescued from the water, and the whole of it was saved.[103]

Such disasters were infrequent, however. Usually the boat brigades reached Fort Nez Percés rapidly and safely and, following a day's stopover to embark the post's returns and repair the boats, they began the descent of the most perilous stretch of the river route.

CHAPTER 8

Boating down the Columbia

The Hard Leg from Walla Walla to the Sea

*The Dalles Rapids force their way thru a number of
Crooked Channels bounded by high Masses of Rock in various
grotesque forms giving the scenery a Wild & singular appearance,
they are a succession of strong rapids, extending about 2 Leagues
[six miles], and very dangerous in many places.*

– LIEUTENANT AMELIUS SIMPSON, 1826[1]

*The Cascades are a chain of strong rapids or falls – presenting
a broken & foaming surface from their commencement to their foot.
The River forms a sudden bend while following its course forming
this chain of cascades – which adds to their violence.*

– LIEUTENANT AMELIUS SIMPSON, 1826[2]

WALLA WALLA

Fort Nez Percés, where the boat brigades usually stopped overnight, had been conceived by the NWC in the summer of 1811, when David Thompson erected a claim pole at the junction of the Columbia and Snake Rivers and promised the local Walla Walla chief (Yellepit?) that he would establish a "House" there.[3] It was not until 1818, however, that the Nor'Westers realized Thompson's intention, building the post at the mouth of the Walla Walla River as a strongpoint on the Columbia route and as a gateway to the promising Snake Country.[4] In the summer of that year the new establishment boasted a complement of ninety-seven, including thirty-eight Iroquois, thirty-two Hawaiians, and twenty-five Canadiens.[5] In 1824 the HBC, acting on the assumption that the Columbia would become the international boundary, ordered that the fort be shifted to the right ("northern") bank of the river; however, Chief Trader Samuel Black was unable to do so on account of "the determined opposition raised by the numerous bands of Indians that frequent that place to the change, who being unaccustomed to the use of Canoes would have some difficulty in crossing the River, which at that part is very thinly peopled and quite destitute of Timber."[6] McLoughlin added that the discontent of the Indians "would make our Communication with the Interior more difficult and hazardous."[7] The possible disruption of the "main communication" was too great a risk, so the fort stayed on the left ("southern") bank, five miles below the Columbia-Snake forks.

The fort was built of wood (squared timbers) plastered with adobe and roofed with sod. Measuring 120 feet square, it was surrounded by a stockade 18 feet high and flanked by two bastions, with a gallery 10 feet above the ground. It was "the best place for defence against an Indian attack on this side the Mountains," for there were sometimes as many as 2,000 natives around the post. The buildings comprised a house, a storehouse, an Indian shop, and a barracks. They were staffed by an officer and eight men in the winter of 1825-26.[8] In 1827 there were eight men, five children, and two women at the post.[9] The following year it was inspected and described by Governor Simpson:

> Fort Nez Perces, the next Establishment down the main River, is situated at the mouth of the Willa Walla River, about Six Miles below the junction of Louis & Clarks River or the South branch of the Columbia with the main Stream. This Post has never been very productive, as the country in its neighbourhood is not rich, and the Natives who are a bold Warlike race do little else than rove about in search of Scalps, plunder and amusement. It is necessary however, on many accounts, to keep on good terms with them, and to maintain a Post for their accommodation whither it pays or not, as in the first place, they from their numbers and daring character command the main communication; in the next place, our Snake Expedition usually passes through their Country to its hunting grounds, which they could not do if we were not on good terms with them; in the third place, we depend on them principally for an annual supply of about 250 Horses, and finally, the Trade in Furs altho' falling off pays tolerably well, as Outfit 1825 yielded about £1800 profit, Outfit 1826 £2200 Outfit 1827 £1100: the accounts of Outfit 1828 are not yet closed, but we think the profits may be estimated at about £1500.[10]

In 1842, shortly after its bourgeois, Chief Trader Pierre Pambrun, was killed by a fall from his horse in the middle of May, the fort was levelled by fire. In the summer it was rebuilt on a "new and more secure" site "of bricks baked in the sun with a stone foundation and is therefore nearly safe from the danger of fire," according to Clerk Archibald McKinlay. The new fort measured 110 feet square with walls 10 feet high and 22 inches thick and two bastions 12 feet square (and it was intended to add 3 or 4 more feet to the height of the walls).[11] When Lieutenants Warre and Vavasour visited the post in the fall of 1845, it was located nine miles below the Columbia-Snake junction and measured 120 feet square; they noted militarily that it was "better adapted than any of the other Posts to resist a sudden attack."[12] "The Fort," they added, "is built of large blocks of Mud hardened in the sun & forming a Wall solid enough to resist musket or even small scale pieces ... and has two Mud bastions or towers at the Angles."[13] Paul Kane was less impressed in the summer of 1847, dismissing it as "a small mud fort in the most barran cuntry I evar saw."[14]

Walla Walla's importance lay in its Snake ventures and its transport services, not the local fur trade (which yielded only seventeen packs of eighty-six pounds each in 1830, for instance[15]). Alexander Ross, the ex-Astorian, considered the post the "Key to the Snake Country" because of its ready access by river and land.[16] It was conveniently located for the dispatch of trapping parties to the east and south, and the locale abounded in native horses for those parties; the first such NWC venture of 55 men, 195 horses, and 300 beaver traps left the post in September 1818.[17] The Snake Country's potential was also recognized by the HBC, John Stuart reporting in 1822 that it "is the fairest field for extending the Trade to advantage of any in the Indian Country."[18] The Honourable Company proceeded to "scour" it by means of annual trapping forays ("expeditions"), mostly under Peter Ogden or John Work. The "trapping party" of 1830, for instance, left Fort Nez Percés on 22 August under Work with 115 persons, 337 traps, 272 horses, and 21 "lodges" (tents); the venture lasted eleven months, going at least 2,000 miles and losing 82 horses.[19] In the Snake Country the Bay men encountered stiff competition from American mountain men – 500-600 annually from 1832 to 1838 and 50 annually in the middle 1840s.[20] Already by the early 1830s, however, the Snake Country had been depleted, while Walla Walla's transport function remained.

The harsh environs and the many natives made Fort Nez Percés an uncomfortable and unpopular posting. At the end of the winter of 1824-25, bourgeois John Dease, whose brother Peter was to become chief factor of New Caledonia, "begged" Governor Simpson during the latter's stopover for a transfer from what Simpson himself rated "the most anxious charge in the Columbia" on account of the hot, dry summers and the numerous and sometimes unfriendly Indians. Simpson granted Dease's request, "as a four years residence among the troublesome visitors of Walla Walla is quite enough for any man of peaceable habits."[21]

Alexander Ross deemed the post "the most hostile spot on the whole line of communication," as well as "the most barren of materials for building."[22] Initially, at least, the Indians (Nez Percés and Cayuses) were indeed intractable. Dease called them the "most turbulent sett of Indians on the communication,"[23] and Ross termed Walla Walla the "centre of all the Principal and hostile Tribes of that part of the Columbia."[24] But the natives refrained from blocking the "main communication," and they did not refuse to trade their horses. Familiarity bred tolerance, if not contempt, on both sides, and disease eventually took its heavy indigenous toll. By 1831 the Indians occasionally stole horses, uprooted vegetables, and mooched tobacco at the post but nothing more serious.[25] The initial threat, however, ensured that the fort was securely sited between the Columbia and the Walla Walla on what was a peninsula at low water and an island at high water, and it was so strongly constructed and so strongly defended that Ross called it "the Gibralter of the Columbia."[26]

Walla Walla's physical geography did not change. It was very hot and dry in the summer and quite cold and dry in the winter, and windy year round, with scant vegetation. The post endured a "bad Climate," acknowledged bourgeois Simon McGillivray in 1831.[27] Paul Kane visited the establishment in the middle of summer, 1847, and described the horrific heat:

> [20 July 1847] I left [the nearby Whitman Mission] for walla walla ... the Dr [Marcus Whitman] wished me to take a dog of Mr. McBanes down with. me I left after beackfast the dog following me the day was dredfull hot on gowing a bout 8 m. I found the dog was so warm that he could not go I put him on the hors but that would not do and let him down again when the pure brute laide down and died absalutely burned to deth in the hot sand. A gentalman tould me that he saw a rattle snake burned to a sinder in trying to pass from one small bush to an other in not more than 10 yards nere walla walla.[28]

Summers were windy and dusty, too, and the fact that "a great number of Indians & Horses are blind of an Eye" was ascribed by McGillivray to the not infrequent "sandstorms."[29] On 29 March 1831 he reported: "The strongest wind I have seen here, the waters of the river splashed on the Pickets – all hands employed putting Posts around the Pickets of the Fort, which are going with the wind to & fro. Part of the East Side of the Platform has fallen in." The next day, he continued, "the wind moderated a little, but our Fort is falling down in all directions of yesterday's gale."[30]

The hot, dry wind seared vegetation. In the middle of May 1831 McGillivray wrote that "the grass around here, which bore a fine green appearance, and other plants, are now turning red, having been parched by the Sun." "This is a dreadful country for heat," he added.[31] So timber was absent, and it was "a matter of importance to procure" as much driftwood as possible from the Columbia and Snake Rivers at high water (late May).[32] In the summer of 1825 the Columbia's level was lower than usual, and the post was "at a loss" for driftwood for burning and building.[33] The climate was not conducive to farming either, so fish and game dominated the post's diet. In 1827 the ten adults and five children consumed 3,000 salmon, 5 sturgeon, 200 pounds of venison, and some rabbits and roots.[34] In 1831, 1,570 dried salmon were stocked.[35] Some provisions were received from Fort Colvile, as in the fall of 1831, when fifteen bags of corn (1½ bushels each), ten bags of flour (100 pounds each), and one keg of pork arrived from upriver.[36]

From Interior Plateau to Coastal Lowland

The more than 200 miles from Walla Walla to tidewater at Fort Vancouver (or the more than 300 miles to Fort George at the Columbia's mouth) marked the transition from the arid interior with its warmer summers and colder winters to the damp, mild coast (see Map 5). The magnitude of the change in landscape struck Duncan Finlayson in 1831:

> The country from Walla Walla to the Chutes [Celilo Falls] consists of high steep masses black rock & stones resembling lava – it presents a picturesque but desolate & sterile landscape amidst which the eye seeks in vain for some spot capable of producing vegetation – nay a solitary tree is to be seen – we had even [to] purchase pieces of drift wood from the natives to supply our daily wants – From the Chutes down to [Fort] Vancouver the country assumes a different character – The tall & stately timber of various kinds thickly interspersed on each side of the River their strongly defined shadows upon the placid surface of the water presented a strikingly splendid contrast to that which we had shortly passed – The effect which so total a change of climate & scenery produced is really astonishing.[37]

Below Walla Walla the Columbia turned sharply westwards away from the rain-shadowed plateau. "The Fort," noted Lieutenant Warre, "is at the head of the Great Bend in the Columbia and at the foot of high Volcanic Mountains, through which the River has forced itself in a narrow channel with high perpendicular banks – after which it again

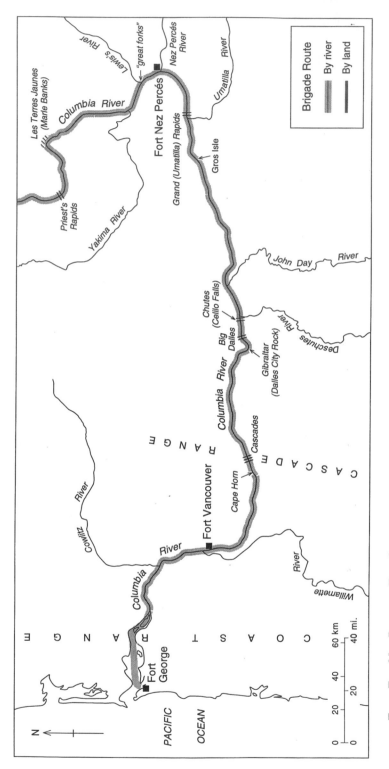

MAP 5 From Fort Nez Percés to Fort George

expands and remains the same dry, sandy hilly desert till we reached the Dalles."[38]

Gouging the Columbia Plateau and cutting the Cascade Range as it descended, the Columbia created a series of waterfalls, rapids, and canyons – what might be called a millrace – to challenge the brigaders. The first was the Grand (Umatilla) Rapids, "a long and very dangerous rapid" at the foot of some high cliffs eighteen miles below Fort Nez Percés and seven miles above the mouth of the Umatilla River.[39] Half-way between this and the next major left-bank tributary, the John Day River (named after a member of the Astorian overland party who was robbed here by the natives), lay Gros Isle (Big Island, later Blalock Island, now submerged by the John Day Reservoir), which extended for six miles.

Twenty-five miles farther downstream, and 100 miles upstream from Fort Vancouver, the Columbia received the Deschutes River, so called not for having waterfalls (*chutes*) but for being close to the Chutes (the Columbia, or Celilo, Falls) on the main river. The Chutes marked the upper end of the thirty-mile-long obstacle course of the Narrows of Lewis and Clark, what later came to be called the Columbia Gorge, or The Dalles (from *dalle*, meaning either "sluice" or "flagstone," referring to the columnar basaltic rocks carved by the river[40]), stretching from Celilo Falls on the east to the Big Eddy on the west and dropping 81½ feet at high water and 62½ feet at low water. The Chutes were the "Great Falls" of Lewis and Clark (and the Astorians, too), who reported that they rose twenty feet but were almost completely flooded during the spring freshet.[41] Ross Cox estimated that the main fall did not exceed fifteen feet in height at high water but stood much higher at low water,[42] when, reported Alexander Ross, it dropped some twenty feet.[43] Lieutenant Simpson described this barrier in the fall of 1826: "The Shoots falls is formed by a number of fine cascades descending into a number of Deep chasms in an extensive Bed of Rock stretching quite across the Bed of the River, & in which the whole body of the River becomes hid from view urging its way with awful force thru these deep channels, untill they again extend in one grand stream at the foot of these foaming Shoots."[44] The Chutes appeared less fearsome to Father Modeste Demers in the fall of 1839:

> These falls are a series of rocks, a mile or two long, which extend across the Columbia and leave but a small channel on the left shore. These rocks rise ever so little in an amphitheatre and are divided by a great number of channels which the mass of water has cut for a passage, in the course of time.

The first *chute* is pretty regular and from 20 to 30 feet wide. I went as far as possible to examine them more closely. Their number and variety are surprising. They are not equally deep. Some are dry, whereas in others, passes a large volume of water. The falls are from 3 to 12 and 15 feet high. One may be astonished to learn that these *chutes*, so terrible at low water, are smooth and still at very high water, which does not happen every year. Then it is that, instead of fearing them, the voyageurs hasten to approach them, to light their pipes and rest.[45]

So in spring the falls were submerged by high water, and the boats shot them "with ease and safety," in Wilkes's words,[46] but in summer, autumn, and winter they had to be bypassed, of course. The portage measured half a mile across a rocky point on the right bank.[47] The Chutes, which lay on the boundary between the Shahaptian and Chinookan territories, were a busy fishing, meeting, and trading place for the natives. "This is the Great Mart of all this Country," noted Lewis and Clark.[48] Below the Chutes the Columbia contained harbour seals (the "sea otters" of the two American explorers).

Three miles below the Chutes were the "short narrows" – Les Petites Dalles, the Little (or Upper) Dalles (the Ten Mile Rapids before 1957, when they were inundated by Lake Celilo behind the Dalles Dam), the middle portion of the obstacle course. They were a mile long and 250 feet wide.[49]

Ten miles downriver were the "long narrows" (the "Great Narrows" of Lewis and Clark) – Les Grandes Dalles, the Big (or Lower) Dalles (the Five Mile Rapids before 1957), where the Columbia's channel narrowed to seventy-five feet. At their foot lay the Dalles Rapids, one and a half miles long and some fifteen feet in descent. No other feature of the river, save its bar, aroused as much comment as the "Grand Dalles." After Lewis and Clark, the next whites to describe them were the Astorians. Franchère was the first to record the name of Les Dalles, "where the river passes through a two-mile natural gorge in the rock, with sheer perpendicular sides.[50] Ross Cox wrote that the Big Dalles stretched more than three miles, "the whole of which is a succession of boiling whirlpools."[51] Alexander Ross was more specific about what he called the "great bend or elbow of the Columbia":

At the upper end, during low water, a broad and flat ledge of rocks bars the whole river across, leaving only a small opening or portal, not exceeding forty feet, on the left side, through which the whole body of water must pass. Through this gap it rushes with great impetuosity; the foaming surges dash through the rocks with terrific violence; no craft, either large or small, can venture there in safety. During floods, this obstruction, or ledge of rocks, is covered with water, yet the passage of the narrows is not thereby improved.[52]

Lieutenant Simpson was more succinct, describing the Big Dalles in 1826 as "a long & intricate chain [of rapids] rushing with great force thru a number of narrow & crooked channels, bounded by huge masses of perpendicular rock."[53] Eight years later John Townsend, an American ornithologist, observed in late summer that "the entire water of the river here flows through channels of about fifteen feet in width, and between high, perpendicular rocks; there are several of these channels at distances of from half a mile to a mile apart, and the water foams and boils through them like an enormous cauldron."[54] Probably the best description of what the local Indians called "Wascopam" came from Father François Blanchet in the fall of 1839:

Here the Columbia is intercepted by a chain of solid rocks, through which — wonderful to say and see — the strong mass of waters have opened a channel to themselves. The *Grandes Dalles* are 4 miles long, impassable in the high water of May and June, but passable in the low waters of the Fall; and even then, not without a discharge of persons and baggage for the first two miles. The first part is a canal of about 150 feet wide, walled with basaltic columns about 50 feet high, ending in a platform about 30 feet broad, and terminating with other basaltic columns 60 feet high. During the high water the swollen Columbia passes over the platform. In low water it only runs through the lower channel; projecting points and recesses in the walls form waves and whirlpools very dangerous, even for light boats managed by 8 men; 6 at the oars, one at the stern and the other at the prow, with long and wide paddles used as rudders; nevertheless, they are never passed without dread.[55]

To Lieutenant Wilkes the Big Dalles was "one of the most remarkable places upon the Columbia," which was here compressed into a narrow channel 300 feet wide and half a mile long with perpendicular, flat-topped walls of basalt. The river, he found, dropped fifty feet in two miles and its level rose as much as sixty-two feet at high water, the great amplitude being caused by the impoundment of spring run-off by the constriction, and the compression created a loud roar and many eddies and whirlpools.[56] In the spring of 1846 Lieutenant Warre was likewise awestruck by "this most extraordinary formation of Rock," where, he corroborated, the river rose sixty-one feet during the spring freshet in June and July. "Many is the unfortunate boats," he added, "that has been doomed to destruction in the Whirlpools of this frightful Cataract."[57]

The "dry and sandy" portage around the Big Dalles was up to nine miles in length and took the brigaders more than a day to cross.[58]

The obstruction was a popular Indian fishery. Alexander Ross labelled it the "great rendezvous" of native traders, gamblers, and rustlers – "the great emporium or mart of the Columbia, and the general theatre of gambling and roguery."[59] Wilkes asserted that the Chutes, Big Dalles, and Cascades were the "three great salmon-fisheries of the Columbia"; the Big Dalles, he added, "is appropriately called the Billingsgate [a famous London fish market] of Oregon." The fishing season here lasted five months, from May through September; every hour each of the native men hooked and speared up to twenty-five salmon, which the women skinned, gutted, and dried in the sun and wind on the rocks and then mashed finely and stuffed tightly into long baskets weighing eighty pounds whose contents kept three years.[60] The Big Dalles was also a rendezvous in the first half of the 1840s for American migrants, who crossed to the right bank here and followed it to a point just below the Cascades, where they recrossed.[61]

It was fifty miles from the Big Dalles to the Cascades, the lowermost obstacle in the Columbia millrace. Now the river was, in Cox's words, "broad, deep, and rapid, with several sunken rocks, scattered here and there, which often injure the canoes." There were also several prominent islets and points, such as Gibraltar (Dalles City Rock),[62] so called because of the stormy conditions that often prevailed there, according to Father Blanchet.[63] The landscape became noticeably hillier and greener, too, as Lieutenant Simpson remarked in 1826:

> Along our Days Track the face of the country gradually underwent a change – from a low country, as we descend the River becomes skirted by Hills which attain a greater elevation as we continue our descent, untill at the Cascades they are nearly two thousand feet – & from a country free from Wood, we arrive in one richly cloathed with Forest – It is a singular remark made upon the Climate of the Columbia, that this spot the Cascades, forms a sort of dividing point, that here & below here we have the rainy season in its greatest force while above the climate is dry nearly the whole year round.[64]

Similarly, in 1845 Lieutenant Warre noted that "the River between the Dalles and the Cascades is in many parts very beautiful high lands covered with Pine Trees & the low ground thickly wooded with several kinds of hardwood."[65] Some of the dominant volcanic peaks of the Cascade Range now came into view. Warre added that "the Views of some of the distant country were magnificent Mount Hood towering in all its majesty & snowy Grandeur high above the surrounding ranges of Mountains."[66]

The Cascades, which marked the cutting of the mountain range by the Columbia, excited almost as much comment as the Dalles. They were the "Great Shute," or "Grand Shute," of Lewis and Clark and the "Great Rapids" of Alexander Henry. Clark wrote: "This Great Shute or falls is about ½ a mile with the water of this great river Compressed within the Space of 150 paces in which there is great numbers of both large and Small rocks, water passing with great velocity forming & boiling in a most horriable manner, with a fall of about 20 feet."[67] According to the Astorian Alexander Ross, this "first barrier of the Columbia" measured two and a half miles. He added:

> We were now [late July 1811] encamped at the head or upper end of them, where the whole river is obstructed to the breadth of one hundred or one hundred and twenty feet, and descends in high and swelling surges with great fury for about one hundred yards. Then the channel widens and the river expands, and is here and there afterwards obstructed with rocks, whirlpools, and eddies throughout, rendering the navigation more or less dangerous; but there are no falls in any part of it, either at high or low water, and with the exception of the first shoot, at the heads of the cascade, where the water rushes with great impetuosity down its channel, they are, with care and good management, passable at all seasons for large craft, that is boats.[68]

A year later another Astorian, Ross Cox, found the Cascades to be longer. He wrote: "The upper part of the chain of rapids is a perpendicular fall of nearly sixteen feet; after which it continues down nearly one uninterrupted rapid for three miles and a half. The river here is compressed by the bold shore on each side to about two hundred yards or less in breadth. The channel is crowded with large rocks, over which the water rushes with incredible velocity, and with a dreadful noise."[69] John Townsend was no less impressed:

> These cascades, or cataracts are formed by a collection of large rocks, in the bed of the river, which extend, for perhaps half a mile. The current for a short distance above them, is exceedingly rapid, and there is said to be a gradual fall, or declivity of the river, of about twenty feet in the mile. Over these rocks, and across the whole river, the water dashes and foams most furiously, and with a roar which we heard distinctly at the distance of several miles.
>
> It is wholly impossible for any craft to make its way through these difficulties, and our light canoes would not live an instant in them. It is, therefore,

necessary to make a portage, either by carrying the canoes over land to the opposite side of the cataracts, or by wading in the water near the shore, where the surges are lightest, and dragging the unloaded boat through them by a cable.[70]

Lieutenant Warre believed that the Cascades had been formed as a result of subsidence. He wrote:

> The "Cascades" are a very curious & interesting part of the River & formed evidently by the settling of an immense tract of ground, which must have dammed back the River till it forced a passage through the broken Rocks ... from the perfectly new appearance of the immense Avalanches on the Mountains in the rear, I think the theory ... of the River being stopped, is correct; that the land has subsided is apparent, not only on the face of the Hills, but also on the Waters Edge, Vast Forests of Trees appearing now, in a upright position some of them in 20 feet of water. A great many of them are almost become petrifactiory and the whole of them are broken off a little above the highest water mark.[71]

The Cascades, where in four and a half miles the river dropped forty-five feet at high water and thirty-six feet at low water, were unnavigable for three to four miles.[72] The portage, which lay on the right bank, varied in length from season to season (and from author to author). Lewis and Clark reported in the spring of 1806 that it measured from one to two miles "along a narrow rough and slipery road"; they also reported that the river here was at least twenty feet higher than in the autumn of 1805.[73] Ross Cox found in late July 1812 that the portage was from three to four miles long, and that "the path was narrow and dangerous, one part greatly obstructed by slippery rocks and another ran through a thick wood."[74] A year earlier, Alexander Ross – always more trustworthy than Cox – took a day to negotiate the portage, which proved to be 1,450 yards (five-sixths of a mile) long. He wrote: "To say that there is not a worse path under the sun would perhaps be going a step too far, but to say that, for difficulty and danger, few could equal it would be saying but the truth."[75] Lieutenant Wilkes described portaging at the Cascades in 1841: "The load is secured on the back of a voyageur by a band which passes round the forehead and under and over the bale; he squats down, adjusts his load, and rises with ninety pounds on his back; another places ninety pounds more on the top, and off he trots, half bent, to the end of the portage." Each boat was carried by eight men bottom upwards, the gunwale resting on their shoulders. Because the brigaders "in general have not the appearance of being very strong men," at this and the other portages they were assisted by the Indians "for a small present ['potlach'] of tobacco."[76] In 1846 Paul Kane's party took two days to portage the Cascades.[77]

Like the Chutes and the Dalles, the Cascades attracted the local natives. In 1811 Ross recorded three Wishram Indian villages whose occupants were "the lords of the falls."[78]

The Columbia River left the Columbia Gorge just above Cape Horn, a windy high rock on the right bank. At Fort Vancouver it merged with the left-bank Willamette River, and then it veered northwards and, after meeting the Cowlitz River, westwards again to the sea. In the thirty-five miles from the foot of the Cascades to Fort Vancouver, the landscape became less rugged and more lush, as Lieutenant Warre noted in 1845: "The River below the falls [Cascades] is very beautiful the Banks very high & very steep & broken by Volcanic action into every variety of form. This continues for several miles the River gradually becomes wider the Banks more level & more extended. Trees increase in size & in beauty of appearance."[79] Below the Cascades, too, there were no rattlesnakes to bother the brigaders.[80]

Six miles upriver from Fort Vancouver stood its saw mill, and one mile below that (at the mouth of a stream) its grist mill. From Fort Vancouver at the forks of the Willamette to Fort George at the sea, the Columbia flowed sluggishly some 100 miles in a wide, deep channel broken only occasionally by islands and sandbars. It presented no formidable obstacles to the brigaders; indeed, this stretch was even navigable by 300-ton ships.

Boating the Columbia Millrace

Before the logistical switch from the Peace to the Columbia route, the boats, having to await the horse brigade from Thompson's River only and not from New Caledonia, left Fort Nez Percés as well as Fort Okanagan much earlier, usually in early May. In 1824 the brigade of sixty-three men in eight boats left Walla Walla on 5 May. It soon encountered one of the millrace's features – a high swell (a large, long, crestless rolling wave, or succession of such waves). As David Douglas noted a year later, the combination of a rapid and heavy downriver current and a strong westerly (upriver) wind produced "a swell like an inland sea; frequently we had to take shelter in the creeks, and although our canoes were considered good, yet we could not see each other except at a short distance, so great was the swell."[81] The 1824 brigaders were likewise delayed. "The wind blew strong up the river so that we made but little way," reported

John Work. "The swell became so heavy that we had to put ashore early in the evening." On the 8th the brigade made the Chutes – "the banks about the shoots high, and in many places abrupt, the river tumbling down through rocks and precipices." There were Indian villages on either side of the river. "The Portage at the shoots is pretty long, [over] part of which the boats have to be carried," continued Work. The next day, Sunday the 9th, the wind and swell resumed. "Blew strong all day, the swell in the river was so heavy that it was deemed prudent to remain ashore." At the Dalles Work noticed the changing landscape: "The country appears hilly, The woods are beginning, the few trees here are oak, pine, and poplar, the hills are green, and of a more fertile appearance than farther up the river." Work's brigaders ran the Little Dalles but had to portage the Big Dalles. "At this place [Big Dalles] the river is confined to a narrow span bounded on each side by steep rocks between which the water rushes with great violence and forms numerous whirlpools which would inevitably swallow any boat that would venture among them." On the 11th the Cascades were reached. They, too, could not be run: "At the Cascades all the property had to be carried, but the boats were towed by lines." Below the Cascades "weighty" rain began. By the time the brigade reached the Willamette forks on the 12th, the change in the landscape was complete. Work noted: "The Country appears flatter than hitherto, but still hilly, and thickly wooded along the shore. The river is broad and has a fine appearance, with some fine islands, the current not very strong. The tide runs up to near the cascades a distance of 90 Miles." Work was somewhat relieved that the Columbia stayed that way to Fort George. "The river has still a fine appearance," he noted on the 13th, "& is very broad as we get near the sea, the shores still a little hilly."[82] Upon reaching the depot the pieces had to be carted up to the fort, opened and checked, and the furs beaten and dried.

The 1825 "brigade from the Interior" was the last early run. Indeed, it arrived at the new depot of Fort Vancouver on 24 April,[83] three weeks earlier than the previous year's brigade had arrived at the old depot of Fort George.

From 1826 the boat brigades normally left Fort Nez Percés in the first week of June, at least a month later than previously. The 1826 brigade added two boats and forty-five packs of furs at Walla Walla and left on 9 June in eight boats with fifty-five men. It included William Connolly and John Work, who kept separate journals of the trip. The first day the brigade met an express from Fort Vancouver with news of the "safe arrival" there of the supply ship *Dryad*, Captain James Davidson, with the "Columbia Outfit"; however, "for want of Hands and no proper craft [lighters]" its cargo would have to be unloaded by the brigaders them-selves. Camp was made just below the Grand Rapids; subsequently, camp was broken at daybreak or even earlier, e.g., 3:00 a.m.

One hundred Indians were found at the Chutes and 200 to 300 at the Big Dalles, where "the men had a hard days labour carrying across the two Portages." On the morning of the 10th at the Chutes Portage, which was crossed between 9:00 a.m. and 12:00 p.m., "the assemblage of Indians was such, that it was necessary to place an armed guard at each end of it, whilst the Men were carrying the Property." It took "a hard days labour" to portage both Dalles. The Big Dalles Portage was reached at 1:00 p.m. and crossed by nightfall. The "concourse of Indians at this place was much greater" than at the Chutes, and the "same precautions" were taken "to preserve the property from depredation." The "rascally" natives "to all appearances are the outcast of God's North," remarked Connolly, owing to their lack of "decency" and their "propensity to theft." Abundant salmon was traded from the Chutes and Big Dalles Indians for tobacco, beads, and knives.

On the 11th "it blew so fresh that we had to put ashore before noon and could not [travel] during the day." Connolly wrote: "From thence [Big Dalles] to the Cascades no rapids of any consequence occur, and the distance could have been performed in little more than one day had the weather been favourable. But the contrary was the case. A westerly wind prevailed, which blowing against the current occasioned a suck [whirlpool] which no Boat could have withstood, and confined us to the same spot for two whole days."[84] Petty theft by the natives continued. Just below the Big Dalles, wrote Work, "the Indians were very quiet dur-ing the night, but before they could be all sent off from the camp they made a hole in the sand under the edge of one of the boats & stole a capot [parka] from under one of the mens head when he was sleeping." After crossing the Portage Neuf (lower Cascades Portage) on the 15th, the brigade reached Fort Vancouver on the 16th, forty-three days from Stuart's Lake (and a week from Walla Walla). At the depot "the New Caledonia people and those from the Interior of the Columbia" were busy from the 16th to the 27th unloading the *Dryad*, so that the out-going brigade did not leave until 5 July.[85]

The 1827 brigade left Fort Nez Percés on 2 June (its leader, Connolly, before leaving asked bourgeois Black to obtain fifteen horses from the Indians for the returning horse brigade). On the way to Fort Vancouver, reported Connolly, the brigaders felt "a good deal of want" because of "our longer stay at [Fort] Okanagan than was expected," and bourgeois Dease "not having brought any [dried salmon] from Fort Colvile";

moreover, "the [fresh] Salmon are much later coming up than usual." On the 4th the brigade encountered a familiar problem: "our progress was much impeded by a strong head wind." At the Cascades and Neuf Portages the cargoes were carried and the boats were "run down," although "they were certainly exposed to some risk." Fort Vancouver was reached on the 5th with the property in "excellent condition." Upon their arrival, the "first duty" of the brigaders was "untying the Packs, dusting & storing their Contents," which took two days.[86]

The 1828 brigade left Walla Walla on 2 June. It, too, was short of provisions, some having been lost in the fatal accident in the Priest's Rapids and "unaccomodating" bourgeois Black having provided only "three bags of corn & pease & a little grease," in Work's words. So the brigade, wrote Connolly, was largely dependent "upon the supplies which the Natives along the route may be able to furnish." On the 3rd a head-wind "blew with such violence as precluded all possibility of proceeding against it," and the brigaders were forced to make camp at the John Day River and stay there for two days. On the 5th they crossed the Chutes Portage, "which in consequence of the low state of the Waters, is much longer than I found it the two preceding years." There seems to have been less to fear from the natives this year. "There are not many Indians about the Dalls now," wrote Work, "the most of them are out in the plains collecting roots." On the 6th, reported Connolly, one boat "by some accident got loose" at the head of the Cascades and descended the rapids unloaded and unmanned but was recovered at the foot of the rapids with "but little injury." Fort Vancouver was reached on the 7th; the supply ship from London, the brig *Eagle* under Captain John Grave, had arrived "some time ago" but with a "very deficient" cargo for the outfits. On the 8th the boats were unloaded and "the men received the regale usually given to them on arrival at the chief Depot." They spent 9-11 June "unpacking, dusting & storing" the furs. All were in "good condition" save the marten skins, which were "materially injured," having "considerably shrunk in drying."[87]

The 1829 brigade left Fort Nez Percés on 2 June. It comprised nine boats and six men per boat, plus passengers, but was still deficient in boutes. On the 3rd at the Chutes the cargoes were carried and the brigaders ran the rapids in the empty boats. Camp was made at the lower end of the Big Dalles, and "the Baggage, as usual, was secured within an inclosure formed with the Boats, and four Gentlemen [the term including chief factors and chief traders, who were 'commissioned gentlemen,' or shareholders, and also clerks, or postmasters, who were 'salaried gentlemen,' or non-shareholders] appointed to watch during the night," the "men" being too tired from boating all day to stand guard. Here the brigaders had to make a long portage, and because the "place of debarkation" was too confined to allow the unloading of all of the boats at the same time, two of them had to make the portage on the opposite side of the river. On the 6th the brigade reached Fort Vancouver, whose occupants were "busily engaged in removing from the old to a new Fort which has been erected in a more eligible situation [higher and drier] than the former." The London ship *Ganymede*, Captain Leonard Hayne, had arrived in May and had already discharged its cargo. On the 7th and 8th the furs were unpacked, beaten, dried, and stored; one pack was missing and presumed stolen by the Indians at the Big Dalles.[88]

The 1831 brigade had a new leader, Chief Factor Peter Dease, but the same schedule. After staying a day at Fort Nez Percés and getting its returns and leaving provisions from Fort Colvile for the Snake Expedition, it departed on 7 June in nine boats with 273 packs of furs and 13 kegs of castoreum. That evening it "put up" at Gros Isle. On the 8th and 9th, three portages were made at the Big Dalles, where, Dease noted, the Indians were infamous for "their well known propensity to theft." On the 9th the brigade was halted by a "violent head wind, the boats shipping Water." On the 11th the brigaders ran the Cascades and Neuf Portages before making Fort Vancouver, where they were given their regale.[89]

And so it went until 1847, the only change being the waning of the Indian threat at the portages with the decrease of native and the increase of white numbers. But until the 1840s, this threat was very real. Numerous Indians congregated at the cataracts, and they regarded the brigaders as trespassers. In 1825 the incoming brigade encountered up to 500 Indians at the Big Dalles and up to 200 at the Chutes.[90] During the "Salmon season" in the middle 1820s, there were some 2,000 Indian men along the lower Columbia between the Big Dalles and the sea.[91] Expecting payment, the natives harassed the brigaders, who tried to mollify them with presents of tobacco and purchases of fish, and sometimes they hired them as portagers.

Whenever numerous Indians were present, the brigaders camped at night in a square formed by the boats around the property to prevent theft.[92] But goods were still stolen, the Indians being daring and adept. Lewis and Clark reported that "these are the greates theives and scoundrels we have met with."[93] And Alexander Ross lamented: "It is a singular fact, that we [Astorians] have never yet once been able to pass this Charybdis [Cascades] without paying tribute either to the natives or the whirlpools."[94] He noted, too, that passing the Big Dalles was risky because they were the "great rendezvous" of so many interior natives, who "infested the communication."[95] Their main camp lay at the head of the rapids and had a population of 3,000 or more during the fishing season.[96]

In the spring of 1817 the Cascades Indians tried unsuccessfully to fix a "perpetual tribute" for the brigades.[97] By the middle 1820s, however, they posed less of a threat. David Douglas wrote in 1825 that they "were only a few years since very hostile" and that "the [Hudson's Bay] Company's boats were frequently pillaged by them and some of their people killed." Douglas's visit to the Cascades in late summer with a Canadien voyageur and a Cascades chief "was the first ever made without a guard."[98] Governor Simpson – ever distrustful of natives – still took the threat seriously, however. He told Beaver House in 1826 that "any serious misunderstanding" with the natives between Fort Vancouver and Fort Nez Percés "might be fatal to our prospects in the Columbia, they being numerous, warlike, and masters of the South shores."[99] Chief Factor McLoughlin advised Simpson in 1828 that loaded boats could not safely ply the Columbia with fewer than thirty-four brigaders, "and even with this number it is running risks and to attempt it with less, I will not say is impossible, but I am of [the] opinion would be hazarding too much both for the people and the property."[100]

In order to safeguard the "main communication" the HBC even tried to resort to a marriage alliance. In the spring of 1825 Simpson told McLoughlin that it was "desirable" that the daughter of the Cayuse chief intended for bourgeois John Dease of Walla Walla be taken by John Work instead, "as he is likely to be employed on the communication for some time to come," and the "connexion will be a protection to a certain degree to our Brigades and the Lady ought to be a passenger every trip." McLoughlin was to see that Work "discharges his Chinook and takes this damsel to Wife the expense to be defrayed by the Coy." This measure, Simpson added, would avoid "trouble with those powerful and dangerous Indians."[101]

By the early 1840s travel on the lower Columbia was much safer. In 1843 McLoughlin recalled that "until 1834 it was not considered safe to travel up or down this river with less than 60 men, armed with muskets and fixed bayonets." But "now even strangers can come down the River from the Snake Country by twos and threes," although it was "improper and imprudent for strangers to do so, and they ought not, as it will lead to trouble."[102] By 1845 the natives had been co-opted to the extent that in the summer of that year Lieutenant Warre found that most of those at the Big Dalles attended church on Sunday, 24 August, so that his party had to wait an hour before enough could be recruited to help them portage.[103]

The only other dangerous obstacle to brigade transport on the lowermost Columbia was the series of cataracts themselves. Headwinds could slow the brigaders, but whirlpools and waterfalls, if not portaged or cordelled, could kill them. Surprisingly, however, very few boat accidents occurred, probably owing to the skill of the brigaders and their reluctance to take chances with the property, which did, after all, represent the HBC's *raison d'être*. The exceptions occurred in 1829 and 1830 at the Big Dalles. At low water the boats often shot the Big Dalles but with much risk because, as Wilkes explained, "such is the peculiar nature of the rush of waters through the Dalles, that for some minutes the whole will appear quite smooth, gliding onwards as though there were no treachery within its flow, when suddenly the waters will begin to move in extended and slow whirls, gradually increasing in velocity until it narrows itself into almost a funnel shape, when having drawn towards it all within its reach, it suddenly engulfs the whole, and again resumes its tranquil state."[104] This is what happened to Ogden's Snake party in the summer of 1829. Ogden himself related the incident to Wilkes:

Mr. Ogden was descending the river in one of the Company's boats with ten Canadian voyageurs, all well experienced in their duties. On arriving at the Dalles, they deemed it practicable to run them, in order to save the portage. Mr. Ogden determined, however, that he would pass the portage on foot, believing, however, the river was in such a state that it was quite safe for the boat to pass down. He was accordingly landed, and ascended the rocks, from which he had a full view of the water beneath, and of the boat in its passage. At first she seemed to skim over the waters like the flight of a bird; but he soon perceived her stop, and the struggle of the oarsmen, together with the anxious shout of the bowman, soon told him that they had encountered the whirl. Strongly they plied their oars, and deep anxiety if not fear was expressed in their movements. They began to move, not forwards, but onwards with the whirl: round they swept with increasing velocity, still struggling to avoid the now evident fate that awaited them: a few more turns, each more rapid than the last, until they reached the centre, when, in an instant, the boat with all her crew disappeared. So short had been the struggle, that it was only with difficulty Mr. Ogden could realize that all had perished. Only one body out of the ten was afterwards found at the bottom of the Dalles, torn and mangled by the strife it had gone through.[105]

Ogden also lost 500 beaver skins and all of his papers.[106] In the spring of 1830 the same mishap befell Ogden again. Returning with less than half of the usual Snake returns, he lost twelve members of his party (including a wife and two children) "in running down the Rapids" of the Big Dalles, it "not being a place that is fit to be run in any season much less when the water is high," in the opinion of John Stuart.[107] And in the autumn, seven men, one boat, and most of its cargo were lost in a rapids just above Fort Okanagan when it "struck on a stone and upset."[108] Such mishaps were uncommon, however, and the brigades almost always reached the depot safely with all of the batteaux and cargoes still intact and all of the voyageurs and passengers still alive. Nevertheless, the loss of lives and goods by company brigades in running rapids, especially on the Columbia, prompted the Council of the Northern Department in 1840 to pass a resolution forbidding guides and steersmen from running rapids that posed the least danger.[109]

Upon their arrival at the depot, the brigaders, after unloading the boats, feted and rested themselves. At Fort George the Nor'Westers, according to Ross Cox, enjoyed "a fortnight of continual dissipation" in the company of Chinook women. "On the arrival of the spring and autumn [express] brigades from the interior they pour in from all parts," he added, "and besiege our *voyageurs* much after the manner which their frail sisters at Portsmouth adopt when attacking the crews of a newly arrived India fleet."[110] They were greeted the same way at Fort Vancouver. Duncan Finlayson observed in 1831: "Some of the Chenook women are so licentious as to renounce matrimony & the hopes of progeny & assemble here to meet the Brigade & distribute their favours indiscriminately among all those who are well provided with the staple commodity [of] blankets."[111] Not surprisingly, the brigaders were loath to leave the pleasures of the depot for the hardships of the interior.

PART 3

The Incoming Brigade

*The communication between the Depot and the Posts in the
interior [of the Columbia Department] receiving supplies from it is
so short & easy, that the Trade may be carried on at a cheap rate.*

– CHIEF FACTOR ALEXANDER KENNEDY, 1825,
in HBCA, B.76/e/1, Fort George (Columbia River) –
District Report, 1824-25, fos. 3v.-4.

CHAPTER 9

At the Sea

The "Grand Depot" and "General Rendezvous"

*Fort Vancouver is situated upon an elevated Bank, with
a low Margin of Meadow land extending about ¾ of a Mile
between it & the River, which is subject to be flooded during the
rise of the River in the Month of June generally – otherwise it
might be made very productive. the Country behind is a Thick Forest,
but the face of the Bank is finely ornamented with Trees thinly
scattered over its surface, which with the extensive Meadow gives it
the rich appearance of a gentlemans lawn. – along the Banks of the
River there is a fringe of Poplars & Ash, & also Oak a short distance
below here – in the distant view you see Mounts Hood & Jeffery
[Jefferson] projecting their snow clad Summits, & the Columbia
flowing majestically, the whole forming a very rich Landscape."*

– LIEUTENANT AMELIUS SIMPSON, 1826[1]

THE DEPOT

Until 1825 the outbound destination of the brigades was Fort George,
which had been established by the PFC in 1811 as Astoria at the mouth
of the Columbia on its left bank. It stood on the southern side of the
river about seven miles from the sea by a small bay, "where ships are in
great safety out of the strength of the tide," according to Peter Corney,
first mate of the NWC's brig *Columbia*. There was, he continued, "a very
good wharf with a crane for landing or shipping goods." The fort itself
measured 150 feet by 150 feet; it was enclosed by pickets fifteen feet high
and protected by two corner bastions, each mounting eight guns. In the
autumn of 1817 there were up to 150 employees, nearly all of whom were
Canadiens (the clerks and partners were Scots) and most of whom kept
native wives. Some 200 acres were cleared, of which about twenty were
in potatoes "for the use of the gentlemen," and a dozen cattle and some
pigs and goats were tended. The men were not allowed to have private
land for fear of becoming freemen.[2]

Actually, however, Fort George was not well located with respect to shipping, trading, farming, or even fishing. The Columbia's mouth was shallow and exposed; the local coast offered few furs; arable land was limited; and fish were only seasonally abundant.[3] The NWC was quick to recognize these shortcomings. In early 1814, only a few months after its takeover of Astoria, the company contemplated relocating the post a hundred miles upriver to the Columbia-Willamette forks, that locale being better suited to provisionment (game hunting and crop growing) and to defence against naval bombardment.[4] Point Vancouver, below which Fort Vancouver was to be sited a decade later and above which Lieutenant Broughton had not sailed, proved especially promising.[5] Alexander Henry the Younger explained why the NWC wanted to move its headquarters from Fort George: "The impropriety of forming a permanent establishment on this spot [is] well known, it would always be too much exposed to an enemies Ship, and the unlevel state of the ground is much against it, the soil is bad, and no pasture ground for cattle of any kind, the whole surrounded by a rough unlevel country, thickly shaded by enormous large Pine trees of various kinds which renders the situation very unpleasant." He added:

> A meeting was held to determine whether or not it was proper to remove our Head Quarters from this spot or not, the result was a removal up to the entrance of the Willamette River, for various reasons, *Viz.* Less Dangerous and expensive &c. Requires fewer men Summer and Winter. Men would like the place and remain on the Columbia, whereas they are all disgusted at Fort George. More healthy and pleasant. Better gardening. Cattle of all kinds, horses &c live well. Less labour at the end of three years. The good will of the Indians above. The property kept in a better state. More secure from Enemies Ship. Stronger for defence. More central for trade. A Ship to winter could be kept in better repair and less damage to her Sails and Rigging. Would save the expences of a Fort at the Willamette.[6]

Despite the advantages of the proposed locale, however, it was not occupied. The reason, apparently, was the "want of a commanding situation,"[7] that is, a promontory along the river with fresh water, arable land, and usable timber. So Fort George remained the depot until 1825, when it was replaced by Fort Vancouver at the same time that the Peace supply line for New Caledonia was replaced by the Columbia route. At that time its population comprised thirty-seven men (plus twenty extra men [brigaders], eight express men, and nine men belonging to Governor Simpson's light canoe), thirty-seven women, thirty-five children, and eleven slaves; eighteen of the thirty-seven men, incidentally, were Hawaiians.[8]

In 1824 Beaver House ordered the relocation of the Columbian headquarters to the northern side of the river at "the most convenient Situation" because the United States was "to have possession of Fort George whenever they please" under the terms of the Treaty of Ghent of 1818.[9] The company, expecting that the course of the Columbia, Snake, and Clearwater Rivers would become the international boundary, planned to move Fort Nez Percés to the Columbia's right bank, too. Fort Vancouver's situation was economically as well as politically superior to that of Fort George. It had much more farmland, was more central to trade, and had a more convenient landing. The site, Jolie Prairie to the Canadiens and Katchutequa ("the plain") to the Indians, lay on the northern bank three miles above the Willamette's mouth and one mile from the Columbia itself on a terrace above a two-mile-long floodplain. In the spring of 1826 the fort measured 250 feet in length and 150 in width and was surrounded by a stockade seventeen feet in height, flanked by two bastions, each with three pieces of artillery; there was one house, one Indian trading hall, one workshop, one powder magazine, and two storehouses.[10] Its population jumped from thirty-two in the winter of 1825-26 to eighty-two – seventy-eight men (including ten gentlemen), two women, and two children – a year later.[11] Fort George continued to be "kept up" for the local Indian trade and the local salmon fishery but languished, while "King George," as Fort Vancouver was dubbed by the Chinooks, quickly became the hub of HBC operations on the Columbia, impressing visitors with its grandness, bustle, neatness, productivity, and hospitality.[12] It was inspected by Lieutenants Warre and Vavasour in the summer of 1845. Warre penned the following description, which, although rather soberly expressed from a largely strategic perspective, clearly depicts the post's large size and vital role:

> Fort Vancouver about which so much has been said & written, the head quarters of the Hudsons Bay Company on the West of the Rocky Mts. is situated near the lower end of a small plain, which is partially flooded by the Spring freshets. These prevent the Soil from being cultivated, but afford excellent pasturage for the numerous herds of Cattle horses & Sheep which the Company keep and accumulate for their own purposes. The Fort is badly situated as regards defence being commanded by a ridge of Ground running the whole length of the Plain & extending along the bank of the River. On this ridge the Fort was formerly placed but as defensive operations were not so necessary as the convenience of transport for stores etc to & from the River the Buildings were removed to their present position. It is surrounded by strong pickets 15 ft

in height 220 yds long by 700 deep at the N. West Angle is a square block-
house, supporting an octagonal upper story containing several small Guns. The
Stores are large and capacious, well built and contain in addition to the stock
of trading articles for the Year, a supply for the succeeding Year to prevent the
possibility of the trade being impeded by an accident to the Vessels in their
long Voyages from England. There are also stores of Wheat large quantities of
which are exported to the Russian Settlement at Sitka and to the Sandwich
Islands. There are several dwelling houses within the Stockade a Kitchen Oven
Blacksmiths house & Shop Coopers ^{Do.} & in fact contains within its own walls
all that can be required to keep in motion the vast mercantile machinery of
which it is the head. There is a Village occupied exclusively by the servants of
the Company on the West side extending to the River bank and a Roman
Catholic Church is in the course of Erection at the head of the principal thoroughfare. The Hospital is on the bank of the River near the landing and altho
generally the place is healthy, there are many cases of fever & ague [malaria]
at certain seasons, which have proved fearfully fatal to the Indian population.
Dysentery also is prevalent during some seasons & on account of the humid-
ity of the Climate Colds and complaints of the Lungs also are frequent.

Warre added that at the depot the company cultivated some 1,200 acres
and produced "large quantities" of wheat, potatoes, and turnips, in addition to keeping "very immense" herds of pigs. It also had a grist mill five
miles upriver and a saw mill another mile farther upstream.[13]

Fort Vancouver was crucial to Governor Simpson's program of self-
sufficiency. Indeed, he considered the establishment "a more important
charge, if well conducted, from the saving of expense it will yield and
the advantages it will afford in other points of view than that of one half
the Posts on either side the Mountain."[14] Simpson acknowledged that
the "principal Depot" was moved from Fort George to Fort Vancouver
in order "to command the means of subsistence," which were "here,
perhaps more than any where else, the main Spring of the business."[15]
In 1825 Fort George's forty men had thirty-one cattle, seventeen swine,
and 1,800 bushels of potatoes;[16] in the fall of the same year Fort Vancouver's first potato crop totalled 900 kegs (720 bushels), and a year later
its cattle herd numbered eighty to ninety head.[17]

But the new depot did not become self-sufficient until the end of the
decade. When William Connolly arrived with the brigade on 5 June 1827,
he found that the scarcity of provisions was a source of "much uneasiness" to Chief Factor McLoughlin.[18] However, in the autumn of 1828
the post's twenty men reaped 4,000 bushels of potatoes, 1,300 of wheat,
1,000 of barley, 400 of corn, 300 of peas, and 100 of oats, and in the
spring of 1829 they tended 200 pigs, 153 cattle (not including calves), and

50 goats.[19] In 1830 McLoughlin reported with satisfaction that "this is the first year since I am here … in which I have been able to supply our people adequately." He added that the farm's output was advantageous in two respects: "the freight it saves us, and it has been raised at no expence … as, if the people had not been doing that [farming], they would have been unemployed."[20] By the middle 1830s, under George Allen, Fort Vancouver's farm comprised 1,500 ploughed acres and 1,500 pastured acres.[21] In 1833 more than 10,000 bushels of grain were grown.[22] Upon going on furlough in the spring of 1838, McLoughlin told his temporary replacement, James Douglas, that he had "always considered the farm as an object of primary consideration as without provisions the different Branches of the Business cannot be carried on," and he advised Douglas to have in store in the fall 5,000 bushels of wheat, 4,000 of peas, 2,000 of oats, and 1,500 of barley (the oats and barley for feeding work horses and fattening pigs) – enough for two years.[23] When Lieutenant Wilkes visited Fort Vancouver in the spring of 1841, he found it to be "a large manufacturing, agricultural, and commercial depot" with "few if any idlers, except the sick." The farm, he added, encompassed nine square miles and comprised some 3,000 cattle, 2,500 sheep, and 300 brood mares, plus four dairies supplied by 250 milk cows, as well as a vegetable garden of four to five acres.[24] Governor Simpson underlined the significance of the "farm at the sea": "The Farm at this place is an object of vital importance to the interests of the business on the west side the mountains, generally, as it has enabled us to dispense with imported provisions for the maintenance of our shipping and establishments, whereas, without this farm, it would have been necessary to import such provisions, at an expense that the trade could not afford."[25]

"Intermittent Fever"

Fort Vancouver faced only one major problem – the Columbia River itself. Opposite the fort the river was about a mile wide in the summer of 1845,[26] but in the spring it rose higher and wider. Between 24 May and 16 July 1825, for example, it rose 12 feet, 8 inches at the post.[27] It could rise as much as twenty feet in late spring and flood up to one-half of the farmland, including most of the best ploughland.[28] The 1830 crop was "very much" injured by the "extraordinary height" of the river.[29] In June 1840 it rose "very much" and destroyed at least half of the crop.[30] One year later Lieutenant Wilkes witnessed the spring freshet at the fort, where during the night of 29 May the Columbia rose one and a half feet in ten hours. He described the scene:

The flood is a very grand sight from the banks of the river at Vancouver, as it passes swiftly by, bearing along the gigantic forest trees, whose immense trunks appear as mere chips. They frequently lodge for a time, in which case others are speedily caught by them, which obstructing the flow of the water, form rapids, until by a sudden rush the whole is borne off to the ocean, and in time lodged by the currents on some remote and savage island, to supply the natives with canoes. I also witnessed the undermining of large trees on the banks, and occasional strips of soil: thus does the river yearly make inroads on its banks, and changes in its channels.[31]

More seriously, the receding floodwater left pools of stagnant water – ideal breeding grounds for anopheline mosquitoes, the vectors of malaria. This "dreadful visitation," variously termed "intermittent," "remittent," or "trembling" fever or "cold sick," struck the lowermost Columbia every year from 1830 through 1836.[32] It occurred semi-annually, and whites suffered less and less with each successive attack.[33] Usually the disease only incapacitated the whites but annihilated the natives, who suffered a mortality rate as high as 75 percent (their remedy – alternating hot and cold baths – was more harmful than helpful). "During the time of the greatest mortality," declared Wilkes, "the shores of the river were strewed with the dead and dying."[34] It was no accident that malaria first struck in 1830 after the "extraordinary height" of the Columbia in the spring (although the Indians were convinced that it had been brought by Captain John Dominis of the American brig *Owhyhee*[35]).

That autumn McLoughlin told Beaver House that "the Intermitting Fever (for the first time since the trade of this Department was Established) has appeared at this place and carried off three fourths of the Indn. population in our vicinity: at present there are fifty two of our people on the sick list."[36] In late September half of the post's employees were "laid up" with malaria.[37] Subsequently, Clerk Frank Ermatinger recalled that "almost all caught it more or less" and that "80 men besides women" were bedridden. But only three of these men died, whereas some Indian villages were "entirely depopulated," and the venerable Chinook Chief Concomly and "most of his subjects" died.[38]

In 1831 malaria raged so fiercely that company business was completely halted for a time.[39] At Fort Vancouver all but seven were afflicted, and some had three and even four bouts with the disease.[40] By the middle of October, reported bourgeois Simon McGillivray of Fort Nez Percés, it was "subsiding" at the depot, "but it is [still] raging at the Dalles among [the] Indians, and many are dead." McGillivray himself succumbed on Friday, 7 October and described the attack the next day: "The illness was very sudden. On Friday Evening just as I had seated myself to Tea [supper], all at once, the Head-Ache attacked me, sever[e] pains, as burning in the Chest, and gripings – it continued so till 10 O'Clock PM, when I was constantly obliged to go to the Privy, every stool was attended with most excruciating Pains, about the loins and testicles. It continued so all night & today, – and all Saturday night." A day later he added: "On Sunday, the evacuations & Pains somewhat abated, but I am weak, and it is only this morning I have been able to relish my Breakfast, with any degree of appetite."[41] The following March, Duncan Finlayson recollected the outbreak:

> The fever, which had raged here during the summer with unabated fury had partially receded before the approach of winter, symptoms of it occasionally appeared ever since, but when the warm weather sets in, I am afraid the effects of it may prove fatal to some of us – It is, however, tho' very lingering & shatters the constitution much, not considered with care & attention very dangerous. – But its effects may be seen on those who have suffered under its influence, as they never after have that external appearance of health & solid strength, which characterises the inhabitants of wholesome climates.[42]

In the summer of 1832 malaria "raged with great violence" at Fort Vancouver, and McLoughlin himself "who had hitherto escaped it had a severe attack."[43] "Several" of the brigaders were struck by the "Fever" after leaving the depot and had to be left at Fort Okanagan to recuperate; in fact, they were the company's first cases of the year. The death toll among the natives below the Cascades was "very great."[44]

The contagion erupted again in 1833. Three-quarters of John Work's Southern Expedition, a trapping foray into California involving nearly one hundred men, was incapacitated.[45] But again it was the Indians who suffered the most. McLoughlin reported in 1834 that "the Mortality among the Natives has been Immense."[46] Missionary estimates of native mortality on the lowermost Columbia ranged from almost two-thirds (Father De Smet) to nearly nine-tenths (Fathers Blanchet and Demers).[47] And the survivors, according to Lieutenant Warre, were "from all accounts and judging from appearances" reduced by one-half in the first half of the 1840s by liquor and disease (influenza).[48] Consequently, the Indian threat to brigaders in the Columbia millrace (as well as to settlers in the Willamette Valley) virtually disappeared by the middle 1830s.[49] During the last half of the 1830s malaria waned. McLoughlin lamented in the summer of 1835 that "the Fever afflicts us much," but he reported in 1836 that there were "very few cases of fever," and in 1837 that there were "fewer cases of Fever than in any year since 1830" – only five, including McLoughlin himself once more.[50]

THE "LONDON SHIP"

The Fraser-Columbia brigade route was but the overland section of a logistical system that linked New Caledonia and Great Britain. The longer and easier overseas section ran around Cape Horn between the departmental depot (Fort George until 1825, Fort Vancouver until 1847, and Fort Victoria thereafter) and the company's headquarters in London. It was plied annually by a supply ship that brought trade goods for both the interior and coastal business, as well as some provisions, luxuries, and passengers, and took furs and castoreum for the European market, and occasionally "country produce" (salmon, lumber, hides, tallow) for export to Russian Alaska (Sitka), the Hawaiian Islands (Honolulu), California (San Francisco), and elsewhere.[51] The imported goods were sold at Fort Vancouver in the early 1840s for 180 percent of the London wholesale price and at the other posts for 200 percent in order to cover expenses, mainly transport; nevertheless, they were no dearer, and perhaps even cheaper, than the same goods being sold in the Eastern United States.[52]

The London ship usually left Gravesend on the Thames in late summer or early autumn in order to be able to round the fearsome Horn in the middle of the less tempestuous summer of the Southern Hemisphere and reach the depot in late spring (early June) just before the brigade. It then could service the coastal posts or even sail to Sitka, Honolulu, or San Francisco and back before embarking for London in the autumn, again in order to be able to navigate the Horn in mid-summer and reach England in time for the spring fur auction. This schedule was reinforced by the fact that, as McLoughlin pointed out, "from the 1st November to the month of February it is seldom there is an opportunity to enter, or go out of the Columbia River, and it is particularly dangerous for a large vessel at that season [of unfavourable winds and tides]."[53] However, with the rerouting of New Caledonia's furs to the Columbia in 1826, the returns reached the new depot of Fort Vancouver later than they had reached the old depot of Fort George, so it was necessary for the London ship not to arrive too early in order to avoid paying demurrage of £5-10 per day.[54] The London ships were outfitted and dispatched one year in advance in order "to provide against [the] loss of ships with outward freight."[55] Beginning in 1841 the company sent two supply ships to the Columbia every other year and two to York Factory on Hudson Bay every other year, the two sailings alternating.[56] In fact, three ships were kept for the Columbia: one going, one coming, and one in reserve at the depot.[57]

The NWC had set a precedent for the London ship, sending the *Isaac Todd* (1812), *Columbia* (1814), and the *Colonel Allan* (1816) to Fort George.

The Nor'Westers, however, found that it was cheaper to send their returns to Canton on an American ship for 25 percent of the proceeds than to buy a China trade licence from the EIC. This device was inherited by the HBC with the merger of 1821, when the last NWC supply ship, the *Alexander*, arrived at Fort George from Boston on 5 May and departed in early June with 16,000 beaver skins.[58] It was followed by the *Houqua* in 1822, the *Lively* in 1823, and the *Vigilant* (Captain James Davidson) in 1824. The *Vigilant* was the HBC's last chartered supply ship, the company finding it cheaper in the long run to buy a sound used vessel than to pay the going freight rate (up to 26 shillings per ton of register per month) on chartered vessels.[59] So it bought the *William and Ann*, a six-year-old brig of 161 tons built of cedar in Bermuda.[60] It was the first of thirty-five London ships to leave Gravesend for Fort Vancouver between 1823 and 1847; three of them – the *Cadboro* in 1827, the *Dryad* in 1830, and the *Nereide* in 1836 – remained there for coastal service, and two of them – the *William and Ann* (Captain John Swan) in 1829 and the *Isabella* (Captain William Ryan) in 1830 – were wrecked at the mouth of the Columbia.[61]

Both shipwrecks occurred on the Columbia Bar. The *William and Ann* lost all of its twenty-six crewmen and most of its cargo.[62] When he reached Alexandria in early May 1829 en route to the depot as brigade leader, Chief Factor Connolly heard the "disturbing intelligence" of the "total wreck" of the brig; however, he also heard that, thanks to the "interposition of a kind providence," a second supply ship with the "bulk" of the Columbia outfit had also been sent, otherwise "we would have found ourselves destitute not only of every means of carrying on the Trade, but also of many necessaries essential to the preservation of our lives."[63] This second ship, the 213-ton barque *Ganymede*, narrowly escaped the same fate when its master, Captain Hayne, mistook Chinook Bay for the Columbia River.[64] A year later the *William and Ann*'s replacement, the 195-ton brig *Isabella*, was lost on the bar, but all of its crew and most of its cargo were saved.[65]

The bar was the sole major barrier to safe navigation of the lowermost Columbia. Below the Cascades the river was a "fine smooth stream, from half a mile to a mile broad," in the words of Fort George's first and last district report (1824-25).[66] Ships of 300 tons burthen were able to make Fort Vancouver; the only obstruction was the occasional sand bar, and the flood tides were weak and short, so that a "fair breeze" from the southwest or northwest was necessary.[67] Even at low water the river at the depot could accommodate a ship of fourteen feet of draught.[68] The only "serious obstacle" was the bar, as Lieutenant Vavasour noted: "The

navigation of the [lowermost] Columbia River is obstructed by numerous sand Banks, which are constantly shifting, and Vessels are often
detained a long time in ascending and descending it, as also in Bakers
Bay waiting for a favourable opportunity of crossing the Bar. The H. B.
Company's Barque Vancouver was one month from Vancouver to Bakers
Bay, and 45 days laying in the Bay, before an opportunity offered for
leaving the River."[69]

The Columbia Bar (or Peacock Bar, or Spit, in commemoration of the
wreck thereon in 1841 of the sloop-of-war of the same name belonging
to the United States Exploring Expedition) comprised what John Dunn
called the "foaming and tumultous breakers" on the shoals at the river's
mouth. According to Governor Simpson, "in the whole Navigation of
the outward and Homeward Voyage [between London and the depot]
I do not believe there is so much danger to be apprehended as in
making & leaving the River," even more so than notorious Cape Horn.
Simpson was so impressed that he even recommended that "some expence
should be incurred" for the installing of buoys and beacons on the bar
and the stationing of a pilot there.[70] Alexander Ross sounded an early
warning on behalf of the Astorians in 1811:

> The mouth of [the] Columbia River is remarkable for its sand-bars and high
> surf at all seasons, but more particularly in the spring and fall, during the
> equinoctial gales: these sand-bars frequently shift, the channel of course shift-
> ing along with them, which renders the passage at all times extremely dan-
> gerous. The bar, or rather the chain of sand-banks, over which the huge waves
> and foaming breakers roll so awfully, is a league [three miles] broad, and
> extends in a white foaming sheet for many miles, both south and north of the
> mouth of the river, forming as it were an impracticable barrier to the entrance,
> and threatening with instant destruction everything that comes near it.[71]

Two years later HMS *Racoon*, Captain William Black, the first war-
ship to enter the Columbia, arrived to take formal possession of
Astoria and to enforce British authority. Upon leaving the river in early
1814, the sloop-of-war struck the bar several times and was so severely
damaged that it subsequently had to limp into San Francisco Bay "in a
sinking state, with seven feet water in her hold."[72] Captain Black seems
to have learned his lesson: "The Bar of this River ought never to be
attempted but in very fine weather, and then the greatest precaution is
necessary either going in or out, particularly by Strangers, the rapid
Tides & very heavy Sea which often breaks with great violence right
across the channel makes it very dangerous; during the winter it is

seldom possible to get either in or out."[73] Captain Black's warning was echoed in 1842 by the Catholic missionary Father Jean Bolduc, who crossed the bar in the HBC barque *Cowlitz*: "The bar located at the mouth of the Columbia is formed by a sand bank which is covered by only four or five fathoms of water and often less. The sea there is almost always in a turmoil, and if it is driven by the wind, it is impossible to cross it. When the weather is very favorable, it is not crossed except with the sounding line, and, in spite of all precautions, there are frequent wrecks."[74] One of these wrecks was that of the U.S. Exploring Expedition's *Peacock*, whose sister ships, the *Vincennes* and *Porpoise*, as well as its replacement, the *Oregon* (the former *Thomas Perkins*), crossed the bar at the beginning of November 1841. The expedition's commander, Lieutenant Charles Wilkes, described and explained the perils of the bar:

> Mere description can give little idea of the terrors of the bar of the Columbia: all who have seen it have spoken of the wildness of the scene, and the incessant roar of the waters, representing it as one of the most fearful sights that can possibly meet the eye of the sailor. The difficulty of its channel, the distance of the leading sailing marks, their uncertainty to one unacquainted with them, the want of knowledge of the strength and direction of the currents, with the necessity of approaching close to unseen dangers, the transition from clear to turbid water, all cause doubt and mistrust.[75]

The harrowing experience of the 780-ton sloop-of-war *Vincennes*, the expedition's flagship, was recounted by the commander, who had, in fact, already crossed the bar en route to the Hawaiian Islands:

> We accordingly got under way and stood to sea, but the wind left us & fell calm so that I was obliged to anchor without, or to seaward of the Bar. The two Brigs *Porpoise* and *Oregon* had obtained an offing of about three miles when the Signal was made to anchor. The sea was perfectly smooth and the weather fine. We lay perfectly quiet until towards midnight when the rollers began to form and rapidly increase until we found the ship was tossed high in the breakers which ensued and finally broke over us in vast rollers rendering our situation very dangerous, at times breaking over our bow and sweeping our decks fore and aft. The cable was at times torn from its stoppers and several fathoms of it escaped, but it served the purpose of gradually easing the ship and the cable which at times seemed that it must part from the violent strain. Although some eighty fathoms had escaped, the depth of water at the ship was but seven fathoms. The roar of these breakers was awful and their violence & magnitude beyond conception, estimated to be some thirty feet in height and with a progressive motion of [blank] feet per minute. For upwards

of an hour these continued, and each breaker gave us additional apprehension that the ship must part her cable. Fortunately the flood tide was strong and enabled me to keep the Ship head on. Each breaker as it rolled on curved over the sides of the ship and filled our upper deck which descended through the Hatches to the gun deck. Several larger rollers struck the Ship full on the bow and was so large and high that it washed the runing rigging out of [the] fore top and tore away the lashing of our booms and swept the deck, and much of it passed over the taffra[i]l carrying with it boxes of plants and every thing movable. The whole was a scene of desolation. Unfortunately a marine of the name of [Joseph] Allshouse was ascending the deck ladder at the time and was caught by the booms and so badly injured that he died the next day of his injuries. There was no other accident to anyone. About two o'clock the rollers became less frequent and ceased to break and my mind became satisfied we had escaped injury to the ship. The Sea became again smooth, but the calm continued with a dense fog. This phenomenon generally occurs at the full and change of the moon on this coast but is little thought of and, I suppose, little experience of its effects have been noticed. I had been informed of its action, but its vast breakers were said to be confined to [the] Bar on which there is but 4 fathoms. The depth of water we had anchored in outside the bar gave me confidence the ship was beyond the influence of these Rollers. The swell proved otherwise and might have caused us serious disaster. All we had to do was keep the Ship end on and this was a very difficult matter. If unfortunately we had already swung broad side to the breakers, great damage must have ensued. The *Vincennes* behaved beautifully and rose to each Successive breaker & then plunged again into the trough of the Sea. Her motions were easy and graceful and few can believe how it became possible for her to over come such a force as these mighty waves offered her hull. I was very greatly relieved when I perceived that the Sea was subsiding and deemed we had been very fortunate to have escaped without greater damage, and all rejoiced over it. There was nothing to be done in the way of seamanship, the ship kept head on. At times the roar of the advancing breakers was awful, and it continued to increase until they struck the ship. Not the faintest air was felt during the time we were subjected to this trial (some five hours). In a few cases when the waves struck the bow fairly it caused the vessel to tremble throughout, and the complete silence of the noise of the breakers [surrounding] the ship after a heavy wave had broken over her was no less frightful than its bursting and enveloping her whole hull, the spray being thrown to the height of her tops and mast head. It was one of the most exciting and anxious hours I passed during the [five-year] cruize.[76]

Wilkes's experience prompted him to urge Washington to press for an international boundary (the forty-ninth parallel) that would grant the superior harbours and channels of Puget Sound to the United States (and none to Great Britain) – which, of course, is exactly what happened under the terms of the Treaty of Washington of 1846. Wilkes declared: "Nothing can exceed the beauty of these waters, and their safety: not a shoal exists within the Staits of Juan de Fuca, Admiralty Inlet, Puget Sound, or Hood's Canal, that can in any way interrupt their navigation by a seventy-four gun ship. I venture nothing in saying, there is no country in the world that possesses waters equal to these."[77] The HBC was well aware of the situation. Indeed, in 1835 the Governor and Committee recommended to Chief Factor McLoughlin that the Columbia Department's "principal Depot" be relocated from Fort Vancouver to an "eligible situation easy of access" on the coast, possibly Whidbey Island, because they considered the "danger of crossing the Columbia Bar, too great a risk to be run by the annual Ships from and to England with the Outfits and returns."[78] But Fort Vancouver remained the depot until the 1846 treaty, whereupon Beaver House decided to remove to the superior port of Camosun (Fort Victoria) on Vancouver Island.

Ships could wait days, weeks, or even months to cross the Columbia Bar, only to be wrecked in the attempt by the breakers. James Douglas and Duncan Finlayson told the American adventurer, Captain Nathaniel Wyeth, in the winter of 1832-33 that ships sometimes laid off the bar for seven weeks before they could enter the river;[79] and two American migrants, Thomas Farnham and Joel Palmer, asserted that ships were often detained in the river for thirty to forty days, and occasionally for two to three months, before they could leave.[80] In 1841 the company's *Columbia* spent one month of a five-month voyage from Fort Vancouver to the northern coast in the river itself.[81] The *Cowlitz* took eighty days in 1844 to cross the bar (although admittedly there was "much culpable neglect" on the part of Captain William Heath).[82] And in 1845 the *Vancouver* waited one and a half months to cross the bar outbound, and inbound it tried for a month without success to cross it and was nearly lost on it.[83]

Even after finally crossing the bar and escaping shipwreck, a vessel could take up to a month to make Fort Vancouver because of absolute calms and contrary winds. Shifting sand bars also slowed navigation. The upriver voyage usually took up to a fortnight.[84] The downriver voyage was presumably faster, although in the summer of 1845 the *Vancouver* took a month.[85]

The London ship had to reach the depot before the brigade to avoid delaying the latter's return. Only once, apparently, did the vessel arrive late. In 1826 the *Dryad*, Captain Davidson, did not arrive until 1 June, and his lateness, plus the necessity of brigade leader Connolly trading horses from the Snake River Indians on his inbound journey, prevented him from extending his New Caledonia trade as much as he had expected upon his return, which was delayed until late September.[86]

More problematical was the condition of the cargo, which at first was at least partly inferior or damaged. The *William and Ann*, the first of the company's own Columbia supply ships, reached Fort George on 11 April 1825 with part of its cargo wet. Six-sevenths of the flour and meal were spoiled. The flour, meal, pork, beef, and gunpowder barrels were "very bad," the pork and beef being "not so good" as, and the gunpowder "damper" than, that "we have hitherto had"; and the bricks were of a "very inferior quality."[87] The *Dryad*, a chartered vessel, arrived on 1 June 1826 with "several" categories of its cargo damaged. The corn had been "much Injured by Insects," some of the dry goods were "much Injured," the gunpowder was "very coarse," and the iron, especially that for use in beaver traps, was "of a Worse quality than any hitherto sent."[88]

The year 1830 marked the first in which Chief Factor McLoughlin received an outfit that was both suited to the trade and enough for his personnel.[89] But the outfit continued to arrive scathed. Both the 1830 and 1831 outfits reached Fort Vancouver in a "damaged state"; a "considerable proportion" of the 1830 outfit, brought by the *Eagle*, was injured.[90] And the cargo of the *Ganymede* was delivered "in a damaged condition" in 1835.[91] Thereafter the problem seems not to have recurred.

Once a sufficient amount and suitable array of goods of adequate quality had arrived at the depot in sound condition, an equally difficult task remained – their conveyance in safety by the return brigade to the interior posts as far as New Caledonia before the onset of winter.

CHAPTER 10

Boating up the Columbia

The Hard Leg from
the Sea to Walla Walla

JULY 1ST − *The nine boats composing the brigade had now
completed their outfit, and were all prepared for their different
destinations. Mr. Lewis [Chief Factor John Lewes] was to command
until he arrived at his own post, Colville; but we had great
difficulty in collecting the men, between sixty and seventy in number: some wanted their allowance of rum, or regale, before they
started, given to the Company's men only preparatory to a long
voyage. Others were bidding farewell to their Indian loves, and
were hard to be found; in fact, all hesitated to give up the life of
idleness and plenty in which they had been luxuriating for the last
two or three weeks for the toils and privations which they well
knew were before them. However, towards evening we succeeded in
collecting our crews, and Mr. Lewis promised them their regale on
the first fitting opportunity. The fort gave us a salute of seven guns,
which was repeated by the Company's ship lying at the store-house.
The occupants of the fort crowded round us; and at last, amidst
cheers and hearty wishes for our safety, we pushed off.*

− PAUL KANE, 1847[1]

THE TURNAROUND

After reaching the depot, the brigaders spent from two to three weeks
unloading the returns, recuperating and celebrating, and embarking the
outfit. Governor Simpson estimated in 1825 that ten days would be sufficient to outfit the brigade at Fort Vancouver, and he advised Chief
Factor McLoughlin to observe the "greatest Expedition" in order "to save
Provisions" − meaning in order to minimize expenses.[2] That very year,
however, the brigade was detained six weeks at the new depot, from 26
April until 11 June, mainly because the men and boats were needed to
help move the property − sixty-four boat loads − from the old depot of
Fort George to Fort Vancouver.[3]

More importantly, the longer the brigade stayed at the depot, the shorter the trading season at the inland posts following its return. Chief Factor Connolly complained to Simpson that his brigade had been obliged to spend six weeks at the depot in 1828 because the goods and their containers were prepared "only after our arrival."[4] The main cause of the delay, however, was the recruitment of most of the brigaders for a punitive expedition of sixty-four men against the Hood Canal Indians for having killed five company employees; the expedition left Fort Vancouver on 17 June for Puget Sound and returned on 15 July. This one-month hiatus, Connolly complained, deferred "my departure from Fort Vancouver, and consequent arrival in New Caledonia to a much later period than the situation of affairs in this District would admit of, without subjecting the Trade to some loss, and, what was more to be dreaded, exposing the lives of the people inland to much risk."[5]

Connolly hoped that in 1829 his stay at the depot could be limited to eight days because "the safety and well doing of the [New Caledonia] District depends so much upon our early return to it."[6] His hopes were dashed, however. The departure of the 1829 brigade was "much" delayed (five weeks) by the "confusion" over the move from the old to the new fort at the depot, by the loading of the *Cadboro* for a voyage to Fort Langley near the mouth of the Fraser and of the *Vancouver* for a voyage to the mouth of the Columbia, and by a "fruitless" attempt by Connolly to recover the twenty bales of freight that had been salvaged from the wrecked *William and Ann* by the Clatsop Indians.[7] This delay "prevented our return to the District in time to pay with our reduced force the requisite attention to its various duties."[8]

Even the two-week stay of the 1831 brigade at Fort Vancouver was too long for Clerk William Kittson of Fort Colvile. He was "anxious for the arrival of the Brigade in order to get up [the Columbia's headwaters] in time for making the Summer trade of the two Out Posts [of the Colvile District – the Flathead and Kootenay Posts], Knowing that the Americans are, on their way to the Flat Heads, for the purpose of taking all the Skins." He added that in general "in fact the Americans have every advantage over us [in the Flathead Country], owing to the long stay of our men at the Sea."[9]

When the brigade served only the Columbia District and not New Caledonia, too, and used only the Columbia and not the Fraser River (that is, from 1811 until 1820 and from 1823 until 1826), it was able to reach and leave the depot (Fort George) much earlier – early enough, in fact, to avoid the freshet of late spring.[10] Otherwise, however, the brigade usually made Fort Vancouver in the first or second week of June and left at the end of the month after a stopover of two to three weeks (see Table 1).[11]

TABLE 1 Dates of the brigade's arrival at, and departure from, Fort
Vancouver, 1825-47

Year	Arrival	Departure
1825	24 April	20 or 21 June
1826	16 June	5 July
1827	5 June	14 June
1828	7 June	22 or 23 July
1829	5 June	11 July
1830	11 June	29 June
1831	13 June	27 June
1832	20 June	5 July
1833	15 June	1 or 4 July
1836	3 June	25 June
1837	7 June	26 June
1838	5 June	20 June
1839	6 June	22 June
1840	10 June	29 June
1842	8 June	?
1843	4 June	28 June
1844	4 June	29 June
1845	12 June	28 June
1847	? June	1 July

Sources: Bagley, *Early Catholic Missions*, 1: 76; Elliott, "Journal of John Work," (1914):
84, (1915): 27; HBCA, B.188/a/8, Fort St. James – Post Journal, 1826-27, 5 July 1826;
HBCA, B.188/a/10, Fort St. James – Post Journal, 1827, 5, 14 June 1827; HBCA,
B.188/a/12, Fort St. James – Post Journal, 1828, 9 June 1828; HBCA, B.188/a/14, Fort
St. James – Post Journal, 1829-30, 11 July 1829; HBCA, B.188/a/17, Fort St. James –
Post Journal, 1831-32, 27 June 1831; HBCA, B.188/b/5, Fort St. James – Correspon-
dence Book, Connolly to the Northern Department, p. 7; HBCA, B.223/b/1, Fort
Vancouver – Correspondence Book, 1825, McLoughlin to Simpson, 20 June 1825;
HBCA, B.223/b/3, Fort Vancouver – Correspondence Book, 1827-28, McLoughlin
to the Governor, Chief Factors, and Chief Traders of the Northern Department, 17
August 1827; HBCA, B.223/b/8, Fort Vancouver – Correspondence Book, 1832-33,
McLoughlin to Simpson, 12 September 1832; HBCA, D.4/6, Governor George
Simpson – Correspondence Book Outwards (General), 1825-26, McLoughlin to the
Governor and Committee, 6 October 1825; HBCA, D.4/119, Correspondence Book
Inwards, 1824-26, McLoughlin to the Chief Factors and Chief Traders of the
Columbia Department, 20 June 1825, Connolly to the Governor, Chief Factors, and
Chief Traders of the Northern Department, 18 July 1826; HBCA, D.4/120, Corre-
spondence Book Inwards, 1827, McLoughlin to the Governor, Chief Factors, and
Chief Traders of the Northern Department, 17 August 1827; HBCA, D.4./121, Cor-
respondence Book Inwards, 1827, Connolly to the Governor, Chief Factors, and Chief
Traders of the Northern Department, 20 September 1827; HBCA, D.4/126, Correspondence Book Inwards, 1833-34, Dease to the Chief Factors and Chief Traders of
the Athabasca District, 19 September 1833; Kane, *Wanderings of an Artist*, 178; Lewis
and Meyers, "Journal of a Trip," 110; MacLaren, "Journal of Paul Kane's Western
Travels," 39; [Work], "Journal of John Work," 21 June 1825, 5 July 1826, 23 July 1828.

A late arrival kept the London ship waiting at the company's expense. This problem arose in 1826 with the inclusion of New Caledonia in the brigade's hinterland. Consequently, complained Chief Factor McLoughlin, the Governor and Committee did not seem "to be aware that the Interior returns are not at this place [Fort Vancouver] so early in the Season as they used to be at Fort George" because they now had to come from farther north and farther away, so that a waiting London ship had to be paid demurrage (detention charges) of £5-10 per day.[12]

During their stay at the depot, whether brief or long, the brigaders added a colourful and hedonistic dimension to its routine. Lieutenant Wilkes described the "voyageurs" of Ogden's 1841 brigade as "decked in gay feathers, ribands, &c., full of conceit, and with the flaunting air of those who consider themselves the beau-ideal of grace and beauty; full of frolic and fun, and seeming to have nothing to do but to attend to the decorations of their persons and seek for pleasure; looking down with contempt upon those who are employed about the fort, whose sombre cast of countenance and business employments form a strong contrast to these jovial fellows." At the fort, he added, "a voyageur occasionally was to be seen, decked out in all his finery, feathers, and flowing ribands, tying on his ornamented leggins, sashes, and the usual worked tobacco and fire pouch ... and it has usually several long tails to it, which are worked with silk of gaudy colours."[13]

THE UPRIVER VOYAGE

Upon their departure, the brigaders, Wilkes found, were still "all gaily dressed in their ribands and plumes; the former tied in large bunches of divers colours, with numerous ends floating in the breeze." After their departure, however, they "doffed their finery, and ... appeared more prepared for hard work." And afloat "the boat and voyageurs seemed a fit object to grace the wide-flowing river."[14] The lieutenant was describing Ogden's inbound brigade of 1841. Three-quarters of its members were Canadiens and one-quarter were Iroquois – "all strong, active, and hardy men."[15] The depot itself did not normally furnish any men for the brigade (except occasionally to assist it as far as Walla Walla), for in spring and autumn in particular they were more sorely needed at the headquarters for other duties (farming, manufacturing, trading).[16] An exception occurred in 1826, when thirty-one men were added to the inward brigade, comprising eleven "Fort Vancouver men to Return in the Fall But in the mean time to be Employed at Spokane and in going to the Rocky Mountains [Portage]" (including the guide Pierre L'Étang and five Hawaiians), ten "Thompson River Men" (including the boat-builder Pierre la Course), and ten "Spokane Men."[17]

It commonly took the brigaders about ten days to go from Fort Van-couver to Fort Nez Percés. The first day of the upriver voyage from the depot was usually short. For one thing, there were often some last-minute hitches that delayed the send-off. For another, as Wilkes noted, the practice was "to go only a few miles the first day, in order that they may discover if any thing has been neglected, and be able to return for it."[18] Lieutenant Warre confirmed that "it never is usual for the Boats, start-ing on so long a Voyage, to go far, on the first day, in case any articles should have been forgotten."[19] In addition, the brigaders were impatient to receive their "regale," the gift of grog that was issued at the end of the first day and far enough from the depot to avoid disrupting its routine. Under the NWC, according to Corney, the brigaders were regaled upon arrival, not departure. He wrote: "the boatmen encamp out-side the fort [George]; they are each served out with a half pint of rum, and their year's clothing, and orders are issued, that those men who do not get drunk, must go to the wood and cut timber." "The liquor shop is then opened," he continued, "and kept by one of the clerks; a scene of drunkenness and all manner of vice follows."[20] The HBC changed the timing of the regale, apparently in order to minimize the risk of bac-chanalian disturbances at the depot. No longer were brigaders issued liquor while travelling or sojourning, and they were not allowed to buy liquor. At the outset of their journey, however, they were each given one pint of rum, which they were not permitted to drink until they were some distance from the post – at a point, explained Kane, "where those who are entitled to get drunk may do so without interfering with the resident servants of the establishment."[21] So camp was struck early the first day, usually at one of the mills several miles above Fort Vancouver, and there the brigaders enjoyed their "customary debauch." The drink-ing began with various amusements – e.g., running, jumping, wrestling, dancing, singing – and progressed, as the drinking increased, to boast-ing and eventually fighting, which ended amicably. Hangovers the next day delayed their departure until the afternoon, but the men were ami-able and obedient.[22]

The change in the landscape was the reverse, of course, of that of the downriver voyage but just as dramatic. Above the Big Dalles, trees yielded to grass, hills to plains, and wetness to dryness, as well as canoe Indians to horse Indians. And rattlesnakes appeared.

The upriver voyage occurred after high water, which would have entailed fewer and shorter portages but a stronger current. Lower water was less arduous, although if the river's level was very low, the brigaders sometimes had to resort to poling. Of even greater assistance was the chinook wind, which blew upstream as far as the Snake forks. It not only moderated the summer heat but also enabled the use of sails. Whenever possible, the incoming boats went *à la voile* – under sail. They used a square sail, "as the wind blows generally either directly up or down the river," explained Lieutenant Wilkes.[23] The very first Nor'Wester on the Columbia, David Thompson, remarked the "very strong head wind" on his way down the lower Columbia in the second week of July 1811. Below the Snake it strengthened to a "strong head Gale" and then to a "very Storm of Wind," and his men "could not advance without great fatigue." On Thompson's return upriver at the beginning of August it was "always blowing a Gale," and a sail was used so much that it interfered with his observations.[24] In the forty miles between the Cascades and the Big Dalles, noted Wilkes, "it usually blows a gale from the westward in the summer season, almost daily."[25] He reported that the upriver brigade of 1841 made only sixteen miles on 4 July by tracking (cordelling) from the Chutes to the John Day River but fifty-seven miles on the 5th with the wind from the John Day River to Gros Isle.[26]

Despite the low water and the tail wind, "the most arduous part of the [brigade] route was the voyage up the Columbia," according to the son of John McLeod, onetime bourgeois of Thompson's River.[27] The cause was, of course, the contrary current of the Columbia, powerful even at low water and especially in the defile of the millrace. As Lieutenant Warre wrote, "the River is contracted for some Miles below Walla Walla, by high Basaltic Scarps forming very peculiar & fantastic shapes through which the Current rushes at all seasons with considerable Violence causing much delay in ascending."[28] From Fort Vancouver to the Cascades the river was navigated, as Wilkes put it, "by seeking out the eddies." "The great diffi-culty," he added, "is found in doubling the points [rounding the river bends], which are at times impassable, except by tracking and poling."[29] Wherever the river was too rapid for rowing, the boats had to be tracked, especially between the Chutes and the Snake forks – and here the track-ers risked being bitten by rattlers.[30] The natives lent welcome assistance. In 1841 from fifty to one hundred Indians were "constantly following the brigade, and aiding the men" from the Cascades to the John Day River – at the cost of two leaves of tobacco for half an hour's help.[31] The Indians also sold pieces of firewood to the brigaders for tobacco.[32]

Lower water usually – but not always – meant longer portages. Rapids were weaker at low water, tempting brigaders to run them, thereby saving time but risking lives and goods. An example was the Cascades, as noted by Wilkes en route upriver with Ogden's inbound brigade of 1841:

> This is the head of ship navigation, where the river takes a turn northward, and for upwards of two miles is comparatively narrow – four hundred and fifty yards wide. It falls in this distance about forty feet, and the whole body of water drives through this narrow channel with impetuosity, forming high waves and fearful whirlpools, too dangerous to be encountered by any boat. When the river is low, these rapids are sometimes passed by skilful boatmen, but there have been many lives lost in the attempt.[33]

Normally the Cascades were so tumultuous that they had to be portaged regardless of the water level. Wilkes described this operation:

> There are two portages here, under the names of the new and the old. At the first, only half of the load is landed, and the boats are tracked up for half a mile further, when the load is again shipped. The boats are then tracked to the old portage. A strong eddy occurs at this place, which runs in an opposite direction; and here it is necessary to land the whole of the cargo; after which, the empty boats are again tracked three quarters of a mile beyond.[34]

Some accidents were inevitable, particularly when the brigaders tried to navigate rather than portage the Cascades, Big Dalles, and Chutes. In 1829 an incoming boat filled in the Big Dalles and lost seventeen pieces.[35] Two years later one boat, two men, and twenty pieces of the upriver brigade "went to the bottom" at Portage Neuf, and the brigade had to return to Fort Vancouver to restock.[36] And in 1843 an incoming boat with one man and most of its property was lost in the Big Dalles, and another man drowned while poling in rapids.[37] At first, too, the brigaders had to be wary of Indian attacks. The Nor'Westers commonly wore clamons – Willamette Valley elkhides, sometimes folded double – as far as the Snake forks as armour against native arrows and even musket balls. If the brigade were short of hands, the danger of accident or attack was increased, as in 1825 ("weaker manned than usual and as heavily loaded as formerly")[38] and in 1828 when the brigade was short seven men by the time it reached Fort Okanagan (three had drowned, three had fallen ill, and one had been left at Fort Vancouver, and between Forts Nez Percés and Okanagan at least two men had constantly been incapacitated by disease).[39] Occasionally the brigade was undermanned by virtue of desertion, as in 1846, when six brigaders deserted after leaving Fort Vancouver, forcing the brigade leader to leave one boat and its cargo at Walla Walla for subsequent forwarding overland to Fort Colvile or Okanagan.[40]

All of these circumstances are reflected in the extant accounts of the upriver brigades. The 1822 brigade, which served both the New Caledonia and Columbia Districts, left Fort George on 8 July in ten boats; another four boats were added at Fort Nez Percés.[41]

The 1824 brigade, which did not serve New Caledonia, did not have to be as early or as large. It left Fort George on 2 August in only six boats with nine men each, and four more men joined it the next day. John Work described the regale at the end of the first day:

> a few miles from the Fort where we encamped for the men to take what is called the regale, which is a pint of rum & some bread and pork p^r man. In a short time the greater part of the men were drunk and began to quarrel when several battles ensued, & the after part of the day was spent drinking and fighting however none of them was much injured as they dont make good use of their fists.

Below the Cascades "the wind was weak so that but little was done with the sail." On 5 August "in consequence of my boat being broke on a stone we had to stop earlier than usual to get it repaired." The accident arose from one boat trying to pass another; fortunately, none of the cargo was damaged. At the Cascades "a good deal of time was occupied crossing the portage but there being a good breeze of favourable wind we made good way with the sails in the afterpart of the day." Now higher temperatures and pesky natives were encountered. On 7 August on the portage around the Big Dalles "the day was very warm and carrying the property very fatiguing to the people." Here the skilful pilfering of the Indians impressed Work: "There were a great many Indians about the portage but they were not very troublesome yet a strict watch was kept to prevent them from stealing any thing Notwithstanding which they contrived to steal the iron clasp that we used to keep the mast fast to the shaft from one of the boats, twisting it off must have been a laborious job & taken some time." The tail wind persisted but was offset by the contrary current. On the 9th, just above the Chutes, "altho the wind was pretty favourable yet some strong rapids kept us considerably back." However, on the 10th there was a "fresh gale all day," so that the brigade made "great way," even though the wind was "sometimes rather too strong." The rough water and high wind were hard on the boats. On the day before reaching Fort Nez Percés, "we also encamped early in the afternoon to get the boats gummed."[42]

The 1825 brigade was the last to leave from Fort George and the last to serve the Columbia District only. It left the new depot of Fort Vancouver on 20 or 21 June under John McLeod, bourgeois of Thompson's River, in five boats with thirty-two men and 262 pieces; a sixth boat with twelve or thirteen men assisted the brigade as far as the Chutes. Six of the brigaders were from Fort Vancouver and would return in the fall. Although it was the last day of spring, the river was still in freshet. "The water is very high and the current strong," wrote Work. An early stop (4:00 p.m.) was made the first day in order to gum some leaky boats. At the Cascades the brigaders took seven hours to cross a new portage. On the 24th "on approaching the [Big] Dalls the current was very strong and the boats being deep laden it was difficult getting them up." "My boat," Work added, "was caught in a whirlpool and very near sunk she was whirled around three times before the men got her out." They found 400-500 Indians on the Big Dalles Portage, which likewise took them seven hours to cross. The Chutes Portage, where they found 150-200 Indians, was short "on account of the high water." Between the Chutes and Gros Isle the brigaders "were detained two hours gumming the boats." On the 29th they reached Fort Nez Percés, where all 262 pieces were left.[43]

Before 1826 the brigade comprised fewer boats, fewer hands, and fewer pieces than it would when it had to supply the distant New Caledonia District as well as the nearby Columbia District. As Chief Factor Alexander Kennedy reported from Fort George in 1825, six or seven boats were needed annually to carry the outfits to the interior and bring the returns to the depot. Each boat was loaded with from forty to fifty pieces and was manned by eight men; it took two crews to portage one boat. More than half of their cargo comprised provisions for the interior posts; for example, in the summer of 1824, 10,328 pounds of flour, 1,985 pounds of tallow, 1,258 pounds of sugar, 990 pounds of pork, 772 pounds of beef, 244 pounds of butter, 92 pounds of rice, 69 pounds of tea, 12 pounds of chocolate, 53 bushels of peas, 20 bushels of beans, 20 bushels of corn and meal, and 57 gallons of molasses were boated inland. Kennedy considered these victuals "a considerable drawback on the profits."[44] Governor Simpson agreed, and thereafter fewer "European provisions" were carried to the interior posts, which now relied more on their own "country produce." As a result, fewer boats were required, although Simpson found that the 1825 upriver brigade of four boats with thirty-two men were "rather heavy" for the portages, and he therefore recommended that in 1826 their loads be reduced by eight pieces (leaving each boat to carry from thirty-two to forty pieces rather than forty to fifty pieces) and that five instead of four boats, each with six instead of eight men, be used.[45] However, this scenario had to be revised with the decision to outfit both the New Caledonia and Columbia Districts from the depot. From 1826 the brigade had to be nearly twice as large as before.

The first reunited brigade did not make an auspicious beginning. The outgoing party did not arrive at Fort Vancouver until 16 June, brigade leader William Connolly reporting that a "deficiency in our means ... occasioned us some trouble" from Alexandria to Thompson's River (meaning a shortage of horses as a result of the very severe winter in New Caledonia), and below Fort Okanagan the "unfavorable weather ... occupied more time than was expected." The London ship had preceded the brigade at the depot, "but for want of hands and the distance she was from the Fort" only a small part of its cargo had been unloaded, so that the brigaders were employed unloading it. They did not finish until 27 June, and they did not leave on the incoming brigade until 5 July, "altho' no time was lost in packing up the several Outfits and equipping the Men." The upriver brigade comprised nine boats, each manned by six men and each loaded with forty-four pieces, plus passengers of five gentlemen, three women, and nine children; each person was allotted four bags of corn, one bag of rice, one keg of corn meal, and half a keg of "grain" (possibly wheat), as provisions for the voyage. More than one-third of the cargo was destined for New Caledonia. Including private goods, the cargo consisted of 60 pieces for Fort Nez Percés, 72 for Fort Colvile, 52 for Thompson's River, 106 to 120 for New Caledonia, and 1 for York Factory, as well as 126 pieces of provisions, 4 cases of muskets, 1 trading chest, and passengers' luggage. The New Caledonia outfit, to which a few pieces would be added at Forts Nez Percés and Okanagan, revealed the articles in demand there for both living and trading. It comprised thirty-eight bales of dry goods, two baskets of copper kettles, six cases of guns, five cases of irons, three cases of sundry goods, five cases of traps, six bags of beaver shot, four bags of ball shot, nine bags of flour, five kegs of gunpowder, nine kegs of sugar, nine kegs of tallow, two kegs of brandy, three kegs of spirits, three kegs of salt, two kegs of butter, and nine rolls of twist tobacco, plus one trading chest of articles for barter for salmon en route and four rum chests of muskets and ammunition for self-defence en route.

Despite the lateness of the season, noted John Work the first day, "the water is very high & the current very strong." Connolly concurred: "the water is unusually high, and our progress consequently slow." He added that "such weak crews [six per boat] were not well calculated to proceed with much celerity against the strong current they had to contend with, occasioned by the uncommon height of the Water." The boats proceeded with half loads from the Cascade Rapids to Portage Neuf, over which everything was carried, and with half loads also to the Cascades themselves, where everything was again carried. Fortunately, as Work noted, "the portage at the cascades was not so long as when the water was low." The Cascades natives were, in Connolly's words, "like all those who inhabit the banks of this River, noted Thieves." Their "principal demand" in exchange for salmon was tobacco, half a twist fetching the largest fish. On the evening of the 9th the brigade reached the Big Dalles, where there was a "swarm of Indians," from whom some driftwood was bought. Connolly wrote: "And the natives here [were] too numerous to admit of our force being divided, the whole being required to guard the Encampment which was formed by the Boats into an oblong square in the Centre of which the different Cargoes were placed, the tents pitched, and a regular watch appointed for the night." By 12 July two days of "excessive heat" had "tended much to spoil our fresh Fish," although roots were available locally in "considerable variety & abundance." An upriver breeze moderated the heat and assisted the boats. On the 12th the brigade "had a nice sail wind all day" between the John Day River and Gros Isle, and on the 13th "a fair aft Breeze throughout the day assisted our progress very considerably." Fort Nez Percés was not reached until the 15th. Here, Connolly observed, "the Heat is really oppressive, and were it not for the westerly breezes which generally prevail, would be intolerable."[46]

The 1827 brigade left Fort Vancouver on 14 June after a stopover of only nine days, "the scarcity of provisions which prevailed there not admitting of our making a long stay," according to brigade leader William Connolly. The brigade had arrived on 5 June "with our Furs in excellent condition." However, the London ship, the *William and Ann*, which had entered the Columbia on 10 May, did not make the depot until 8 June, three days after the brigade. It brought "sufficient" trade goods for the natives but "not near sufficient" supplies for the servants. Connolly complained that "the scarcity of Goods generally at Fort Vancouver would not admit of the Men being supplied as well as they required, and is a cause of discontent which is out of my power to remove." The interior outfits were particularly deficient in capots, which were "entirely wanting," and in ironware, whose quality was "very inferior." So both necessities and luxuries were insufficient for the servants, "and they could not therefore be allowed such indulgences as they expect at a Depot, and which generally make them forget the hardships & Privations of the preceding year." Connolly especially lamented the shortage of capots: "Capots which are an essential article of our Trade and of which at least

One hundred would have been required were totally wanting, and unfortunately materials for making them were equally scarce, this important deficiency will I fear sensibly effect [affect] the Returns of the current year, and will be productive of still more injurious results should a similar omission occur the ensuing Outfit."[47] Initially, the brigade comprised seven boats, "but it not being considered safe to embark all the property in them … without overloading them," an eighth boat was added by Chief Factor McLoughlin with six men, who "are to be sent back together with the Guide, after the most dangerous parts of the River are passed." The outfits totalled 313 pieces: 140 for New Caledonia, 85 for Fort Colvile, 57 for Fort Nez Percés, and 31 for Thompson's River, plus 21 pieces of provisions for the brigaders from Fort Okanagan to Stuart's Lake, since "from our early departure [from Fort Vancouver], we will undoubtedly reach Frasers River before the First salmon [of the August run] is arrived." Each of the boats was supplied with four bags of peas and corn, the latter of a "very bad quality." Walla Walla was not reached until the 23rd, nine days after leaving the depot. The early departure meant high water for the brigade. "The waters were exceedingly high," wrote Connolly, "which occasioned some retardment, but the greatest loss of time occurred from the frequent repairs two of the old Boats required." These craft were "so entirely worn out" that they could not carry their full share of the "ladings."[48]

The 1828 brigade was much later leaving Fort Vancouver. It was not late arriving (7 June), but most of the brigaders were assigned to the large posse that was dispatched to Hood Canal in the middle of the month and did not return until the middle of July. During the posse's absence, the interior outfits were packed, so that when the brigaders returned they had only to be equipped, "which was a tedious and unpleasant business," reported Connolly, "the quantity of Goods which could be spared for that purpose being not only very small, but also badly assorted." Again, too, he lamented the insufficiency of his own outfit:

> The New Caledonia Outfit for the Trade is also very defective. Several articles, particularly shirts, are entirely wanting, nor could any substitute for them be procured. That article is of much importance as it frequently is not only the means of saving others of greater consequence, but also by its cheapness often induces idle fellows to hunt a few furs to pay for it, who would never muster resolution enough to endeavour to provide the means of purchasing one of higher value. Of Files we are equally as destitute as of shirts, and unfortunately they are a more indispensable article, as without them the Ice chisel and the axe, the only implements used by the Indians to hunt Furs in the

winter season, can be of little use. Of Tobacco we are one third short of what is required, but this deficiency I understand is to be made up from York Factory. Several other items, which altho' of minor importance, are nevertheless essential to the successful prosecution of the Trade, are either totally wanting, or in such trifling quantities as to be but of little use.[49]

It took most of the 22nd to haul the cargo on two wagons from the fort to the riverside. Late the same day the brigade left in nine boats with forty-six pieces and fifty-four hands, plus from six to ten passengers, including two Indian slaves and one servant with a large family and baggage that was a "great incumbrance upon the Boats" but whom Chief Factor McLoughlin was anxious to remove from the country. Brigade leader Connolly was dissatisfied with the size of the boat crews, which consisted of six men each with no extra hands except the two Indian slaves:

> Such is the scarcity of disposable men in the Columbia, that no possibility existed of replacing the three New Caledonia men who were lost on the passage down, nor was one sick man I was obliged to leave at Fort Vancouver. Thus I find myself with four hands less than I had on the voyage out, and as the number then was barely sufficient to conduct the Horses, and for the navigation in Frasers River, I may [as well] in consequence make up my mind before hand to meet the difficulties I have reason to expect upon my return.

Of the nine boats, two were manned by Fort Vancouver men who were to return from Fort Nez Percés or, more likely, Fort Okanagan because the former's outfit did not exceed one boat load and the boats were "all too heavy loaded." Corn, peas, and grease were the brigaders' provisions.[50]

The brigade left so late in the day that camp was pitched only two miles upstream from the depot at one of the "prairies" (grassy river terraces), where the men were given their regale. On the second day, reported Connolly, "the men still feeling the effects of their regale, were more inclined to sleep than to work, our progress would therefore have been very slow, had we not been assisted by a good Breeze." But the boating was harder and the portages were longer, owing to the low level of the river. The same day, the 24th, the brigade made the Cascades, where, John Work wrote, "the water is very low and it was very difficult dragging the boats." "The line broke," he added, "and one of them ran down the rapid again and a considerable time was lost recoving [recovering] it." The Indians at the Cascades were catching "plenty of salmon" but would not dispose of any to the brigaders, he explained, "from a superstitious idea that if our people who had been [in the posse] at war would eat of the salmon they would catch no more." The next day at the Big Dalles, some of the cargo could have been carried across the portage before nightfall but not, Connolly recorded, "without separating the Brigade for the night, and thereby exposing the property to the danger of being robbed by bands of rogues who inhabit the neighbourhood." So, he added, none was portaged until the 25th, when the whole day was spent crossing the portage, it "in consequence of the low state of the waters, being double the length that it is when they are of a moderate height." At the Chutes on the 27th Work found that "it was very warm during the day though it blew a storm & the people were nearly blinded with driving sand." Here, too, wrote Connolly, "low water being even more unfavourable to this portage than it was to the last [at the Big Dalles], we had to carry a distance of at least thrice the length of the usual portage." The next day the indisposition of several of the brigaders was partly offset by a "good sail wind." Nevertheless, recorded Work, on the 30th, one day before reaching Fort Nez Percés, "some of them have their hands lamed with the poling."[51]

Again in 1829 the inbound brigade left Fort Vancouver late. Its departure was delayed by the relocation of the fort and by the embarkation of two company ships, and it was not until the end of June that the packing of the interior outfits and the equipping of the brigaders began. The brigade comprised nine boats with fifty-four hands (six each, as usual), including twenty-three for New Caledonia, plus seven passengers, excluding John Harriott and his "deranged" wife, who remained at the depot. One of the boats was to be returned from Walla Walla. The brigade left in the late afternoon of 11 July and made camp at the depot's saw mill. The next day sails were raised on the boats to take advantage of a "strong breeze from the westward." In the Big Dalles, reported Chief Factor Connolly, seventeen pieces of property were lost when a boat being hauled by a line against a very strong current was punctured by a projecting rock and a "large proportion" of its cargo was washed into the river. The salvaged pieces were dried on a "rocky island" in the river that was "less exposed to the intentions of the Indians." The favourable wind continued; indeed, on the 19th it was "so exceedingly high" that the brigade could not embark until it diminished in the evening. Fort Nez Percés was reached on the 21st.[52]

From 1830 the upriver brigade was almost always on schedule. By then company shipping and farming had much improved at Fort Vancouver, whose activities were now well regulated, and the united brigade system of the Fraser and Columbia was well tested and proven. Malaria did commence that year, but it does not seem to have deterred the brigade; indeed, it likely eased its operation by eventually depopulating the natives of the lower Columbia. Nevertheless, delays and accidents still occurred occasionally. The 1831 brigade is a case in point, arriving at Fort Vancouver about a week later than usual and suffering a fatal accident during its return. The arrangements for its departure upriver lasted from 11 to 26 June. It left on the 27th in nine boats with forty-six to forty-eight pieces (five to six each) and sixty-three men (seven each). Brigade leader Dease opined – presciently – that "the Boutes are not all so good as could be wished & would be required for such a navigation as this is." The first day the brigade went only as far as the end of the fort's plain to camp and regale. The next day, three hours were lost awaiting a boat that lagged "from the Intoxication of most of the Crew." On the 29th at Portage Neuf a "great throng" of natives obliged the brigade to watch the property "very narrowly" at either end of the portage. On the same day two men, both boutes, were drowned in the Cascades when trackers lost hold of the line to their boat, which then "was drawn into the Rapid & went down, upsett below the Portage." The boat and fourteen pieces were recovered. As a result, two boats were sent back to Fort Vancouver to inform Chief Factor McLoughlin and to replenish the outfit, and the brigade did not leave the Cascades until 4 July, when another man died in a boat accident. On the 5th the west wind was so strong that the boats had to stop for three hours. On the 8th another three hours were lost repairing a boat that had been "broken considerably" in a collision under sail with another. Walla Walla was reached on the 11th, three days later than the 1830 upriver brigade.[53]

Another case in point was the 1841 brigade, which was accompanied by Lieutenant Wilkes as far as Fort Okanagan. It left Fort Vancouver – probably on 27 June – in nine boats with sixty hands, as well as brigade leader Ogden, three passengers, and eight native wives. Eight of the boats carried sixty pieces each and Ogden's boat forty (in order to leave room for his and Wilkes' baggage). On 30 June, between the Cascades and the Big Dalles, the brigade caught a favourable wind, "but it blew so hard that they were obliged to reef their sail, and afterwards found the waves and wind too heavy for them to run without great danger; they in consequence put on shore to wait until it abated." On 2 July they portaged the Big Dalles. The Chutes were portaged on the 3rd, and the entire distance from there to the John Day River was tracked because the river was "filled with rocks." The Grand Rapids were tracked on 6 July, and Walla Walla was hailed at sunset.[54]

Until the cessation of the Fraser-Columbia brigade system in 1847, the number of incoming boats and hands remained constant, e.g., nine boats with sixty hands in 1835,[55] nine boats with fifty-seven hands (plus Peter Ogden, the brigade leader, and Samuel Black, bourgeois of Thompson's River) in 1839,[56] and nine boats with sixty hands (plus Ogden) in 1841.[57] The last upriver brigade of 1847 was no exception. On 1 July it left Fort Vancouver, now located on American territory following the signing of the Treaty of Washington on 15 June 1846, under brigade leader John Lewes in nine boats with sixty to seventy hands and 450 pieces of cargo (and a seven-gun salute from the fort and a company ship). The brigaders were, as usual, loath to leave. According to Paul Kane, "all hesitated to give up the life of idleness and plenty in which they had been luxuriating for the last two or three weeks for the toils and privations which they well knew were before them." The first day's camp was made eight miles upriver at the depot's saw mill, and the second day's twenty-eight miles upriver at Prairie du Thé, where the brigaders had their "regale of rum" and kept Kane awake all night. At the Cascades the boats were dragged and the pieces carried over the portage. At the Big Dalles Portage, Indians were hired to carry the boats at the rate of five musket balls per boat, each of which was borne by thirty Indians. Kane noted in his peculiar brand of phonetic English that "grate quantites of salmon are cot here." He also observed that "at this plase the cuntry commences to be barran and devested of wood." At the Chutes, too, the brigade found "amence quantaties of Indians." It also found its best ally for the hard upriver haul. Kane wrote: "left the Shoots with a strong fare wind [on 9 July] they boats ran up the rappeds under sale oure boat had the water curling over her bows and would have filled her if we had not taken in sale." On the 10th, he added, "we cilled a grate menny rattle Snakes," and on the 11th they reached Fort Nez Percés – to Kane "a small mud fort in the most barran cuntry I evar saw."[58]

Walla Walla, despite Kane's aversion, offered the brigaders a much desired and much deserved respite – if only for several days – after the toilsome and hazardous upriver voyage. At least it was much less so from here to Fort Okanagan, where the boats yielded to horses. Those horses, however, came from the vicinity of Walla Walla, whose bourgeois helped the brigade leader upon his arrival to buy enough from the local Indians and to drive them overland to the Columbia-Okanogan forks. Owing to Walla Walla's small complement, this operation had to be manned mostly by the brigaders themselves, so their respite was minimal.

CHAPTER 11

Boating up
the Columbia

The Easy Leg from
Walla Walla to Okanagan

*The Nez Perces Camp at Lewis's River I understand
is a regular Horse fair.*

— GOVERNOR GEORGE SIMPSON, 1825[1]

THE NEZ PERCÉ HORSE FAIR

Upon arrival at Fort Nez Percés the upriver brigade halted while some of the hands accompanied the brigade leader to the Nez Percé camps along the lower Snake River in order to buy Indian ponies. Arrangements for the purchase of these animals were usually made beforehand by the brigade leader during his voyage down the Columbia in the spring. The bourgeois of Walla Walla facilitated the horse trading, but he could not spare any of his few men for the venture. The brigade leader, or his subaltern, and a couple of the hands drove the band of horses overland along the Palouse River and through the Palouse Hills, mostly to Fort Okanagan for the horse brigade and partly to Fort Colvile for the trapping expeditions to the Flathead Country (some were also retained at Fort Nez Percés for the Snake Country ventures). The rest of the hands returned to Walla Walla and rejoined the brigade of boats (usually leaving one at the post with its outfit) and continued up the Columbia to Fort Okanagan, where they had been preceded several days by the hands with the new horses.

The horses were bought from the Nez Percé Indians, both at a "Horse Fair" at Fort Nez Percés itself and, more commonly, at their own camps, which the brigade leader had to visit in order to negotiate a price and then collect the animals. Unlike the Walla Walla Indians of the Columbia-Snake forks, who were mostly fishers, the Nez Percés to the east and the Cayuses to the south were, in the words of bourgeois Samuel Black of Walla Walla, "Hunters & rich in Horses."[2] The pedigree of their horses was Spanish, and since the middle of the eighteenth century the

Indians had been trading and stealing them, as well as capturing them from bands of mustangs.[3] In both the autumn of 1805 and the spring of 1806, Sergeant John Ordway of the Lewis and Clark expedition noted that the natives in the vicinity of the Columbia-Snake forks had "a great number of horses"; on its return journey the expedition bought more than a dozen horses from these Indians, and Ordway judged that "most of them are good to ride or pack."[4] Lieutenant Warre reported in 1845 that the Nez Percés "are possessed of immense droves of horses and it is not an uncommon circumstance for one Indian to own 500, and even it is said, some have as many as 1000 horses."[5] Theirs was "the best Horse Market in the Columbia," asserted Governor Simpson.[6]

This source was certainly sufficient to meet the needs of the HBC, including the brigade. In the spring of 1825 Governor Simpson told Chief Factor McLoughlin that at least 150 horses would be needed that spring and summer for New Caledonia (70) and the Snake and Umpqua trapping expeditions (80);[7] McLoughlin subsequently increased the brigade's requirement to 100 (including 20 for Thompson's River).[8] Many of these died during the severe New Caledonia winter of 1825-26 and had to be replaced. In anticipation of such a contingency, McLoughlin had in the summer of 1825 advised bourgeois John Dease of Walla Walla that "as many Horses especially mares ought to [be] purchased as you can conveniently," and in the spring of 1826 – following New Caledonia's high winter toll – he ordered Black, Dease's successor, "to Buy as many Horses as you can."[9] McLoughlin knew that horses would cost trade goods that would otherwise fetch furs, but the horses were essential. "I am aware that purchasing Horses must Effect very materially your Trade," he told Black, "But we cannot carry our Business on without them."[10] Enough animals were obtained for the brigade.

In August 1826 James Douglas bought sixty horses at the Nez Percé horse fair and drove them to Fort Okanagan, where they joined seventy-five already there (fifteen of the sixty were assigned to Thompson's River, but a quarter of these were "unfit to proceed on the journey").[11] Additional horses were required for Ogden's trapping expedition to the Snake Country (whose furs were in 1826 rated the "finest" in the Columbia Department, comparable to those of Rupert's Land); that same summer McLoughlin ordered bourgeois Dease of Spokane House to send "all the Horses you can dispense with to Walla Walla so as to supply Mr Ogdens party Amply with these usefull Animals … as without Horses Hunters in that Country can do nothing."[12] According to Governor Simpson in 1828, the annual supply of Nez Percé horses to the company totalled some 250.[13]

At Fort Nez Percés, horses were traded regularly from the Indians – 106 altogether in 1831, for instance. In the words of bourgeois Simon McGillivray, "as the Indians are poor in furs, they trade Horses, and a good moderate Horse, will always cost a Large Blkt. with other Items to the amount of 20 to 22 [beaver] Skins." Summer was the horse trading season. In the spring of 1831 McGillivray received a request for twenty-five horses for New Caledonia and twenty-five for Thompson's River; he replied that "the number of Horses required, is what I cannot well spare, as the Horse Trade will not commence before July ensuing and some must be Kept for the Snake Trappers." Nevertheless, he managed to select forty from his stock (twenty-five for New Caledonia and fifteen for Thompson's River). There was a "Horse Guard" as well as a "Horse Fair" at the fort; on 16 March 1831 the guardsman monitored 116 horses at the guard. Horse rustling was a persistent problem. McGillivray complained on 20 August that the post's complement was only three men but that ten were needed, including four who would do nothing but pursue horse thieves.[14]

Thus, when the upriver brigade arrived at Fort Nez Percés – usually in the middle of July – it was in time for the opening of the horse trading season. The first reunited brigade reached Fort Nez Percés on 15 July 1826. Brigade leader William Connolly found that bourgeois Black had succeeded in trading sixty to seventy horses, which, Connolly asserted, would "fully answer our [New Caledonia's] purpose." Chief Factor McLoughlin, however, had made "a large demand of those Animals" for several purposes. Not enough could be obtained in the immediate vicinity of the post, so a party of twenty-eight to thirty-two men under John Work was dispatched on 18 July to the "horse fair" of the Nez Percé camps to buy, if possible, eighty more horses, twenty of which would be taken by three men under Work to Fort Colvile for the Flathead Country ventures and the rest by four men under James Douglas to Fort Okanagan for the horse brigade. They managed to trade seventy-seven horses, which with three acquired at Fort Nez Percés totalled eighty, "the exact number we require." This number, however, was not acquired without some difficulty, which was described by bourgeois Black:

The trading party to Nez Perce River traded about Eighty Horses twenty of which are gone to Kettle Falls [Fort Colvile] and Sixty to New Caledonia that Scamp Charley [a Nez Percé chief] (who from an ungovernable spirit never properly checked or [a desire] to Exact property) is always after some one or another fell on [Jean] Toupin [a company interpreter] and [was] near Raising a dust [disturbance] for refusing him something But by the prudence of the

Gentlemen and some Tobacco Charley was pleased to be a Good Boy Its suspected that a party up Snake River to Whom Tobacco had been sent to bring their Horses to Salmon River Forks to trade had after trading their Horses and thinking themselves they had not got much for them regretted the Bargain plotted carrying them off and it was principally these fellows Charley got to join him the others behaved well although a number of the Nez Perces have Strong Bands of Horses and Tobacco had been sent Early and far for them to bring up their Horses to trade at the time appointed yet at the End the trade was at a stand nor could they have got many more with Goods moreover they were displeased at the price and we can only Expect much fewer Horses and at a higher price next trip But I surely hope and trust you [McLoughlin] will not want a number next year for with this Horse Business and all its consequences amongst the natives I shall Loose Ground at Nez Perces in place of Keeping Order amongst such Scamps – Real free Booters in their Hearts.

The Work party proceeded to Fort Colvile with twenty animals and the Douglas party to Fort Okanagan with sixty. Douglas reached Fort Okanagan on 5 August (five days before the last of the boats from Fort Nez Percés) with his band of horses "all safe, tho' many of them are too lean to proceed any further until they recover their Flesh." They were rested and "baited" (fed) for a week before they departed with the brigade for Thompson's River. The band that Connolly had left there in the spring en route to the depot "are all recovered of their sores, and in good order, excepting some of those that were lately gelded, an operation it was necessary they should undergo to avoid the immensity of trouble they gave us in the spring, being again repeated." Gregoire, the horse keeper, had repaired all of the "horse appointments." When the horse brigade left Fort Okanagan on 13 August, it numbered up to 120 animals (75 left there in the spring and 45 of 60 traded from the Nez Percés, the other 15 staying at Fort Okanagan) – enough to offset the heavy toll of the previous winter in New Caledonia. Connolly subsequently reported that a "sufficient band of horses" had been traded at the "Nez Percez Forks" to meet his estimate of 120 that were needed for the brigade.[15]

The 1827 upriver brigade, again under Connolly, reached Fort Nez Percés at the end of the third week of June, three weeks earlier than in 1826 and prior to the horse trading season. So it was just as well that Connolly needed very few horses, New Caledonia's band having been restocked the previous summer. On his way downriver at the beginning of June, Connolly had asked Walla Walla's Black to get fifteen horses for the return brigade. That early in the season Black was able to trade only twelve animals, which were in "very poor condition"; two men took them overland to Fort Okanagan. Fortunately, however, by the time Connolly returned there with the boat brigade on 3 July, they had been recovering for a week, and all of the horses – those that had been left there and those that had been driven there – were "Healthy and in good Condition" (although one had died), and the horse gear had been "all thoroughly repaired."[16]

In 1828, the upriver brigade reached Fort Nez Percés at the end of July. Three men left the brigade there and drove thirty horses to Fort Okanagan, including twenty destined for the horse brigade. All of them arrived "safe" on 7 or 8 August, two or three days before the boat brigade, but "few" were fit to pack (presumably because they were unbroken or exhausted).[17]

In the summer of 1836 some 70 horses were required from Walla Walla, and bourgeois Pambrun was instructed to "purchase as many horses as you can at a moderate price."[18] One year later, however, when there were 60-70 horses at the post, it was expected to provide 35 for the brigade, 40 for the Willamette Valley, and 60 for a fall trapping venture – 135 altogether, or double its stock.[19]

The Upriver Voyage to the Columbia-Okanogan Forks

While several of the incoming brigaders were driving Nez Percé horses to Fort Okanagan, the remainder (and majority) of them were boating there via the less direct and longer (in terms of both miles and days) river route. The river passage above Walla Walla was relatively uneventful after the gauntlet of the millrace below, and Fort Okanagan was normally reached in a week to ten days.

From 1826 the boat brigade usually spent a day or two at Walla Walla discharging one boat and refreshing the crews before resuming the upriver voyage in eight boats. However, the 1822 brigade, the last of the three consecutive united brigades, added four boats at Fort Nez Percés to the ten that had left Fort George, so that fourteen boats reached Fort Okanagan; moreover, thirty-five horses were driven to Fort Okanagan for the brigade but from Spokane House rather than Fort Nez Percés. The four additional boats may simply have been returning empty to Fort Okanagan (where batteaux may have been built before the founding of Fort Colvile three years later) after having gone downriver the previous year to help found Walla Walla. And the latter may have been too recent to have been able to organize horse trading with the Nez Percés.

The 1825 brigade, the last of the three consecutive disunited brigades, reached Fort Nez Percés on 29 June in five boats. Two boats and 262 pieces remained at Walla Walla; the other three boats inexplicably stayed three weeks before proceeding to Fort Okanagan, which was reached eight days later on 28 July. One of these boats remained there with the outfits for it and Thompson's River; the other two with eighteen men continued to Spokane House and Flathead Post. John Work described the arduous tracking on the upstream route from Fort Okanagan to the Columbia-Spokane forks: "the road was tolerable though the current was very strong till afternoon they got on with the poles but afterwards the boats had to be towed the greater part of the way with lines ... sometimes the united strength of two crews was required to take up one boat." The next day, 31 July, he added: "at the dalls [Grand Rapids, or 'Little Dalls'] it was very bad, the men had to pass the line over high projecting rocks where had they missed a foot they would have been killed ... at the upper end of the dalls the boats had to be lightened and the one half of their cargoes carried."[20]

The 1826 brigade left Fort Nez Percés in two groups, having arrived in nine boats on 15 July. While half of the hands were still trading horses from the Nez Percés, three of the boats with six men each and Fort Colvile's outfit were dispatched upriver under William Kittson on 19 July because Colvile's John Work had told brigade leader William Connolly that "the detention of the Fort Colvile Outfit for any considerable time would be highly injurious to the Trade of that post," meaning that the Flathead trade would suffer for a want of goods. The three boats took ten days to reach Fort Okanagan (29 July) and another two days to make Fort Colvile (31 July). The remainder of the boat brigade, comprising four boats, each manned by six hands and loaded with thirty-six pieces (excluding provisions), did not leave Fort Nez Percés until 2 August (so two boats stayed at the latter post). From Walla Walla they took sixteen bags of corn and peas for provisions beyond Fort Okanagan, plus a "couple" of bales of sundry goods and a "number" of trap springs. They reached Fort Okanagan on 10 August, five days after the band of Indian horses. Three days later the horse brigade departed for New Caledonia.[21]

The 1827 brigade made Fort Nez Percés on 23 June and left the very next day in one fewer boats (seven) under Chief Factor Connolly. The river, he wrote, was "very high, which added much to the difficulties usually attending the Navigation." Three of the boats reached Fort Okanagan on 3 July and the other four on 4 July, when two of them proceeded to Fort Colvile with its outfit. On 5 July the horse brigade left.[22]

The belated 1828 brigade left Fort Nez Percés in eight boats on 1 August, again only a day after arriving and again less one boat, which stayed at Walla Walla, and less three hands, who conducted the Nez

Percé horses overland. The ascent of the brigade, reported leader William Connolly, was "slow, owing principally to disease in our crews which prevailed to such a degree that for several days we had no less than nine men at the same time unable to perform any duty." From Walla Walla to a point just above the Columbia-Yakima forks "the men worked with the poles all day," wrote John Work. On 2 August between the mouth of the Yakima River and the Priest's Rapids, he added, "the current during the day was strong and the poles were employed all day," for "the water is very low." Not surprisingly, on 4 and 5 August "several more of the men are off work with sore hands or other diseases." The boats reached Fort Okanagan on two separate days (9-10 August or 10-11 August) with the cargo "safe and apparently in good condition." The boats were disembarked and the pieces redistributed; 123 pieces were forwarded on 11 August to Fort Colvile in three boats with six men each. The Nez Percé horses had arrived two or three days earlier.[23]

The 1829 brigade spent one day at Fort Nez Percés, leaving on 22 July in eight boats. The boats were more heavily laden upon their departure than they had been upon their arrival because the outfit left at Walla Walla with one boat was less than one boat load, so that the remainder had to be added to the loads of the other boats. The heat was "oppressive," according to brigade leader Connolly, but the men were in "excellent health & spirits" and did their duty with "vigour and alacrity." Fort Okanagan was reached on the 30th with the cargo "correct and in good condition." The next day two loaded boats under John Work proceeded to Fort Colvile.[24]

The 1831 brigade did not arrive at Fort Nez Percés until 11 July, having been delayed by the fatal accident in the Cascades. It, too, spent only one day at Walla Walla, delivering the post's outfit and rearranging the loads, and left with one fewer boats. The eight boats reached Fort Okanagan on 21 July. En route at the Priest's Rapids the brigade was befriended by the "Old Priest," an Indian shaman whose compatriots often returned lost cargo to the brigaders or assisted them up the rapids.[25]

At Fort Okanagan most of the boats (six or seven of the nine that usually left Fort Vancouver) were unloaded and stored until the following spring, when they would be repaired or replaced. Their cargo was then reloaded onto the pack horses, some of which had been waiting since the departure of the boats downriver and some of which had been resting since their arrival several days earlier from the Nez Percé "horse fair." There now began the long return trek by pack horses to the boat landing on the Fraser River at Alexandria.

CHAPTER 12

Packhorsing between the Columbia and the Fraser

From Okanagan to Thompson's River

A beautiful sight was that horse brigade, with no broken hacks in the train, but every animal in his full beauty of form and color, and all so tractable!

– MALCOLM MCLEOD, 1872[1]

To conduct a Horse Brigade is the most irksome duty imposed upon me.

– JOHN STUART, 1822[2]

SEEKING A BETTER MEANS OR A BETTER ROUTE

The horse brigade between Fort Okanagan and Fort Alexandria may indeed have been a "beautiful sight" to Malcolm McLeod, son of the onetime bourgeois (1822-26) of Thompson's River, but he exaggerated the condition and disposition of the pack horses. Half-wild cayuses derived from Spanish riding, not packing, stock, the horses were unwilling pack animals. Sometimes undernourished at the outset of the brigade, they might be emaciated at its finish. And the long, hard route frequently lamed and sometimes killed them. Stuart, who actually conducted a brigade, unlike McLeod (although his father had), was most likely much nearer the mark. McLeod himself admitted that the horse brigade, especially the leg from Fort Okanagan to Thompson's River, was second only to the boat brigade up the Columbia in arduousness, even though the Okanagan Valley route was "beautiful pasture country."[3]

The difficulties of packhorsing between Fort Okanagan and Thompson's River, notably along the rugged shore of Okanagan Lake, prompted thoughts of, and attempts at, either rerouting the horse brigade to easier terrain or switching to another means of transport altogether. The latter seems to have been the first option, the idea being to exploit the waterways linking the two posts by changing from horses to boats. This suggestion was made as early as 1823 by Chief Trader John McLeod, bourgeois of Thompson's River. On 1 February of that year he made the following entry in his post's journal: "Spoke to [boatbuilder Pierre] La Course to day about getting a Boat build for taking the property [packs of furs] passe[d] the Big Okanagan Lake as there is great work in carrying it on Horses along it, but after I examined the materials necessary for building a craft I found we were short of nails and several [other] things so that I was obliged to drop my project."[4]

The matter was raised again three years later, when the re-linking of New Caledonia to the Columbia District greatly increased the volume of traffic on the horse brigade route. In the summer of 1826 Archibald McDonald, McLeod's successor at Thompson's River, took the same La Course with him to his new post in case boats were to be built there for brigade transport in lieu of horses. La Course found, however, that the hauling of boats between Okanagan and Shuswap Lakes would be "attended with difficulty," and McDonald reported to Chief Factor McLoughlin that "I am afraid the transport of Boats from Big OK. Lake to the Shewhops Lake will be attended with unsurmountable difficulties." McDonald added that "nothing will be attempted towards Boat Building Untill I hear from you or some other again." The plan was abandoned, and at the end of the year La Course was "recalled to Fort Colvile for it is supposed that Crafts will still be required next Summer for the Columbia." Meanwhile, noted McDonald, at Thompson's River "we have all the wood necessary for two new ones brought home & sawed – they may possibly be of service in the Spring to meet the New Caledonians up [the] North [Thompson] river," rather than send them south to add to the brigade of boats on the Columbia (the eight left at Forts Colvile [two], Okanagan [four], and Nez Percés [two] in the fall).[5]

The available sources do not explain in detail why the plan was dropped. Indeed, its abandonment is somewhat puzzling, given the availability of suitable timber for boats and of expertise on the part of the servants in building and handling boats, which, moreover, were already in use in the brigade system to the south and could have been easily extended to the north. Furthermore, boats would likely have saved the company money, since horses had to be bought and broken, as well as rested and baited (including foddered during the long winter). Also, boats would have moved the property faster, especially downstream on the rivers, of course, but perhaps even upstream, too, as well as on the lakes. Finally, the water route (Okanogan River-Lake Osoyoos-Okanagan River-Vaseux Lake-Okanagan River-Skaha Lake-Okanagan River-Okanagan Lake, and then either Deep Creek-Otter Lake-Deep Creek-portage of four miles-Shuswap River-Mara Lake-Sicamous

Narrows-Shuswap Lake-South Thompson River-Little Shuswap Lake-South Thompson River, or Deep Creek-portage of seven miles via Round and Spallumcheen Lakes-Salmon River-Salmon Arm-Shuswap Lake-South Thompson River-Little Shuswap Lake-South Thompson River) between Fort Okanagan and Thompson's River was almost as direct as the horse trail, and it offered few obstacles, at least none of the magnitude of those that were regularly overcome in the Columbia millrace. The sources specify only the "unsurmountable difficulties" of transport between Shuswap and Okanagan Lakes. These probably refer to the excessive length of either portage or to the insufficient depth of the tributary streams or to both. Both "difficulties" may well have been "unsurmountable" without enough hands to carry and track the boats, and the small complements of Fort Okanagan and Thompson's River together would not have sufficed. More "extra men" from the depot would have had to have been used, and presumably their wages would have offset any savings from the substitution of boats for horses.

Having resigned itself to packhorse transport between the two posts, the company attempted to find a better route for the horse brigade. No sooner had bourgeois McDonald of Thompson's River concluded in the summer of 1826 that boats could not be substituted for horses than he sought an alternative track to Fort Okanagan, one that would avoid the steep shore of Okanagan Lake. On 17 October he left with two men to reconnoitre the "Schimilimash [Similkameen] trail," reaching Fort Okanagan on the 22nd and returning to Thompson's River on 7 November. The Similkameen Country had not been visited by whites since 1812, when the PFC had probed it. The Similkameen Trail may have followed the Shumway Lake-Trapp Lake-Stump Lake-Nicola Lake-Nicola River-Coldwater River-Otter Creek-Tulameen River-Similkameen River route, or, more likely, the Shumway Lake-Trapp Lake-Stump Lake-Nicola Lake-Quilchena Creek-Summers Creek-Similkameen River route. McDonald reported that "the greatest part of the road is good but many hills & rocks are to be met with also: and about the height of land [the water divide between the Fraser and Columbia drainage basins] a good deal of fallen wood is in the way, which however with some labour can be much improved."[6] McDonald's largely positive assessment seems to have elicited no reaction from his superiors, however. But the following summer Chief Factor Connolly wrote from the Traverse (the North Thompson River crossing) to Chief Factor McLoughlin to suggest that either James Yale (a clerk at Fort Okanagan) or Frank Ermatinger (a clerk at Thompson's River) – whichever was to go from Fort Okanagan to Fort Alexandria later that year – travel "by the southern track [presumably the Similkameen route], of which the Indians spoke to me in the spring and represented it as not only much finer, but also considerably shorter than the road we at present follow" and thereby "ascertain whether these advantages really exist."[7] Neither Yale nor Ermatinger seems to have done so, however, and the Similkameen route was not developed to replace the Okanagan route, probably because the former, although shorter, would have required costly improvement.

PACKHORSING BACK TO THOMPSON'S RIVER

The incoming horse brigade usually left Fort Okanagan in late July and took from twelve to fourteen days to reach Thompson's River,[8] encountering the same obstacles as the outgoing brigade, except that in the middle of summer temperatures were higher, water levels were lower, and grass was less succulent en route. For example, the 1822 brigade under John Stuart departed on 22 July, three days earlier than the 1821 brigade (which, incidentally, left on only fifty-six horses). It made Fort Kamloops on 8 August "all safe," wrote Stuart; "the Horses however are getting fagged and owing to bad saddles many of them have sore backs."[9]

In 1826 the horse brigade left Fort Okanagan in the middle of August in two groups, presumably because it was already three weeks late and Chief Factor Connolly was anxious to proceed with the larger group with New Caledonia's outfit and reach Stuart's Lake in time to distribute the property before the onset of winter; the smaller group could follow later with the outfit for Thompson's River. Two days (11-12 August) were spent at Fort Okanagan, reported Connolly, "completing the arrangements for our departure from hence, i.e., in tying up the various packages, dividing the Men & Horses into Brigades, etc. etc." The brigade left on the 13th, "conveying a complete Outfit for the district, and a competent supply of provisions for the journey." It comprised twenty-four men and 80 to 108 horses, excluding 15 animals that were left at Fort Okanagan but including 9 "light Horses, which tho' very poor, will occasionally serve to relieve such as may fail along the way." The men were also "all mounted." Six bales of dry goods (mostly damaged and unsaleable), four kegs of tallow, one case of ironware, and one bag of shot from Fort Okanagan were added to the outfit for New Caledonia.

On the first day the brigade suffered some "inconvenience" from the unbroken horses, "many of the Horses having never before carried loads." Connolly explained: "By kicking and prancing, they contrived to throw off their burthens, to which the bad quality of the Cords tended not a little, being too weak to resist the violent motions of these wild Brutes.

In the course of an hour the Plain of Okanagan was covered with Pieces, and three Bags of corn which some time in the confusion were entirely lost." The weather was "fine," and "was not the air refreshed by frequent gales, the heat would be insupportable." Care had to be taken of the loaded horses in the withering heat. "The benefit we derived from allowing the Horses to rest daily on our way out, was so eminent," noted Connolly, "that the same practice will be observed on our return. Washing their backs with cold water is also of much service to the poor Animals." He felt that "too much care cannot … be taken of the Horses," and he added: "I mean to go on quietly until the Horses are inured to fatigue, and sufficiently advanced on their journey to insure their being able to accomplish it without failing, for experience sufficiently teaches that when a Horse is once jaded, he cannot recover during the continuance of a voyage." The brigade usually started at 4:00 a.m. Twenty-one miles were covered on the 14th of August, twenty-two on the 15th, eighteen on the 16th, twenty-six on the 17th, twenty-eight on the 19th, twenty-four on the 20th, twenty on the 21st, twenty-five on the 22nd, and twenty-four on the 23rd for an average of twenty-three miles per day (at least for nine of the twelve days of the trip).

The brigaders passed the Little Chutes of the Okanogan River on 16 August, and later the same day they crossed the river in canoes at the Barrière, meaning "gate" or "barrier," where it exited Lake Osoyoos. The horses swam across, and one drowned; Connolly was relieved that "he happens luckily to have been one of the worst we had." The campsite at the Barrière had "abundant" feed for the horses, but "the flies are numerous & annoy them much." By now the animals were more tractable, Connolly noting that "the Horses being now rather fatigued go on quietly and in regular order."

On the 17th the brigade crossed the Rivière au Thé, fifteen miles north of the Barrière; eleven miles farther north it passed Bute du Sable. The animals continued to suffer. On the 18th, when the brigade camped at the Rivière au Serpent, Connolly wrote: "The Horses are much fatigued, & many of them have swellings on their sides occasioned by the Kegs and other hard pieces they carry." The vicinity was "completely parched up, & in many places has been lately overrun by fire," so that it afforded "scanty subsistence" for the horses, which were also being "tormented night and day" by "miryads of insects."

On the 19th the brigade crossed first the Rivière du Poulin and then the Rivière de la Fruite and rested the horses for four hours at the Prairie de Nicholas one and a half hours south of Okanagan Lake. On the 20th the brigade passed the Rivière à Jacques et du Borgne, rested the horses at L'Anse de Sable, and camped at The Bute, fifteen miles north of the southern end of Okanagan Lake.

On the 21st, in passing the Mauvais Rocher, "one of the Horses slipped & fell over the precipice, when he was literally dashed to Pieces." Connolly noted that "several" such accidents had already occurred at this "dangerous spot." Camp was made at the Rivière a la Biche, where, happily, there was "excellent feeding" for the horses.

On the 22nd the brigade passed the Rivière au Paquets, Rivière de Aguires, Rivière de Borgnes, and Rivière de Talle d'Épinette. The route was "particularly rugged, & fatiguing to the Horses." The brigade left Okanagan Lake on the 23rd, passed Lac en Ronde, and camped at Grand Prairie.

On the 24th the convoy passed Campement du Poulin and reached the South Thompson River, where it camped. Here on the following day the "Baggage [and] 7 people" were ferried across the river in borrowed Indian canoes, and the horses swam across. So Fort Kamloops was reached in the evening via the right, not the left, bank of the South Thompson. Here Connolly found that the property left in the spring had been stolen. He also found it "expedient" to give a present to a local chief, a "notorious rogue," in order to dissuade his followers from horse rustling.[10]

The smaller part of the 1826 brigade under bourgeois Archibald McDonald arrived at Thompson's River two weeks later on 9 September with an outfit worth £200, mostly guns, ammunition, tobacco, blankets, strouds, hatchets, traps, and axes, plus "the usual Stores allowed the Gentlemen in charge." McDonald was accompanied by eight men, who with three others would constitute the post's complement, in addition to seven women and ten children. The brigade comprised forty horses and ten colts (yearlings), which, McDonald noted, was

> a much greater number than is required either for bringing in the Supplies or taking out the returns, but the nature of the living here is such, as to render us entirely dependent on remote parts of the country for dried Salmon: especially to the main Stream commonly called Fraser's river which occupies in one trip from 12 to 15 days, & afterwards transport [of] part of that Salmon even to the mouth of the Columbia; consequently fewer horses would be puting a great deal at hazard.[11]

Thus, the 1826 incoming brigade returned fifty horses to Thompson's River and double that number to Fort Alexandria.

The 1827 brigade left Fort Okanagan on 5 July, accompanied by Clerk Frank Ermatinger of Thompson's River with part of its outfit and three men. It comprised eighty-two loaded horses divided into ten strings of seven horses and two men each, and one string (Chief Factor Connolly's) of twelve horses and five men. During the previous night four horses had been stolen by "Rascally Indians." And during the previous day the freight had been packed thus, in brigade leader Connolly's words:

> Early in the morning the Brigade [of boats] arrived, and immediately after the Pieces constituting the different outfits were separated, and we began to tye up the Guns & Traps into Pieces suitable to Horse Carriage. The former are made up into Bundles of 12 each, and two such packages will form one Horse load, and being well wrapped up in Blankets & Leather I hope they will receive no injury. Last year they were made up into Bundles of 5 each, and added as top pieces to the loads, but in this manner they were exposed to many bad blows, by which two of them were irreparably broken & several others very much damaged. The Traps are tied up into Bundles of 5 each, and will be given as top pieces to the usual loads, for some of the Horses are able to carry much more than two pieces, whilst others with difficulty manage that number.

Again the horses were troublesome on the first day. "The Horses having been for such a length of time idle [i.e., since their arrival at Fort Okanagan two months earlier]," wrote Connolly, "some of them were on the outset rather unruly, & contrived to throw off their loads, which occasioned some little delay, & prevented us from advancing above fifteen miles from the Fort, where we encamped in a fine Plain which afforded abundance of food for the Horses."

On the way to Thompson's River, fodder for the horses was "abundant," and the "march" was not marred "either by bad weather or accident." The animals made the trip with "ease," save a few colts and those got at Walla Walla, which, although "much fagged," were nevertheless "all Healthy" and bound to "entirely recover" after a couple of days of rest. On 6 July, Ermatinger was sent ahead to Fort Kamloops to hire fresh horses from the local Indians in order "to relieve such of our own as most require it" and to have a canoe sent to the North Thompson Traverse. The brigade reached Thompson's River on the 15th and was reinforced by two company horses and nine Indian horses, the latter hired at the rate of two beaver skins each and the former bound only as far as the Traverse.[12]

The 1828 brigade, like that of 1826, was late leaving Fort Okanagan for Thompson's River. After it had reached the Columbia-Okanogan forks, the boats had been beached but left exposed because there still was no boat shed to shelter them from "the inclemency of the weather," noted brigade leader Connolly. On 12 August the horses were caught and shackled and the animals and the brigaders were divided into strings, "which in consequence of the scarcity of men, consist of a larger number of Horses than usual." Three men had drowned in the Cascades, two were so unwell (probably with venereal disease) as to be unfit for duty "for a long while to come," and one had such sore hands as to be of no service "at all for the present." The horse brigade, comprising eighty-three loaded animals and twenty-two men (including the sick), left Fort Okanagan on the 13th and reached Fort Kamloops on the 23rd.[13]

The 1829 upriver brigade made Fort Okanagan on 30 July and found the horses "all safe and in good condition," according to brigade leader Connolly. There were not enough of them, however. Seven more were obtained from Fort Colvile, and another seven were taken from Fort Okanagan, but the total was still insufficient for the transport of the outfit to New Caledonia. Consequently, two pieces had to be left at Fort Okanagan for later conveyance to Thompson's River and retrieval from New Caledonia in the fall.

The brigade comprised eleven strings of eight horses and two men each, except Connolly's (three men). This arrangement left a few spare horses, which were "of a very inferior quality and unfit to carry loads" anyway but which were taken nevertheless "for the purpose of giving the men a lift occasionally and to relieve such of the Horses as may become jaded before the end of the journey."

The brigade left on 2 August and made its first camp at the Monté on the lower Okanogan River. On the 3rd the horses were rested at Rat Lake and camp was made at the Rapids (Little Chutes?). Grass for the horses was "not only scanty, but also very dry, a consequence of the unusual drought this season," wrote Connolly. The brigade crossed the Okanogan River on the 4th not at the Barrière but at the Forks (presumably those of the Okanogan and Similkameen) without canoes, "the water being sufficiently low to admit of our tallest Horses fording it without wetting their loads." Thompson's River was reached on the 12th after ten days, a normal duration.

The 1831 boat brigade stayed on schedule. It returned to Fort Okanagan on 21 July but found that during its absence three horses had fled, two had died, and two had been so disabled by injury or disease as to be unable to pack. Four replacements (and ten pieces of provisions – corn and peas) came from Fort Colvile on the 21st and ten replacements from Fort Okanagan on the 26th. After four boats had proceeded to Fort Colvile with its outfit on the 22nd, the horse brigade left four days later in a "long line" with 110 loaded animals, ten to every two men. For want of enough horses, some pieces had to be left at Fort Okanagan.

The trip was uneventful until the northern end of Okanagan Lake. On 2 August, the last day along the lake, the trail was "bad." Two horses broke their loads and lost half a bag of flour and half a bag of corn, "not having good Wrappers for such Pieces & the Cords very bad." By the 3rd some of the horses were "very sore galled," and two of them had to be unloaded. On the same day in the "strong [thick?] woods" between Okanagan Lake and the Salmon River the brigade encountered a "fire Raging in all directions, and ... the smoak so thick as almost to darken the atmosphere."

Thompson's River was reached on the 5th. The pieces were canoed across the South Thompson and the horses were driven across, the river's level being low.[14]

The incoming brigade did not stay long at Thompson's River – only long enough (overnight) to unload its outfit and to rest and feed the horses before proceeding to Fort Alexandria. This overland leg was nearly as difficult as that from Fort Okanagan, so much so that attempts were made to replace it, too, with a water route.

CHAPTER 13

Packhorsing over the Mountain

From Thompson's River to Alexandria

*Several of our Horses being too low to carry their loads all the
way from here [crossing of the North Thompson] to Alexandria,
without sacrificing more time than we can spare – Lolo is dispatched
to Alexandria for the purpose of bringing every horse and Mare
which can be mustered, to our relief, which I request you will deliver
and send him back immediately – If he loses no time, he will meet
us about half way. It is also directed to hire a few Horses from the
Indians of the Rapid at the rate of two Plues [made beaver] Each –
We are at present occupied crossing our Baggage and Property
over this River, and to night we encamp at the foot of the Mountain ...
Until yesterday no accident occurred, but at that time by the
falling of one of the Horses over a rock into the River, his load
consisting of [the] best part of Two Bales, were lost.*

– BRIGADE LEADER WILLIAM CONNOLLY
to bourgeois Joseph McGillivray of Fort Alexandria,
18 July 1827[1]

Seeking a Better Way

Chief Factor Connolly's remarks underline the difficulties of packhorsing
between Thompson's River and Fort Alexandria. Those difficulties
prompted a search for a better way of hauling freight between the two
posts, just as similar difficulties had induced a search for a better route
or a better mode between Fort Okanagan and Thompson's River. That
search occurred at the very time when New Caledonia was switched from
the Peace to the Fraser-Columbia route in an attempt to make the new
route as expeditious and as economical as possible.

There did not seem to be a better land route for pack horses, with the
possible exception of the Kamloops Lake-Thompson River-Bonaparte
River-Green Lake bypass of the North Thompson-Mountain stretch of
the brigade trail (a bypass that was used in 1833 to drive livestock
[accompanied by botanist David Douglas] from the Columbia District

to New Caledonia). So attention was turned to the Thompson-Fraser river route between Fort Kamloops and Fort Alexandria. Simon Fraser had demonstrated the unusableness of the Fraser in 1808, but his demonstration referred to the river below the Fraser-Thompson forks, mainly the Fraser Canyon and particularly Simpson's Falls (Hell's Gate). For this reason Governor Simpson felt certain in 1825 that "the Columbia is the only navigable River to the interior from the Coast, we are acquainted with, it is therefore the only certain outlet for the Companys Trade west of the Mountains, comprehending that of thirteen Establishments now occupied."[2]

However, the Fraser and Thompson above their junction might be navigable; in that case, boats would be faster and cheaper than horses. So in July 1826 Chief Factor McLoughlin ordered Archibald McDonald "to Examine the nature of the Water Communication" via the Thompson and Fraser Rivers between Fort Kamloops and Fort Alexandria. Between 18 and 25 September McDonald with eight men, plus Chief Nicola, explored the Thompson between the forks of its North and South branches and the Fraser-Thompson forks, and the Fraser from these forks to the "Bridge" – Simon Fraser's *Rapide Couvert*, either French Bar Canyon or Chisholm Canyon, where the river is pinched between the Camelsfoot and Marble Ranges (and shortly afterwards he reconnoitred the Similkameen River Valley as a possible alternative to the Okanagan Lake trench as a horse brigade route). McDonald had "no hesitation" in reporting that this stretch was navigable by boats, although not at all seasons. He even opined that the Fraser below the Thompson junction was navigable by boats with the use of the line. "The fact is," he wrote, "that the Nature of those two Rivers Rolling down with Great Rapidity in a narrow Bed between Immense Mountains generally speaking Renders their ascent most Labourious and in places in the main River [Fraser] perhaps Impassible but not at Low Water." Chief Factor Connolly learned of McDonald's findings in early November:

> I received by this opportunity [a servant returning to Stuart's Lake from Fort Vancouver via Alexandria] a letter from Mr. Ar^d McDonald, informing me that he had visited Frasers River, from the mouth of Thompsons River to the [Moran] rapids above, and also a few miles below which he finds navigable. This point I believe has been long before ascertained. The greatest difficulty was supposed to exist in the long chain of Rapids from the foot of which Mr. McDonald returned. From all we have been able to learn these rapids are impassable by any kind of Craft at all periods of the year. But this will soon be ascertained, and correct information obtained in regards to the best means

of obviating the above difficulty, by a party I intend shall proceed from Alexandria for the express purpose of examining that part of the Rapid.[3]

Following McDonald's exploration, then, the only part of the river route that needed to be checked was the Fraser from Fort Alexandria to the foot of the Moran Rapids; the rest of the route was usable. In late summer Connolly had acknowledged that "another duty to be performed this Autumn is to examine this River between the head of the Rapids & the Mouth of Thompsons River, in order to ascertain whether the Navigation is practicable, and if found not to be so, to enquire into the easiest mode of overcoming this difficulty." Accordingly, in November, Clerk James Yale and eight other men from Alexandria reconnoitred the Fraser from that post to the Thompson forks. Yale reported that "the river thus far is navigable with Boats, but not without much difficulty and danger." He added: "From Alexandria to the Falls [?] / close to what is called the Bridge / there are 27 Strong rapids: at 8 or 10 of them ascending the current, the laiding [lading] must be carried, but the Boats can be hauled up all except 4 – descending I believe loaded Boats can run all except 4 or 5 without risk – Upon the whole I do not think there will be so much difficulty in navigating the river as its bad appearance would induce me to believe."[4] Yale recorded his findings in a journal, which Chief Factor Connolly read at the end of the year and summarized by writing that "it appears that the navigation between Alexandria and the mouth of Thompsons River is unobstructed by any obstacles which could not be easily surmounted in the season when the water is low." However, "in high water," he added, "some parts are perfectly unnavigable this channel running between perpendicular rocks, over which it is impossible to carry. And the agitation of the water is such, that no Craft made in this Country could pass those places in safety."[5]

Connolly elaborated this summation somewhat in the spring in his district report:

> The Navigation of Frasers River between Alexandria and the mouth of Thompsons River was examined last Fall, and according to Mr. Yales report (the Gentleman who performed this service) it presents no insurmountable obstacles – During the height of the waters, from June to the latter end of July, it would be altogether impracticable, but after they subside, with craft of a proper description, little or no danger would exist – Canoes are supposed too weak to resist the violent motion of the waters at any period of the season – And for this navigation therefore Boats such as are used in the Columbia, will be required.[6]

The sole obstacle, then, to the use of batteaux instead of horses for hauling company property between Thompson's River and Fort Alexandria was the Fraser River between Alexandria and the Thompson forks during spring freshet, when the waters were too tumultuous for safe navigation and the banks were too high and steep for easy portaging. So boats could have been used only during low water, that is, for the outgoing brigade in May and the incoming brigade in August. Certainly the obstacles to safe navigation in this stretch of the Fraser were no worse than those in the millrace of the lower Columbia. However, the shallow streams and the lengthy portages between Okanagan Lake and Shuswap Lake, that is, between the Fraser and Columbia drainages, were apparently sufficient to negate the replacement of horses by boats on the Fort Okanagan-Fort Alexandria section of the brigade system (but only apparently, for the streams *were* navigable and the portages *were* crossable). Otherwise the system could have dispensed with horses altogether and depended solely upon batteaux between Fort Vancouver and Fort St. James.

Packhorsing back to Fort Alexandria

The incoming horse brigade left Fort Kamloops in the middle of August, retraced the route of the outgoing brigade along the left bank of the North Thompson to the Traverse, over the Mountain to the Fraser, and along its eastern side, and reached Fort Alexandria in late August. There the horse "appointments" were dried, and the "cutting & cleaning" of the injured horses were done. Unlike the outgoing brigade, the incoming brigade was not troubled by cold weather or meagre fodder, but it still suffered from the rugged terrain, which continued to tire, lame, and kill horses, especially along the North Thompson and over the Mountain.

The 1822 brigade under Chief Factor John Stuart left Thompson's River on 9 August and did not cross the North Thompson at the Traverse until the 14th. On this stretch one horse – "our best Mare," wrote Stuart – was killed (broken leg) and another was perhaps fatally injured. The brigade leader added that "many of the others are getting Low and their backs much hurt." Alexandria was reached on the 16th.[7]

The 1826 brigade was late, having been delayed at the depot. It did not leave Thompson's River until 26 August. On the first day the horses were rested at the Rivière du Milieu (Heffley Creek?) and camp was made at the Pines after the brigade had covered twenty-one miles. On the 27th, twenty-five miles were made, although the "road," noted brigade leader Connolly, was "exceptionally bad, and fatiguing for the Horses," one of which tumbled "a considerable height into the river" but, miraculously, escaped injury. Thirty miles, "the longest day march we have yet performed," were covered on the 28th as far as the Traverse on trails "equally as bad as those we passed through yesterday." The morning of the 29th was spent crossing the North Thompson in canoes; afterwards ten miles were made until camp was pitched at the foot of the Mountain.

On the 30th, wrote Connolly, the trail across the Mountain "being very much obstructed with fallen Trees, and many marshes which are almost impassable, Mr. Douglas with Six Men proceeded ahead to clear away the former, & to throw bridges [corduroy] over the latter to prevent the Horses from sinking." The "swamp" was the only place on the Mountain that afforded feed for the horses. The brigade travelled twenty-four miles.

On the 31st the brigade covered fifteen miles and reached the western end of the Mountain, where "we have now got into quite a different Climate from the other side of the Mountain, the nights are frosty and the days cool & pleasant." On the Fraser side of the Mountain, too, grass for the horses was "abundant, and of an excellent quality."

The brigade made twenty-eight miles on 1 September to Lac Tranquil and twenty-seven miles on the 2nd to Drowned Horse Lake. On the 3rd, first the Beaver Dam River and then the Bridge River were both low enough to be crossed by the horses with their loads, and camp was made at White Earth Lake. Because the weather was "cool and pleasant" and grass was "very abundant" for the horses, explained Connolly, "they can perform long days marches without any risk of endangering their making the end of their Journey in safety." The brigade covered thirty miles on the 4th, passing Axe Lake in the morning, and thirty miles again on the 5th, passing McBean's Lake; on the 6th it covered thirty-four miles, making the banks of the Fraser early in the morning.

Fort Alexandria was reached on 7 September, twenty-five days from Fort Okanagan, as fast a trip as it was possible to make without more horses. "Every article" of property was in "excellent order," except two broken guns, and the horses were "all healthy" and in "good order" and "not much reduced," although "many of them have sore backs & sides, which will take some time to cure." They had plenty of time until next spring.

On the 8th "the Goods were unpacked, and what is required to form the Outfit of this post was laid aside." On the 9th Alexandria's outfit was "all delivered" and found to be complete except for leather, which was lacking altogether, and capots, which were "rather scarce." The remaining goods were repacked and "put in readiness for our departure [upriver to Stuart's Lake]."[8]

The 1827 brigade was early, leaving Thompson's River on 15 July. On the 16th the brigaders passed several camps of Indians, "all anxiously expecting that the Salmon would make their appearance," reported brigade leader Connolly, "and visibly with good reason, for a set of more emaciated & half starved wretches I never saw before." The horses were rested from 11:00 a.m. until 2:00 p.m.

The 17th was "a day of misfortunes." The trail was "the most fatiguing of any part we have hitherto passed," and "several" horses were "much fagged & with difficulty reached the Encampment [the Traverse]." Two horses fell into the North Thompson, and one of them with its load (two bales of dry goods, mostly blankets) was lost, for the blankets "imbibed the water immediately, which sank them to the bottom." A raft had to be made to cross the river and catch the other horse.

On the 18th it took six hours to cross the men, horses, and property over the North Thompson. A man was sent ahead on the 19th to Fort Alexandria to fetch the horses left there in the spring and to hire eight to ten Indian horses and return with all of them to meet the brigade in order to relieve the "lean & small Horses." On the Mountain the "swamp" was the only place where fodder was available for the animals.

On the 23rd Clerk Pierre Pambrun of Fort Alexandria met the brigade with nineteen horses, ten of which had been hired from the Indians. Of the mares left at Alexandria in the spring for breeding, two had died from overwork and their foals from starvation; the remainder were in worse condition than any horse in the brigade, although they were "not fatigued" and were therefore serviceable.

Fort Alexandria was reached on the 26th. "Considering the long voyage the Horses look lively and Smart," noted the keeper of the post's journal upon their arrival. However, he added on 12 August that "our Horses are sufering after the Fatigues of the Voyage" and on 22 August that "the Horses were brought to the House to *Doctor*, a few of them who have sore Backs – and Tails [chafing from cruppers?]."[9]

The 1828 brigade was a couple of weeks late. It did not leave Thompson's River until 24 August, taking five horses as far as the Traverse to allow some of the "fagged" horses to recover. On the first day brigade leader Connolly sent two men ahead to Fort Alexandria to fetch fresh horses and to inform its bourgeois of the imminent return of the brigade so as to dispel "much anxiety" on the part of New Caledonia's servants over its lateness and to undercut any "villainous schemes" on the part of the natives. Eleven horses from Alexandria met the brigade on the 31st shortly after it had broken camp at Bridge River. On 2 September a horse fell from a precipice along the Fraser and broke its neck; its meat was taken to Alexandria for food for the brigade.

Fort Alexandria was reached on the 3rd with all of the property. Some of it, however, particularly the guns, had suffered "much injury"; six guns were "irreparably broke." The bales, added Connolly, were "much torn, and a considerable number of the blankets which happened to be [on the] outside, are greatly damaged." He continued: "Mischances of this nature are, it is true, almost inseparable from horse carriage, but they would occur less frequently and to a less extent, if the packages which require it were covered with more durable stuff than the miserable trash which is at present used for that purpose, and means supplied for repairing the injuries which happen almost daily."[10]

The 1829 brigade was more or less on schedule. It left Thompson's River on 12 August without having overnighted. Two horses that had been "quite knocked up" by the trip from Fort Okanagan had to be left at Thompson's River. A few others were fagging, so several fresh animals were hired from the Indians to pack as far as the Traverse. Not wanting to risk crossing the property in pine bark canoes at the Traverse, brigade leader Connolly sent a wooden canoe with three men there from Fort Kamloops. En route to the Traverse a horse fell into the North Thompson "from a considerable height" but was rescued with its load, and the contents were dried. The brigade reached Fort Alexandria on the 22nd. The property was "complete & in good order," and the horses were in "very good condition," with only two or three having "any serious sores."[11]

The 1831 brigade was somewhat early. It made and left Thompson's River on 6 August. Four of the horses were unable to continue, so five were hired from the Indians to go as far as the Traverse. The brigade encountered a forest fire near Grande Prairie between Fort Kamloops and the Barrière River. Some of the horses being "much Galled & Exhausted," on the 12th brigade leader Dease sent two men ahead to get fresh animals at Fort Alexandria and return. On the 18th the brigade reached Alexandria, where forty-four pieces were delivered.[12]

Thereafter the horse brigades from Thompson's River were more or less on schedule, reaching Alexandria in the third or fourth week of August. For example, the 1833 brigade arrived under Dease on 17 August, the 1837 brigade under Ogden on 20 August, the 1842 brigade under Ogden again on 24 August, the 1846 brigade under Lewes on 23 August, and the 1847 brigade under Lewes again on 26 August (after horses had been sent from Alexandria to meet it because its own horses were in such a "miserable state").[13]

Because Alexandria was a transshipment point where the property was switched from horses to canoes, it was more than an overnight stopover for the brigade. Up to two weeks were spent here unloading the horses and treating the injured and fatigued animals, delivering the post's outfit and arranging the remaining outfits, and repairing and embarking the canoes. Usually it was the end of August before the brigaders left for Stuart's Lake on the final stretch of their journey.

CHAPTER 14

Canoeing up the Fraser

From Alexandria to Stuart's Lake

*Our voyage hither [Stuart's Lake] from Alexandria was
unattended with any material accident – I arrived here on the
8th Inst. [of August] and the Brigade on the 13th – The Indians
along the communication not having the means of supplying us with
the smallest quantity of Provisions the men were therefore confined
to their bare and very short daily allowance of a Pint of Pease, and
another of bad Corn, which was so insufficient for the support of
men labouring so hard as they did, that when they reached this, they
were much reduced, and required some recruiting which however
they obtained more by rest than good living.*

– CHIEF FACTOR WILLIAM CONNOLLY, 1827[1]

THE HOME STRETCH

Following a layover of a week or more at Fort Alexandria, the refreshed
brigaders left at the end of August or the beginning of September in
canoes or boats for Stuart's Lake. This upriver run took up to three
weeks, the main obstacles being, besides the contrary current, the Grand
Rapids (between the Quesnel and West Road Rivers), the Stony Island
Rapids (stretching half a mile just below the junction of the Stuart and
Nechako Rivers), and a long series of rapids on the Stuart River, as well
as scarce provisions in the event of a delayed or deficient salmon run.
The sooner New Caledonia's depot was reached, the sooner supplies
could be issued to the servants and articles could be traded to the natives
before the onset of the long, cold winter. From four to six craft, each
bearing six brigaders and hauling up to one hundred pieces of property
altogether, performed this last leg of the brigade route. Sometimes in the
middle of August one vessel went from Fraser's Lake to Fort Alexandria
to meet the horse brigade, and upon the return of the boat brigade it
was left at the Chinlac Forks (Stuart River-Nechako River junction) to
proceed directly to Fraser's Lake while the remaining craft returned to
Stuart's Lake, the district depot.[2]

During the early 1820s the brigades returned late to New Caledonia – too late for the comfort of the posts and the conduct of the trade. Their tardiness arose from their late departure – at the end of May instead of the middle of April. The 1820 brigade was a case in point, as Clerk George McDougall noted in the post journal of Stuart's Lake on 1 June of that year:

> About 9 A.M. Mr. Faries took his departure for the Columbia with J.B. Bouché our only Interpreter & eleven Men in three Canoes light with the exception of a few sundry articles Mr. Faries has taken for trade and only three hundred Salmon for Provisions, as Mr. Larocque [bourgeois of Thompson's River] promised to send a man to this end of the [North Thompson-Fraser] Portage [between] this place & Fraser's River [that is, Fort Alexandria] with Horses & provisions between the 4th & 6th Instant [of June] which will be about the time he will reach that place & by all accounts he will be at [Fort] Okanagan where he will meet his Outfit from the Sea [Fort George] on or about the 20th, But there owing to the heighth of the Waters [spring freshet on the Columbia] & want of Provisions [that is, before the salmon run on the Columbia] they will have to remain untill the 25th of July at least so that we cannot well expect them here before the beginning of October, at which time we will be anxiously looking out for them and not without reason.

The brigade did not return to Stuart's Lake until 19 October.[3]

The next three brigades were also late. The 1821 brigade arrived with ninety pieces of cargo (mostly axes, blankets, capots, beads, cloth, files, mirrors, gun flints, knives, needles, ribbon, clothing, utensils, medicines, ammunition, and provisions, plus leather) on 11 October, the 1822 brigade on 2 October after an absence of five months and two days (meaning that it, too, had departed on 1 June) "without any accident," and the "ample Outfit" of 1823 (the last from the Columbia until 1826) likewise on 2 October.[4]

Apparently it was Governor Simpson who not only redirected the brigade from the Peace to the Columbia but also rescheduled the brigade to depart New Caledonia earlier in order to return before autumn. The 1826 brigade, which had left Stuart's Lake at the beginning of May, returned to Fort Alexandria on 7 September. By the next day the damage to the canoes from the "summer heats" was repaired, but the boat brigade did not leave until the 10th. It comprised four canoes, three with twenty-eight pieces and five men each and one with eighteen pieces and eight men (including brigade leader William Connolly and James Douglas), with provisions for ten days. Twelve pieces of "sundry" and non-essential property had to be left at Alexandria because they "could not be embarked without overloading the canoes and endangering their safety in the rapids." En route the Fraser's current was "extremely strong" and the brigade's progress "proportionally slow." It reached Stuart's Lake on the 23rd and found George McDougall, the temporary bourgeois, and his men "all well – or at least alive, for they have passed a wretched Summer which their appearance sufficiently bespeaks," wrote Connolly. The pieces were opened and checked on the 24th, sorted and dried on the 25th, "laid aside" on the 26th, packed on the 27th, and forwarded on the 28th (including twenty-four pieces to Fraser's Lake and twelve pieces to Fort Kilmaurs). By 5 October all of the outfit had been distributed to the district's posts.[5]

The 1827 brigade, which had left Stuart's Lake on 1 May, returned on 13 August for a "very expeditious" trip "with every thing safe and in good order" but "with an Outfit by no means complete." The pack horses had reached Fort Alexandria on 26 July. There it took two days to overhaul the canoes, for "having passed the summer exposed to the Sun, they entertained much injury" and were "not in a proper state to receive their ladings." By the 28th "the Canoes were repaired and ready, but to[o] late in the Evening for departure." The brigade of four or five canoes and sixteen or twenty-four men, plus seven bags of corn and peas (a "very small allowance," according to brigade leader Connolly), left on the 29th. On the 31st it took the brigaders half a day to ascend the Grand Rapids, "which from the height of the waters at present was so strong as to oblige us to unload the Canoe & carry the lading in two different places." After reaching Stuart's Lake on 13 August, Connolly reported: "The Men are all in health but their appearance is wretched from the privation they suffered. Our poverty obliged us to put them upon a short allowance from the time they left Okanagan, and for several days passed they were reduced to one meal pr. day. And here unfortunately we have nothing to give them but very bad dry salmon, and even that in very moderate quantities."[6]

The 1828 brigade arrived at Fort Alexandria under Chief Factor Connolly at the beginning of September to find that three of the four canoes were "tolerable" and the other unusable. Five canoes were needed to convey the entire outfit, but, Connolly noted, "even if that number could be provided we have not a sufficient number of hands to man them," so several pieces had to be left at Alexandria for forwarding "before the close of the navigation." The canoes were repaired on the 2nd and 3rd. The brigade left on the 4th in four canoes, three with five men each and one with six men. Two canoes carried twenty-eight pieces each, one carried twenty-five pieces and Clerk Yale, and one carried twenty-three pieces and Chief Factor Connolly (making twenty-three men altogether). The brigaders had a "sufficient stock" of provisions – the meat of three horses that had been slaughtered at Alexandria and four bags of leftover peas. Stuart's Lake was reached in two weeks on the 18th with the property in "no very great condition." The brigade had been delayed at least one day by heavy rain but mostly by the desertion en route of one man ("the most useless carcass I ever knew," in the opinion of Connolly) and by the "awkwardness" of another who twice broke his canoe, the second time irreparably, and soaked its cargo. Connolly adumbrated one of the brigade system's foremost obstacles – namely, the shortage of proficient manpower – when he subsequently reported from Stuart's Lake that the brigade's return trip from Fort Vancouver had been "not unattended with difficulties arising from the weakness of the Boats crews in the Columbia, the disproportion of our complement to the number of Horses we had to conduct from Okanagan to Alexandria, and a little inconvenience occuring in our Canoes from Alexandria to this place."[7]

The last of the 1829 brigade, comprising only one canoe with six men and twenty-four pieces (the "largest proportion" of which was intended for McLeod's Lake), left Fort Alexandria on schedule on 23 August but took, according to Chief Factor Connolly, an "extraordinary length of time" to reach Stuart's Lake. It did not arrive until 10 September, owing to "the height of the waters, [the] weakness & sickness of his [Clerk John Tod's] crew, and the badness & overloading of his canoe," although Connolly himself dismissed the second and third of these excuses of Tod's. The chief factor attributed his clerk's "very tardy passage" to his "inexperience as a voyageur." And Tod took eight days to go by horse from Stuart's Lake to McLeod's Lake on account of the "badness of the roads," a condition, moreover, that "he did not endeavour to remedy."[8]

The 1831 brigade, upon reaching Fort Alexandria, found the canoes in a "very bad state " and in need of a "thorough" overhaul, but the post did not have any of the "indispensable Articles" of gum, bark, and watap. The brigade was unable to leave until 24 August, six days after arriving, there being only two men capable of repairing the canoes. It comprised four bark canoes with twenty-five pieces each and one bark canoe (the worst) with eighteen pieces; forty-four pieces had to be deposited at Alexandria and forwarded later. One canoe was lost, but its cargo saved, in the Grand Rapids. Stuart's Lake was not reached until 13 or 14 September, the canoes being "very leaky" and "unmanageable," so that frequent stops had to be made in order to bark and gum them.[9]

The remaining brigades kept more or less to the foregoing schedule. For instance, the 1833 brigade reached Fort Alexandria on 17 August and departed on 26 August in six canoes, the interval being spent unpacking the horses, sorting the goods, preparing the canoes, and writing and copying letters; the 1837 brigade arrived on 20 August and, after gumming the boats, departed on 25 August; the 1842 brigade arrived on 24 August and departed on the 29th in five boats with twenty-two men; the 1846 brigade arrived on 23 August and left on the 29th in five boats; and the 1847 brigade, the last from the Columbia, arrived on 26 August and left on 2 September.[10]

Occasionally the principal impediments between Fort Alexandria and Stuart's Lake – high water, unsound canoes, and inept crewmen – combined to delay the brigade considerably, as in 1844, when it did not return until the last day of September. Its lateness, reported Chief Factor John Lewes, was caused "entirely by the uncommon high state of the water in Frasers River together with the deficiency & awkwardness of our Bow & Steersmen in that part of the route, & I may add the wretched state of the Boats, two of which we could scarcely keep afloat."[11] The 1848 brigade was even later, but it, of course, followed not the Fraser-Columbia route but the new all-Fraser River route to Fort Langley rather than Fort Vancouver and did not return to Stuart's Lake until 11 October.[12] This very lateness demonstrated the superiority of the Fraser-Columbia route, even though it was much longer.

Conclusion

We go this year as last, to the Columbia for our Outfit,
and it will be for you [Governor and Council of the Northern
Department] to Consider and determine from what quarter this
Department [New Caledonia] will in future receive its necessary
supplies. Either quarter will be attended with difficulties and great
expences, and I will not presume to give an opinion, not from any
apprehension that I might be supposed more partial to the one than
the other, but because I am no way Competent [to] judge and have
not the vanity to place my own judgment in Competition with
yours, which though I do not hold it to be infalible I conceive to be
superior to that of any Individual whatever. But if the East side of
the Mountains is to be prefered as the place from which supplies are
to be received some method must be found to bring them ... at least
to Cumberland House. It being absolutely impossible for the New
Caledonians themselves to go further and return in time to supply
the Department by water, and equally impossible to do it in Winter
across land. The Department could not maintain half the number
of men and Dogs, that would be required to effect it and to
convey the Returns to the place of embarkation.

– CHIEF FACTOR JOHN STUART, 1822[1]

Notwithstanding Stuart's modesty, he was indeed competent to judge the relative merits of the Fraser-Peace and Fraser-Columbia supply routes, having opened the latter and helped to open the former and used both. But now he equivocated on the resolution of what he aptly described as New Caledonia's problem of "the distance from any Port of entry and the difficulty of getting the necessary supplies."[2] The HBC, which had successfully used a Hudson Bayside depot in its intense struggle with the NWC, and which held a negative view of the Columbia quarter anyway, opted for the Peace route. A year after the coalition of March 1821, the Council of the Northern Department ordered Stuart to transport his returns to, and his supplies from, Norway House.[3] The northern route was followed for only three years (1823-25), however. Governor Simpson found during his 1824-25 tour of the Pacific Slope that the work of the New Caledonia brigade was "the most tedious harrassing and expensive transport in the Indian Country," requiring the stationing of twice as many servants as necessary in the district; he also found that the Columbia Department's trade, "if sufficiently extended and properly managed," could yield twice as much profit as any other part of North America.[4] Meanwhile, Stuart, who had always preferred the southern link, was urging the company to abandon the Peace in favour of the Columbia route because the latter would save time and men and in particular would obviate the necessity of distributing New Caledonia's outfit to its five posts throughout the winter by sled dogs from McLeod's Lake, the "place of embarkation" that in 1822 had replaced the more central Stuart's Lake as the winter residence of the chief factor.[5] So in 1825 Simpson ordered the reopening of the southern supply line.[6]

Thus, from 1826 the Fraser-Columbia route served as the main line of transportation and communication for the Oregon Country – the united New Caledonia and Columbia Districts – until it yielded to the Oregon Trail with the influx of American migrants in the middle 1840s, and to the Fraser route with the final political partition of the Oregon Country along the forty-ninth parallel in 1846. During those two decades the brigade system seems to have worked with a minimum of misfortune and a modicum of expense – no mean achievement, given the long hauls and high risks. Outfitting New Caledonia from the Columbia depot (about 1,000 miles away) instead of the Hudson Bay depot (about 2,000 miles away) saved up to six weeks of time and consequently allowed the distribution of the district's outfit before the onset of winter, thereby equipping the natives to hunt earlier and freeing the servants to mount exploring and trading expeditions.[7] On the southern route, too, fewer hands brought as much cargo in fewer craft. Via the Peace route thirty-six men brought 130 pieces in six canoes on 30 October 1824, and thirty-two men brought 108 pieces in six canoes on 31 October 1825; by contrast, via the Columbia route twenty-three men returned with 102 pieces in four canoes on 23 September 1826, and twenty-six men returned with 118 pieces in five canoes on 13 September 1831 (another forty-four pieces were brought later).[8]

Although the sources do not allow an accurate calculation of the cost of brigade transport,[9] presumably its efficiency helped to make the Columbia Department a profitable enterprise for the HBC. At the Columbia depot the markup on goods, that is, the advance on their "invoice cost" (prime cost), was 75 percent in 1814-16 (expenses amounted to 57 percent) and 100 percent in 1817-20 by the NWC, and 70 percent in 1821-29 and 80 percent in the early 1840s by the HBC,[10] but these advances reflected the cost of overseas transport to the depot, not interior transport by the brigade.[11] More germane is the fact that at the posts of the Columbia Department these goods were advanced one-third above their Fort Vancouver price in 1833 and one-quarter in 1841.[12] If this markup truly reflected the cost of brigade transport, then that cost was moderate.

The moderation of the cost of the brigade system was, of course, but one of the various reforms undertaken by Governor Simpson in the middle 1820s in an effort to minimize the expenses and maximize the returns of company business in the Oregon Country. Those reforms were so successful as to make the department one of the HBC's principal moneymakers; in the 1825-46 period it contributed up to one-third of the company's total profits.[13] Increasingly from the 1821 coalition that one-third was derived from the New Caledonia as opposed to the Columbia District, which was deliberately overhunted on the prescient assumption that most or all of it would eventually be lost to the United States. From 1826 until 1847 New Caledonia's share of the Columbia Department's fur returns rose steadily from less than one-half to three-quarters; more importantly, the district's share of the take of beaver, the company's mainstay, doubled, increasing from one-third to two-thirds.[14] Chief Factor Ogden told Lieutenant Wilkes that New Caledonia's 1840-41 returns were worth $100,000, which was "much less than the usual amount," whereas the Columbia District "was scarcely worth the expense of an outlay for a party of trappers."[15] It was, of course, imperative that this growing share be handled as safely and as cheaply as possible by the brigade system, whose primary function increasingly became the exporting of returns and the importing of supplies for New Caledonia.

That district's returns languished between 100 packs (of 90 pounds each) in 1815-16 and only 73 packs in 1820-21,[16] when, by stark contrast, the Columbia District returned more than 15,000 furs, or about 275 packs at roughly 55 furs per pack (the most and the best from the Spokane Country).[17] But then New Caledonia's returns improved sharply to 103 packs of furs and 6 kegs of castoreum in 1821-22, 112 packs (about 6,000 furs) and 8 kegs (387 pounds) in 1822-23, 105 packs (again about 6,000 furs) in 1823-24, 125 packs and 9 kegs in 1824-25 (13 packs more than any previous year), 125 packs (weighing 11,007 pounds and worth £11,000, £700 more than those of 1824-25) and 8 kegs in 1825-26, 113 packs (yielding a gross profit of £8,000, which would have been £10,000 if the books had been closed on the usual date of May instead of 1 March) in 1826-27, 138 packs (each weighing 86 pounds and all worth £12,000 gross and £9,000 net, the "most favourable which New Caledonia ever produced") in 1827-28, 136 packs (again each weighing 86 pounds and all grossing £12,616 and netting £9,748) in 1828-29, 162 packs and 10²/₃ kegs in 1830-31, and 163 packs and 15 kegs (worth £11,000 gross and £8,000 net) in 1833-34.[18] In the outfit year of 1836-37, when New Caledonia yielded 150 packs (two-thirds of them beaver), the entire Columbia Department's gross returns of £41,057 were fairly evenly divided among New Caledonia (30 percent), the Columbia District (34 percent), and the coast trade's ships and posts (36 percent).[19] Thanks largely to the department's performance, HBC shareholders, after having seen their annual dividends reduced to 4 percent in 1800-7, nil in 1808-13, and 4 percent in 1814-21 by NWC competition, received half-year dividends of 5 percent in 1825-37 (plus bonuses of 10 percent in 1828-32 and 6 percent in 1833-36).[20]

In 1837, however, no bonus dividend was paid – an indication that the fur trade was faltering. The Columbia Department's average annual returns decreased by more than one-fifth from 76,100 skins in 1835-39 to 59,900 in 1840-44.[21] The depletion of fur bearers, the depopulation of fur trappers, the disaffection of fur traders, and the defection of fur buyers were conspiring to effect what Chief Factor James Douglas termed "the decline and wreck of fur trade affairs."[22] Like the sea otter of the coast, the beaver had been overhunted. The country south of the Columbia had been "scoured" in the 1820s, and even the "nursery" of New Caledonia had been "overdone." And more and more habitat was being usurped by white settlers, who cleared and drained for homesteads, especially from the 1840s with the influx of American migrants: 137 men, women, and children in 1842, 875 with 1,300 head of cattle in 1843, 1,475 in 1844, and 3,000 in 1845.[23]

Meanwhile, the natives, who trapped the beaver and swapped their pelts for goods, were devastated by disease, alcoholism, and perhaps anomie. Malaria on the lowermost Columbia in the first half of the 1830s and smallpox on the northern coast in the last half exacted a particularly heavy toll. In the fall of 1831 at Fort Vancouver, Duncan Finlayson recorded that "there has been & still continues a great mortality among the natives" from "fever and ague," and "consequently, the [fur] trade is not so brisk as at former periods."[24] Malaria and smallpox together may have halved the Columbia Department's native population, which Warre and Vavasour estimated to be 87,000 in 1840.[25]

There was a decrease of fur traders as well as trappers as more and more men declined to sign HBC contracts, opting instead for more promising livelihoods, particularly homesteading. In a personal letter to Governor Simpson in the spring of 1842, Chief Factor Archibald McDonald of Fort Colvile reported that although the Columbia

Department's 1841-42 outfit was the most profitable yet – returns of £40,000 and expenses of £20,000 for a net profit of £20,000 – he admitted that "it is evident everything must be deranged" by the depletion of beaver, the influence of missionaries, and "the reluctance of the Servants to renew their Engagements," for "no fewer than five & thirty of the most efficient Men in the Country go out this Spring, most of them with the avowed intention of returning free & independent by some defile of the R. Mountains" to homestead.[26] And later the same year Letitia Hargrave, the daughter of the epistolary bourgeois of York Factory, James Hargrave, told her father that "there is a universal spirit of discontent all over ... Many are leaving the Service, old & young & going to Upper Canada [Ontario]."[27]

Finally, by the 1840s the demand for fur was disappearing. There had been sags before – e.g., in 1823, when the fur market was "in a very depressed state," as Governor Simpson put it[28] – but those had been temporary reverses. Now, however, fashion had changed, replacing the felt (beaver) hat with the silk hat. As John Tod was to recall, "beaver were valuable before silk hats came into use."[29] Letitia Hargrave noted this basic shift in a letter of 1845 to her father from York Factory: "Hunting beaver has again been put a stop to as the silk hat manufacture has pushed them out [of] the market. This will be a great loss as they have been what they call nursing the country for many years & the people at home not getting beaver were driven to try silk & now that there are plenty skins they won't buy them."[30] Beaver House was only too well aware of the situation, and it kept Chief Factor McLoughlin informed. At the end of the summer of 1843 the Governor and Committee wrote McLoughlin that "the furs [from the Columbia Department], with the exception of Beaver, realized tolerable prices at the [London August] sale." "In that staple article [beaver] there has been we regret to say, a further depression to a considerable extent." They added that "this continually decreasing price when considered in connexion with a constantly decreasing supply, holds out no very cheering prospect for the future, unless the tide of fashion change[s], and the consumption of Beaver in the manufacture of hats becomes more general than it has been for some time past." Realistically, however, "economical management" was the only way of curtailing expenses.[31] Nevertheless, revenues continued to fall with the price of beaver. Two years later the Governor and Committee told McLoughlin that beaver was "at present unsaleable." Other furs had brought "high" prices at the summer 1845 auction but "not so high as formerly," and the quantity was "small" because of the "general dimuni-tion of the returns."[32] Between 1826 and 1846 the price of large beaver skins on the London market fell threefold from about 30 to about 10 shillings each.[33] James Hargrave reported from London in 1847 that furs "are sold at about ¹/₃d from the prices of last year – and our late valuable staple – Beaver – is literally a drug in the market." All of the company's last shipment of furs to the London market (some 65,000 pelts, excluding those from the Columbia Department) were still unsold, he added.[34] Later the same year, Chief Factor John Work acknowledged "the almost worthlessness of beaver."[35]

Little wonder that the fur trade became less and less remunerative. In early 1837 Archibald McDonald observed that "the general profits are annually decreasing & will continue to decrease."[36] A chief trader's annual income fell from about £500 at the end of the 1820s to about £300 at the end of the 1830s.[37] The 1839-40 outfit of the Columbia Department revealed a growing difference between gross profit (£44,000) and net profit (£24,000), the reason being that, as Chief Factor John Rowand of Fort Edmonton lamented, "the country is getting poorer every day the Beaver is disappearing fast, and our expence is getting greater every day."[38] Governor Simpson himself "was sorry to find the profits dwindling away to nothing."[39] Nevertheless, the department's profits in 1841-42 were "higher than ever," and those of 1842-43 promised to be equally as high, according to Chief Factor Douglas, undoubtedly owing to economic diversification, especially the opening of markets for "country produce" (grain, fish, timber) in Russian America, the Sandwich (Hawaiian) Islands, and Alta California.[40] Hides, for example, were by then "as valuable as Beaver in the London Market," in the words of Fort Vancouver's Clerk Dugald Mactavish, the brother-in-law of York Factory's James Hargrave.[41] Despite the program's success, diversification was scorned by some veteran servants, such as Hargrave himself. In a letter to him of 1839, Archibald McDonald wrote from Fort Colvile that "I find you all throw cold water on every other laudable exertion we make to find you substitutes for Beaver."[42] The critics particularly disdained what Chief Factor John Tod of Fort Kamloops dubbed the "soap bubble" of the Puget's Sound Agricultural Company, which was founded partly for political reasons and which did not show a profit for some time.[43] All were agreed, however, that, as Tod said, the Indian Country's old mainstay of "the Fur Trade is evidently declining in all quarters, while its expenses appear, in an equal ratio, to be annually increasing."[44] McDonald voiced their common lament: "the universal cry is that the old H.B. gold dust is gone for ever."[45]

Thus, by the time the Fraser-Columbia brigade system was severed – *de jure* in 1846 but *de facto* in 1848 – by the drawing of the international boundary along the forty-ninth parallel, it loomed less large in Oregon Country transport. With the decline of the fur trade, its logistical role likewise declined, and it did not really serve the movement of the diversification program's "country produce," which was produced primarily on the coast rather than in the interior and was shipped abroad rather than inland, or the movement of American migrants, who came overland. Before the negotiation of what Douglas and Work called "this monstrous treaty"[46] of 1846, Governor Simpson had alerted the company's London directors that it would be "well to be prepared for the worst,"[47] that is, the loss of the Columbia routeway. His concern was somewhat exaggerated, however. Admittedly, the treaty was, as Douglas and Ogden feared, not explicit enough to protect the property of those British subjects left on American territory and would be a pretext for the commission of "every species of oppression" on the company's trade via the Columbia, so that it became necessary to open an alternative supply route for New Caledonia via the Fraser in order to avoid the payment of American import duties, as well as to move the depot from Fort Vancouver to Fort Victoria and the affiliated Puget's Sound Agricultural Company from the Puget Sound-Cowlitz River portage to Vancouver Island (which was granted to the HBC by the Crown in 1849).[48] But the loss of the territory to the south of the new boundary meant that even fewer trade goods had to be brought in, and even fewer furs had to be taken out, by the brigade than before 1848, when the volume of traffic had already decreased in the wake of the fur trade's decline. So the new all-Fraser route was less crucial than the old Fraser-Columbia route, which for two decades had been the "main communication" of the Oregon Country. In the middle 1850s both routes would be dramatically, if temporarily, rejuvenated by the rush of fortune seekers to the goldfields of the upper reaches of the Columbia and Fraser Rivers.

William Connolly's Journal of the Brigade from New Caledonia to Fort Vancouver and Return, 5 May-23 September 1826.[1]

The Governor and Council of the Northern Department of Rupert's Land decided in 1825 to reroute the New Caledonia brigade from the Peace to the Columbia route once and for all, although the shortage of pack horses at Fort Alexandria – resulting from the unusually cold and snowy winter of 1825-26 – forced the district to send some of its returns via the Peace. The rerouted brigade was led by Chief Factor William Connolly, who had recently succeeded John Stuart as bourgeois of New Caledonia. Connolly kept a daily journal, one of only two with much detail that have survived; the other was kept in 1831 by Chief Factor Peter Warren Dease, and both are published here for the first time.[2] These fascinating eyewitness accounts provide the most authoritative and the most comprehensive information we have on the brigade system, and as such they deserve to be made more widely available.

1826

May 5th Friday – Every arrangement being completed both for the voyage to York Factory & to Fort Vancouver, at 8 oclock this morning Mr James McDougall with 8 Men took their departure from Stuarts Lake for Fort Simpson (McLeods Lake) where they will join Messr^s Brown & McBean with the people already there with whom they will proceed, under the command of Mr Brown, for York Factory – The party going by that route consists of the three above-mentioned Gentlemen & 13 Men – As detailed in the last Journal, they are to convey to Hudson's Bay about 44 Pieces of Furs & Castorum, and in order to accelerate their passage from hence to the East end of the Rocky Mountain Portage, and to add strength to the party in case of an attack from the Beaver Indians, four additional Men accompany them as far as the last mentioned place – from whence they will return & will bring up whatever Leather may be procured from the Secaunees [Sekanais], and also the Arms taken out for defence, and what property may remain of what I send to Trade with those Indians –

After the return of these four Men the summer Establishments of the different Posts will be as follows – viz

Fort Simpson	John Tod	Clerk with two Men		
Frasers Lake	John M^cdonell	"	"	two "
Babines	Charles Ross	"	"	two "
Alexandria	J. M. Yale	"	"	two "
Stuarts Lake	Geo. M^cdougall	"	"	three "

Forming a Total of five Gentlemen and eleven Men, exclusive of two Men who are left inland for the purpose of going for the Leather at the Sources of Frasers River – And until they depart upon that Service, one of them will be stationed at the Babines, & the other at Stuarts Lake – They are to proceed from the latter place accompanied by two Indians, to be hired for the purpose – And the Iroquois guide who remained sick at Alexandria (but who will be sent up) about the 10th September in order to reach the Sources of Frasers River (where the Leather is to [be] brought by the Sascatchuwan [Saskatchewan] people) in time to clear the road between that place and Jaspers House, which M^r McMillan reports being much obstructed with fallen trees –

M^r McDougall is directed to send the Interpreter Waccan Bouché in [the] course of the Summer to Beaver Lake a Country with which we are acquainted only by report – And as far as that goes, it seems well worthy of closer examination. He will endeavour to find out some of the Inhabitants in order to form some idea of the advantages which might result from an intercourse with them, and in the event of favourable appearances, to promise them that our visit will be repeated in the Fall, and in the mean time to engage those whom he may see, to collect the rest of their Tribe, and appoint a certain place, & period, for the general meeting – He will also make the necessary enquiries in regards to the means of subsisting an establishment, and of the most convenient spot on which it should be formed, both for ourselves & for the accomodation of the Natives – For this voyage Waccan will build a Canoe of sufficient Size for the purpose –

These are the only services, exclusive of the common duties of the Several Establishments, which are to be performed during the Summer –

The Brigade consisting of three Canoes, were dispatched for Alexandria on the 3rd Instant – And myself with Mr Douglas (who is to accompany me to the columbia) embarked from Stuarts Lake at one oclock PM to proceed to the same place – The weather was fine and we encamped at half after seven PM in Stuarts River – The water is very low, none of the Snow in the Mountains being yet dissolved, and the Current is therefore not strong – And our progress altho we have a crew of nine Men, is not so great as might be expected.

6th Saturday – At half after two A.M, we left our Encampment and passed the Forks formed by the junction of the two Rivers which flow from Stuarts & Frasers Lakes, at a quarter past twelve – And encamped below the rapids of *Chal a oo chicks* at half an hour after 7 – The weather was fine –

7th Sunday – Proceeded at the same time as yesterday, and shortly after, passed the Forks formed by the union of the East or main branch of Frasers River, with that we have hitherto followed – where we saw an Indian from whom, for a small quantity of Ammunition and cash, we procured 20 Martens and a Silver Fox – Below this place the Country exhibits some Signs of Spring, which are more evident the farther we advance – At two oclock PM passed the West road [Blackwater] River, and five hours after we reached Quesnels River, below which we Encamped – The weather continues fine –

8th Monday – pursued our route at the usual hour – at seven we passed *Sto-ni-yâ* and at nine reached the Fort of Alexandria, whither the Brigade had preceded our arrival a couple of Hours, & had delivered their cargoes in excellent Condition –

Mr Yale had returned from Kamloops on the 1st Instant with 49 Horses, 29 of which had been furnished by Mr Ermatinger, who is in charge of that Post, and the remainder were hired from the Indians for the voyage hither, and back again, at the rate of Eight [beaver] Skins each – These added to 14 which have escaped the general destruction [the heavy toll taken by the very cold and snowy winter], and five that are hired from the Indians of this place for the whole Summer forms a Total of 68 – which number will just answer to carry out the Returns, and Provisions requisite for our Support from hence to Kamloops – where a supply of fresh Horses will be furnished in lieu of the Indian Horses, which are to be returned there to assist us on from thence to Okanagan. The letters relative to these Matters, and to what further arrangements are in contemplation to assist our progress out, are entered in Letter Books Nos 1 & 2 [not extant] –

Most of these poor Animals are extremely lean however with proper attention, and slow Marching, I hope they will be able to carry out their respective loads – which are made up into packages to suit their strength, from 45 lbs to 85 lbs weight – To Mr Yale every credit is due both for the expedition he used, and in having brought over the band of Horses without losing one, either in crossing the Mountain, in which he found from three to four feet of snow, or from the Scarcity of food, the ground being in most places yet uncovered – And when that did not occur the grass was yet so short as to afford the Poor Brutes but a very scanty subsistance – In compliance with my request Mr Ermatinger sent over with Mr Yale, two of their own Men who are experienced Horsemen, and whose assistance we require – And in place of whom Mr Yale left three of the Men who accompanied him from hence – The former Gentleman is to wait our arrival at Kamloops and has a sufficiency of salmon to supply us from thence to Okanagan – He will also provide Canoes at the North River for the purpose of crossing our Property – by which much time will be saved – and the danger to which it would be exposed in crossing it over on rafts, avoided –

Mr Pambrun I am sorry to observe, continues so unwell, that I consider his life would be in danger if he remained in land. He will therefore accompany us out in hopes of his being able to obtain medical assistance at F^t Vancouver – altho' in the state he is in, the voyage I fear, will aggravate his Complaint –

All the Indians belonging to this place [trading at Alexandria] being off to their Fishing Lakes, no opportunity offerd of using my endeavours to disuade them from an expedition I understand they are intending to make against the Chilcotins – Mr Yale will however do every thing in his power to stop them and in this I trust he will succeed – as further Hostilities can only tend to widen the breach between them, and protract an accomodation of their dispute, which it is most desirable should be effected as soon as possible – as the welfare of this Post depends almost entirely upon that – as well as the projected establishment in the Chilcotin Country, which cannot be formed until tranquillity is restored between the two Tribes –

The fatal effects of this unfortunate business are already severely felt – The Natives are in a state of too great alarm to admit of their hunting with much success – And indeed they have all fled in a contrary direction to their usual Hunting Grounds, where Beaver are scarce, and where they could not do much, even if the agitation they are in did not exist – Since the Commencement of this contest not one fifth of the quantity of Furs usually obtained during the same period, have been procured – A proof of what may be expected until peace is reestablished –

Mr Yale, as already noticed, passes the summer at Alexandria – And I am truly grieved not to have it [in] my power to leave him more than two Men – Under existing circumstances four would not be too many – Trusting to chance in such a case, is hazarding too much – there is however no alternative, and he must depend upon his own caution & firmness for the security of himself, People and property – The work to be done here this summer is to complete if possible, the store which is already considerably advanced – but the principal duty is to attend to the Safety of the people – As any misfortunes which might occur would independant of the mournful feelings they would create, involve the Department in trouble and confusion –

The Day was occupied in laying up the Canoes in such a manner as will secure them so much as possible from the injury they would unavoidably receive from exposure to the weather – until such time as a Shed can be erected over them – The climate is far more favourable than above [upriver] – the weather has been fine for some time passed [past], and vegetation, of which at Stuarts Lake there was not the least vestige on the 5th Ins^t, is here pretty far advanced, and warrants a hope that our Horses will find tolerable good feeding along the way –

9th Tuesday – Some Loon [?] Furs we brought down were packed, and also the Provisions for the voyage which completes every arrangement connected with our departure from hence, tomorrow, on our Journey to the shores of the Pacific – The Horse appointments were examined and found in good order, those which required it having been repaired by Mr Pambrun, who was in charge of this place from the departure of M^r McDougall, until Mr Yales arrival – The weather continues fine –

10th Wednesday – At an early hour the Horses were mustered, but before their loads were adjusted – (a duty with which most of our Men are unacquainted) it was ten oclock – at which hour we moved off from Alexandria – The Brigade consists of myself and two clerks, with 24 Men & 68 Horses, and ladings of 83 Packs of Furs, 6 Kegs Castoreum & 15 Bales of dry Salmon, besides our voyaging apparatus – For the greater Convenience of Travelling, the Brigade was subdivided into twelve Brigades [strings] of two Men each, with from five to Six Horses each – By this arrangement much confusion will not only be avoided, but if any of the Horses are injured the offenders will be easily discovered –

Some of the Horses having never before carried a load, did not much like their Burthens which they contrived by Kicking to throw off their backs. Some time was therefore lost in readjusting their loads, and prevented our proceeding above 15 miles, when we Encamped on the Banks of a rivulet Skirting a plain of considerable extent which afforded the Horses very good feeding – The Morning was fine, but in the afternoon it Rained –

11th Thursday – At a quarter after 4 oc[lock] AM we were on the march, and reached the head of the Grand Rapid at nine, when one of the young Horses in passing on the side of a high & almost perpendicular Bank took fright, & rolled down the precipice into the River. Any attempts on our part to save him were impossible, and I thought it equally so that he should save himself, which however to our surprise he effected after being carried by the Current to the foot of the Rapids, a distance of at least four miles, where he succeeded in landing on the opposite side with his load, consisting of two packs of Beaver, safe upon his Back. These by their Buoyancy, were, I conceive, the means of his preservation. A Canoe was procured with which the Packs were brought over, and the Horse of course swam across – but the Poor Brute was too much exhausted to proceed any farther, which added to the necessity of drying the Packs prevented our proceeding any farther to day – In the evening the Furs were dry and repacked, and every thing in readiness to resume our Journey early tomorrow morning –

12th Friday – We were ready to start at an early hour, but much time was lost in climbing up a steep Hill forming the bank of the Gully in which we had Encamped – Some rain that fell during the last night had softened the mud, and rendered the Hill so extremely slippery, that several Horses reached the summit only after repeated efforts, in each of which, after ascending some distance, they rolled back again to the imminent risk of their Necks – At length this difficulty was overcome, and we continued to follow the left Bank of Frasers River until half an hour after nine, when we left it to pursue the shortest route to Kamloops – At Twelve we reached a small lake with excellent grass in its vicinity, which of itself was a strong inducement to Encamp for the night – even if the fatigued state the Horses are in from the unevenness of the roads we passed through to day, did not require it – The weather was fine –

13th Saturday – & 14th Sunday – We proceeded from our Encampments both these days at our usual hour – (ie) at half an hour after four oc[lock] AM – The Country we passed through is beautiful, the roads level & unobstructed, and food for our Horses plentiful, which enabled us to perform excellent marches – Pheasants [grouse or quail?] and water Fowl, were also in tolerable abundance, of which we procured a few – And from the Indians, who frequent the lakes that lay on our route, for the purpose of Fishing, we obtained a few Trout, Carp, & some roots – These fellows being notorious Horse Thieves, we began on the night of the 13th to keep watch, a practice I mean to observe as long as any danger may be supposed to exist – With these people we exchanged a mare and a Horse that were miserably poor & unable to proceed much farther for two Horses in good condition by giving a few trifles in the bargain – We also found it expedient to allow the Horses a few Hours rest each day, by which means they are never exhausted. They are soon refreshed and enabled to perform longer days journey with less fatigue than they possibly could by going from one Encampment to the next without Halting – We had frequent showers of rain, but none of sufficient violence to retard our march or injure the Furs –

15th Monday – Two Hours after leaving our Encampment we passed a small river sufficiently deep to wet the lower part of some of the Packs. At a Small Lake suitable to our purpose we Halted to give the Horses their usual rest, and to dry the furs. In the afternoon we pursued our route in [the] course of which we passed a river too deep to be forded, but its breadth not exceeding ten yards we threw a bridge across, over which the Horses passed with their loads – At four oc[lock] PM we reached the Beaver dam River which was also too deep to ford – The Horses swam across, & the property was carried over a Bridge formed by drift wood. At this place we Encamped for the night – The progress of vegetation is less, the nearer we approach the Mountain, and the Horses now feed for the most part either upon very young grass, or the stubble of last year, which does not afford much nourishment – The weather was fine –

16th Tuesday – Pursued our route, and Baited the Horses at the drowned Horse Lake, at ten oc[lock] AM – At two PM we resumed our Journey, and Encamped at Six – Passed a couple of camps of Indians who gave us a few Fish for Tobacco & Ammunition – They appear to be the most wretched people in the creation – Their whole time is occupied in procuring food, consisting of Fish & Roots, and very seldom kill either Beaver or any other fur bearing animals – What furs they do procure are carried to Alexandria – Indeed the Country seems entirely destitute of Beaver, and it appears from the few Signs either old or new that those animals were once numerous in this quarter – The weather continues fine –

17th Wednesday – Early in the morning we left our Encampment, and at nine oclock reached *lac Tranquille*, which we found covered with Ice – And vegetation in the neighbourhood consequently but little advanced – We here stopped to allow the Horses their usual rest – but they had scarcely dispersed to feed, when it was discovered that two of them were missing – And there being no doubt that they had been stolen, Mr [James] Douglas [Connolly's future son-in-law and subsequent first governor of British Columbia] and three Men set out immediately in pursuit of the Thieves – And in the mean time several Indians who [had] followed us since yesterday were put under arrest, as I was determined in the event of Mr Douglas being unsuccessful in uncovering our Horses, to replace one of them with the only Horse these people have in their possession; At the usual Hour the Brigade moved off, and with them the Indian Horse, together with its owner, and encamped at the East end of the Lakes, where Mr Douglas & party arrived at night with our two Horses which they recovered after pursuing the Thieves to the borders of a lake which the lat[t]er crossed over in Canoes, and thus escaped the chastisement they so well deserved – A Short distance from the lake Mr Douglas met two Indians (sons of the Chief of the North [Thompson] River) who were on their way to our Camp with the two Horses which they had taken from the Thieves in order to restore them to us – An instance of honesty and good will towards the whites which I endeavoured to requite by giving them as large a proportion of our small stock of supplies, as could be well spared – The weather continues the same –

18th Thursday – Pursued our route at the usual hour, and stopped at *Lac du Rocher* (which is also covered with Ice,) to rest the Horses – In the afternoon we resumed our march and reached the foot of the Mountain at 5 oc[lock] PM where we Encamped – The road we passed through this day is very rugged, and many obstructions occasioned by fallen woods occur – For an hour before encamping, and for some time after, it snowed considerably – The old Chief, Father of the young man who recovered our Horses, came up with us at night – And as a mark of my approbation of his childrens conduct, I gave him a piece of Tobacco with some Ammunition & promised on my return to make him a more valuable present –

19th Friday – It being impossible to cross the Mountain in one day, and there being only one place, about midway, which affords food for Horses, we did not therefore leave our Encampment until twelve PM & just to have time to be able to reach the above place, which we did at about 7 oc[lock] – Our route was through Marshes & very deep snow – in the former of which the Horses Sunk in many places up to their bellies & were with difficulty extricated – This is the most fatiguing march they have yet performed, and they were entirely exhausted when they reached the swamp, which unfortunately afforded but very poor means of recruiting their strength. One of the poor animals was left along the way, being unable to proceed any farther – In such roads it was impossible to avoid wetting some of the Packs, but none of them are sufficiently so to injure the Furs – The weather was fine, but we were too much elevated to feel any heat –

20th Saturday – Early in the Morning we pursued our route in order to reach a good feeding place for the Horses as soon as possible – A man was sent to see after the one we left yesterday, he returned shortly after, & reported that he had found him dead – Another of our Horses being unable to rise, we therefore under the necessity of leaving him behind. At nine oclock we reached the heights [summit] from whence we had a view of the North River – In our descent the Horses fatigued a great deal, and when we reached the small River it was necessary to Halt, in order that they might rest & replenish themselves – After which we resumed our Journey and arrived at the North Branch of Thompsons River at 5 oc[lock] PM, where we found three of the Kamloops Men, and two Indians, waiting our arrival with Canoes to cross over the property, and two fresh Horses to relieve such of our own as most require it – I received letters from Messrs Ar^d McDonald & F. Ermatinger informing me of the steps taken to assist in the Transport out of our returns – And with which I am satisfied – Mr Dease had the goodness to send twenty of his Horses to our relief which are now at Kamloops – And from this date we may consider our greatest difficulties at an end – For Copies of these letters see Correspondence [Books] N°s 3 & 4 –

By sun set all the property was ferried over the River but the Horses were so much fatigued that it was judged necessary to allow them a nights rest before they crossed.

The weather was fine, and the Climate being here much more moderate than on the other side of the Mountain, vegetation is therefore farther advanced, and we have a fair prospect of finding good feeding for our Horses during the remainder of our Journey –

21st Sunday – The two Canoes being of sufficient size to carry a considerable proportion of our Baggage, they were loaded each with 12 pieces, manned with two Men & immediately sent forward for Kamloops, which without much exertion they can reach to day, as they will descend the current which is very strong – By 8 oc[lock] AM our Horses were all crossed over to the south [east] shore [left bank], and having a considerable number more than are required to carry our Property, the weakest were therefore not needed, and will be allowed to go light until they recover strength, & in their turn will occasionally relieve others who may fail along the way – At nine oc[lock] we left our Encampment & proceeded along the Banks of the North River which are extremely rugged and fatiguing to the Horses – At one oc[lock] PM we reached a small plain where I resolved on passing the remainder of the day, in drying the Furs that were wet & for which purpose the weather was particularly favourable – A thorough examination of the Packs was made, and a smaller quantity of Furs was found wet than I expected – At Sun set they were all dried & repacked. And at day break

22ᵈ Monday – The Horses were collected, and as soon as they were loaded we set off, and at 10 oclock we reached the *Barière*, where [there] was a camp of Indians from whom I procured a sufficiency of Trout, for a meal to the whole Brigade, in exchange for Tobacco & Ammunition – After allowing the Horses four Hours rest we continued on through a country equally as bad as that of yesterday, & got to a place called the *Pineux* where we Encamped at Sun set – The weather was Beautiful & vegetation being here in full vigour the horses have therefore excellent feeding –

23ᵈ Tuesday – Set off at the usual Hour, and proceeded without Halting until two oc[lock] PM, when we arrived at the Fort of Kamloops, where we found Mʳ Ermatinger & the people with him all well – The people I sent down with the canoes arrived on the day expected, & delivered their Cargoes in good order – The [Nez Percé] Horses from Spokane [House] which are here are fat – but from bad usage on their way from [Fort] Okanagan to this place, they have very sore backs, which is even worse than being low in flesh – However with the number here to be added to our own we will certainly get to the end of our Journey without much Trouble. The Horses that were borrowed from the Indians were all returned, and the nine [?] paid for – which ammounts to a sufficient sum to have purchased, at least, one half of them – This expense will I trust not again occur – And under all [the] Circumstances I may consider myself very fortunate in being so far on my Journey with the Returns, and without any apprehension of meeting with further difficulties – In the morning the weather was fine – but towards evening it rained

24ᵗʰ Wednesday – To Allow our Horses a complete rest & Mʳ Ermatinger to make the necessary preparations for his departure from hence with all the property at this place [that is, to close the post for the summer] I determined on passing the day here – But towards evening Every thing was crossed over the South Branch of Thompsons River, to avoid any loss of time tomorrow – From the uncertainty in regard to the probable period of my reaching the Banks of the Columbia – Mʳ Dease I am informed had resolved on retaining his people at Fort Colvile until he should hear from me. It is therefore necessary in order to avoid any further loss of time, to forward to him information of our movements – In consequence [I] addressed a few lines to him acquainting him therewith and requesting that his people may find themselves at Okanagan by the 5ᵗʰ Proxº, at which period I expect to be there – With this dispatch Mʳ Ermatinger will proceed a head to the Little Okanagan Lake [Lake Osoyoos], from whence he will forward it over land to Mʳ Dease – And there is no doubt if due expedition is made, that it will answer the intended purpose. Rained considerably throughout the Day –

25ᵗʰ Thursday – Although the Horses were crossed early in the morning, yet before they were caught, tackled & loaded it was Eleven oclock, & we therefore were not able to proceed farther than the *Monté*, where we Encamped – For want of Cords to tie them with, I had to leave about 1100 Salomn, with a few Appichimonts & Pack saddles, at Kamloops – which were put in charge of an Indian called Nicholas [Chief Nicola] – who is said to be an honest fellow; & possessed of sufficient influence over his Tribe to secure them from being stolen – The weather was fair & warm –

26ᵗʰ Friday – At Break of day Mʳ Ermatinger with three Men set out for Okanagan – He expects to reach the Small Lake of that name on the third day, from whence he will forward an express to Mʳ Dease – At the usual Hour the Brigade moved off. And at nine the Horses were allowed to rest until two PM, when we resumed our Journey, and got to the furthest extremity of the *Grand Prairie* [Westwold Valley] at Sun set, where we Encamped – Weather the same as yesterday –

27ᵗʰ Saturday – Proceeded from four until eleven oclock AM when we reached the Salmon River, when a heavy Shower of rain detained us for five hours – We then went on until Dark, when we Encamped at the Entrance of Okanagan Lake –

28th Sunday – Set out as usual – Our route lay along the Okanagan Lake, which is rugged & fatiguing to the Horses, we reached Red Deers River at 11 oc[lock] AM, where we remained until 4 in the afternoon, from which hour until seven we proceeded on, & passed the Mauvais Rocher without accident – a little beyond which we put up for the night – We had several showers of rain, but none of sufficient consequence to arrest our progress, or injure the property –

29th Monday – Rainy weather, which retarded us much, but as it increased towards the afternoon we were obliged to Encamp at an earlier Hour than usual –

30th Tuesday – At an early hour we moved off but stopped for some time at Jaques River, where the Packs were examined from a suspicion of their having received some damage during the late rains – They were however all in excellent order – After this we pursued our route, and Encamped a few miles from the Prairie de *Nicholas*. Weather fine –

31st Wednesday – Left our Encampment at four AM and continued along the Lake until five, when we left it and at ten stopped to rest the Horses until two PM, when we went on, and marched till seven, when we Encamped a Short distance from the Bute de sable. Weather continues fine –

June 1st Thursday – On leaving the Encampment much delay occurred in passing through a Long Miry [boggy] Prairie in which the Horses sunk to their Bellies, and many of them could not be extricated without being unloaded. They were allowed to rest at the Little Okanagan Lake, from whence we proceeded in the afternoon to the *Barière*, or entrance of Okanagan River, where we encamped after having crossed the Property & Horses to the opposite shore – The former was crossed over in Canoes, which a band of Indians we found here lent us for the purpose – These people also supplied us with some fresh Carp, & roots – I here found a note from M[r] Ermatinger informing me of his having arrived on the 28th Ult[o], and that the next day he had dispatched an Indian over land, with my letter to M[r] Dease. The weather continues fine –

2[d] Friday – In counting over the Horses this morning it was discovered that four of the Colts were missing – Gregoire, the Horse Keeper, with an Indian, was sent in search of them –
   No danger either by accident, or otherwise, being to be apprehended between this & Oka-nagan, I left the Brigade in charge of Mess[rs] Douglas & Pambrun, and with one Man proceeded for that place where, after a pretty hard ride, I arrived at five oclock PM – I here found Mess[rs] [John] Work & Ermatinger, but not a word has been received from M[r] Dease, and I fear that some time will be lost in waiting for his people – The Boats, Eleven in number, are Pitched [or gummed, i.e., their seams chinked with resin] & ready to take in Cargoes – Which is all that can at present be done – The weather continues fine –

3[d] Saturday – At Eight oclock P.M. Mess[rs] Douglas & Pambrun arrived with the Brigade – The property is all in excellent order – And the Horses, considering the length of the voyage most of them have performed, & the condition they were in when they left Alexandria, are as well as can possibly be expected –

4th Sunday – Having as yet no intelligence from M[r] Dease I am therefore apprehensive that something has occurred to prevent the express forwarded to him on the 28th Ult[o] from reach-ing its destination – A fresh express was in consequence dispatched to day, informing him of our arrival at Okanagan – and at the same time requesting of him a supply of Horses, in addi-tion to those he has already sent, if he can spare any. We have here at present, including five belonging to the Indians of Alexandria, and the twenty sent by M[r] Dease, fifty seven – And we require altogether about a hundred – If the deficiency could be made up without having recourse to the Nez Percez Camps, it would be the means of saving much time, and of enabling me to perform the Services I have in view this summer, and which depend entirely upon my early return to New Caledonia – Leather & Cords are also requested of M[r] Dease, if he can spare any –

6th Tuesday – This Evening M[r] Dease's people arrived under the direction of M[r] [William] Kittson – They left Fort Colvil yesterday morning, which place the express forwarded on the 28th Ult[o] reached only a few minutes before their departure – for [a] copy of M[r] Deases Letter, see Correspondence [Book] N[o] 6 – by which it will be observed that no assistance in Horses is to be expected from him – indeed it is what I might have expected from the number he has already given –

The remainder of the day was occupied in appointing the people to the different Boats, and other necessary preparations for our departure from here tomorrow morning – The weather is fine & excessively warm –

7th Wednesday – This Morning the Brigade, consisting of Six Boats manned with seven men each, & loads of 35 Pieces left Okanagan for Fort Vancouver, under the Guidance of an experienced man – Pierre L'Etang – The passengers are besides myself Messrs Work, Douglas, Pambrun & Kittson – The last proceeds only to Walla Walla where he is to pass the summer with M^r [Samuel] Black – The day was fine, & the strength of the Current being proportionate to the usual height of the watters, we went on with much rapidity until seven oclock PM, when it was necessary to Encamp in order to Pitch some of the Boats that are very leaky – From some Indians we saw, a few Salmon were procured of an excellent quality –

8th Thursday – At three A.M. we were on the water and at nine reached the lower part of the Priests Rapids, where we breakfasted upon Salmon we obtained from the Indians who inhabit that place – Reembarked at ten, and arrived at Walla Walla at eight oclock PM, where we found Mr Black & people all well –

It being impossible to complete the necessary arrangements this night, connected with our departure from hence – they were therefore deferred till next day – We are here to add two Boats to the Brigade – to man which we will have to reduce the crews of the whole to Six Men, as Mr Black cannot furnish a sufficient number of hands for these two Boats – They are to Convey the returns of this place, and a quantity of Gum required for the use of Fort Vancouver – The latter part of the day was rainy, which being accompanied by a strong head wind, impeded our progress much –

9th Friday – Early in the morning the Men began to put the two Boats we take here in order, which was not effected until 11 oc[lock], when the ladings were given out & we immediately after pursued our voyage to Fort Vancouver – Having mentioned to Mr Black our necessities in regard to Horses – he informed me that the number we required he thought could be obtained without being under the Necessity of visiting the Nez perces camps, which are at a considerable distance up Lewes's [Lewis's] River [i.e., the Snake] – And a voyage to which, & time taken up in Trading – could not occupy less than fifteen or eighteen Days –

Shortly after our departure from *Walla-Walla* we met an express from Mr C. Factor McLoughlin carrying the intelligence of the Safe arrival of the ship Dryade [*Dryad*], Capt Davidson, from England, with the Columbia Outfit – But for want of Hands, and no proper craft being yet provided for the purpose her Cargo had not been yet discharged – a duty which must necessarily fall upon the people of the Brigade – And will occasion a longer stay at Fort Vancouver than I had calculated upon –

The weather was fine, and we Encamped at eight PM below the grand Rapid –

10th Saturday – At an early hour we embarked, and reached the Portage, called the *chutes*, at nine, where the assemblage of Indians was such, that it was necessary to place an armed guard at each end of it, whilst the Men were carrying the Property; this place we left at twelve PM, and got to the next portage called the Dalles at one – The concourse of Indians at this place was much greater than at the former – and the same precautions were therefore taken to preserve the property from depradation – This portage is so long that it was too late when we reached the west end to proceed any farther – and we were under the necessity of passing the night amongst these rascally Indians – Who to all appearances are the outcast of Gods Earth – They have not the smallest idea of decency, and their propensity to theft is such that nothing is safe which they have an opportunity of taking – Although a Strict watch was Kept at night, they contrived to steal a Capot and Hat from the Men – We procured from these people, and those at the Chutes, an abundant stock of Salmon for the whole Brigade for two days – in return for which they received Tobacco, Beads, Knives, and other articles of the like description – The weather was fine & very warm –

11th Sunday – Left the Portage at break of day, and proceeded down the small *dalles*, which were passed without accident – From thence to the Cascades no rapids of any consequence occur, and the distance could have been performed in little more than one day had the weather been favourable. But the contrary was the case. A westerly wind prevailed, which blowing against the current occasioned a swell which no Boat could have withstood, and confined us to the same spot for two whole days – On the Morning of the

15th Thursday – The weather moderated sufficiently to allow us to proceed – At seven oc[lock] AM we reached the portage of the Cascades, at the west end of which we Breakfasted upon excellent Salmon, which the natives gave us in abundance, on the same terms, & for Similar articles as those we procured before – At twelve PM we left the *Portage Neuf*, from whence to Fort Vancouver no danger existing I left the Brigade, and proceeded on a head with my Boat for that place, which I reached at nine oc[lock] in the Evening – Making it 42 days since I left Stuarts Lake, including three lost at Okanagan in waiting for the Fort Colvile People – M[r] C. Factor M[c]Loughlin, and the Gent[n] with him viz – Messr[s] Ar[d] M[c]donald, [Alexander] M[c]Kenzie [Donald] Manson & [Edward] Ermatinger – I found all well –

16th Friday. At 8 oclock in the Morning the Brigade arrived, and delivered their Cargoes in excellent condition with the exception of a few Furs which recently got wet –

As I have already stated, the [London] Ship was not yet unloaded – And several articles required to complete the Inland Outfits & Equipping the Men, being on Board of her – The New Caledonia people and those from the Interior of the Columbia [District] were employed upon this service – which occupied them until the 27th – The several outfits for New Caledonia, Fort Colvil, Thompsons River & Walla Walla were Packed, the Men received their advances, and in the Evening of July 4th Every thing was in readiness for our departure from Fort Vancouver –

July 5th Tuesday – Early in the Morning the ladings were given out and at twelve PM the Brigade set out on its return – It consists of nine Boats manned with each six Men including the Guide – The ladings amount to 44 pieces each, making a due allowance for the passengers consisting of myself, Messr[s] Ar[d] M[c]donald, Work, Douglas and [François] Annance, and their Families – The provisions allotted to each for their voyaging is 4 Bags Corn, 1 of Rice, 1 Keg Indian Meal and ½ Keg grease – and they are all well supplied with the requisite agrés [gear] – M[r] Pambruns indisposition continuing, I was under the necessity of leaving him at Fort Vancouver for the recovery of his Health – One of my Men was also too unwell to embark, and was therefore left behind also –

The outfit for New Caledonia, to which a few Pieces are to be added at Walla Walla & Okanagan, consists of the following Pieces – viz –

38 Bales dry Goods, Including Summer Mens orders
2 Baskets copper Kettles
6 Cases Guns
5 "   Irons
3 "   Sundry Goods
5 "   Traps
6 Bags Beaver Shot
4   Ball
9   Flour
5 Kegs Gunpowder
9   Sugar
9   Tallow
2   Brandy
3   Spirits
3   Salt
3   Butter
9 Rolls Twist Tobacco
TOTAL 120 PIECES

We are also provided with a Trading chest containing such articles as are most in demand with the natives along the route for the purpose of buying salmon which will be the means of saving a considerable quantity of our European provisions – We have also four arms chests, containing muskets & Ammunition for defence in Case of necessity – The weather was rainy and we proceeded no farther than Johnsons Island where we Encamped –

6th Wednesday – Left our Encampment at an early hour. The water is unusually high, and our progress consequently slow – Weather cloudy with some occasional showers – put up for the night three miles below the Cascades rapids, where we were visited by several Indians from whom we obtained an abundance of excellent salmon for Supper –

7th Thursday – The Boats proceeded with half cargoes to portage Neuf, over which every thing was carried – From thence they proceeded to the Cascades with half loads also – An efficient force having been left at the last portage for the Protection of the Property, the Natives being here numerous and like all those who inhabit the banks of this River, noted Thieves – They supplied us with as many Salmon as we chose to take, for which the principal demand is Tobacco a leaf of which is considered a sufficient equivalent for the largest Fish – The weather was fine and cool –

8th Friday – The people brought up the Goods from Portage Neuf early in the Morning – And after carrying over the Cascades which occupied us until three oclock PM – we departed from thence, after having procured a Stock of Salmon to last us until we get to the Dalles – And marched till seven oclock PM when we Encamped opposite the Horse Point – In the morning we had some rain, the remainder of the Day was fine –

9th Saturday – Embarked at Break of Day. And assisted by a fine aft Breeze we came almost within sight of the Dalles at Six oclock PM, when I thought it best to Encamp to avoid being pestered by the swarm of Indians who inhabit that place – One of the Boats received a Slight injury by striking on a shoal – which was however soon repaired, & occasioned but little loss of time. The weather continues fine & very pleasant –

10th Sunday – Proceeded at an Early hour – And with much labour tho' without accident in ascending the Dalles, we reached the portage of that name at five oc[lock] PM, which was too late an hour to undertake carrying over – as the whole of the property could not have been carried across – And the natives were too numerous to admit of our force being divided, the whole being required to guard the Encampment which was formed by the Boats into an oblong square in the Centre of which the different Cargoes were placed, the Tents pitched, and a regular watch appointed for the night. We here obtained a sufficient supply of Salmon for the Brigade for two days – And were also under the necessity of purchasing wood to cook our supper – an article this barren [i.e., lacking in trees, and therefore to a Bay man lacking in fur bearers, too] Country does not produce – What we procured was drift wood brought down by the floods [spring freshets] from the upper parts of the River, and drawn up by the natives for their present & winter Consumption –

In the Evening Mr Finian McDonald arrived at our Encampment, having left Messr^s McKay & Dease with their Men & property, at the East end of the Portage. These Gentlemen and Men, formed a part of the Snake Trapping Expedition under Mr Ogden – They took their Horses to Walla Walla, & are now on their way by water communication, with their Hunts, to Fort Vancouver – Mr Ogden departed from thence on the 29th Ult^o to proceed direct across the Mountains [Cascade Range], to Fort Vancouver. The success of this expedition, altho' they encountered none of the disasters they met with last year, has not been more successful in collecting Beaver – The Country they had to pass through being destitute of large animals, and not being able to Kill a sufficiency of Beaver for their subsistence – they consequently suffered much from starvation, which their appearance sufficiently bespeaks; and were obliged to return much sooner than they would otherwise have done – The weather continues fine

11th Monday – At dawn of Day the Men commenced carrying, and by eight oclock the Property and Boats were at the East end of the Portage – from whence we departed at two. Mr Finan M^cdonalds Family being on one Boat as passengers, he expressed a strong desire of accompanying them as far as Walla Walla – from whence he consented to return to Fort Vancouver, should C. Factor McLoughlin require it. To this request I did not *think proper* to oppose myself, particularly as M^r M^cdonald can be but of little service to the Boats going down, which will be quite as secure with Messr^s McKay & Dease, and he will be at Walla Walla to follow such instructions as M^r McLoughlin may think necessary to give him – he therefore embarked with us – And the last mentioned Gentlemen with their two Boats & property, left the Portage on their way down some time before we did – Passed the Chutes at five PM – And encamped two hours after some miles above them – The weather was fine & very warm –

12th Tuesday – At 4 oc[lock] AM we pursued our voyage – And in the evening passed John Days River, and encamped a few miles above it – In our progress to day we saw several small parties of Indians who appeared from their reluctance to part with their salmon, to be not very successful – The excessive heat experienced these two Days has tended much to spoil our fresh Fish, part of which it was necessary to throw away, and a bare sufficiency remains for tomorrows consumption –

13th Wednesday – A fine aft Breeze throughout the day assisted our progress very considerably –
Several Bands of Indians were seen encamped by the River who appear destitute of every
species of food excepting Roots which this Country provides in considerable variety &
abundance – The weather continues fine

14th Thursday – The wind was again in our favour, and enabled us to proceed a much greater distance than we could have done without its assistance – Encamped above the Grand Rapid –
Weather the same and heat excessive –

15th Friday – Early this Morning proceeded on our route and reached Walla Walla at twelve oclock
P.M., where I received a letter from Mr Dease, C.F. informing me that he would forward ten
horses from Ft Colvile to Okanagan for the use of New Caledonia – which number he cannot spare without inconvenience & expresses a wish that they may be replaced by Mr Black
before the Fall – This Gentleman has succeeded in Trading about 70 Horses – which would
fully answer our purpose, but Mr McLoughlin having made a large demand of these Animals,
the number required cannot I suspect be completed without making a visit to the *Nez perces*
camps – Mr Black however thinks otherwise, & I sincerely wish he may not be mistaken –
I shall wait a Day or two to ascertain the result, & then act as circumstances may require –
The Heat is really oppressive, and were it not for the westerly breezes which generally prevail,
would be intolerable –

16th Saturday – Mr Black Traded a few Horses – but at the rate he goes on, it would be far preferable to go up the *Nez perces* [Walla Walla] river at once, for every moment we remain here
I consider as lost, particularly as Mr Black is determined not to remove this Post [to the right
bank of the Columbia] at present, consequently our stay here can be of no service – The weather
continues the same –

17th Sunday – Being now convinced of the impossibility of procuring from the natives in this neighbourhood, the Horses we require – The necessary preparations were made for a visit to the
nez perces Camps – The property required was furnished out of Mr Black's outfit, and Messrs
Work, Ard Mcdonald, Douglas & Annance with 28 Men, are to depart from here tomorrow
for the above purpose – Mr Work who is appointed to conduct this business, is directed to
trade if possible 80 Horses with twenty of which he will proceed direct to Fort Colville from
the Horse Fair – And Mr Douglas in like manner will conduct the remainder to Okanagan –
The former is to be accompanied by two, & the latter by three Men – The Nez perces Chiefs
who are at present here, are to accompany our people to their Camps, & have promised to use
their influence to have the object of the Trip as speedily accomplished as possible – The weather
is the same –

18th Monday – The above party embarked in two Boats this morning to proceed on their Trip –
The period of their returning is very uncertain, and cannot be much less than twelve or fifteen
days –

Mr Work having represented to me that the detention of the Fort Colvile Outfit for any
considerable time would be highly injurious to the Trade of that post, I in consequence made
the necessary arrangements to dispatch the Boats conveying the same, from hence tomorrow
morning. In proceeding above, no danger exists farther than what is incident to the navigation, and as the Guide & Mr Kittson accompany this Brigade, I am therefore under no apprehension of serious accidents occuring in their passage – Weather as usual –

19th Tuesday – Early in the morning the Brigade under Mr Kittson, consisting of three Boats, took
its departure from Walla Walla – They are manned with 19 Men including the Guide and are
well provisioned for the voyage – The Fort Colvile outfit not being sufficient to load them,
their ladings were completed by adding a few Pieces belonging to New Caledonia & Thompsons River –

By this opportunity I forward a letter to the Governor C. Factors & Traders of the
Northern Department, giving an account of our Proceedings, so far – For [a] copy see No 9
of [the] Letter Books –

From this last date to the 24th nothing worth mentioning occurred. This day a courier arrived
from Fort Vancouver with a dispatch from C. Factor McLoughlin addressed to the Govr, C.
Factors & Traders relating to the affairs of his District, and which will be forwarded from
hence by Mr Finan McDonald who has permission to proceed upwards until he meets Governor Simpson, who is expected to revisit this Department this year – Mr McDonald therefore

prepared himself to start tomorrow, he will go direct to the Nez Perces Forks, where I expect he will arrive in time to accompany Mr Work from thence to Fort Colville

25th Thursday – Early in the morning M^r McDonald took his departure accompanied by an Indian – The Interval between this period and the return of the People from above was as barren of occurrences worth repeating as the former – And was borne by me with no small degree of impatience, reflecting that the time so idly spent might have been employed in advancing to our destination, where our early arrival this season in particular, would have been attended with beneficial results – But we could not possibly proceed without Horses, and the number required it was equally impossible to provide without recuring [resorting] to the measures we have adopted –

August 1. Tuesday – Messr^s McDonald & Annance returned from the nez perces Forks, and I was happy to find that the Object of the voyage thither had been fully accomplished. They Traded 77 Horses, which added to the two taken from hence by M^r McDonald, & one I got in exchange from Mr Kittson, forms the exact number we require – With this Band of Horses Messr^s Work, F. McDonald & Douglas proceeded yesterday morning to their respective destinations, viz the two former for F^t Colvile with 20 Horses, and the latter for Okanagan with 60 – Having nothing further to detain us here, the necessary arrangements were made for our departure tomorrow Morning –

2^d Wednesday – The day was pretty far advanced before all the Boats were in readiness – We immediately after Embarked – This Brigade consists of four Boats manned with Six men each & loaded with 36 pieces, exclusive of the Provisions required for our voyage from hence to Okanagan – For the purpose of Supplying the New Caledonia Brigade with provisions for the journey beyond Okanagan, 16 Bags of Corn & Pease were taken from this place – also a couple of Bales of sundry goods, with a number of Trap Springs of an excellent quality & which we much require, and a few other Irons [Items?] –

The Passengers are Messr^s Ar^d M^cdonald, & Annance, & myself –

Our voyage from Walla Walla was unattended with any disagreeable occurrences – And favoured with fine weather – We reached Okanagan on the

10th Thursday – Where Mr Douglas had arrived five days before with the Band of Horses all safe, tho' many of them are too lean to proceed any further until they recover their Flesh – The Band of Horses I left there in the Spring are all recovered of their [pack saddle] sores, and in good order, excepting some of those that were lately gelded – An operation it was necessary they should undergo, to avoid the immensity of trouble they give us in the spring, being again repeated – Gregoire the Horse Keeper had with the assistance of Mr F. Ermatinger repaired all the Horse appointments as well as his means permitted –

The two following Days were occupied in completing the arrangements for our departure from hence, i e, in tying up the various packages, dividing the Men & Horses into Brigades &tc &tc – And on the

13th Sunday – Every thing being in readiness, the Brigade consisting of 80 loaded Horses and 24 Men, moved off – We have also nine light Horses, which tho' very poor, will occassionally have to relieve such as may fail along the way – Our Men are likewise all mounted, having sold a Horse, of the most inferior Kind, to such as had none, a few of them having been provided by the Thompsons River people who had Horses to spare – To the outfit from F^t Vancouver we added at this place 6 Bales of dry Goods, including a considerable proportion of damaged and unsaleable property, which I take in hopes of being able to dispose of it to some advantage, also 1 Bag Shot, 4 Kegs Tallow & 1 Case Iron works –

Many of the Horses having never before carried loads – a similar inconvenience to that experienced on leaving Alexandria, again occurred, By Kicking and prancing, they contrived to throw off their burthens, to which the bad quality of the Cords tended not a little, being too weak to resist the violent motions of the wild Brutes – In the course of an hour the Plain of Okanagan was covered with Pieces, and three Bags of Corn which were torn in the confusion were entirely lost – It was night before they were all collected & every thing readjusted. In this case, as in all others where his services could be of use, we received every possible assistance from Mr Ermatinger – Who even deprived himself of his own private property to repair our damages, and enable us to get on –

From this place I addressed a letter to the Governor, C. Factors & Traders, for [a] Copy of which see Letter Book N° 11 – Amongst other matters, I notice our vantages from the Columbia

Gentlemen for the ensuing spring – in order to avoid any misunderstanding or disappointment – The weather continues fine, indeed since we left Vancouver the sky has been seldom
clouded, and was not the air refreshed by frequent gales – the heat would be insupportable –

14ᵗʰ Monday – This morning I left Okanagan & overtook the Brigade at seven oclock – Mʳ
Douglas who encamped with it last night was going on as well as could be expected – The
Horses were not so troublesome as yesterday – And after proceeding a distance of about 21
Miles we Encamped near the River *de la Guère* –

Mʳ Annance & two of the Thompsons River Men accompany us – This person is sent on
ahead to Kamloops – Mʳ Arᵈ Mᶜdonald who is appointed to the charge of that place remains
at Okanagan to wait Governor Simpsons Arrival – The weather is fine & pleasant –

15ᵗʰ Tuesday – At an early hour the Horses were caught & loaded without much trouble, and few
of them seemed inclined to repeat the pranks of the two preceding days – We proceeded on
for four Hours, when we stopped at the little *chutes* to refresh the Horses, after which we went
on and encamped beyond the hill of the little chutes – The benifit we derived from allowing
the Horses to rest daily on our way out was so eminent, that the same practice will be observed
in our return – Washing their backs with cold water is also of much service to the poor
Animals. This was begun to day and shall be continued – We have a long Journey to perform
without the least hope of obtaining succours along the way, too much care cannot therefore
be taken of the Horses –

We made to day about 22 Miles – I mean to go on quickly until the Horses are inured to
fatigue, and sufficiently advanced in their Journey to insure their being able to accomplish it
without failing – for experience sufficiently teaches that when a Horse is once Jaded, he
cannot recover during the continuance of a voyage – Weather continues fine –

16ᵗʰ Wednesday – At four oclock AM, (the hour at which I am to commence every succeeding
Days march) we proceeded from our Encampment – passed two Rivulets one of which is
distinguished by the name of Bonaparte – And at Eleven reached the Bariere, or entrance
of the Okanagan River, which we crossed by means of Canoes we hired from a small party of
Indians we found here – The Horses swam over and got safely across, excepting one which
was unfortunately drowned – He happens luckily to have been one of the worst we had –
Encamped for the night at this place, where feeding for the Horses is abundant but the flies
are numerous & annoy them much – Advanced to day about 18 miles – Our march was through
a fine level Country – And the Horses being now rather fatigued go on quietly and in
regular order – Weather the same as yesterday –

17ᵗʰ Thursday – The Horses having strayed to a considerable distance, it was rather later than usual
when we left our Encampment – After advancing about 15 miles we Stopped for a few Hours
at *Riviere au Thé* – In the afternoon proceeded 11 miles farther to the Bute de Sable, where
we put up for the night – Weather continues fine –

18ᵗʰ Friday – At four we were on the march – And proceeded on without Halting (having met with
no place in our route where the Horses could feed) to Riviere au Serpent, when we Encamped
– The Horses are much fatigued, & many of them have swellings on the sides occasioned by
the Kegs, and other hard pieces they carry – The country we are now in is completely parched
up, & in many places has been lately overrun by fire, consequently affords but scanty subsistence for the Horses, which added to the miryads of insects by which they are tormented night
and day, reduces the poor beasts very much –

19 Saturday – The Country through which we now pass being inhabited by Horse thieves, we
commenced last night to mount guards – At an early Hour pursued our route in the course
of which we passed *Riviere du Poulin, Riviere de la Fruite*, & rested the Horses for four Hours
at the little River that runs through the *Prairie de Nicholas* – At three oc[lock] PM our march
was resumed, and at half an hour after four reached the Banks of the Okanagan Lake, which
we followed about nine miles & then Encamped – Feeding for the Horses now better than
usual – Distance to day about 28 miles – Weather continues fine, & very warm –

20ᵗʰ Sunday – On mustering the Horses this morning two of them were missing. [An] immediate
search was made for them, and in the course of an hour they were brought back – This
accident retarded our departure beyond the usual hour – Passed *Riviere au Jaque, aux des Borgne*,
and allowed the Horses some repose at *L'Ence [Anse?] de Sable* – In the afternoon proceeded
to the *Bûte*, where we Encamped – Distance about 24 Miles – Weather the same –

21st Monday – Before reaching the *Mauvais Rocher*, the Horses were allowed to rest – In the afternoon we went on, & in passing the above mentioned place one of the Horses Slipped and fell over the precipice, where he was literally dashed to Pieces – His load, consisting of two Bales of dry Goods, received no other injury than having the corners very much torn – This misfortune having roused our attention, this dangerous spot, where several accidents of the same nature as just described have already occurred – was so far improved in the course of half an hour as to divest it of all its terrors, and the remainder of the Brigade passed it in safety – Encamped at *Riviere a la Biche* at an earlier hour than usual – The excellent feeding we found here, and of which the Horses have been deprived for some days, will fully compensate for the few Hours we lose – Distance to day 20 Miles – Weather as usual –

22^d Tuesday – At an early hour commenced our march; passed *Rivière au paquets*, and rested for a few hours at Mr Jacques Encampment. In the afternoons march we passed *Rivière de Squirés*, *Rivière des Birges*, and Encamped at *Riviere de Table d'Epinette*, where we found excellent feeding for the Horses – Our route to day was particularly rugged, & fatiguing to the Horses – Distance about 25 Miles – Weather the same –

23^d Wednesday – A Heavy Shower overtook us at *Lac en Rond* where it detained us for four Hours – The weather after that became Settled, and we proceeded on to the Entrance of the Grand Prairie, where we encamped – Distance to day about 24 Miles

24th Thursday – Set out an early hour, and rested the Horses at *Campement du Poulin* – from thence we proceeded on & reached the south Branch of Thompsons River at Six oclock PM, where we Encamped – A man was sent to a fishing place above, to which the natives generally resort at this season, in order to procure a Canoe or two to ferry over our Baggage – he returned at night with information that the Indians would be with us early tomorrow morning with the Canoes requested – The roads to day were pretty good, & weather fine –

25th Friday – The Indians were as good as their word, and came down with the canoes early in the morning – And by Eleven oclock the Baggage & people were all ferried over – The Horses crossed by swimming, and tho' the river is of course double breadth, they all reached the opposite shore in safety – At one pm we resumed our Journey – having previously given the Indians a suitable recompense for the loan of their canoes, as well as for some fresh Salmon with which they had supplied us – At sun set we reached the Fort of Kamloops, where I received a visit from *Constipatte*, the chief of the gang who inhabit the adjacent Country, to whom I made a present of a calico Shirt, a little Ammunition and Tobacco – Altho' he is a notorious rogue it is however expedient to Keep on good terms with the fellow, as perhaps otherwise our Horses might suffice, his followers being well Known for their dexterity in stealing those Animals – The property we left here in the Spring, was Stolen during the summer, which gives me but a poor opinion of *Nicholas'* influence over his Tribe, & for which he is so much celebrated –

Weather the same as yesterday – Distance from this crossing place to Kamloops about 16 Miles –

26th Saturday – Early in the Morning the Horses were mustered, but before we set off, an Indian who had sold a Horse to one of our Men in the Spring, being dissatisfied with his bargain, or from some other motive, attempted to take the Horse back, and had the insolence to take hold of him with that intent – for which offence he got what he deserved a good drubbing; the impudence of these rascals has been too long borne, and to such a reprehensible degree – that I am resolved they shall meet with no unmerited indulgence from me –

Our route was through level country, and at night we encamped a short distance from the *Pineux*, having baited our Horses at Rivière du Milieu – Distance about 21 Miles – Weather Beautiful –

27th Sunday – The road we passed through this morning was excessively bad, and fatiguing for the Horses, one of which rolled down with his load from a considerable height into the river, but without having received any apparent injury – Allowed the Horses their accustomed rest after which we proceeded on to the Bariere where we put up for the night – A Small Band of Indians we found at this place supplied us with Salmon for supper, & for the consumption of the next day – Weather the same as yesterday – Advance about 25 Miles –

28th Monday – Pursued our route at an early hour, and stopped to rest the Horses at the Grand Prairie from whence we proceeded at one oclock PM – and at dark reached the Traverse of the North Branch of Thompsons River, where of course we Encamped – The roads were equally as bad as those we passed through yesterday – And this was the longest days march we have yet performed – about 30 Miles – We here found the old Chief & his Family, who furnished us with an ample supply of fresh Salmon for Supper – I applied to him for Canoes to cross over our baggage – which he promised to bring the next morning – Weather as usual – fine; –

29th Tuesday – Agreeable to the promise made last night the Chief brought us three Canoes, & himself, & his young Men, assisted to cross our property to the opposite side, which was accomplished by one oclock P.M. – The Horses also got over without accident, and at four oclock PM we left Thompsons River, and proceeded about eight miles beyond it, when we Encamped – The Chief and some of his followers accompanied us to the Encampment, whither they brought a sufficiency of dry Salmon for the consumption of two days, which I paid for with ammunition & Tobacco – And in consideration of his services this day, & of his childrens good conduct in the spring (the particulars of which are related in page 10 [17-18 May]) I made him a present of a Shirt, with some Ammunition and Tobacco; and to each of his Sons I also gave a handsome supply of both the latter articles – Weather continues fine – Advance to day about 10 miles –

30th Wednesday – The road in the Mountain which we are now about to cross being very much obstructed with fallen trees – And many marshes which are almost impassable – Mr Douglas with Six Men proceeded ahead to clear away the former, & to throw bridges over the latter to prevent the Horses from sinking – About three hours after the Brigade moved off, and at five oclock PM, reached the swamp, the only spot in this Mountain which furnishes any Kind of subsistence for Horses, and where of course we Encamped – The road we have passed through, tho' naturally bad, is susceptible of much improvement, which however can never be effected by a passing Brigade – Weather fine & cool – distance to day about 24 Miles –

31st Thursday – Mr Douglas & Party set out again early in the morning for the same purpose as yesterday, the remainder of the Mountain being equally in want of repairs as the part we have already passed – At nine AM The Brigade moved forward, and reached a fine Plain at the west end of the Mountain at two oc[lock], PM, where we Encamped for the night; none of the Horses appears at all exhausted, and there can now be little doubt of our reaching the end of our Journey in perfect safety – We have now got into quite a different climate from the other side of the Mountain, the nights are frosty and the days cool & pleasant – And vegetation being still in full vigour, affords the Horses a luxurious abundance – Distance performed to day, about 15 miles –

September 1st Friday – The Horses having strayed during the night to a considerable distance, the Sun was up before they were collected and loaded – We then moved through a rugged country to the western extremity of *Lac du Rocher*, where we baited the Horses – We then went on & reached *Lac Tranquille* at Six oc[lock] PM, where we Encamped – It was here observed that the light, or extra Horse, belonging to *Plessés'* and Thomas' Brigades was missing – The former was therefore sent in search of him. In the morning muster, he was amongst the rest but it is suspected that he Skulked off before the Brigade started; and he must be at our last Encampment – The weather continues beautiful; and food for the Horses abundant, and of an excellent quality – Distance about 28 Miles –

2d Saturday – Plessés overtook us this morning but without the Horse; And in conformity to what was all along held out to them, that their own Horses would be taken to replace any that should be lost by negligence, Plessés' Horse was in consequence added to the Brigade – Our route this morning was much obstructed by fallen Trees – but in the afternoons march we found the roads excellent, and reached the drowned Horse Lake at six oclock PM where we Encamp – Fine weather continues, distance about 27 Miles –

3d Sunday – Started at an Early hour, and reached the Beaver Dam River at nine AM, the water of which has sufficiently subsided to admit of the horses fording it with their loads – A Short distance from this, is the Bridge river, where we halted for three Hours; when we resumed our Journey, and got to the White Earth Lake at seven PM, where we Encamped – The weather being cool and pleasant, and food for the Horses very abundant, they can perform long days marches without any risk of endangering their reaching the end of their Journey in safety –

4th Monday – After proceeding four hours and a half we baited the Horses at the western extremity of Axe Lake, where we saw a few Indians, who had nothing to dispose of but a few Berries – In the afternoon we went on and Encamped at seven oclock – Days march about 30 Miles

– The roads are beautiful, the weather equally so, and food for our Horses in such abundance they generally graze as they go along – And some who were rather weak when we left the Mountain, have now recovered their strength, and carry their burthens with sufficient Ease –

5ᵗʰ Tuesday – Frasers River being at no great distance, I sent off the Interpreter *Lo-Lo* this morning to go and visit the Indians who Inhabit its Banks, to procure some salmon, with which he will rejoin us at the Encampment – The Brigade went on at the usual hour; baited the Horses at McBeans Lake, after which we proceeded on until half after seven PM when we [made] Encampment on the same spot where we passed the night of the 12ᵗʰ May – *Lo-Lo* overtook us here with a party of Indians from whom we received a good supply of Salmon for two days, which we paid for with Ammunition & Tobacco – From these people we learn that several Bloody Battles had been fought in [the] course of the Summer between the Natives of Alexandria, and the Chilcotins – I trust these reports are exaggerated – but even after making due allowances for Indian stories, I dread much that Hostilities between these two Tribes have not yet ceased – Weather continues fine – Days march about 30 Miles –

6ᵗʰ Wednesday – The Indians who Encamped with us having contrived during the night to steal a Bundle containing the whole of Joseph Porteur's property – And all our endeavours to discover the Thief & recover the property having proved ineffectual – we took two of their Horses from them as some Kind of equivalent for the Stolen property and as a punishment necessary to be inflicted to prevent a recurrence of similar practices – At the same time they were told that their Horses should be returned when the stolen property was restored –

This affair occupied some time & prevented our departure until Six oclock – At eight we reached the Banks of Frasers River, and at two Halted for a couple of Hours – when we resumed our Journey, and got to our Encampment of the 10ᵗʰ of May at eight oc[lock] PM – where we put up for the night – The Little *Atnah* Chief, with a few of his followers, paid me a visit – To the first I gave a Shirt and a piece of Tobacco – and to the rest each a piece of Tobacco – These people are employed curing Salmon, which they complain is rather scarce – however it is Still early in the season, and they may yet be abundant – They also in some measure, confirm the reports we had yesterday in regard to the Alexandrians & Chilcotins – but this will be cleared up tomorrow, when I expect to arrive early at the Fort – Weather Beautiful – March about 34 Miles –

7ᵗʰ Thursday – Early in the morning I left the Brigade in charge of Mr Douglas, and proceeded towards Alexandria, where I arrived at Seven oclock AM, and the Brigade two Hours after – with every article of Property in excellent order, excepting two Guns, one of which was broken by accident – And the other by the negligence of one of the Men – Our Horses are, to appearances, all healthy and those that left Okanagan in good order, are not much reduced – but many of them have sore backs & sides, which will take some time to cure – Our voyage has occupied from Okanagan to this place exactly 25 Days, during which the weather was particularly favourable – And I believe it hardly possible for a Brigade consisting of the same number of Horses, and with equal loads, to perform it in less time –

Mr Yale and his two Men, I was happy to find in perfect health, but they have passed a most anxious summer in consequence of the disturbances between the Indians of this place & the Chilcotins –

The former unfortunately could not be prevented from going on a war excursion against the latter in the early part of the summer, when by their own account they Killed nine of their Enemies and took two women prisoners – The Chilcotins in return have paid them two visits, in the first of which they Killed the only Talk-o-tin in this vicinity – And in the second, which happened yesterday evening, they killed two women, & desperately wounded a Man almost within sight of the Fort – The Indians here are Encamped within fifty yards of the Fort Pickets, & were preparing, when I made my appearance, to pursue the Chilcotins – This ardour I have however endeavoured to check, by desiring them not to move until they had heard my opinion on the subject – This delay will give them time to cool, and it will then be less difficult to persuade them to relinquish their intention – which if executed, could only tend to widen the breach between the two Tribes, and destroy every hope of Peace being restored this season – An object of the utmost importance to us as experience now confirms that the injury I apprehended would result from this unfortunate warfare, has been realized and [not] until its termination, can we expect any great alteration in our favour – The returns of this season amount to about 3 Packs, being hardly a fourth of what was usually procured during the same period, and that which has been obtained from some Indians of *Klu-Kuz* who visited the place, unconscious of the existing disturbances – Since that period no stranger has been seen about the place – Those Indians who usually inhabited the banks of River above, and which they deserted at the commencement of these troubles – still continue in their retreats in the mountains to the Eastward and about Bears Lake – where it may naturally be supposed that but a Small portion of their time has been occupied in Hunting Beaver –

The Talkotins, or Indians who inhabit the plains, it may be immagined have done nothing in the Fur way – nor do they even appear disposed to provide Salmon for their Support the ensuing winter – They have no other means of procuring subsistence but what the waters supply – And if the opportunity is lost, no other resource is left them, and they must inevitably starve – I shall endeavour to rouse them to a sense of the calamities which must overtake them by continuing in the state of inaction in which they at present are –

The *Atnahs* below are busily employed in curing Salmon and it is hoped will be able to spare us a few thousand, which added to 7,000 remaining of the last years Stock, will suffice for the Consumption of this Establishment –

To Mr Yale every praise is due for having preserved the Establishment from insult – Neither of the Contending parties offered the least violence, and notwithstanding their invitracy [?] towards each other – And the Jealousy it might be supposed the Chilcotins would entertain from an idea that their Enemies were supported by the whites, they made no attempt to injure us – The first party of Chilcotins that came across showed themselves on the opposite side of the River. They were thirty Six Men. They spoke for a long while but the distance was too great to distinguish what they said – And Mr Yale could not with any degree of prudence trust himself amongst them – It is however pretty certain that they had no hostile intentions against us – for if they had, opportunities offered of perpetrating the murder of Mr Yale's two men, who were daily employed at a considerable distance from the Fort –

The Store has been completed – all but the upper flooring which is not quite finished – And a new House to lodge the Men is considerably advanced – In Short Mr Yales conduct gives me entire satisfaction –

8th Friday – The Goods were unpacked, and what is requisite to form the outfit of this post was laid aside – in addition to the usual supplies, a sufficiency is also left for the Chilcotin Tribe in case an opportunity should occur of renewing our intercourse with them –

In the Evening the Indians were invited to the House, where my opinion in regard to the existing troubles as well as the course to be followed which I conceived the best calculated to restore peace between them and the Chilcotins, was stated – As a preliminary, I insisted upon their relinquishing all ideas of retaliation for the last aggression, thereby setting an example of moderation, which could not fail of convincing their Enemies of the sincerity of their intentions to heal up the breach between them – In the mean time I proposed to send one of the *Atnah* chiefs (who are on friendly terms with both parties) to inform the chilcotins of this, and to require that on their part a similar conduct should be observed; and that in the event of their compliance – to assure them that another excursion to their Country should be made by us in the Early part of the winter – And that the promise I made them of giving them a Post, should positively be fulfilled next summer. On the other hand, if they refused to come to terms – we would in that case be compelled to take the part of those who were disposed to be quiet, and we would not, as hitherto, allow them to be Butchered at our very gates without assisting them with the means of defending themselves –

These proposals appeared satisfactory to the *Talkotins*, but they required time to consider of them, and I allowed them till tomorrow to return me an answer –

The *Atnah Chief* who has offered to be the bearer of the above message to the chilcotins, was present during this conference, and as he perfectly understands the language in which the Indians were addressed, he will therefore be able to give a correct account of what passed to those people – which he promises faithfully to do – This is all that can be done at present in relation to this unfortunate affair, & I trust these steps will tend to bring on the so much desired reconciliation – And by quieting the minds of the Indians of this place, they will pay more attention to their Fishing, and avert the calamity which must unavoidably attend a continued neglect of that important object –

Salmon appears to be scarce, but the Fishing weirs are so badly attended to that it is probably more owing to that circumstance, than to real scarcity, that so few are caught – The natives have large quantities of dry berries (which this season has produced in great abundance) and as they are disposed to part with them at a moderate price – I have directed Mr Yale to purchase all they have to spare – They will, in the event of Salmon being scarce, answer as a substitute for that article – The Gardens look well – And their produce will likewise assist to weather out the Winter –

The Men were employed repairing the injuries the Canoes received from the summer heats – And tomorrow I expect that every thing I have to do here will be accomplished –

9th Saturday – The Indians returned me their answer to day – which was that they agree to be guided by my advice on every point – The *Atnah Chief* who has undertaken to act as a mediator, took his departure to execute his mission, which he promises faithfully to perform – And return with the answer of the chilcotins as soon as the sense of the Tribe was obtained on the subject – To *Chin las nel* the principal Chief I made a present of a Shirt, with a Hat, and Leather – To the father of two of the young Men who were Killed in the Spring, a shirt, and to *Pa-han* the second chief whose brother was killed this summer, a p^r Leggins – And to each of them a piece of Tobacco – with which they all appeared satisfied – by the bye their presents were more than they had any right to expect – And were made mainly on account of their ready compliance with my wishes –

The Outfit was all delivered, and is as complete, excepting in the article of leather, which cannot at present be furnished, as can be desired – Capots are rather scarce but we have [an] abundance of cloth to make them with – before night every thing was repacked & put in readiness for our departure from here tomorrow morning –

A Omnipotent Gentleman [Governor George Simpson] being expected in this year – this place from its importance, & existing circumstances, is the best suited for his residence – And ought to be his station, unless the Council [of the Northern Department] point out some other post for that purpose – being uncertain by which route he may come in. I leave a letter for him here, in case of his passing by Okanagan, conveying my opinion relative to the present state of affairs at this Post – The measures I have thought it proper to adopt, and suggesting the principal duties to be attended to – for the rest I refer him to Mr Yale, who in the interval, will continue in charge of the place, and on whose statements he may perfectly rely –

The only method which holds out any prospect of recovering our lost ground here, will be to visit the natives on the grounds where they at present hunt, to carry them Supplies, receive their Furs, and encourage them to make future Hunts by a promise of repeating our visits whenever necessary – By this means they will probably be induced to do something – but if this plan is neglected, little can be expected from them – And the failure in the returns will be complete – The experience of this summer proves conclusively, that during the continuance of the present troubles they will not frequent the Fort – And without the expectation of obtaining supplies, it is equally certain that they will not Hunt – Another duty to be performed this Autumn is to examine this River between the head of the Rapids & the mouth of Thompsons River, in order to ascertain whether the Navigation is practicable, and if found not to be so, to enquire into the easiest mode of overcoming this difficulty – But the chief duty to be attended to, is to endeavour to restore peace amongst the Natives – on which the present prosperity of Alexandria, and our future prospects of advantage from our extension of the Trade in this district, entirely hang – To the attainment of this most desirable object, every other consideration must be sacrificed –

Five Men will remain for the present with Mr Yale – the rest being required to take up the canoes – besides it would be imprudent to have a greater force than is wanted from the appearance of a Scarcity of provisions being experienced – A Force competent to all the duties which are to be performed here, will be furnished by the time it is required –

To avert as far as lays in our power similar disasters to those of last year [the heavy loss of horses to winter snow and cold in early 1826] – Mr Yale is directed to provide as much hay as possible for the support of such of the Horses as may require it – The grass in this neighbourhood is far more luxuriant than last year – And as this season can hardly be expected to be so severe, I have sanguine expectations that our Horses will pass it in safety – It behoves us nevertheless, to take every possible precaution by which their preservation may be ensured –

A few of those Atnahs belonging to the Camp from whence we took the Horses on the 6th Ins[t] having accompanied us to the Fort, I thought it most consistent with Justice & policy, to restore them their Horses, exacting at the same time a promise from them, to return the Stolen property if they could discover the Thief – In the first place it appears to me that the person to whom the Horses belong was not concerned in the theft – And secondly they would no doubt attempt to steal back their Horses, & with them probably take some of ours, which would unavoidably lead to a quarrel which at this time particularly, it would be highly injurious to enter into – For [a] Copy of the above Letter see Correspondence [Book] N° 12, –

10th Sunday – In the Morning we departed from Alexandria to proceed up the River to Stuarts Lake – The Brigade consists of four Canoes, three of which are loaded with each 28 pieces and manned by five Men, and mine with M[r] Douglas who embarks with me, has 18 pieces, and Six Men – I was under the necessity of leaving 12 pieces of sundry property (none of it however essential to complete the Fall Outfits,) which could not be embarked without overloading the Canoes and endangering their safety in the rapids – These goods shall be sent for before the closure of the Navigation [i.e., before freeze-up], if possible – We are provided with provisions for ten days – And expect to procure a sufficiency for the Completion of our voyage along the way – A short time after our departure it commenced raining, which continued all day – After the extraordinary series of fine weather we have had I fear we will experience a proportionate duration of bad – At seven P.M. we Encamped at *Sto-ni-yâ*

11th Monday – At Break of day we embarked, and in the course of it passed two small parties of Indians who appeared to be not sufficiently apprehensive of the Chilcotins to induce them to quit the banks of the River – They are occupied Fishing, & are pretty successful – from them we procured a few fresh Salmon – Encamped at Quesnels River – Cloudy weather –

12th Tuesday – Early in the night it commenced raining which continued by intervals throughout the day – In passing at the Rascals village we saw only a couple of Indians – They confirm the reports that the numerous body of Indians who usually inhabit this place had retreated from the Banks of the River towards Bear Lake, and the sources of Quesnels River, but whether they have done any thing in the Fur way is not known – To both those places salmon ascends – And they will I hope be able to provide the means of subsistence for the ensuing Winter – Encamped at the foot of the Rapid above Rivière au Liard –

13th Wednesday – Embarked at an early hour – Rain again best part of the day – Reached the head of the Rapid at 9 oc[lock] AM, having carried part of the Cargoes over – The Current is extremely strong, & our progress proportionately slow – Encamped at the West road River –

14th Thursday – Rained heavily all day – It did not however prevent us from proceeding – At nine AM we came up with a band of Indians, whom we found employed in curing salmon, of which they already have a considerable quantity – These people altho' too distant from the Scene of Action to be under any apprehension from the Chilcotins, are nevertheless too much in dread of those people to venture to visit Alexandria – to which place they belong – I therefore promised them in conformity with the plan laid down, that the people of that establishment should bring them their usual supplies either late this Fall, or in the commencement of the Winter – These people have a few skins – And promise to endeavour to make up their usual Hunts – At two PM we came up with old *chilquettes* Band, whence after remaining about an hour, we went on to a third [band], where we Encamped – These like the first are all occupied curing Salmon, & have also a few skins – The latter they offered to give me, but as they have all debts at Alexandria – to avoid any confusion in their accounts, I left them their furs to be delivered to the people of that post, when they come up with their supplies – Of Salmon I procured a sufficiency which without any other help, would serve the Brigade to Stuarts Lake – by the means of which and some given gratis – they were all supplied with Ammunition for their Fall Hunts – on which they are to go as soon as the Salmon Fishing ceases –

15th Friday – At Break of day we Embarked – found the Current exceedingly strong – the river in this part being confined within a very narrow channel – Reached the Stony Islands at too late an hour to attempt ascending the Rapid, we therefore encamped below it – Cloudy weather, but no rain –

16th Saturday – Passed the Rapids without accident tho' one of the Canoes occasioned us some loss of time by having taken a wrong channel –

In the Evening we met *Ho del to*, the Chief of the west road river – who was on his return from Bear Lake where he had made his Hunt – in which however he was not very successful, from the extraordinary height of the waters during the spring months (An evil of which every Indian I have hitherto seen has complained). He informed that the Natives who are about Bears Lake, have not been altogether idle – that most of them have Furs, and that they all intend to make Fall Hunts – If their reports are correct, I have less reason to despair of Alexandria, than I at first suspected – I will endeavour to inform them of our intentions of visiting them early in the winter – it is important that they should be acquainted with this, as they would otherwise perhaps feel a disinclination to work, from the small hope they would have of receiving any supplies –

From this Indian I learn that the people, as was directed in the spring, are on the way up to the sources of the east branch of this River [i.e., the uppermost Fraser] to fetch the Leather which is to be furnished by the Sascatchewan people – They slept last night at the Forks [Fraser-Nechako junction], and departed from Hodelto this morning – Waccan is one of the party, having been, as I am informed in a letter from M^r McDougall of the 11th Ins^t, sent to procure a Guide, in place of that old Rogue Tete Jaune who has deceived us – I also received letters from Messr^s Ross & McDonald of the 5th & 7th Ins^ts – which contain nothing of an agreeable nature – The returns have failed throughout the Department [New Caledonia], owing it appears to the uncommon height of the waters during the most favourable period for Hunting Beaver – for Copies of these letters see Correspondence [Books] N°s 13, 14, 15. – I shall make no comment upon the summers Transactions, until I have an opportunity of being better acquainted with them – To *Holdelto* I gave a shirt & some ammunition, and he is to proceed immediately to his old Hunting grounds about the Salmon River, together with his Band – where he expects to make well out – These Indians are all supplied with the means of Hunting – until such time as we can again replenish their stock –

In the evening we came up with old *Chu tiass* & his small party who also gave us Salmon – The old fellow had Eleven Skins, and being their only furs, I advanced him a Blanket of 3 p^ts, upon which he now owes five Beaver – We proceeded a little farther where we Encamped about two miles below the forks – The weather was fine, the first entire fair day we have had since leaving Alexandria –

17th Sunday – Early in the morning we passed the Forks, and at nine AM came up with a couple of Indians, who are, as all those we have hitherto seen Employed curing Salmon. from these also we procured a few, both fresh and dry – The Chief *Tu-ar* is off a hunting Beaver with a few of his followers; and the rest are to follow shortly – These Indians during the existence of Fort George made excellent Hunts, but since the first year after the abandonment of that Post they have done but little – Nor can it be reestablished until the Cause which induced this measure is removed – (ie., the death of the Rascal who perpetrated the murders at that place – In the Evening we met an Indian called *Tal-pay* who informed me that he had a few Furs which he was desirous of giving in part of his debt at Frasers Lake – He was requested to go for them, and in the mean time the Brigade continued on, and reached a place called *Hamilto* where we Encamped – The Indians we found here also supplied us with Salmon – And have a greater quantity than any of those we have hitherto seen – Weather cloudy –

18th Monday – Rained during the last night, and occasionally throughout the day, but not sufficiently to arrest our progress until towards evening when it increased to a complete pour, which obliged us to encamp at an earlier hour than we wished – At *Chal-a-oo-cheeks* which we passed in the morning we saw *Naw-whalh-Tele*, the Chief, and his band, who have very few furs, and no less abundance of Salmon – All we could get from them was a sufficiency for one meal – In the afternoon we were overtaken by *Telpay* who proceeded in company & Encamped with us – He delivered me nine Beaver Skins in part of his debts – And I advanced him two steel Traps which he expressed a wish of obtaining to enable him to Hunt – I also made him a present of a little Ammunition & Tobacco – He bears the character of being an industrious Indian, but for some time passed has been very unwell – he is now on the recovery, & promises to exert himself – I have thought it advisable to reduce the steel Traps from 15 to 8 Beaver each – The former price was so exorbitant that it put it out of the power of many to procure any each – And of the whole to provide themselves with the number they require to make successful Hunts –

19th Tuesday – Embarked at dawn of day. In our progress we passed two small parties of Indians, from whom we got a few Fresh Salmon. They tell us it is only within these eight days that they are caught here in any abundance – Encamped about ten miles below Chinlac – on the forks formed by the Rivers issuing from Stuarts and Frasers Lakes – Rained at intervals throughout the Day –

20th Wednesday – Proceeded early in the morning, & reached the forks of Chinlac at ten oclock, where a small band of Indians have Encamped who also supplied us with Salmon – At Eleven we proceeded from thence, and Encamped at Seven, in the midst of a long chain of Rapids, the upper end of which we will not gain until tomorrow night – The day was fine, but in the Evening it recommenced raining, with an appearance of its continuing all night –

21st Thursday – Rained best part of the night, and during the Day we had several showers – In the Evening we got to the head of the Rapids, from whence to Stuarts Lake the water is smooth and Current weak, with the exception of a couple of small Rapids –

22d Friday – At Break of day we Embarked, and having met with no obstructions we proceeded a long distance, and Encamped a few miles below *Qua*'s old village – We again had several showers of Rain –

23d Saturday – Two Hours before Day light we proceeded from our Encampment, and reached the Entrance of Stuarts Lake at 12 oc[lock] PM, & the Fort an hour after – where I found Mr George Mcdougall & people belonging to the Establishment all well – or at least alive, for they have passed a wretched Summer which their appearance sufficiently bespeaks.

Chief Factor Connolly had, in fact, left the brigade on the evening of the 22nd and proceeded ahead. The brigade itself arrived in the afternoon of the 23rd "and delivered all the property Complete." Connolly feared that "the goods are not all in very good order" because of the rainy weather since Alexandria; however, all of the next day was spent "opening and Examining the Bales and different Packages of Goods, which were found in better Condition than I had reason to expect." "A few only of the dry Goods are wet," he added, "but not an article was found any ways damaged." On the 25th "the Property was all assorted, and Every thing completely dried," and the 26th "was occupied in Laying aside the different outfits, which tomorrow I expect will be packed ready to be forwarded to their respective destinations the day after." The brigade had taken but four and a half months to go to Fort Vancouver and back, and it had returned to Stuart's Lake a month and a half earlier than that from York Factory. Moreover, no returns, supplies, or lives had been lost. And all this in spite of the heavy loss of pack horses at Alexandria in the winter of 1825-26 and the fact that the outfits were not ready and waiting for the brigade at Fort Vancouver but had to be unloaded from the London ship by the brigaders themselves. The new brigade route had definitely proven a success.

There was little else for Connolly to celebrate, however, for he was immediately confronted by some worrisome problems. Most important, he found "with the greatest concern ... that the [summer's] Trade has been less productive than was perhaps ever before known," owing to the very high water level in the spring. He anticipated alleviating this "General and unfortunate failure," incidentally, by tapping the furs of the natives of the Babine Lake region, "a large proportion of which, we understand, are yearly disposed of to the Indians of the Sea Coast, by whom they are visited at regular periods" (23 September). Connolly was referring to the diversion of beaver skins to the coast from the interior by native middlemen for sale to American shipmasters, who in this way had been sustaining their atrophic sea otter trade. Governor Simpson was about to undermine this traffic through a policy of dispatching ships to, and establishing posts on, the coast and deliberately underselling the American traders.

Connolly was also facing a shortage of servants and victuals. At "Fort Simpson" (McLeod's Lake) one of Clerk John Tod's two men had died in July, and the other "from his age hardly deserving the name of a Man," so that "Mr Tod may therefore be said to have passed the summer alone" (23 September). Also, "from the extraordinary height of the waters, the Men who accompanied the Brigade for York Factory as far as the Rocky Mountain Portage, experienced on their return, the utmost difficulty, and from the unexpected Length of time they took suffered much from starvation" (23 September). The summer salmon run was disappointing. It was early but light, and "in Consequence of no fresh fish having been caught the people had to live upon the old Salmon which originally was of a very bad quality, and suffered as much privation as if they had occasionally been entirely without any thing to eat, for nothing worse can be immagined than this bad old dry salmon" (23 September). To make matters worse, the garden at Stuart's Lake, at least, "exhibits a poor appearance, and does not promise a very good Crop" (23 September). There was obviously much work to be done before the onset of New Caledonia's long, cold winter.

Peter Warren Dease's Journal of the Brigade from New Caledonia to Fort Vancouver and Return, 7 May-13 September 1831[1]

This was the first brigade to be conducted by Chief Factor Peter Warren Dease, who succeeded Connolly as bourgeois of New Caledonia in 1831. As usual, preparations were completed at the end of April. Canoes were gummed and paddles and poles were made, furs were packed and provisions were stocked, and "summer appointments" were made and instructions left. Leaving Stuart's Lake in charge of Thomas Dears with three men, Dease departed on Saturday, 7 May in three canoes (two of which had actually left the day before) with the returns of 77½ packs of furs and 4²/₃ kegs of castoreum from the four posts of Stuart's Lake, McLeod's Lake, Connolly's Lake, and Babine Lake; 19 packs and 1 keg, plus 4,000 dried salmon "for the voyage & Lower Posts [Forts George and Alexandria]" from Fraser's Lake, were added en route. Dease kept the following journal, which is slightly less detailed, as well as less literate, than Connolly's.

Saturd 7 Every thing being settled & Instructions given to Mr Dears for his Conduct during the summer & the transports to be effected of 1800 Salmon from Frasers Lake which are to be sent to McLeods Lake as a Stock for that Post and provisions for the Party that will go for Leather in the Fall to Peace River – I embarked at 1 P.M. with 7 men & the remaining Packs and Leather to be taken down for the Lower Posts – towards Evening saw Ahtshesil, Quaus second son who gave us 2 bustards [grouse?]. encamped at 8 P.M.

Sund. 8 Started at an Early hour and got to Chinlac Forks, where the Canoes got down safe – also the Batteau & Canoe from Frasers Lake, accompanied by Roi & 2 Indians in a wooden Canoe who is to take up any property that Mr [Alexander] Fisher may have sent from Alexandria for those Posts which are Short of Ammunition & Tobacco – here I received a letter from J Bte [Jean Baptiste] Bouche Stating that previous to sending off the Returns Provisions now here, he had Counted the Stock of Salmon on hand which he says is 3400[2] – That Quantity, far from affording the Supply required for McLeods Lake is not Sufficient to Subsist the Establishment and the Dogs sent there for the Summer say 24 Dogs. this is a deficiency no ways Expected & never mentioned by Mr Dears when spoken to on the subject of getting that Quantity brought from there which is rather astonishing, as he should Know the Contents of the Store this will Cause a derangement by obliging us to get what will be required from Babines instead of Frasers Lake – The Canoes being Gummed & loadings given out, Embarked at 4 PM, after having received a few furrs from Deh [an Indian chief] & 3 young men & proceeded to the head of Stony Island Rapids where we put up for the night

Mond. 9 The Boat & Canoes got down the Rapids safe and we arrived at Fort George at 2 P.M. found all safe from Charles Chase who was left in charge of the House during Mr McGillivrays absence I learn that Brunelle & Brassard refused to do the work they had received orders to do during his absence & were called to account for it The Little Chief & Party have brought in their Hunts lately and are here now – they have worked well & have 3½ Packs – The men since the beginning of the month have taken 10 Sturgeons of a large size most of which are on hand – The Packs were made up & pressed and the Canoes gumming ready for Embarkation tomorrow one of them was changed being unfit to take a load. The Returns of this Post form 27½ Packs fine furrs & 2 Kegs Castoreum – Another disappointment occurs here in finding no arrivals from Alexandria which renders it necessary that Roi should go down to Alexandria, as the Post of Frasers Lake is quite destitute of Tobacco & Ammunition and this retardment of getting supplies will be the loss of part of the Indians hunts, which they might have made by getting timely supplies of those articles

Tuesd 10 Embarked at 2 P.M. leaving M^r McGillivray with his Interpreter & 2 men for the summer Establishment of the Post, the Brigade consisting of 1 Batteau, 5 men & 5 Canoes at 4 men including Roi. put up after sunsett. had a Snow storm but not of long duration

Wednesd 11 This morning at 9 A M. got to the Big Rapid which L^s[Louis] Paul who was leader of the Brigade was Sent to Examine previous to going down the Water being in a fine State he led the way with the Batteau, the Canoes following each other at a moderate distance – L^s Paul after having got down Safe with his batteau observed in looking back one of the Canoes taking the Eddy Current too soon, fearing it would be driven against the Rocks turned round to warn them to take Care, when the Sweep oar fixing in the water threw him over the Boat after a Short Struggle the poor man sunk to rise no more – By this melancholy Event I have to regret the Loss of the Best Boute in the District, which cannot easily be replaced – After stopping for some time to Endeavour to find or see the Body but in vain, we proceeded and arrived at Alexandria at 5 P.M. where Mr Fisher & his people are all Safe – Received a letter from Kamloops by the return of the men who accompanied the Express, which had got safe to Okanagan – with Assurances that a Canoe will be found at North River for us & Provisions at Kamloops to take us to Okanagan The Horses are all in Excellent order and none lost during the season [winter] – their Agres although not Sufficient for the augmentation of returns we have, will I hope with proper arrangement Serve – Gave the leather & Siffleu Robes intended for the Post, & tomorrow will have the furrs that are on hand made up –

Thursd 12 This afternoon Sent off Roi with J B^{te} Lapierre & 2 Indians to take up 1 Roll Tob^o, 1 Bag Flour, 1 Bag Balls, $^2/_3$ Bag Shott, to be divided between F^t George, Frasers Lake & Stuarts Lake, for which directions are given to M^r McGillivray, to make the separation there – Gregoire & others working at Horse Agres – Wrote Messrs Dears & Roussain regarding the Transport –

Frid 13 Preparations making for Departure tomorrow, the Horses Collected and fettered that they may not stray – The returns of the Post amount to 38 Packs and a remainder with 3 Kegs Castorum – These are far better than was Expected and procured at much less Expense than less returns have been obtained at. The Natives seem well disposed and are at Same time Kept in order – Not many are on the Ground at present this being the season at which they go to the inland Lakes to fish & at same time make spring Hunts – Lapierre was sent some time back to the Chilcotins, to Explain to them our motives for withdrawing the men from there in March to do away with any bad impression it might have made upon their minds – Very few of them were seen, but the visit will have I hope a Good Effect upon them as they were told at Same time, they would be visited in Summer – We are rather short of Horses to enable us to Supply the men with each one as they cannot otherwise attend to their Brigades – with all we have there are 6 wanting to Complete the number to mount each man –

Saturd 14 The Returns of the District being now all Collected and the arrangements for the Summer Establishments taken I shall enter them, as also the trade since Closing the accounts in March belonging to outfit [18]31, but taken out with those of outfit [18]30 at Present on hand. The Settlements of the different Posts are as follows

Summer Arrangements

McLeods Lake
Mr John Tod Clk.
Louis Gagnon   labourers
Jos Letendre

Connollys Lake
Mr C^s Ross Clk.
Ant^e Normandin Labourer
Joseph a Lefevre   "
Francois Duhaime   "

Babine Lake
Mr Ch^s Roussain P.M.
Wastayap Campbell Int^r.
Andre Dubois Labourer
J B^{te} Poirier   "
Alexis Belanger Ap. Int^r.

Fort George
M^r W^m McGillivray Clk.
J B^{te} D Bouche fils Int.
Joseph Martel labourer
J B^{te} Branconnier "

Stuarts Lake | Alexandria
M^r. Th^s Dears Clk.
Joseph Porteur Native Int^r.
Aug^n. Lafleche Blks. & labourer
Joseph Bonnin   "

Alexandria
Alex^r Fisher Esqr C T.
J B^{te} Lapierre Int^r
Lac [Luc] Gagnon labourer
Jacques Bibeau   "

Frasers Lake
J B^{te}. Boucher c Inter^r.
Thomas Roy labourer
David Donpiere "

Our Complement of Men for the transport is twenty four 3 of these are indeed so wretchedly poor that they cannot be called Efficient for the Duty they have to perform – the Whole Amount of Returns and the provisions required from hence to Kamloops amounting to upwards of 180 Pieces, the Party was divided into 20 Brigades of 9 horses each 2 men with Exception of Bellecque who had two for one and one Brigade of 6 horses for my Baggage & Extra Pieces with 2 men as Gregoire the Horse Keeper cannot be said to belong to it having to attend to all, when required – each horse having 2 Pieces all being ready, the loads were given out and the Whole made a move to break Ground about 2 P.M. as much difficulty Existed in putting loads upon Some of the Young Horses not yet broken in they Expected to get to a little River where the Horses may have Water and good grazing – as their Encampment is not such a distance but I may overtake them Early in the morning I passed the remainder of the day at the House and will Join them in the morning – Our Deficiency of Men renders it out of our power to Keep up the Chilcotin Establishment but Mr Fisher intends sending occasionally during the Summer by which means he will secure their hunts, give them some Encouragement to work in the Expectations of having again the Post established of which they appear to be very desirous – from the General Peaceable behaviour of the Natives I do not think that any danger Exists for any of the Establishments from any of the Natives and I have hopes that they will Exert themselves to give Satisfaction which they promise to do at the different Posts where an opportunity of hearing their Sentiments offered –

Sunday 15 This Morning at an early hour took leave of Mr Fisher and joined the Brigade who were ready to start, rather late through the awkwardness of some of the men in Catching and tackling the Horses – proceeded and put ashore [halted] at 11 A M, it being an advantage to allow the Horses about 3 hours rest to feed, and less liable in warm Weather to get their backs injured by the loads – In the afternoon one of the men Louis Jeronquay was seriously lamed by the Kick of one of the Horses upon the leg while riding near, from which unfortunate accident he is rendered incapable of any Duty I fear for the voyage. 2 of the Packs got a little wet by the Horse fording a Small River but not to Cause any damage. Warm day, put up near Sunsett at a River Called Riviere a Joseph about 12 miles after leaving Frasers River at the Barge –

Mond. 16 Left our Encampment at an Early hour & put ashore at the South End of first Lake where the Packs were Dried – here we found a few Indians from whom some Roots & a few fish were traded for Tobacco & a few Pairs Shoes – proceeded at 2 PM and encamped at 6 at Lac en Long –

Tuesd. 17 This day without any accident brought us to Salmon River where a family of 7 Atnahs came to us with some Roots & fish, from them I traded 7 Beavers 1 Fox & a few musquash for Leather, Am^n & Tobacco – The weather fine & Warm & the Rivers not being in a high State, is a great advantage, having numerous Streams to ford which at high Water Causes much difficulty & Delay besides the risk of Wetting the Packs.

Wednesd 18. Put ashore to bait the Horses as usual at a River called Beaver River, from whence we Proceeded & Encamped along Lac des Chevaux which is so named from the Circumstance of 18 horses having perished in it by breaking through the Ice some years ago, some Indians were Seen in Course of the day from whom we procured some Roots and a few fishes being the only articles they have to subsist upon during the Season –

Thursd 19 The roads not so fine to day as we have had nor the Country so open Our usual routine of traveling brought us to Lac Tranquil where we put up for the night –

[Statement of the returns of the different posts in New Caledonia District, Outfit 1831]

| | Alexandria | | | Fort George | | | Frasers Lake | | | Stuarts Lake | | | McLeods Lake | | | Babine Lake | | | Connollys Lake | | | Total |
| | Outfit | | | Outfit | | | Outfit | | | Outfit | | | Outfit | | | Outfit | | | Outfit | | | |
	1830	1831	Total	1830	1831	Total	1830	1831	Total	1830	1831	Total	1830	1831	Total	1830	1831	Total	1830	1831	Total	
Bears																						
Lar. black	31	2	33	11	5	16	4	6	10	8	2	10	18	0	18	4	0	4	3	0	3	94
Cub black	17	0	17	9	1	10	6	0	6	18	0	18	11	0	11	0	0	0	2	0	2	64
Lar. brown	1	0	1	2	0	2	0	0	0	2	0	2	1	0	1	0	0	0	0	0	0	6
Cub brown	2	0	2	0	0	0	0	0	0	0	0	0	0	0	0	0	0	0	0	0	0	2
Lar. grizzly	0	0	0	0	0	0	0	0	0	1	0	1	0	0	0	0	0	0	0	0	0	1
Cub grizzly	0	0	0	0	0	0	0	0	0	1	0	1	0	0	0	0	0	0	0	0	0	1
Beavers																						
Lar. fine and com.	1,309	4	1,313	1,012	181	1,193	646	84	730	876	90	966	1,224	67	1,291	88	5	93	934	0	934	6,520
Small fine and com.	600	31	631	273	61	334	184	29	213	311	70	381	427	38	465	26	0	26	255	0	255	2,305
Coating and cuttings (lbs)	184	0	184	49	0	49	11	0	11	13	0.5	13.5	1	0	1	0	0	0	66	0	66	324.5
Castoreum (lbs)	127	8	135	95	5	100	55	3	58	90	7	97	40	0	40	5	3	8	27	0	27	465
Cats or lynx	186	14	200	46	4	50	134	8	142	189	47	236	15	2	17	199	17	216	30	0	30	891
Fishers	22	1	23	4	0	4	32	10	42	17	15	32	0	0	0	21	21	42	0	0	0	143
Fox																						
Silver grey	8	3	11	5	1	6	23	4	27	7	4	11	0	0	0	2	0	2	0	0	0	57
Cross	11	3	14	4	1	5	0	12	12	25	0	25	0	0	0	13	4	17	1	0	1	74
Red	13	0	13	2	0	2	10	2	12	11	0	11	0	0	0	7	1	8	0	0	0	46
Martens prime	423	12	435	307	20	327	285	62	347	279	90	369	20	52	72	282	271	553	109	0	109	2,212
Minks	12	1	13	0	0	0	22	0	22	16	0	16	2	0	2	14	4	18	1	0	1	72
Musquash	673	89	762	35	4	39	708	10	718	600	148	748	27	0	27	240	18	258	20	0	20	2,572
Otters																						
Prime lar.	22	6	28	18	7	25	12	11	23	32	0	32	10	6	16	5	0	5	5	0	5	134
Prime com.	22	0	22	10	0	10	22	0	22	23	0	23	16	0	16	1	0	1	0	0	0	94
Wolverines	3	1	4	0	2	2	4	1	5	8	7	15	1	1	2	7	5	12	8	0	8	48
Wolves	6	1	7	1	1	2	0	1	1	1	2	3	0	0	0	1	0	1	0	0	0	14

Friday 20 – Stopped at Lac des Rochers where we saw some Indians among whom is the Chief of North River from whom we got some fine Trout which is a Great treat what has been heretofore procured being only Carp fresh or Dry. One of the Horses, this Evening was found missing having been allowed to go light to relieve him – the Country during this days progress being very rugged & Rocky, the Animal was recommended to the Old Chief to Catch & Keep untilol our Return – when he would be recompensed – Slept at Grand Muskeg – a Large Swamp. an Indian from our Breakfast place accompanies us to north River having his Canoe there for Crossing our Baggage – at the request of Lolo by Mr Blacks orders this is a very precarious dependance, and am surprised a Canoe was not sent from the Establishment as requested by our letter of March to that Effect. we are hereby left to depend upon the Indians good will who by any Caprice or unwillingness would subject us to great trouble, risk of losing property, and loss of time –

Saturd 21 From our Encampment we reached North River at Midday when we found the Indians Canoe – One of the Horses to day on the Mountain was so completely Knocked up, that any Endeavours to bring him on were unavailing – he was therefore left and recommended to the Care of the Indian who accompanies us – the Baggage was crossed but the horses could not be collected on time. Here we found 169 salmon, deposited under Ground by Lolo for us – out of 200 intended. Some no doubt have been taken by Indians –

Sund 22 The Horses were Collected & crossed – Hired the Indians Canoe for the purpose of Crossing at the River below Called the Barrier and at same time to relieve some of the Horses that are much fatigued. Sent down Thomas Tehontawasse & Louis Jeronquay with the Canoe & 6 Pieces to wait for us at the Barriere – having lost some time Crossing the Horses we put up at a large Plain about half way to the River mentioned.

Mond 23. – Got to the River about 10 A M, where we were joined by the men with the Canoe, the stream being very swift, and Canoe containing but 7 Pieces at a time, with 2 men – occupied the Remainder of the day – here we found some Indians, who traded a few Carp & trouts.

Tuesd 24. Some time was taken to Collect the Horses this morning, part of the way being very bad along the River, going over a Point of Rocks which is dangerous on account of broken stones ascending and descending on each side of the Rocks very Steep. One of the horses with his load of Packs rolled down from a height of about 80 feet & fell in the River. fortunately received but little hurt by the fall and swam down to an Eddy where the Packs were taken off safe and the Animal got ashore – the Packs were dried, and we put up for the night below the Pi[n]eux –

Wednesd 25. Reached Kamloops about midday – found Lolo in Charge of the House, and is to proceed with us to Okanagan – took 1008 Salmon for our voyage hence to that Place & with the assistance of Some Indian Canoes hired – All the Baggage & horses were Crossed over with the Exception of those of this Place, that will be crossed in the morning – two horses were hired from Indians of this Place for the voyage to & from Okanagan at the rate of 10 M B^r. value for each – the Property remaining was put in Security by Lolo and an Indian appointed to take Care of the Establishment untill our return, which he promised to do. Rained in the afternoon

Thursd 26 Being rather late before the Kamloops, horses were Crossed over, and the Indians settled – began our march at 11 A M & put up for the night at the River where we leave the South Branch of Thom[p]sons River to strike across for the Columbia – Here 2 Indians from the upper Posts of the River came with 17 M B^rs value in furrs which were traded by Lolo, fine day –

Frid 27 The Weather very Warm put ashore at Salmon River East end of Grande Prairie – afternoon passed the Strong woods recrossed the River and put up for the night at the beginning of the Hills – Had a Shower of Rain in the Evening –

Saturd 28 At the End of Okanagan Lake saw some Indians from whom a few furrs were traded by Lolo – put up for the night at Riviere la Biche where An Exchange was made with an Indian who Came to our Camp gave him a young filly for a young horse – Brunelle one of the men sick of a Swelling about the Groin – unable to do any duty –

Sund 29 – Put ashore at a Small River called Bear River – and afternoon we proceeded saw some Indians, who had nothing to trade – put up at a Small River called Riviere a Jacques – Rained about Sunsett accompanied by a Strong gale of Wind.

Mond 30 – Rained most part of the night which retarded our Departure this morning, that the Water may fall from the trees – 2 Packs got a little wet in fording the River this morning, but not to cause any damage put up for the night at Beaver River – saw 3 Indians who have nothing Brunelle getting worse, suffers much riding & Cannot Walk –

Tuesd 31. – Baited the Horses at Fourche du Chemin – and put up for the night at Riviere au Thé – Louis Jeronquay getting better a little begins to walk a little – had a Shower of Rain in the Evening –

June

Wednesd 1 Got to the narrows of Little Lake Okanagan where we found Indians who lent us Canoes to Cross the Baggage – after which I traded one from them to send down [the Okanogan River] Louis Jeronquay & Brunelle being a safe navigation from this to the Establishment traded some Roots from a Party of Indians and put up for the night about three miles below the Forks of the Chemilcomeen [Similkameen] River – The Canoe came & Encamped with us.

Thursd 2nd The travelling from this to the Columbia being fine without any dangerous Places, with a view of having Every thing prepared at Okanagan for Embarkation – I left the Brigade in Charge of Gregoire and with Lolo proceeded to the Fort where I arrived at 2 P M. and had the pleasure of finding C[hief] T[rader] Black with Mr Kit[t]son and the Brigade from Upper Posts [Kootenai, Flathead, and Colvile] all well and Every thing safe. a Good supply of provisions has been sent down by C[hief] T[rader] [Francis] Heron from Colville for N[ew] C[aledonia] District and also for the Snake Expedition, 9 Boats ready –

Frid 3 The Brigade arrived safe to day at about midday – the Packs all safe and in good order & the horses in Excellent Condition considering the long voyage they have performed – the men were appointed to the different Boats and will have them gummed & loaded tomorrow

Saturd 4th The Boats were prepared, loading[s] given out, and all loaded ready for an Early Start – Gregoire, with Lolo are appointed to take Care of the Horses, all the N[ew] C[aledonia] horse agres given in Charge to the former received the requisition of Horses and Agres applied for by Express - The State of the Water in the Columbia River is fine and we have every reason to hope for a Good passage hence to Vancouver

Sund 5th   This morning at Sunrise the Brigade consisting of 9 Boats loaded with – Ps ea. passengers Messrs. Black, Kitson & Self pushed off from Okanagan & put up for the night above Priests Rapid

Mond 6 Arrived at Walla Walla afternoon, left the Provisions required for the Snake Expedition Party. Ch. Trader Simon McGillivray being in a bad state of health & wishing for Medical Assistance requested to get a passage to Vancouver. Mr Kitson has therefore been appointed to take the Charge during his absence and being Experienced at this Place will not be at any loss to manage its affairs –

Tuesd 7 Embarked the Returns of the Post and gave passage to two freemen to go down to Vancouver. left the Fort at 2 PM & put up at the Big Island. procured some fresh Salmon from Indians in the Course of the day. fine Warm Weather

Wednesd 8. Passed the Chutes and Camped at the End of the first Portage of the Dalles, Boats all Carried across – with the Assistance of the Natives who are very numerous here – less inclination to pilfer was Evinced by them than I had Expected, from their well Known propensity to theft – they were paid for the Assistance rendered and appeared well satisfied – some Salmon was traded from them, Enough to Give a Good Mess to all the Brigade –

Thursd 9 – Made the 2 last of the Dalles portages & encamped below the Plains being stopped by a violent head wind, the boats shipping Water –

Frid 10 Saw many Indians in Course of the day, reached the head of the Cascades in time to encamp, got some fresh Salmon from the Natives

Saturd 11 The Portages of the Cascades & Portage Neuf were made, the Boats all safely run down, the weather fine, arrived at Fort Vancouver at 4 PM, when the Packs were delivered, a few got a little wet but not of any consequence – the men got their Regale for arrival – from this date to the 26th Arrangements were made for Return, the outfits ready & men Equipped for the Winter – Mr F. Annance who is on the retiring list from Columbia, was appointed to pass the Winter in N C. District, having no person then to accompany the men to go for our Supplies of Leather to Peace River, he will be of service for that voyage on Return from Whence he will pass the season untill departure of the Express in Charge of Chilcotin Post –

Mond. 27. The Outfits for the Different Districts being ready they were taken to the Water side on Waggons – The loadings given out to the 9 Boats 46 to 48 Pieces each, 7 men – the Boutes are not all so good as could be wished & would be required for such a navigation as this is – the Regale was Given them & sent to Encamp at the End of the Plain whither they will be Joined in the Morning by the Passengers viz C T^s Black & McGillivray, Mr Annance & Self – An Invalid Bellair gets a passage to Cross the Mountains this fall – Perrault the Carpenter also goes for the same purpose.

Tuesd 28 – Joined the Brigade this Morning when Perrault Changed his mind & remained – Embarked at 8 A M – had aft wind part of the day lost 3 hours Waiting for one of the Boats (Thomas Ogoniasta) that lagged behind from the Intoxication of most of the Crew –

Wednesd 29 – Reached the Portage Neuf at 1 PM – One of the Boats Injured before reaching it & were obliged to repair below (Thomas Ogoniastas) the other boats got safe up the Portage, a great throng of Natives obliged us to watch the Baggage very narrowly at each end while The men were Carrying the Pieces across – the Portage made 6 Boats were Sent to the Cascades to make room for others – 2 boats remained [with] Canoté (the Guide), With Mr Annance untill Thomas boat was brought up the Rapid – One of those that had left the Place to go up Augustin La Boute & J Moreau Boutes – sheered out shortly after the Men on the Line could not bring it in, and let the line go when the Boat with the 2 poor men was drawn into the Rapid & went down, upsett below the Portage – & the unfortunate men drowned Thomas boat which had in mean time been brought up, he run down the Rapid with in hopes of saving them but too late – Mr Annance, Canoté & some of the men went down by land to get Indians if possible, the 2 boats remain at the portage and Mr Black went down with some men who are not yet come back to the Cascades. I am anxiously Waiting to Know the Extent of our Misfortune. Many Indians about but are not very troublesome

Thursd 30 This Morning Messrs. Black & Annance Came back with Thomas & Crew with 14 P^{s.} of the property picked up from the confined Eddy at the Portage a great intermixture of baggages took place the Whole baggages were Examined to ascertain the Pieces lost with an account of which Mr Annance with 16 men will be dispatched to Vancouver – will take the Boat which was found below Tea Meadow [Prairie du Thé] also in order to come up lighter & more Expeditiously – Wrote to C F McLoughlin informing him of the sad events and requesting that the Pieces of which a list is sent May be replaced as it would bear very hard upon the Posts for the trade during the season

July

Frid 1 This Morning Mr Annance left this as mentioned, we are told that some things were found by the Natives, Mr Black with a party of 13 Men went down to the Camp – In the afternoon a Bale was brought by the Natives belonging to Nez Perces outfit, and a part of a Case of Soap Private Orders, N C. District 11^{lb} wanting – Cusenau is very active in the search & bringing in what was found

Saturd 2. To day a Keg Wine was brought of Colville Outfit for which they were recompensed to encourage them in the search.

Sund 3 This Afternoon Mr Annance with the 2 boats came back from Vancouver being late and no room at the upper End of the Portage for the Property the Pieces were not Carried across – the Indians who rendered us service were rewarded and seemed to be well satisfied with us – since our stay here a sufficiency of Salmon has been procured to save our Provisions

Mond 4 At 9 A M we left the Cascades, had aft wind. at 1 P.M. Louis Bellair who was sick Expired on the Boat – and at 4 PM. put ashore to inter the Body which took Place at 5 in as decent a manner as means would permit – after which we proceeded untill Evening.

Tuesd 5 A Strong aft wind, one of the Boats was injured & obliged to put ashore to repair stopped 3 hours by the wind & reached the Islands below the Dalles where we put up for the night –

Wednesd 6 Got to the Dalles in towing the Boats up the little Channel on[e] of the filled, nothing lost – With the Assistance of the Natives got over the Portage at 3 PM, left that and Encamped near the Chutes Portage some salmon was traded here and at the Dalles from the Natives

Thursd 7th After sunsett put up near John Days River – very warm Weather

Frid 8th – One of the Boats was broken Considerably to day by another coming in Contact while under sail lost 3 hours repairing – had a Strong aft wind most of the day –

Saturd 9 Very warm day – put up opposite Big Island, 2 dishes lost on the way down were found & brought by the Natives – were recompensed for their honesty

Sund 10 The Weather very warm – One of the men (Joyale) fell over the side of the Boat & hurt himself off duty –

Mond 11 Arrived at Fort Nez Percé at Midday – delivered the Outfit of the Post – made out a new distribution of the loadings of the Boats. Mr Kitson will Embark in place of C T McGillivray who resumed his charge –

Tuesd 12 Left the Fort afternoon, & put up near Nez Percé River

Wednesd 13 Strong side wind – Encamped below the White Bluffs –

Thursd 14 Encamped above the Bluffs, traded some salmon – learn from Indians that 2 of the N C. horses had run away from Okanagan & could not be overtaken by Gregoire who was out 3 days after them – 2 Ind^s were gone in search of them

Frid. 15 Got up the Priests Rapid – Learn from the Old Priest that the body of a man drowned last fall at Chalifous Rapid was found by him & interred above the Rapid a little – Gave the Old man a present for the humanity he shewed.

Saturd 16 Put up opposite the Tree in the Rock, had assistance from the Natives in getting up the Rapids –

Sund. 17 Got above the Portage of Stoney Islands put up at the upper end

Mond 18 Encamped above the Piscaoos River without any serious accident

Tuesd 19 Had Sail wind afternoon which notwithstanding the loss of 3 hours to wait for one of the Boats brought us near Clear Water River –

Wednesd 20 Encamped above the Big Rapid all safe The day very Warm –

Thursd 21 Reached Okanagan at 10 A M where all was safe – the 2 horses that run away have not been found, and 3 others died since I left there belonging to N C. two others unable from Injury or Disease to perform the voyage, prepared Every thing to send off the Boats with Colville District Outfit – Young Rivet a free man arrived from there with 10 P$^s.$ Corn & peas, & some horse agres requested to be Sent down in Spring, 4 horses are likewise given to enable us to take the Outfit

Frid 22 Mr Kitson with 4 Boats took his Departure for Colville, horses being sent with loads above the Big Rock by Mr Black to lighten them Having no cords for our transport, Cut up 3 hides brought from Vancouver for the Purpose. Gave the men their advances of flour & were busy arranging the Brigade, with agres &c untill the following

Tuesd 26 When the Brigades Consisting of 110 Loaded Horses, 10 to each 2 men with the Outfit Provisions &c left Okanagan, where some Pieces are left (Provisions) for want of Horses – C T Black having lent us 10 – being late before loading &c did not proceed far –

Wednesd 27 Put up at the Tree along the River – rather early one of the Horses having thrown his load some distance behind – there are 3 men for Kamloops with an Indian with their Brigade of Horses in Company – with 25 men of which 2 besides Gregoire have the Charge of the 6 horses for Baggage for N C. District form a long line

Thursd 28 Put up for the night at Farthest Riviere a Bonaparte

29 Baited the horses at the Forks where Exchanged a worn out Mare for a horse with one of the Natives – from the Camp we found at this Place traded some salmon & berries and proceeded to Tea River where we put up for the night.

30 Stopped at our usual hour, at Fourche de Chemin from whence we proceeded to Serpent River & put up having passed a River Called Riviere la Cendri previously –

31 Passed Beaver River, Trout River & Stopped at River Prairi[e]s de Nicholas from whence we put up at the Tree along the Lake –

August

Mond 1 Passed Riviere a Trepagnier, Riviere a Jacques, Riviere d'Ours, the Anse au Sable and put up at Sunsett –

2 Stopped at Riviere la Biche – the roads in this part bad, 2 horses broke their loads – by which ½ Bag Flour & ½ Bag Corn were lost not having good Wrappers for such Pieces & the Cords very bad –

3 Passed Okanagan Lake stopped at Lac Rond – on passing the strong woods found fire Raging in all directions, and had to pass very near it – the smoak so thick as almost to darken the atmosphere some of the Horses very Sore galled – 2 of them were unloaded – passed Salmon River and put up at E end of Grande Prairie –

4 Some of the horses were not brought untill a late hour – Lolo and Party took the lead to go on to the House – put up at Campement du Poulin for the night.

5 Reached the River at 9 A M, and got to the Crossing place by the house at 3 PM – with the assistance of the Natives & their Canoes 7 of the Brigades Baggages were Crossed over to the Fort – the others remain untill morning – all the Horses were driven across Except one –

Saturd 6 This morning the remainder was Crossed & find that 4 of our horses Cannot continue the voyage, they are therefore left here, hired 5 from the Natives to take us to North River, and 6 of those Mr Black has lent us leaving 4 of them here and 10 Ps remain here untill they Can be sent for by Mr Fisher – Sent off the Brigade at 3 PM.

7 Without any accident put up at Pineux Point.

8 Put up at Grande Prairie, the fire Raging on the Woods – passed the Barriere where we saw some Indians, who have nothing

9 Arrived at the Traverse of North River at 10 A M where I found the Old Chief & party with the young horse left in the Spring the Old one Died a few days ago from Old age – Every thing was crossed and being no Grazing for the Horses nearer than the swamp Stopped for the night

10 Put up at Grand Muskeg – 11 Stopped at Rocky Lake and put up at Lac Tranquil – had a shower of Rain in the Evening –

Frid 12 Put ashore to bait at Riviere la fourche, but a heavy Shower of Rain obliged us to stop all day – some of the horses being much Galled & Exhausted – intind [intend] to proceed in the morning for Alexandria in order to send the mares that are there to assist them on – take one Man with me.

13 Left the Brigade under Care of Mr Annance & Gregoire, and Stopped for 1½ hour – had a violent shower of Rain towards Evening – put up for the night at Dusk.

Sund 14 Arrived at Sunsett at Alexandria, where find Mr Fisher and all his people safe and well – the Indians about the house Complain much of the scarcity of Salmon – they have been very peaceable throughout the summer, & the Returns pretty fair, three derouines [forays] were made to the Chilcotins, and produced about 3 Packs – the upper or West Road River Indians have not come down being in dread of those about this Post – the Supplies sent up in the Spring got safe to Fort George whence I think they would have reached Frasers Lake safe the navigation not being so dangerous as below

Mond 15 Sent 2 men with all the Horses that are here to meet the Brigade and to relieve such as are most fatigued – from this nothing of any moment occurred – the Indians taking very few Salmon, are apprehensive that they will suffer during the season as few small salmon come up as yet – they were abundant at this time last year – the Brigade arrived on

Thursd 18 at Sunsett – they were retarded by Rainy Weather rather than wet the Property – the Baggage was put up & Received, all safe except a Beaver trap either stolen by the Indians or lost by Bellisle – the Canoes are in a very bad state and require a thorough repair to be able to take up Cargoes – the Post is without the means of making the necessary repairs – having neither Gum, Bark or Wattap on hand those indispensable articles must be got before we can begin repairs

Frid 19. Some of the men were Employed to go and gather Gum & Wattup, the Canoes being too dry were put to soak – previous to beginning to repair them – some of the Bales untied to make up the outfit of the Post – some of the Indians from Bear Lake came with a few furrs but it appears they are not on the most friendly terms with those of this place.

20 The outfit made out – Want of Bark for the Canoes is a great obstacle to us at the present moment for which the Worst of the Canoes could not be done with to day and but 2 men capable of doing that work properly – 44 Pieces will remain in Depot here untill sent for

Wednesd 24 These impediments retarded us untill the 24th when allbeing ready the Canoes were loaded with 25 Pieces in four of them – the Old one being so bad was loaded with 18 least liable to damage with Mr Annance as passenger – On turning round the Point in passing a fishing Weir the Canoe was allowed to turn in shore too soon – the Stern came against the Weir & broke it off – being near shore fortunately all the property was saved. the Canoe filled but was got out, to repair it the goods put out to Dry and the men sett about mending it which could not be Completed – 25ᵗʰ.The Canoe being patched up as well as means admit Embarked at half past 11 A M. & put up for the night above Big Island rather Early to allow them to gum the Canoe –

Friday 26 Started at an Early hour – the Canoes so very leaky cause a great loss of time, being obliged to put ashore to Gum them – put up at 5 PM on that account.

27. Had heavy rain all night which continued some time this morning – Provisions being scarce got a few fish above Quesnels River which the Indians demand most Extravagant prices for – very few are Caught by them, they are consequently reluctant to part with what they have. put up about Canoe Island –

28 Two of the Canoes were very badly broken, Caused a great loss of time, during which time Mʳ William MᶜGillivray with an Indian and a Boy in a small Canoe arrived from Fᵗ Geo – By him I have the Satisfaction of hearing from the Posts of MᶜLeods, Stuarts & Frasers Lakes where all was well by last accounts. The Returns of Fᵗ George are better than last year – the other Posts rather less – it is reported that the Indians of the upper Forks of Frasers Lake have been towards the Coast and bartered about 100 Beavers with with the natives from that Quarter who bring Goods which they sell at very low prices – The state of that Post did not admit of the Interpreter leaving his Charge otherwise we might have drawn in some of these furrs – as most of those Indians are due Balances to the Coʸ – After repairing damages proceeded & put up at Asco or Liard River having Embarked Mʳ MᶜGillivray & lightened the Canoes by putting 2 Pieces in the Indians Canoe –

29 Got up the Big Rapid where Charleau's Canoe was in such an unmanageable State that it was left & the pieces put on the other Canoes, untill we can find means of Getting a Wooden Canoe from Indians – they being too heavy loaded for safety in such a Strong stream – put up about 6 miles below the West Road River –

30 Rained hard Yesterday & this day also – Passed 2 Villages of Natives from whom we Purchased salmon sufficient for the Canoes to day & tomorrow – Received also some furrs for Debts due at Fᵗ George – the 4 Canoes Cause much delay to Keep the property from getting wet – Put up above West Road River –

Wednesd 31. At an Indian House where we stopped for one of the Canoes which was injured to gum & repair, Hired a Wooden Canoe to lighten the others in which 3 men & 8 Pieces were put – and proceeded – Cloudy with showers of Rain now and then – at another house traded a few fresh salmon & some furrs for Fᵗ George also got 4 pᶜᵉˢ Bark which was Paid for with Tobacco, were twice stopped to Gum the Canoes –

September

Thursd 1 Stopped twice again to Gum the Canoes & put up about 6 miles below the Rapid of Stoney Islands –

2 – Two of the Canoes were broken to require repairs which Caused much delay – got above the Rapids & pushed on ahead of the Canoes which Mʳ Annance remains with – Could not get to the House

3 reached Fᵗ George at 6 A M. All safe and every thing in good Order – the Returns amount to 12 Packs mostly Beaver and the principal Hunters not yet come in – Gardens have produced well – & had the Post been well supplied with # 9 twine for the Sturgeon fishery – would have taken a number of those large fishes – one of which that was Killed during the summer measured 14½ feet in length – We are now very deficient in all Kinds of twine this year – which was not to be got at Vancouver – the other Canoes Cast up at 11 A M and will require thorough repairs before leaving this –

4, 5ᵗʰ were Employed Getting Gum, Bark & Roots & repairing the 4 Canoes – the Outfit of the Post made out and all ready for Departure tomorrow – Very few Salmon are taken here & have received but 3 from the Natives since arrival –

Tuesd 6 Left Fort George at 1 PM & put up above the first village no salmon to be got from the Natives & provisions Scarce –

7 My Canoe was broken badly & filled before it could be unloaded the Bales were opened & Dried While the Canoe was mended which Kept us from 11 A M to 4.30 PM. when we pushed off – passed a village where a few Salmon were procured –

Thursd 8 Breakfasted at White mud portage & put up some miles below upper Stoney Islands

9th Passed Stoney Islands and got to Chinlac Forks at sunsett found 2 families of Indians of Frasers Lake from whom I received a few furrs on their debts & supplied them with a Beaver Trap & some Ammunition to enable them to hunt, these Indians are almost starving no salmon & Stuarts Lake River they say is Extremely low – I therefore hired 2 Wooden Canoes to Exempt the Canoes from making a Double trip to the

10 head of the Rapid – 2 of the Indians take up one of them with 9 Pieces – the other with 2 men in it has 10 – before putting up one of them was broken in the Rapid & were obliged to send back for the Pieces & put up for the night being but about hal way up the Rapids

Sund 11 Got up the Rapids at 10 A M lost 2 hours to Gum the Canoes the Indians were paid for their trouble & went back to their Camp – Yesterday & to day had to deal out rations of Corn & flour to all hands

12 This afternoon passed at Hoolson's Lodge where most of the Indians of Stuarts Lake are assembled to spear Salmon there being only some of the large Kind Called Kase to be got none of the small salmon has Come up the River which is a bad sign – and none can be Expected at this season – procured 12 Salmon from them & having Given each a piece of Tobacco proceeded some distance above where one of the Canoes was broken & obliged to put ashore to repair put up about 9 Miles from the Lake –

Tuesday 13. Arrived at the House at 9 A M. Mr Dears and all the men well. The Indians bring no salmon – but 4 have been hitherto given by them, Received letters from Mr Roussain of the 31st. Ulto informing me that although the salmon is not so abundant as it has been Known he Expects to trade a considerable Quantity – Wastayap Campbell & Alexis (the Boy) are here from that Post. The Returns are only about 3 Packs furrs, but has more Beavers than all last years returns – The Goods were untied to make out the Outfits of the Posts – but very Little salmon in Store of the 4000 Got from Babine Lake – 1800 were Sent to McLeods Lake and there now remains in Store but 1780 and no hopes of getting any either at this Place or Frasers Lake by last accounts from there – they were entirely subsisting upon the Produce of the Gardens – which very fortunately have appearance of a fair increase – the Garden at this place has only produced Turnips in any Quantity – Potatoes have been frozen and the Barley that was sewn has been blighted also by the Frost – From the Post of Connollys Lake no accounts have been received yet – McLeods Lake last news is of the beginning of the month, all well & hopes of having near the same Returns as last year – the Indians will be at the Establishment about the latter end of the month –

Although Chief Factor Dease's brigade had been plagued by canoe breakdowns on the last leg of the four and a half month "voyage," it had returned on schedule (the middle of September). On the 14th the goods were "assorted," and it was found that "some Bales have been wet and damaged by the transport across Land for want of sufficient Coverings," "several Blankets have been worn through by the friction of the Cords," and "several pounds of Tea lost by having got wet on the Way up," but these losses were minor. During the next couple of days the subdivided outfit was distributed to the individual posts by canoes and horses (that for McLeod's Lake was sent on seven horses) and the "winter appointments" were made (seven men were assigned to Alexandria). That part of the outfit that had been left at Alexandria reached Stuart's Lake in one large and two small canoes on 9 October. Meanwhile, on 16 September a party of a dozen men under Annance had left for the Peace River to fetch leather.

As he awaited the winter, Dease's chief worries were the district's usual bugbears – the scarcity of provisions and the shortage of employees. The salmon run of late summer had failed to materialize. "No Salmon comes up Except some large – a bad sign," he lamented on the 18th. Two days earlier he had noted: "Many Indians going and Coming but bring in very few furrs and nothing in the way of Provisions, for which our Prospects are very gloomy – the Natives also very anxious how to get through the Winter." Potatoes and turnips from the company gardens would assist but not suffice. On the 17th a letter from Fraser's Lake informed Dease that twelve of that post's best dogs had starved to death since the spring and that more would likely die soon; the establishment's complement "subsist chiefly now on the Produce of the Gardens which they think will give 300 Kegs of Potatoes," while thirty kegs of barley were grown from three-quarters of a keg of seed. At Stuart's Lake itself forty kegs of turnips were harvested "of a fine size & Quality," but the potatoes were "not much larger than musket balls, having been twice frozen in course of the Summer" (26 September); also, "the Ground was not well ploughed – & the Garden has been Choked up with Weeds" (6 October), so only twelve kegs of potatoes were produced from four kegs of seed on nearly one acre – "a very poor return" (8 October). So Dease began to buy "small fishes" (lake fish) from the natives – five kegs of trout for two made beaver per keg of some 450 fish on 14 September, for example – "Our principal Object at Present being to secure the Posts depending upon Supplies from this [post] from absolute Starvation which I fear we will have much difficulty in Effecting," for "The Scarcity of Dogs and the reduced State they are now in ... will hardly be able to get through the transports required" (30 September). He hoped eventually to get 6,000-8,000 salmon from the Babine post (18 September), it being "our only resource" (5 October). Much to his relief his hopes were more than met. That fall the Babine post traded 20,000 salmon from the natives (22 October) and sent 12,000 to Stuart's Lake at the end of September (16 October). More might be procured from Thompson's River, and in an emergency grain could be expressed from Fort Colvile. By the end of October the chief factor's anxiety abated further with the arrival of ten additional employees (23-24 October).

Within six months it would again be time to mount the spring brigade to Fort Vancouver.

Notes

Preface

1 W.S. Wallace, ed., *John McLean's Notes of a Twenty-Five Year's Service in the Hudson's Bay Territory* (Toronto: Champlain Society 1932), 185-6.

2 Harold A. Innis, *The Fur Trade in Canada: An Introduction to Canadian Economic History*, rev. ed. (Toronto: University of Toronto Press 1970), passim.

3 Lewis and Clark, after crossing the Rockies via the Lolo Pass route in 1805, believed that "we have found the most practicable and navigable passage across the Continent of North America" (Gary E. Moulton, ed., *The Journals of the Lewis & Clark Expedition* [Lincoln: University of Nebraska Press 1990], 6:309), but they had not, of course, the Peace-Fraser-Columbia route proving much superior.

4 W. Kaye Lamb, ed., *The Letters and Journals of Simon Fraser 1806-1808* (Toronto: Macmillan 1960), 76, 77.

5 The Columbia River was found by Captain Bruno de Hezeta in 1775 but not entered until the spring of 1792 by Gray, who named the river after his ship, the *Columbia Rediviva*. Several months later Lieutenant William Broughton of Captain Vancouver's expedition also entered the river. Vancouver himself passed the river's mouth two weeks before Gray but did not detect it. Lieutenant Charles Wilkes, commander of the United States Exploring Expedition of 1838-42, was "at a loss" to understand how the British commander could have missed the mouth of the "great river of the west" in view of "the evidence of a powerful flood of fresh water contending with the tides of the ocean, in a bar turbulent with breakers, in turbid waters extending several miles beyond the line of the shore, and in the marked line of separation between the sea and river water" (Charles Wilkes, *Narrative of the United States Exploring Expedition* [Philadelphia: Lea & Blanchard 1845], 4:293).

6 Cole Harris, "Towards a Geography of White Power in the Cordilleran Fur Trade," *Canadian Geographer* 39 (1995): 132, 133.

7 James R. Gibson, *Farming the Frontier: The Agricultural Opening of the Oregon Country, 1786-1846* (Vancouver: University of British Columbia Press 1985).

8 The records of the Hudson's Bay Company are particularly rich, of course, and they include two especially informative journals of the 1826 and 1830 brigades that are published here for the first time (see Appendices 1 and 2). It should be cautioned, however, that the sources, particularly the post journals and district reports, are much richer on the 1820s than on the earlier or later years. So what might be called the brigade system's halcyon phase – from the early 1830s to the middle 1840s, when the problems of the formative phase had been either mitigated or overcome – is underdocumented and hence underappreciated.

9 The most recent and most scholarly treatment is Mary Cullen, "Outfitting New Caledonia 1821-58," in Carol M. Judd and Arthur J. Ray, eds., *Old Trails and New Directions: Papers of the Third North American Fur Trade Conference* (Toronto: University of Toronto Press 1980), 231-51. Also see William C. Brown, "Old Fort Okanogan and the Okanogan Trail," *Oregon Historical Quarterly* 15 (1914): 1-38; F.M. Buckland, "The Hudson's Bay Brigade Trail," in *The Sixth Report of the Okanagan Historical Society 1935* (Vancouver: Wrigley Printing 1936), 11-22; E.P. Creech, "Brigade Trails of B.C.," *The Beaver* (Spring 1953): 10-15; and Margaret A. Ormsby, "The Significance of the Hudson's Bay Brigade Trail," in *The Thirteenth Report of the Okanagan Historical Society 1949*, ed. Margaret A. Ormsby (n.p., n.d.), 29-37. These older articles, however, tend to lack detail, balance, analysis, or documentation.

Two interesting guidebooks to traces of the Okanagan section of the brigade trail have appeared: Roberta Holt, Alfred Jahnke, and Peter Tassie, *The Okanagan Brigade Trail:*

Central and North Okanagan. A Field Guide to the Remaining Sections of the Trail (Vernon: Vernon Branch of the Okanagan Historical Society 1986) and Bob Harris, Harley Hatfield, and Peter Tassie, *The Okanagan Brigade Trail in the South Okanagan 1811 to 1849: Oroville, Washington to Westside, British Columbia* (n.p., 1989).

Chapter 1: Opening the Oregon Country

1   HBCA, B.119/b/1, McLeod's Lake – Correspondence Book, 1823-24, [Stuart] to McDougall, 15 November 1823.

2   The Russian-American Company (RAC) did not really enter this contest, preferring from its founding in 1799 to preoccupy itself with the maritime fur trade (sea otter and fur seal) of the Pacific coast. Astor's Pacific Fur Company (PFC) did enter the fray in 1811 at the mouth of the Columbia but abandoned it two years later under duress (the War of 1812).

3   Alexander Ross, *The Fur Hunters of the Far West*, ed. Kenneth A. Spaulding (Norman: University of Oklahoma Press 1956), 67.

4   HBCA, B.188/b/1, Fort St. James – Correspondence Book, 1821-2, Stuart to Garry, 20 April 1822. Stuart considered himself "the person who first explored and established this quarter," and he regarded New Caledonia as "a child of my own rearing" (ibid.; also see HBCA, D.4/116, Governor George Simpson – Correspondence Book Inwards, 1821-2, Stuart to the Governor and Council of the Northern Department, 27 April 1822). Nevertheless, he rated James McDougall, who accompanied him to the Cordillera in 1805, "the father of New Caledonia" (HBCA, B.188/b/1, Fort St. James – Correspondence Book, 1821-2, Stuart to Garry, 20 April 1822; HBCA, D.4/116, Governor George Simpson – Correspondence Book Inwards, 1821-2, Stuart to the Governor and Council of the Northern Department, 27 April 1822; also see HBCA, B.188/b/1, Fort St. James – Correspondence Book, 1821-2, Stuart to Leith, 24 April 1822). In 1828, two years before his break with Stuart over their treatment of "country wives," Governor George Simpson declared that Stuart "may be considered, the Father or founder of New Caledonia; where for 20 years of his Life, he was doomed to all the misery and privation, which that inhospitable region could bring forth, and who with a degree of exertion, of which few men were capable, overcame difficulties, to which the business of no other part of the country was exposed; bringing its returns to near about their present standing, and leaving the District as a Monument of his unwearied industry and extraordinary perseverance, which will long reflect the highest credit on his name and character, as an Indian Trader" (E.E. Rich, ed., *Part of Dispatch from George Simpson Esq^R Governor of Ruperts Land to the Governor & Committee of the Hudson's Bay Company London March 1, 1829* ... [Toronto: Champlain Society 1947], 25-6).

5   HBCA, B.119/b/1, McLeod's Lake – Correspondence Book, 1823-4, [Stuart] to McDougall, 15 November 1823.

6   Alexander Ross, *Adventures of the First Settlers on the Oregon or Columbia River, 1810-1813* (Lincoln: University of Nebraska Press 1986), 139.

7   David Thompson, *Columbia Journals*, ed. Barbara Belyea (Montreal: McGill-Queen's University Press 1994), 142.

8   W. Stewart Wallace, ed., *Documents Relating to the North West Company* (Toronto: Champlain Society 1934), 268.

9   W. Kaye Lamb, ed., *The Journals and Letters of Sir Alexander Mackenzie* (Cambridge, UK: Cambridge University Press for the Hakluyt Society 1979), 417.

10 The best secondary work on the Astorian venture is James P. Ronda, *Astoria & Empire* (Lincoln: University of Nebraska Press 1990). The most accessible and reliable primary source is Ross, *Adventures of the First Settlers*; also see Robert F. Jones, ed., *Astorian Adventure: The Journal of Alfred Seton 1811-1815* (New York: Fordham University Press 1993) and Kenneth A. Spaulding, ed., *On the Oregon Trail: Robert Stuart's Journal of Discovery* (Norman: University of Oklahoma Press 1953). Less trustworthy is Ross Cox, *The Columbia River; Or scenes and adventures during a residence of six years on the western side of the Rocky Mountains among various tribes of Indians hitherto unknown* ..., ed. Edgar I. Stewart and Jane R. Stewart (Norman: University of Oklahoma Press 1957). The classic fictional treatment is Washington Irving, *Astoria; or, Anecdotes of an Enterprise beyond the Rocky Mountains*, ed. Edgeley W. Todd (Norman: University of Oklahoma Press 1964), originally published in 1836.

11   Ross, *Adventures of the First Settlers*, 1986 edition, 101.
12   "Astor Papers," BRBML, Western Americana Collection, Astor to Jones, 8 August 1813.
13   Alexander Ross, *Adventures of the First Settlers on the Oregon or Columbia River* (London: Smith, Elder, and Co. 1849), 175.
14   See Ronda, *Astoria & Empire*, 62-4.
15   Earlier, on 2 May, an Astorian party of one canoe with six men under McKay had gone to the Cascades to assure the natives of the PFC's friendship.
16   Ross, *Adventures of the First Settlers*, 1986 edition, 115. Thompson, however, wrote that the Astorian party comprised three canoes and intended to erect a post near the junction of the Columbia and Snake Rivers (Thompson, *Columbia Journals*, 157).
17   Ross, *Adventures of the First Settlers*, 1849 edition, 150.
18   Kenneth Wiggins Porter, *John Jacob Astor: Business Man* (New York: Russell & Russell 1966), 1:530-2.
19   Ross, *Adventures of the First Settlers*, 1849 edition, 283.
20   W. Kaye Lamb, ed., *Sixteen Years in the Indian Country: The Journal of Daniel Williams Harmon 1800-1816* (Toronto: Macmillan 1957), 167.
21   Ross, *Adventures of the First Settlers*, 1986 edition, 244.
22   Ross, *Adventures of the First Settlers*, 1849 edition, 254.
23   Ross, *Adventures of the First Settlers*, 1986 edition, 257. Elsewhere, Ross called the Nor' Westers "the great Nabobs of the fur trade" (Ross, *Fur Hunters of the Far West*, 55).
24   The best primary sources on the NWC's "adventure to the Columbia" are Gabriel Franchère, *Journal of a Voyage on the North West Coast* ..., trans. Wessie Tipping Lamb (Toronto: Champlain Society 1969); Barry M. Gough, ed., *The Journal of Alexander Henry the Younger 1799-1814* (Toronto: Champlain Society 1992), vol. 2; and Ross, *Adventures of the First Settlers*, 1849 edition.
25   Innis, *Fur Trade in Canada*, 260-1.
26   Ibid., 261.
27   Wallace, *Documents*, 262, 266. In 1811 Thompson vainly proposed that the Peace River route be used instead (ibid., 266).
28   Ibid., 271-2. Already by 1814, however, the NWC was hoping that "a favourable connection could be made with an American House ... for facilitating the Business in China," the arrangement with the EIC apparently proving too costly (ibid., 283).
29   Lamb, *Sixteen Years in the Indian Country*, 154-5.
30   Ibid., 159.
31   Ibid.
32   Ibid., 163.
33   Ross, *Adventures of the First Settlers*, 1986 edition, 244.
34   Lamb, *Sixteen Years in the Indian Country*, 163, 164.
35   HBCA, B.188/e/1, Fort St. James – District Reports, 1822-1823, fo. 3v.
36   Lamb, *Sixteen Years in the Indian Country*, 170-1. The brigade brought goods that had been shipped from England on the *Isaac Todd* and the *Columbia*; the former arrived at Fort George on 23 April 1814 and left for Canton with furs on 26 September, while the latter arrived at Fort George on 29 June, traded along the coast as far north as Sitka in the summer and autumn, returned to Fort George at the end of the year for furs, and sailed to Canton via the Hawaiian Islands at the beginning of 1815.
37   Gough, *Journal of Alexander Henry*, 2:633-4, 708-9; Ross, *Adventures of the First Settlers*, 1849 edition, 264-6, 276.
38   Gough, *Journal of Alexander Henry*, 2:735, 745-7.
39   Peter Corney, *Early Voyages to the North Pacific 1813-1818* (Fairfield, WA: Ye Galleon Press 1965), 176.
40   Ross, *Fur Hunters of the Far West*, 58, 59.
41   Corney, *Early Voyages to the North Pacific*, 141.
42   Ibid., 83, 84, 95.
43   For example, the returns from the three interior posts of Thompson's River, Fort Okanagan, and Spokane House for the winters of 1811-12 and 1812-13 totalled only 140 packs of furs (no more than 7,700 beaver skins) (Franchère, *Journal of a Voyage*, 119).

44   Ross, *Fur Hunters of the Far West*, 53, 55, 56, 57, 58, 96, 108, 117. Actually, Fort Nez Percés did
      not replace Spokane House, which was not supplanted until 1826 by Fort Colvile.
            Ross also wrote that under this reorganization the region would henceforth be supplied
      overseas via Fort George rather than overland from Fort William, with the returns being
      shipped to the Canton market via the Columbia instead of Montreal (ibid., 56). In fact,
      however, this was already the case.
45   Ibid., 83.
46   Ibid., 134.
47   HBCA, D.4/116, Governor George Simpson – Correspondence Book Inwards, 1821-22, Lewes
      to Simpson, 2 April 1822.
48   The "Willamette freemen" were vaunted as independent and resourceful farmers, hunters,
      trappers, and guides.
49   Ross, *Adventures of the First Settlers*, 1986 edition, 114, 228, 261. According to the Astorian
      Alfred Seton, elk particularly abounded in the cottonwood bottomlands of the river and deer
      in the prairies and hills of the valley (Jones, *Astorian Adventure*, 116, 121).
            The Astorians did not wait long to tap the Willamette Valley, sending at least four expe-
      ditions there. The first, under Robert Stuart, did a quick reconnaissance in December 1811;
      the second, a party of eight under Donald McKenzie, explored 100 miles up the river in
      April 1812; a third Astorian party of sixteen men under John Halsey and William Wallace
      in two canoes reached the Willamette from Astoria at the end of November 1812 in order
      to winter and found a post (Wallace House near present-day Salem) as a food supply base
      (game) for Astoria, but the unexpectedly mild winters of the valley and the lack of salt
      impeded food preservation, although the post sent seventeen packs of furs (up to 1,020
      beaver) and thirty-two bales of dried venison to Astoria in late May 1813; and a fourth party
      under Duncan McDougall traded 500 miles up the Willamette to its headwaters in the
      spring of 1813 and found the natives numerous but tractable, game (deer and elk) abundant,
      and the Umpqua River Valley the best beaver ground (Cox, *Columbia River*, 218, n. 6;
      Franchère, *Journal of a Voyage*, 112, 116, 119, 144; Ross, *Adventures of the First Settlers*, 1986
      edition, 228, 229, 230, 231).
50   NAC, Map VI-700.
51   HBCA, B.76/e/1, Fort George (Columbia River) – District Report, 1824-25, fo. 1.
52   [John Work], "Journal of John Work," BCARS, MS AB40 W89.1, 24 May 1834.
53   HBCA, B.188/b/1, Fort St. James – Correspondence Book, 1821-22, Garry to Stuart, 17 July
      1821.
54   E.E. Rich, ed., *Colin Robertson's Correspondence Book, September 1817 to September 1822*
      (Toronto: Champlain Society 1939), 96. According to Robertson, a former Nor'Wester, the
      New Caledonia and Mackenzie River districts together accounted for more than half of the
      NWC's returns (ibid., 260); New Caledonia yielded the NWC eighty packs annually, mainly
      beaver, according to Chief Trader John Clarke, who, however, was not known for his integrity
      (ibid., 213).
55   "Remember Gentlemen," wrote Chief Factor John McLoughlin of Fort Vancouver to his
      officers in 1825, "we ought to get all we can from the south side of the Columbia while it is
      in our power" (HBCA, B.223/b/1, Fort Vancouver – Correspondence Book, 1825, McLough-
      lin to the Chief Factors and Chief Traders [of the Columbia Department], 10 August 1825;
      also see HBCA, D.4/119, Governor George Simpson – Correspondence Book Inwards,
      1824-26, McLoughlin to the Governor, Chief Factors, and Chief Traders of the Northern
      Department, 10 August 1825). A year later Governor Simpson reminded McLoughlin that
      the purpose of the annual trapping expeditions to the Snake Country was "to scour the
      country wherever Beaver can be found … to reap all the advantage we can for ourselves,
      and leave it in as bad a state as possible for our successors" (HBCA, D.4/6, Governor George
      Simpson – Correspondence Book Outwards (General), 1825-26, Simpson to McLoughlin,
      10 July 1826).
56   HBCA, D.4/85, Governor George Simpson – Official Reports to the Governor and Com-
      mittee in London, 1822, Simpson to the Governor and Committee, 16 July 1822.
57   HBCA, D.4/86, Governor George Simpson – Official Reports to the Governor and Com-
      mittee in London, 1823, Simpson to the Governor and Committee, 1 August 1823.

58 HBCA, D.4/116, Governor George Simpson – Correspondence Book Inwards, 1821-22, Lewes to Simpson, 2 April 1822.

59 Beaver House complained to Simpson in 1824 after receiving the Columbia's returns on the *Lively* that "there is room for much improvement in the drying and preparing the Skins in the interior [of the district] and in the care and preservation of them previous to being Shipt" (HBCA, D.5/1, Governor George Simpson – Correspondence Inward, 1821-26, Governor and Committee to Simpson, 2 June 1824). According to Chief Factor John McLoughlin of Fort Vancouver, the blame lay partly with the natives, who could "not be got to keep their furs clean and stretch them better," and partly with the freemen, who did not beat their pelts (HBCA, B.223/b/1, Fort Vancouver – Correspondence Book, 1825, McLoughlin to the Chief Factors and Chief Traders of the Columbia Department, 20 June 1825; also see HBCA, D.4/119, Governor George Simpson – Correspondence Book Inwards, 1824-25, McLoughlin to the Chief Factors and Chief Traders of the Columbia Department, 20 June 1825). McLoughlin stated that it was necessary to "beat our furs from time to time," as well as hang them in a cellar in order to keep them pliable and free of moths (ibid.). He told Simpson that "we cannot do without some person to be constantly beating and airing the Furs" (HBCA, B.223/b/1, Fort Vancouver – Correspondence Book, 1825, McLoughlin to Simpson, 20 June 1825). McLoughlin estimated that his furs would bring 25 percent more in the market "if we could get them in the same state as we get them on the other side of the Mountain" (HBCA, D.4/119, Governor George Simpson – Correspondence Book Inwards, 1824-26, McLoughlin to the Chief Factors and Chief Traders of the Columbia Department, 20 June 1825).

60 John Tod, "History of New Caledonia and the Northwest Coast," 1878, BCARS, MS, 21.

61 HBCA, B.188/b/1, Fort St. James – Correspondence Book, 1821-22, Stuart to Garry, 20 April 1822.

62 Ibid. Also see ibid., Stuart to Leith, 25 February 1822; D.4/116, Governor George Simpson – Correspondence Book Inwards, 1821-22, Stuart to the Governor and Committee, 27 April 1822; B.119/e/1, McLeod's Lake – District Report, 1824.

63 HBCA, B.188/a/1, Fort St. James – Post Journal, 1820-21, 27 January 1821.

64 HBCA, B.188/b/1, Fort St. James – Correspondence Book, 1821-22, Leith to Stuart, 19 September 1821.

65 Ibid., Stuart to Brown, 3 November 1821.

66 HBCA, B.188/a/2, Fort St. James – Post Journal, 1823-24, 31 May 1823 (Stuart to McDougall, 5 May 1823).

67 HBCA, B.188/a/1, Fort St. James – Post Journal, 1820-21, fos. 5v.-6.

68 Ibid., 20 October 1820.

69 Ibid., 19 October 1820.

70 HBCA, B.188/b/1, Fort St. James – Correspondence Book, 1821-22, Stuart to Garry, 20 April 1822; HBCA, D.4/116, Governor George Simpson – Correspondence Book Inwards, 1821-22, Stuart to the Governor and Council of the Northern Department, 27 April 1822.

71 HBCA, B.188/b/1, Fort St. James – Correspondence Book, 1821-22, Stuart to Garry, 20 April 1822.

72 HBCA, B.188/a/1, Fort St. James – Post Journal, 1820-21, 25 February 1821.

73 Ibid., 28 February 1821.

74 HBCA, D.4/116, Governor George Simpson – Correspondence Book Inwards, 1821-22, Brown [to the Governor of the Northern Department?], 4 November 1821, Leith to the Governor of the Northern Department, 11 February 1822. For a detailed list of the outfit (imports) received by New Caledonia via the Columbia in 1821 (and via the Peace in 1822), see HBCA, B.188/d/1, Fort St. James – Account Books, 1821-22, "Invoice of Sundries Supplied by the Columbia to New Caledonia on A/c of Outfit for 1821" and "Invoice of Sundries Supplied by the Different Establishments in Peace River Summer 1821 On A/c of Outfit for New Caledonia 1821/22."

75 HBCA, B.74/a/1, Fraser's Lake – Post Journal, 1822-24, 4 May 1822.

76 HBCA, B.188/b/1, Fort St. James – Correspondence Book, Fleming to Stuart, 12 August 1822. For a detailed list of the returns (exports) from New Caledonia in 1822, see HBCA, B.188/d/1, Fort St. James – Account Books, 1821-22, "Contents of One hundred & thee

Packs Weighing 86 lbs Made up in New Caledonia Marked & Numbered as Per Margin Spring 1822" and "Recapitulation of the foregoing Packs & Returns of New Caledonia Spring 1822."

77   HBCA, B.74/a/1, Fraser's Lake – Post Journal, 1822-24, 17 October 1822; HBCA, D.4/117, Governor George Simpson – Correspondence Book Inwards, 1822-23, McDougall to Simpson, 22 October 1822, Brown to Simpson, 3 December 1822. Also see HBCA, D.4/2, Governor George Simpson – Correspondence Book Outwards (General), 1822-23, Simpson to Stuart, 6 February 1823.

78   HBCA, B.188/b/1, Fort St. James – Correspondence Book, 1821-22, Stuart to Garry, 20 April 1822.

79   Ibid., Stuart to Leith, 25 February 1822.

80   HBCA, D.4/116, Governor George Simpson – Correspondence Book Inwards, 1821-22, Stuart to the Governor and Council of the Northern Department, 27 April 1822.

81   R. Harvey Fleming, ed., *Minutes of Council Northern Department of Rupert Land, 1821-31* (Toronto: Champlain Society 1940), 302.

82   Ibid., 343.

83   HBCA, D.4/118, Governor George Simpson – Correspondence Book Inwards, 1822-23, Brown to Simpson, 25 April 1823. The Americans did not reoccupy Fort George, but the possibility of their doing so at any time, plus the implication that the southern side, or left bank, of the Columbia below the Snake junction would become U.S. territory, induced the HBC to replace it as the departmental depot with Fort Vancouver on the northern side. At the same time an abortive attempt was made to move Fort Nez Percés to the northern side of the Columbia. And when the Puget's Sound Agricultural Company, a subsidiary of the HBC, was formed in 1839, all of its operations were confined to the right bank.

84   HBCA, D.4/117, Governor George Simpson – Correspondence Book Inwards, 1822-23, Brown to Simpson, 3 December 1822.

85   Ibid., McDougall to Simpson, 22 October 1822 [1823?].

86   HBCA, B.188/e/1, Fort St. James – District Report, 1822-23.

87   HBCA, B.119/e/1, McLeod's Lake – District Report, 1824.

88   HBCA, B.188/b/2, Fort St. James – Correspondence Book, 1822-23, Stuart to Simpson, 4 January 1823.

89   Ibid., Stuart to Brown, 29 November 1822. Subsequently Stuart and Simpson were estranged by the latter's treatment of his "country wife" (the sister of Stuart's own "country wife") and family, whom he discarded upon his return from Britain in 1830 with his English wife.

Chapter 2: Linking the Oregon Country

1   HBCA, B.5/e/1, Fort Alexandria – District Report, 1827-28, fo. 24v. Elsewhere this quotation is attributed to Chief Trader Samuel Black (Rich, *Part of Dispatch from George Simpson*, 216-17).

2   New Caledonia's outfit year was defined by the time of collection and enumeration of the district's returns prior to their transport by the outgoing brigade – the end of February via the Peace route and the end of March via the Columbia route.

3   HBCA, B.188/a/3, Fort St. James – Post Journal, 1824-25, 22 February 1825.

4   HBCA, B.5/a/1, Fort Alexandria – Post Journal, 1824-25, 21 January 1825.

5   HBCA, B.188/b/1, Fort St. James – Correspondence Book, 1821-22, Stuart to Faries, 25 February 1822.

6   Ibid., Stuart to Leith, 24 April 1822.

7   HBCA, B.188/a/1, Fort St. James – Post Journal, 1820-21, 2 July 1820.

8   Lamb, *Letters and Journals of Simon Fraser*, 84.

9   HBCA, B.223/a/3, Fort Vancouver – Post Journal, 1826, 28 October 1826.

10 Cox, *Columbia River*, 127.

11 HBCA, B.5/a/1, Fort Alexandria – Post Journal, 1824-25, 25 December 1824.

12 HBCA, B.119/a/2, McLeod's Lake – Post Journal, 1824, 27 July 1824.

13 HBCA, B.188/a/3, Fort St. James – Post Journal, 1824-25, 5 May 1825.

14 HBCA, B.188/a/8, Fort St. James – Post Journal, 1826-27, 5 May 1826.

15 HBCA, B.188/e/1, Fort St. James – District Report, 1822-23, fo. 2.

16 Lamb, *Letters and Journals of Simon Fraser*, 185, 230. Governor Simpson also found the navigation of the upper Peace "bad and dangerous" (E.E. Rich, ed., *Journal of Occurrences in the Athabasca Department by George Simpson, 1820 and 1821, and Report* [Toronto: Champlain Society 1938], 384).

17 HBCA, B.119/a/1, McLeod's Lake – Post Journal, 1823-24, 6 and 12 October 1823; ibid., "Journal of Occurrences from York Factory to and at Western Caledonia by John Stuart 1823 & 4," 13 October 1823.

18 HBCA, D.4/125, Governor George Simpson – Correspondence Book Inwards, 1829-31, Connolly to the Chief Factors and Chief Traders of the Athabasca District, 2 September 1830.

19 Rich, *Journal of Occurrences in the Athabasca Department*, 391.

20 HBCA, B.188/b/1, Fort St. James – Correspondence Book, 1821-22, Stuart to Faries, 25 February 1822.

21 HBCA, B.119/a/1, McLeod's Lake – Post Journal, 1823-24, 12 October 1823. Stuart's brigade spent ten days at the portage crossing, measuring, and improving it, repairing their boats, and conferring with the Indians (ibid., 5-14 October 1823). Also see ibid., "Journal of Occurrences from York Factory to and at Western Caledonia by John Stuart 1823 & 4," 12 October 1823.

22 HBCA, B.188/a/3, Fort St. James – Post Journal, 1824-25, 8-17 October 1824.

23 Malcolm McLeod, ed., *Peace River: A Canoe Voyage from Hudson's Bay to Pacific by Sir George Simpson (Governor, Hon. Hudson's Bay Company.) in 1828. Journal of the late Chief Factor, Archibald McDonald (Hon. Hudson's Bay Company), who accompanied him* (Edmonton: M.G. Hurtig Ltd. 1971), 18.

24 Wallace, *John McLean's Notes*, 143.

25 HBCA, D.4/117, Governor George Simpson – Correspondence Book Inwards, 1822-23, McDougall to Simpson, 22 October 1823.

26 McLeod, *Peace River*, 19.

27 HBCA, B.188/a/3, Fort St. James – Post Journal, 1824-25, 5 May, 7 July 1825.

28 HBCA, D.4/88, Governor George Simpson – Official Reports to the Governor and Committee in London, 1825, Simpson to the Governor and Committee, 10 March 1825.

29 HBCA, B.188/a/2, Fort St. James – Post Journal, 1823-24, 3 November 1823.

30 HBCA, B.188/a/3, Fort St. James – Post Journal, 1824-25, 27 July, 30 October 1824. However, the Council of the Northern Department had "resolved" on 1 July that "6 canoes containing 130 ps [pieces] manned by 36 men constitute the current outfit" (Frederick Merk, ed., *Fur Trade and Empire: George Simpson's Journal ...*, rev. ed. [Cambridge, MA; Belknap Press 1968], 220).

31 HBCA, B.188/a/4, Fort St. James – Post Journal, 1824-25, 7 November 1825; HBCA, B.188/a/5, Fort St. James – Post Journal, 1825-26, [5? September], 31 October 1825. The brigade had been ordered by the Council of the Northern Department to transport 108 pieces in six canoes with thirty-two men (Fleming, *Minutes of Council*, 105).

For an account of a brigade journey from York Factory to McLeod's Lake in the summer and autumn of 1824 by William Connolly, see HBCA, B.188/a/3, Fort St. James – Post Journal, 1824-25, 27 July-27 October 1824, pp. 2-26; also see "Journal of Occurrences from York Factory to and at Western Caledonia by John Stuart 1823 & 4" in HBCA, B.119/a/1, McLeod's Lake – Post Journal, 1823-24.

32 HBCA, B.188/a/8, Fort St. James – Post Journal, 1826-27, 23 September 1826.

33 HBCA, D.4/119, Governor George Simpson – Correspondence Book Inwards, 1824-26, Connolly to Simpson, 30 April 1826.

34 HBCA, B.188/e/3, Fort St. James – District Report, 1824-25, fo. 14.

35 HBCA, D.4/119, Governor George Simpson – Correspondence Book Inwards, 1824-26, Connolly to Simpson, 30 April 1826.

36 HBCA, B.188/a/3, Fort St. James – Post Journal, 1824-25, 31 October 1824.

37 Ibid., 1, 2, 3 November 1824.

38 HBCA, B.188/e/1, Fort St. James – District Report, 1822-23, fo. 3.

39 HBCA, D.4/88, Governor George Simpson – Official Reports to the Governor and Committee in London, 1825, Simpson to the Governor and Committee, 10 March 1825.

40 HBCA, D.4/87, Governor George Simpson – Official Reports to the Governor and Committee, 1824, "Minutes of a Temporary Council ... Northern District of Ruperts Land ..."

41 HBCA, B.188/e/3, Fort St. James – District Report, 1824-25, fos. 14v., 15.
42 HBCA, B.188/a/5, Fort St. James – Post Journal, 1825-26, William Connolly, "Report of New Caledonia District 1826." Also see HBCA, D.4/119, Governor George Simpson – Correspondence Book Inwards, 1824-26, Connolly to Simpson, 30 April 1826.
43 The coastal posts – Forts Langley (1827), Simpson (1831-32), McLoughlin (1833), Nisqually (1833), Stikine, or Highfield (1840), Taku, or Durham (1841), and Victoria (1843) – were supplied not by the brigade, of course, but by the "coasting vessel."
44 McLeod, *Peace River*, 113.
45 Ibid.
46 HBCA, B.188/a/3, Fort St. James – Post Journal, 1824-25, 28 October 1824.
47 Ibid., n.d., 152.
48 HBCA, D.4/119, Governor George Simpson – Correspondence Book Inwards, 1824-26, Connolly to the Chief Factors and Chief Traders of the Northern Department, 4 February 1826.
49 HBCA, D.4/7, Governor George Simpson – Correspondence Book Outwards (General), 1824-26, Simpson to the Governor and Committee, 31 August 1825.
50 HBCA, B.119/e/1, McLeod's Lake – District Report, 1824.
51 John Edward Harriott, "Memoirs of Life and Adventure in the Hudson's Bay Company's Territories, 1819-1825," BRBML, Western Americana MS 245, n.p.
52 HBCA, D.4/7, Governor George Simpson – Correspondence Book Outwards (General), 1824-26, Simpson to the Governor and Committee, 31 August 1825.
53 HBCA, D.4/6, Governor George Simpson – Correspondence Book Outwards (General), 1825-26, Simpson to Connolly, 5 July 1826, and Simpson to McLoughlin, 10 July 1826.
54 HBCA, D.4/120, Governor George Simpson – Correspondence Book Inwards, 1826-27, McLoughlin to Simpson, 20 March 1827.
55 HBCA, D.4/116, Governor George Simpson – Correspondence Book Inwards, 1821-22, Cameron to Simpson, 3 April 1822.
56 In 1821 the Willamette freemen sold some 2,000 beaver skins to the NWC at Fort George (HBCA, D.4/116, Governor George Simpson – Correspondence Book Inwards, 1821-22, Cameron to the Governor and Council of the Northern Department, 3 April 1822). And in the middle 1820s the Willamette still produced 1,000-2,000 beaver annually, collected by seven freemen (HBCA, B.76/e/1, Fort George [Columbia River] – District Report, 1824-25, fo. 1).
57 HBCA, D.4/117, Governor George Simpson – Correspondence Book Inwards, 1822-23, Ross to [the Council of the Northern Department?], 10 February 1823.
58 HBCA, D.4/6, Governor George Simpson – Correspondence Book Outwards (General), 1825-26, McLoughlin to the Governor and Committee, 6 October 1825.
59 HBCA, B.45/a/1, Fort Colvile – Post Journal, 1830-31, 31 August 1830.
60 HBCA, D.4/7, Governor George Simpson – Correspondence Book Outwards (General), 1824-26, Simpson to the Governor and Committee, 31 August 1825.
61 HBCA, D.4/119, Governor George Simpson – Correspondence Book Inwards, 1824-26, Connolly to the Governor and Council of the Northern Department, 1 May 1826. Connolly wrote: "But altho' this plan would answer well, a less expensive one might be adopted in its place, which would be to transport the leather etc immediately in the Fall by the Columbia [Athabasca] Portage to Okanagan, from whence it would be taken en passant & brought in with the rest of the yearly Outfits." This route, he said, would save the wages of two men, as well as "much trouble" on the part of the Saskatchewan personnel. In fact, his suggestion was followed in 1826, when fifty-two moose skins reached New Caledonia via this route in the late winter of 1825-26 (HBCA, B.188/a/5, Fort St. James – Post Journal, 1825-26, 23 November 1825, 5 February 1826, 9 March 1826).
62 HBCA, B.188/a/5, Fort St. James – Post Journal, 1825-26, 20 November 1825.
63 Ibid., 23 November 1825; HBCA, D.4/119, Governor George Simpson – Correspondence Book Inwards, 1824-26, Connolly to the Chief Factors and Chief Traders of the Northern Department, 4 February 1826.
64 HBCA, D.4/119, Governor George Simpson – Correspondence Book Inwards, 1824-26, Stuart to the Chief Factors and Chief Traders of the Northern Department, 16 February 1826.

65 A "halfbreed" was a mixed blood, or *brûlé* ("burnt"), so called from his or her swarthiness (Ross, *Fur Hunters of the Far West*, 196).

66 HBCA, B.188/b/5, Fort St. James – Correspondence Book, 1826-27, Connolly to the Commissioned Gentlemen of New Caledonia, 10 September 1826.

67 HBCA, D.4/119, Governor George Simpson – Correspondence Book Inwards, 1824-26, Connolly to the Chief Factors and Chief Traders of the Northern Department, 4 February 1826.

68 HBCA, D.4/127, Governor George Simpson – Correspondence Book Inwards, 1833-35, Dease to the Governor and Council of the Northern Department, 14 February 1835. For more details, see David Smyth, "The Yellowhead Pass and the Fur Trade," *BC Studies* 64 (1984-5): 48-73.

69 HBCA, B.5/a/2, Fort Alexandria – Post Journal, 1827-28, Connolly to McGillivray, 22 August 1827.

70 HBCA, D.4/119, Governor George Simpson – Correspondence Book Inwards, 1824-26, Connolly to the Governor and Council of the Northern Department, 1 May 1826.

71 HBCA, B.188/e/3, Fort St. James – District Report, 1824-25, fo. 16.

72 HBCA, B.188/a/5, Fort St. James – Post Journal, 1825-26, 30 October 1825.

73 HBCA, B.188/a/8, Fort St. James – Post Journal, 1826-27, 3-4 November 1826.

74 Ibid., 6 November 1826. According to Connolly's son, Henry, Waccan had accompanied Simon Fraser on his 1808 journey; he added that his name meant "cracked" in Cree and Ojibwa ([Henry Connolly], "Reminiscences of one of the last desendants of a Bourgeois of the North West Company," NAC, MS MG29 B15, vol. 61, file 34, 9).

75 HBCA, B.188/a/10, Fort St. James – Post Journal, 1827, 21 September, 30 October, 1-2 November 1827.

76 HBCA, B.188/a/12, Fort St. James – Post Journal, 1828, 4 October, 12, 15 November 1828.

77 HBCA, B.188/a/14, Fort St. James – Post Journal, 1829-30, 30 September, 4 October, 26 November 1829.

78 HBCA, D.4/124, Governor George Simpson – Correspondence Book Inwards, 1830-31, Minutes of a Council, 3 July 1830.

79 Ibid.

80 Ross, *Fur Hunters of the Far West*, 200.

81 Ibid., 104.

82 I.S. MacLaren, ed., "Journal of Paul Kane's Western Travels, 1846-1848," *American Art Journal* 21 (1989): 36.

83 HBCA, D.4/7, Governor George Simpson – Correspondence Book Outwards (General), 1824-26, Simpson to the Governor and Committee, 10 March 1825.

84 For accounts of the express route, see, for example, George T. Allan, "Journal of a Voyage from Fort Vancouver, Columbia, to York Factory, Hudson's Bay, 1841," BCARS, MS; James Douglas, "Journal of a Journey from Fort Vancouver to York Factory and Back 1835," BCARS, MS; and C.O. Ermatinger and James White, eds., "Edward Ermatinger's York Factory Express Journal, Being a Record of Journeys Made Between Fort Vancouver and Hudson Bay in the Years 1827-1828," *Proceedings and Transactions of the Royal Society of Canada*, 3rd series, vol. 6 (1912), section II, 67-132. Also see I.S. MacLaren, ed., "Journal of Paul Kane's Western Travels, 1846-1848," *American Art Journal* 21 (1989): 23-62; Amelius Simpson, "Journal of a Voyage Across the Continent of North America in 1826," HBCA, B.223/a/3, Fort Vancouver – Post Journal, 1826; H.J. Warre, *Overland to Oregon in 1845: Impressions of a Journey across North America*, ed. Madeleine Major-Frégeau (Ottawa: Public Archives of Canada 1976); and [John Work], "Journal of John Work," BCARS, MS AB40 W89.1, 18 July-28 October 1823, fos. 1-45 (York Factory to Spokane House). Later accounts include Thomas Lowe, "Journal of trip from Vancouver to York Factory pr. H.B. Express Spring 1847 ...," BCARS, MS AB20.4 L95; Thomas Lowe, "Journal from Vancouver to York Factory with Express, Spring 1848," BCARS, MS AB20.4 L95j; and John Charles, "Journal of the Columbia Express party," 1849, BCARS, MS AB20.4 C38 [transcript: AB20.4 C38A].

85 Edward Ermatinger, "Edward Ermatinger Papers 1820-1874," NAC, MS 19, series A2(2), 2:85; Glyndwr Williams and John S. Galbraith, eds., *London Correspondence Inward from Sir George Simpson 1841-42* (London: Hudson's Bay Record Society 1973), 52.

86 G.P. de T. Glazebrook, ed., *The Hargrave Correspondence 1821-1843* (Toronto: Champlain Society 1938), 371.

Chapter 3: Reforming the Oregon Country

1   Merk, *Fur Trade and Empire*, 72.

2   Ibid., 175.

3   Ibid., 243-4; Roderick Finlayson, "The History of Vancouver Island and the Northwest Coast," 1878, BLUC, MS P-C 15, 72-3.

4   The Snake Country was "much dreaded by all North Westers" because their trapping forays there were rendered laborious and dangerous by the rugged terrain, scanty provisions, and hostile Blackfoot (Ross, *Fur Hunters of the Far West*, 206).

5   HBCA, D.4/5, Governor George Simpson – Correspondence Book Outwards (General), 1824-25, Simpson to McLoughlin, 10 April 1825.

6   Merk, *Fur Trade and Empire*, 65.

7   HBCA, D.4/5, Governor George Simpson – Correspondence Book Outwards (General), 1824-25, Simpson to McLoughlin, 10 March 1825.

8   HBCA, A.12/1, London Inward Correspondence from Governors of H.B.C. Territories – Sir George Simpson, 1823-32, Simpson to the Governor and Committee, 20 August 1826.

9   HBCA, D.4/7, Governor George Simpson – Correspondence Book Outwards (General), 1824-26, Simpson to the Governor and Committee, 10 March 1825.

10 HBCA, D.4/5, Governor George Simpson – Correspondence Book Outwards (General), 1824-25, Simpson to Brown, 4 April 1825.

11 For details, see HBCA, D.4/5, Governor George Simpson – Correspondence Book Outwards (General), 1824-25, Simpson to McLoughlin, 10 March 1825, Simpson to Ogden, 14 March 1825, Simpson to McLoughlin, 10 April 1825; HBCA, D.4/88, Governor George Simpson – Official Reports to the Governor and Committee in London, 1825, Simpson to the Governor and Committee, 10 March 1825.

12 On the coast trade, see James R. Gibson, *Otter Skins, Boston Ships, and China Goods: The Maritime Fur Trade of the Northwest Coast, 1785-1841* (Montreal: McGill-Queen's University Press 1992).

13 Simpson mistakenly believed that the Fraser was "formed by nature as the grand communication with all our Establishments on this side the mountain," particularly in case the Columbia were ceded to the United States, but he changed his mind after attempting to descend it in 1828, discovering – as Simon Fraser (and John Stuart) had two decades earlier – that "it can no longer be thought of as a practicable communication with the interior ... the banks do not admit of Portages being made, and in many places it would be impossible to use the line, on account of the height of the projecting Rocks which afford no footing ... I should consider the passage down, to be certain Death, in nine attempts out of Ten" (Rich, *Part of Dispatch from George Simpson*, 28, 35, 38-9). Archibald McDonald descended the river with Simpson and found the Fraser Canyon in particular a "bad piece of navigation" (McLeod, *Peace River*, 36).

      Alternative river routes to the interior were also found wanting. In 1825 Mackenzie's route from the middle Fraser near Fort Alexandria westwards to the sea along the Chilcotin River proved suitable as a horse trail only. The Lillooet River ("Harrison's River") was explored by Francis Ermatinger from Thompson's River in 1827 and by James Yale (with eight men) from Fort Langley in the spring of 1830, but it was found that this prospective bypass of the Fraser Canyon "presents obstacles too formidable to entertain any notion of opening an easy communication with the Interior by the Lilliwhite now called Harrisons River" (HBCA, D.4/125, Governor George Simpson – Correspondence Book Inwards, 1829-31, McDonald to the Governor and Council of the Northern Department, 10 February 1831). And at the end of the summer of 1832 Donald Manson and ten men from Fort Simpson on the coast ascended the Nass River by canoe and concluded that in the summer the "navigation of this River would be impracticable" (HBCA, B.201/a/1, Fort Simpson [Nass River] – Post Journal, 1832, D. Manson, "Journal of a Voyage up Nass River"). The Columbia remained the HBC's route to the interior and Fort Vancouver the department's depot. "As long as we are free from Opposition and Outfit trappers to the South side of the Columbia," said McLoughlin, the latter was better situated than the Fraser to supply the department (HBCA, D.4/121, Governor George Simpson – Correspondence Book Inwards, 1827-28, McLoughlin to Simpson, 20 March 1828). After 1846, of course, these conditions no longer prevailed.

14 HBCA, B.76/e/1, Fort George (Columbia River) – District Report, 1824-25, fo. 5.
15 John Dunn, *History of the Oregon Territory ...*, 2nd ed. (London: Edwards and Hughes 1846), 216.
16 Ross, *Adventures of the First Settlers*, 1986 edition, 108, 140.
17 Ibid., 108.
18 On post farming, see Gibson, *Farming the Frontier*, chaps. 1-3.
19 HBCA, B.223/b/3, Fort Vancouver – Correspondence Book, 1827-28, McLoughlin to McDolnald, 17 November 1827.
20 HBCA, B.223/b/3, Fort Vancouver – Correspondence Book, 1827-28, McLoughlin to Connolly, 17 November 1827.
21 HBCA, B.223/b/8, Fort Vancouver – Correspondence Book, 1832-33, McLoughlin to Simpson, 12 September 1832.
22 HBCA, B.45/e/3, Fort Colvile – District Report, 1830.
23 HBCA, D.4/7, Governor George Simpson – Correspondence Book Outwards (General), 1824-26, Simpson to the Governor and Committee, 10 March 1825.
24 HBCA, D.4/119, Governor George Simpson – Correspondence Book Inwards, 1824-26, Robertson to Simpson, 10 May 1826.
25 HBCA, D.4/85, Governor George Simpson – Official Reports to the Governor and Committee in London, 1822, Simpson to the Governor and Committee, 31 July 1822.
26 HBCA, D.4/2, Governor George Simpson – Correspondence Book Outwards (General), 1822-23, Simpson to Stuart, 6 February 1823.
27 HBCA, D.4/86, Governor George Simpson – Official Reports to the Governor and Committee in London, 1823, Simpson to the Governor and Committee, 1 August 1823.
28 HBCA, D.4/85, Governor George Simpson – Official Reports to the Governor and Committee in London, 1822, Simpson to the Governor and Committee, 31 July 1822; HBCA, D.4/86, Governor George Simpson – Official Reports to the Governor and Committee in London, 1823, Simpson to the Governor and Committee, 1 August 1823. The Governor and Committee, however, did not accept Simpson's preference for Canadiens over Orkneymen.
29 Rich, *Journal of Occurrences in the Athabasca Department*, 402.
30 HBCA, B.119/a/1, McLeod's Lake – Post Journal, 1823-24, 23 July 1823.
31 HBCA, D.4/7, Governor George Simpson – Correspondence Book Outwards (General), 1824-26, Simpson to the Governor and Committee, 31 August 1825.
32 The shift of the brigade route did reduce New Caledonia's company roster. In 1822-23 the district contained fifty-six employees (comprising one chief factor, one chief trader, eight clerks, five interpreters [three mixed bloods and two Indians], one boatbuilder, four bowsmen, seven steersmen, and twenty-nine middlemen), plus five women (country wives) and three children, at six posts (HBCA, B.188/e/1, Fort St. James – District Report, 1822-23, fos. 4-4v.). The complement for the transition year of 1825-26 was sixty-one (one chief factor, one chief trader, three clerks, four interpreters, one guide, thirty-four canoe men, and seventeen summer men), of whom en route from York Factory three deserted, one was left sick at Fort Chipewyan, one was dismissed for misconduct, and one (the guide, no longer needed) was left at the Rocky Mountain Portage (HBCA, B.188/a/5, Fort St. James – Post Journal, 1825-26, "Report of New Caledonia District 1826," 149-50); the 1826-27 complement was set at forty-two (one chief factor, six clerks, two interpreters, and thirty-three men), a "reduction [of nineteen] which the change of route admits of being effected" (ibid., 150).
33 HBCA, A.12/1, London Inward Correspondence from Governors of H.B.C. Territories – Sir George Simpson, 1823-32, Simpson to the Governor and Committee, August 1825.
34 HBCA, D.4/5, Governor George Simpson – Correspondence Book Outwards (General), 1824-25, Simpson to McLoughlin, 11 July 1825; also see Fleming, *Minutes of Council*, 106.
35 HBCA, D.4/5, Governor George Simpson – Correspondence Book Outwards (General), 1824-25, Simpson to McLoughlin, 11 July 1825. When Simpson had announced his plans in the late winter-early spring of 1825, it was too late "to make any change for the current season in the mode of conducting the New Caledonia transport business"; especially the necessary number of pack horses could not be provided without abandoning an exploratory expedition to the mouth of the Fraser from Fort George (it required forty horses) and a trapping expedition to the Umpqua Country from Fort Vancouver (its forty to fifty men

were mostly the "extra Columbia men" of the Columbia brigade) (ibid., Simpson to Brown, 4 April 1825).

36 HBCA, D.4/5, Governor George Simpson – Correspondence Book Outwards (General), 1824-25, Simpson to Brown, 4 April 1825.
37 HBCA, B.188/a/3, Fort St. James – Post Journal, 1824-25, 19 May 1825.
38 HBCA, B.188/a/5, Fort St. James – Post Journal, 1825-26, [5 September 1825?].
39 HBCA, D.4/119, Governor George Simpson – Correspondence Book Inwards, 1824-26, Connolly to Simpson, 30 April 1826.

Chapter 4: Canoeing down the Fraser

1 Rich, *Part of Dispatch from George Simpson*, 25.
2 Wallace, *John McLean's Notes*, 186.
3 On "country wives," see Jennifer S.H. Brown, *Strangers in Blood: Fur Trade Company Families in Indian Country* (Vancouver: University of British Columbia Press 1980) and Sylvia Van Kirk, *"Many Tender Ties": Women in Fur Trade Society* (Winnipeg: Watson and Dwyer 1980), as well as several articles by the latter.
4 The Willamette Valley (and Vancouver Island) were particularly attractive to those servants who had native wives and mixed-blood children and who consequently could not have retired to the Canadas without becoming social outcasts. The Red River Settlement was another possibility, but it was climatically harsher than the Pacific Coast.
5 John McLeod, "John McLeod Papers 1811-1837," NAC, MS 19, series A23, 1:271.
6 John Work, "Work Correspondence," BCARS, MS AB40, 82.
7 Ross, *Adventures of the First Settlers*, 1986 edition, 85.
8 Lamb, *Sixteen Years in the Indian Country*, 171.
9 HBCA, D.4/125, Governor George Simpson – Correspondence Book Inwards, 1829-31, McLoughlin to Simpson, 16 March 1831; E.E. Rich, ed., *Letters of John McLoughlin from Fort Vancouver to the Governor and Committee* (London: Hudson's Bay Record Society 1941), 1:228.
10 HBCA, B.45/a/1, Fort Colvile – Post Journal, 1830-31, 13 July 1830; HBCA, D.4/125, Governor George Simpson – Correspondence Book Inwards, 1829-31, Kittson to Rowand, 12 August 1830; Connolly to the Chief Factors and Chief Traders of the Athabasca District, 2 September 1830; Rich, *Letters of John McLoughlin*, 1:85.
11 Paul Kane, *Wanderings of an Artist Among the Indians of North America from Canada to Vancouver's Island and Oregon Through the Hudson's Bay Company's Territory and Back Again* (Edmonton: M.G. Hurtig 1968), 109.
12 HBCA, B.45/a/1, Fort Colvile – Post Journal, 1830-31, 29 October 1830; HBCA, D.4/125, Governor George Simpson – Correspondence Book Inwards, 1829-31, Harriott to Simpson, 16 March 1831; Rich, *Letters of John McLoughlin*, 1:97.
13 Ibid., 273.
14 Glazebrook, *Hargrave Correspondence*, 71.
15 [Archibald McDonald], "McDonald Correspondence," BCARS, MS AB40 M142A, McDonald to McLeod, 15 January 1832.
16 Clifford Merrill Drury, ed., *First White Women over the Rockies* (Glendale, CA: Arthur H. Clark 1963), 1:121.
17 HBCA, D.4/106, Governor George Simpson – Official Reports to the Governor and Committee in London, 1839, Simpson to the Governor and Committee, 8 July 1839; Rich, *Letters of John McLoughlin*, 1:293.
18 Daniel Lee, "Articles on the Oregon Mission," OIIS, MS 1211, pt. 5, fo. 5v.
19 MacLaren, "Journal of Paul Kane's Western Travels," 37.
20 Pierre-Jean De Smet, *Oregon Missions and Travels over the Rocky Mountains, in 1845-46* (New York: Edward Dunigan 1847), 235.
21 Pierre-Jean De Smet, *Letters and Sketches: With a Narrative of a Year's Residence Among the Indian Tribes of the Rocky Mountains* (Philadelphia: M. Fithian 1843), 378.
22 Glyndwr Williams, ed., *Hudson's Bay Miscellany 1670-1870* (Winnipeg: Hudson's Bay Record Society 1975), 199.
23 John Work, "Journals" and "Letters," OHS, MS 319, Work to Edward Ermatinger, 10 September 1838.

24 Work, "Correspondence," Work to Edward Ermatinger, 28 March 1829, 5 August 1832.
25 Glazebrook, *Hargrave Correspondence*, 425. McDonald himself liked the Columbia Department, calling it a "blessed country."
    Official British opinion on the eve of the 1846 treaty, incidentally, was likewise unfavourable. Two British army officers, Henry Warre and Mervyn Vavasour, inspected the lower Columbia in 1845 (they did not tour New Caledonia or the northern coast, only the area that was realistically in dispute – that between the lower Columbia and Puget Sound, the so-called "Oregon triangle"). They gave it a negative review, reporting that its posts were "calculated only to resist the sudden attacks of Indians," that the upper country was "desolate in the extreme" and the lower country (with the exception of the "fertile" Willamette Valley, where Americans outnumbered British subjects four to one) "rugged and impracticable," that transport on the Columbia was hampered by the Bar and the Dalles, and that soldiers could reach the region overland more easily from the United States than from Canada (HBCA, B.223/z/4, Fort Vancouver – Miscellaneous Items, 1824-60, Warre and Vavasour to the Secretary of State for the Colonies, 1 November 1845). The views of British naval officers were no more sanguine. Little wonder that in the face of such reports and American insistence on possession of Puget Sound's harbours, the British government, preoccupied with weightier matters, such as the Irish famine and the repeal of the Corn Laws, and disenchanted with the recently rebellious Canadian colonies, accepted the "compromise" of the forty-ninth parallel.
26 Work, "Correspondence," Work to Edward Ermatinger, January 1828.
27 Ibid., Work to Edward Ermatinger, 19 March 1830.
28 Glazebrook, *Hargrave Correspondence*, 424.
29 HBCA, D.4/120, Governor George Simpson – Correspondence Book Inwards, 1826-27, McLoughlin to Simpson, 17 April 1827, quoting William Connolly, the bourgeois of New Caledonia.
30 HBCA, D.4/122, Governor George Simpson – Correspondence Book Inwards, 1828-29, Connolly to the Governor and Council of the Northern Department, 28 February 1829. Connolly added that "the best Men for this Country are young Men from Canada, old hands from other districts are commonly of very plaintive dispositions and seldom fail of infecting those around them with a similar feeling."
31 Peter Skene Ogden, "Peter Skene Ogden's Notes on Western Caledonia," ed. W.N. Sage, *British Columbia Historical Quarterly* 1 (1937): 53. Ogden added that New Caledonia's servants had from the beginning "been represented as [a] most worthless dishonest disolute sett of beings," but he had found from long experience that they were "by no means so bad as represented," given the district's "hard duty," "indifferent" food, and "great" temptations (ibid.).
32 Tod, "History of New Caledonia," 52.
33 HBCA, B.74/a/1, Fraser's Lake – Post Journal, 1822-24, 4 June 1822.
34 HBCA, B.119/a/1, McLeod's Lake – Post Journal, 1823-24, 24 October 1823; HBCA, B.188/a/2, Fort St. James – Post Journal, 1823-24, 13 September 1823 (McDonnell to McDougall, 11 September 1823), 22 September 1823 (Yale to McDougall, 4 September 1823). Fort George was abandoned in the spring of 1824 with the opening of the "navigation" and its property transferred to Fort Alexandria.
35 HBCA, B.188/a/2, Fort St. James – Post Journal, 1823-24, 25 November 1823.
36 HBCA, B.188/a/14, Fort St. James – Post Journal, 1829-30, 20 August 1829; HBCA, D.4/99, Governor George Simpson – Official Reports to the Governor and Committee in London, 1832, Simpson to the Governor and Committee, 10 August 1832; Glazebrook, *Hargrave Correspondence*, 92-3.
37 HBCA, B.188/a/6, Fort St. James – Post Journal, 1825-26, 3 March 1826.
38 HBCA, B.188/a/5, Fort St. James – Post Journal, 1825-26, 30 October 1825.
39 Glazebrook, *Hargrave Correspondence*, 63. Apparently Ross did not fully recover his health until his transfer to the Athabasca District in the fall of 1832 (ibid., 93).
40 HBCA, B.188/a/5, Fort St. James – Post Journal, 1825-26, [5 September 1825?].
41 The NWC estimated in 1810 that its annual expenditure of liquor totalled 10,000 gallons (Wallace, *Documents*, 268). Governor Simpson's "Character Book" of 1832 frequently alludes

to the fondness of the HBC's employees for booze (see Williams, *Hudson's Bay Miscellany*, 169-236).

42 HBCA, B.188/a/1, Fort St. James – Post Journal, 1820-21, 8 July, 3 August 1820. On 20 June Stuart wrote that the oldest natives could recall having seen the river's water level so high only once before, and on 16 July he noted that for the past six weeks the level had been higher than at any time since the post's founding. The flies, incidentally, also decimated the post's cabbages and turnips.

43 Winters did vary, however. For example, the winter of 1825-26 was very cold and snowy but that of 1826-27 very mild and dry. Chief Factor Connolly went even further: "The climate is mild," he asserted, "too much so for the frequent voyaging we have to perform – Intervals of soft and rainy weather often occur, which occasion much delay and add greatly to the difficulties which are at all times experienced" (HBCA, B.188/e/3, Fort St. James – District Report, 1824-25, fo. 14v.). Similarly, the winter of 1824-25 was late, as the post journal of Fort Alexandria noted on 31 December: "the oldest Indians along this [Fraser] River Say they never recollect the *Water* being So *low*, the River So open, So little Snow on the Ground, or So little appearance altogether of Winter at this late Season of the Year, as there is this Year." The journal added that "nor could any thing happen that would prove So detrimental to the Returns of Alexandria, as this – no possibility of going about, in time, in quest of Furs for want of Snow and Ice, and now the Want of Tobacco, (a principal article of trade here), Blankets & Leather" (HBCA, B.5/a/1, Fort Alexandria – Post Journal, 1824-25, 31 December 1824). Another veteran New Caledonian, John McLean, also noted the district's climatic variability: "The climate of New Caledonia is exceedingly variable at all seasons of the year. I have experienced at Stuart's Lake, in the month of July, every possible change of weather within twelve hours; frost in the morning, scorching heat at noon; then rain, hail, snow. The winter season is subject to the same vicissitudes, though not in so extreme a degree: some years it continues mild throughout" (Wallace, *John McLean's Notes*, 172).

All of this serves to remind us that climate (long-term) is but an average of the weather (short-term), with much variation around the mean.

44 HBCA, B.188/a/4, Fort St. James – Post Journal, 1824-25, 17 August 1825.

45 HBCA, B.188/a/6, Fort St. James – Post Journal, 1825-26, 30 October 1825; HBCA, B.188/e/3, Fort St. James – District Report, 1824-25, fo. 3.

46 HBCA, B.188/a/6, Fort St. James – Post Journal, 1825-26, 30 October 1825.

47 Transport was faster by canoe than by dogsled; it took twice as long to haul salmon from Stuart's Lake to Babine Lake by dogsled in winter as by canoe in summer (HBCA, B.188/a/3, Fort St. James – Post Journal, 1824-25, 9 November 1824). Also, dogsled travel was difficult just before spring break-up, when the snow was soft, and just after autumn freeze-up, when the snow was thin. One dogsled drew 200 pounds, according to Lieutenant Wilkes, who reconnoitred the lower Columbia in 1841 (but not New Caledonia); he also asserted that in New Caledonia snowshoes measured six feet in length and one and one-half feet in width, and that a snowshoer could make thirty-five miles in one day (Wilkes, *Narrative*, 4:451). Wilkes's informant was probably Chief Factor Peter Skene Ogden, bourgeois of New Caledonia.

48 HBCA, B.188/e/1, Fort St. James – District Report, 1822-23, fo. 3v.

49 HBCA, B.188/e/3, Fort St. James – District Report, 1824-25, fos. 11-11v.

50 HBCA, B.188/e/1, Fort St. James – District Report, 1822-23, fo. 3.

51 HBCA, B.119/a/1, McLeod's Lake – Post Journal, 1823-24, 6 September, 28 October 1823; also see HBCA, B.119/e/1, McLeod's Lake – District Report, 1824.

52 HBCA, D.4/117, Governor George Simpson – Correspondence Book Inwards, 1822-23, Stewart [Stuart] to Simpson, 4 January 1823; also see B.188/b/2, Fort St. James – Correspondence Book, 1822-23, Stuart to Simpson, 4 January 1823.

53 HBCA, D.4/116, Governor George Simpson – Correspondence Book Inwards, 1821-22, Stuart to the Governor and Council of the Northern Department, 27 April 1822.

54 Ibid.

55 HBCA, B.5/a/2, Fort Alexandria – Post Journal, 1827-28, 3 November 1827.

56 Even at the depot of York Factory as late as 1841, the diet was inadequate. In September of that year the bourgeois's daughter wrote a friend that "we are often short of fresh provisions

in summer, scurvy prevails among the men" (Margaret Arnett MacLeod, ed., *The Letters of Letitia Hargrave* [Toronto: Champlain Society 1947], 100).

57   HBCA, B.188/a/3, Fort St. James – Post Journal, 1824-25, 27 July 1824.

58   Lois Halliday McDonald, ed., *Fur Trade Letters of Francis Ermatinger ... 1818-1853* (Glendale, CA: Arthur H. Clark 1980), 64.

59   Wallace, *John McLean's Notes*, 152. William Connolly's son, Henry, recalled in his retirement that sun-dried salmon was "the principal food for everybody" in New Caledonia ([Connolly], "Reminiscences," 10).

60   Ibid., 186.

61   [Edward and Francis Ermatinger], "Ermatinger Papers," BCARS, MS AB40 Er62.3, Dears to E. Ermatinger, 5 March 1831.

62   McLeod, *Peace River*, 108.

63   Wallace, *John McLean's Notes*, 151-2.

64   HBCA, B.119/e/1, McLeod's Lake – District Report, 1824; HBCA, B.188/e/1, Fort St. James – District Report, 1822-23, fo. 3v. Sturgeon weighing 200-400 pounds each were caught in June and July of the middle 1820s in the Fraser River and in Fraser and Stuart Lakes (HBCA, B.188/a/5, Fort St. James – Post Journal, 1825-26, "Report of New Caledonia District 1826," 145).

65   HBCA, B.188/a/17, Fort St. James – Post Journal, 1831-32, 3 September 1831.

66   HBCA, B.119/e/1, McLeod's Lake – District Report, 1824; HBCA, B.188/e/1, Fort St. James – District Report, 1822-23, fo. 3v. A fresh salmon lost four-fifths of its weight when dried and became crisp and reddish, as well as blackened by smoke (HBCA, B.5/e/1, Fort Alexandria – District Report, 1827-28, fos. 18v.-19).

67   HBCA, B.188/e/3, Fort St. James – District Report, 1824-25, fo. 12v.; also see Ogden, "Notes on Western Caledonia," 52.

68   [Connolly], "Reminiscences," 10.

69   HBCA, B.188/a/2, Fort St. James – Post Journal, 1823-24, 31 May 1823 (Stuart to McDougall, 5 May 1823).

70   HBCA, B.188/a/3, Fort St. James – Post Journal, 1824-25, 21 January 1824; HBCA, B.188/a/5, Fort St. James – Post Journal, 1825-26, 9 January 1826.

71   HBCA, B.188/a/3, Fort St. James – Post Journal, 1824-25, 8 November 1824.

72   HBCA, B.188/e/3, Fort St. James – District Report, 1824-25, fo. 13.

73   HBCA, B.188/a/14, Fort St. James – Post Journal, 1829-30, 21 August 1829.

74   HBCA, B.188/e/1, Fort St. James – District Report, 1822-23, fo. 3v.; also see HBCA, B.119/e/1, McLeod's Lake – District Report, 1824.

75   HBCA, D.4/116, Governor George Simpson – Correspondence Book Inwards, 1821-22, Brown to Simpson, 4 November 1821.

76   HBCA, B.188/a/8, Fort St. James – Post Journal, 1826-27, 12 November 1826.

77   Ogden, "Notes on Western Caledonia," 51.

78   HBCA, B.119/a/1, McLeod's Lake – Post Journal, 1823-24, 3 November 1823; HBCA, B.188/a/3, Fort St. James – Post Journal, 1824-25, 27 October 1824; McLeod, *Peace River*, 29.

79   HBCA, B.119/e/1, McLeod's Lake – District Report, 1824; HBCA, B.188/a/8, Fort St. James – Post Journal, 1826-27, 7 January 1827; HBCA, B.188/e/1, Fort St. James – District Report, 1822-23, fo. 3v.

80   HBCA, B.5/a/2, Fort Alexandria – Post Journal, 1827-28, 25 July 1827.

81   HBCA, B.188/e/3, Fort St. James – District Report, 1824-25, fo. 5.

82   HBCA, B.188/a/4, Fort St. James – Post Journal, 1824-25, 24 July 1825. For ration purposes one berry cake was equivalent to two dried salmon and one keg of potatoes to twenty-six dried salmon; so Fort Alexandria's stock of 3,500 dried salmon, 480 berry cakes, and 53 kegs of potatoes on 21 December 1826 was equal to 5,838 salmon and would last the post's seven men, four children, two women, and one boy 149 days at thirty-nine dried salmon per day, that is, until 19 May 1827 (HBCA, B.188/a/8, Fort St. James – Post Journal, 1826-27, 7 January 1827).

83   Wallace, *John McLean's Notes*, 153.

84   HBCA, B.188/a/1, Fort St. James – Post Journal, 1820-21, 20 April 1821.

85   HBCA, B.188/d/15, Fort St. James – Account Book, 1836-37, "Expenditure of Provisions at

the different Posts in New Caledonia District OT 1836" and "Statement of Men's Accounts New Caledonia District 1836/37."

86 Quoted by McLeod, *Peace River*, 107.

87 HBCA, B.188/a/14, Fort St. James – Post Journal, 1829-30, 16 September 1829.

88 HBCA, B.188/a/3, Fort St. James – Post Journal, 1824-25, 7 November 1824.

89 It seems that more natives than whites starved to death, even though the former were less fastidious in their choice of food sources. "It is well known," reported Clerk John McDonnell in 1823, "that Carriers kill Beaver, as much, at least, on account of the meat as for the Skin" (HBCA, B.74/a/1, Fraser's Lake – Post Journal, 1822-24, 30 June 1823). The starving natives sought relief from the HBC, as the post journal of Fraser's Lake noted in the middle of the winter of 1822-23: "The Indians suffer so much from Starvation that they are become really troublesome from the number of applicants for our *Bounty*, and were there no other inducement Humanity would prompt any man possessed of the least feeling, to alleviate in some degree such extreme wretchedness, as at this season it is impossible for them to better their present forlorn Condition" (ibid., 23 February 1823). Also, when salmon failed, the natives lacked bait for their marten traps, whereupon they resorted to butchering company horses and substituting their meat. The Carriers, incidentally, comprised nine-tenths of New Caledonia's Indians (HBCA, B.188/a/5, Fort St. James – Post Journal, 1825-26, William Connolly, "Report of New Caledonia District 1826," 140).

90 Madge Wolfenden, ed., "John Tod: Career of a Scotch Boy," *British Columbia Historical Quarterly* 28 (1954): 227.

91 HBCA, B.188/a/1, Fort St. James – Post Journal, 1820-21, 26 April 1821.

92 HBCA, B.188/e/1, Fort St. James – District Report, 1822-23, fo. 4; also see HBCA, B.119/e/1, McLeod's Lake – District Report, 1824.

93 HBCA, B.188/a/1, Fort St. James – Post Journal, 1820-21, 23 February, 2, 4 March, 26 April 1821.

94 HBCA, B.188/a/2, Fort St. James – Post Journal, 1822-23, 2 December 1823 (McDougall to Stuart, 17 November 1823); HBCA, B.188/a/3, Fort St. James – Post Journal, 1824-25, 21 January 1824 (Stuart to McDougall and McDonnell, 21 January 1824).

95 HBCA, B.119/a/1, McLeod's Lake – Post Journal, 1823-24, 20 November 1823.

96 McLeod, *Peace River*, 31.

97 HBCA, B.5/a/2, Fort Alexandria – Post Journal, 1827-28, 11 November 1827.

98 HBCA, B.188/a/10, Fort St. James – Post Journal, 1827, 2 November 1827.

99 HBCA, B.188/a/12, Fort St. James – Post Journal, 1828, 13 August 1828.

100 Ibid., 2 September 1828.

101 Ibid.

102 HBCA, B.188/a/14, Fort St. James – Post Journal, 1829-30, 4 September 1829.

103 HBCA, D.4/99, Governor George Simpson – Official Reports to the Governor and Committee in London, 1832, Simpson to the Governor and Committee, 10 August 1832.

104 The keeper of Stuart's Lake post journal, *à la* Governor Simpson, managed to detect an advantage in the failure of salmon: "This scarcity ... cannot be considered an evil, as it is the means of saving a large quantity of Goods which were annually consumed in Trading a superabundance of that article, and by which the natives were supplied with most of their necessaries without the trouble of Hunting [furs]" (HBCA, B.188/a/8, Fort St. James – Post Journal, 1826-27, 12 November 1826).

105 The salmon failure of 1835, for example, forced New Caledonia to turn to Fort Colvile for grain; however, the latter's own consumption of grain was "very considerable," while the demand from elsewhere was "great & incessant" (Glazebrook, *Hargrave Correspondence*, 237-8).

106 For example, at Stuart's Lake 1,600 bundles of hay were mowed and stacked in the summer of 1823; it was fed to the horses and mixed with plaster for the walls of buildings (HBCA, B.188/a/2, Fort St. James – Post Journal, 1823-24, 23 August 1823). In 1827 at the same post, four stacks of hay, each containing 250 bundles, were made in late August (HBCA, B.188/a/10, Fort St. James – Post Journal, 1827, 25, 28 August 1827).

107 HBCA, D.4/126, Governor George Simpson – Correspondence Book Inwards, 1833-34, Dease to the Chief Factors and Chief Traders of the Athabasca District, 19 September 1833.

Incidentally, the botanist David Douglas, the Douglas fir's namesake whom the Cayuse Indians nicknamed "Grass Man" because of his botanizing ([David Douglas], *Journal Kept by David Douglas during his Travels in North America 1823-1827 ...* [New York: Antiquarian Press 1959], 159), accompanied the drive as far as Fort Alexandria and drew a series of sketch maps of the route (David Douglas, "Book of Sketch Maps of Journey from the junction of the Columbia and Okanogan Rivers to Quesnel and North, April-May, 1833," BCARS, Add. MSS 0622).

108   HBCA, B.188/e/3, Fort St. James – District Report, 1824-25, fo. 14. Before 1827, at least, the potato crops at McLeod's Lake were "always abundant, and materially assisted towards the support of the place" (HBCA, B.188/a/10, Fort St. James – Post Journal, 1827, 4 September 1827).

109   HBCA, B.74/a/1, Fraser's Lake – Post Journal, 1822-24, 11 September 1823, for example.

110   Lamb, *Sixteen Years in the Indian Country*, 241.

111   Tod, "History of New Caledonia," 21.

112   HBCA, B.188/a/1, Fort St. James – Post Journal, 1820-21, 10 May, 11 August, 14 September, 17, 28 October 1820.

113   HBCA, B.188/a/12, Fort St. James – Post Journal, 1828, 10 October 1828; HBCA, B.188/a/14, Fort St. James – Post Journal, 1829-30, 13 October 1829. Fraser's Lake's potato crop in 1828 totalled 180 bushels (HBCA, B.188/a/12, Fort St. James – Post Journal, 1828, 9 November 1828).

114   HBCA, B.188/a/19, Fort St. James – Post Journal, 1840-46, 23 September 1841.

115   Wallace, *John McLean's Notes*, 170.

116   Ibid.

117   HBCA, B.5/a/4, Fort Alexandria – Post Journal, 1837-39, 19 October, 3 November 1837; HBCA, B.5/a/2, Fort Alexandria – Post Journal, 1826-27, 10 October 1827; HBCA, B.5/a/5, Fort Alexandria – Post Journal, 1842-43, 27 October 1842, 20 July 1843; HBCA, B.5/a/6, Fort Alexandria – Post Journal, 1843-45, 18 October 1844; HBCA, B.5/a/7, Fort Alexandria – Post Journal, 1845-48, 16 October 1845, 11 October 1847; HBCA, B.188/a/5, Fort St. James – Post Journal, 1825-26, 25 November 1825.

118   HBCA, B.5/a/1, Fort Alexandria – Post Journal, 1824-25, 26, 29 May, 5, 6, 22 July 1824.

119   Glazebrook, *Hargrave Correspondence*, 256.

120   HBCA, D.4/99, Governor George Simpson – Official Reports to the Governor and Committee in London, 1832, Simpson to the Governor and Committee, 10 August 1832. Four years earlier Simpson had found that salmon (the "principal 'stand by'"), carp, "a few" whitefish, "an occasional treat" of native berry cakes, and "a Dog Feast on high Days and holydays constitute the living of nearly all the posts in New Caledonia; and altho' bad, as to quality, would not afford grounds for complaint, if the quantity was sufficient to satisfy the cravings of Nature; but the people are frequently reduced to half allowance, to quarter allowance, and sometimes to no allowance at all, so that the situation of our New Caledonia Friends in regard to the good things of this Life, is any thing but enviable; nor can it be materially improved by attention to agriculture, as Summer Frosts are so frequent as to destroy Vegetation" (Rich, *Part of Dispatch from George Simpson*, 19).

Given the servants' dislike of the fishy diet, one can sympathize with bourgeois John McDonnell of Fraser's Lake when in early November 1822 he was invited to a Carrier funeral feast but was able to stay only half an hour because of his revulsion at the "Quintessence of putrefaction" exuded by the salmon roe, which had been buried for some time (HBCA, B.74/a/1, Fraser's Lake – Post Journal, 1822-24, 5 November 1822).

121   HBCA, B.119/a/1, McLeod's Lake – Post Journal, 1823-24, 28 December 1823, 11 January, 6 February 1824.

122   Glazebrook, *Hargrave Correspondence*, 28.

123   Merk, *Fur Trade and Empire*, 221.

124   Rich, *Part of Dispatch from George Simpson*, 71.

125   Generally the district's "establishment" in the middle 1830s numbered up to fifty, comprising one chief factor, one chief trader, six to seven clerks, and forty men (mostly Iroquois and Métis) (Wallace, *John McLean's Notes*, 186).

126   HBCA, B.188/a/1, Fort St. James – Post Journal, 1820-21, 22 June 1820.

127   HBCA, B.119/b/1, McLeod's Lake – Correspondence Book, 1823-24, [Stuart] to the Governor, Chief Factors, and Chief Traders of the Northern Department, 30 October 1823.

128   HBCA, B.188/a/12, Fort St. James – Post Journal, 1828, 4, 6, 17, 18 September 1828; also see
       HBCA, D.4/122, Governor George Simpson – Correspondence Book Inwards, 1828-29,
       Connolly to the Governor and Council of the Northern Department, 28 February 1829.
129   HBCA, B.188/a/3, Fort St. James – Post Journal, 1824-25, 6 December 1824.
130   HBCA, B.188/a/14, Fort St. James – Post Journal, 1829-30, 3 May 1829.
131   HBCA, D.5/8, Governor George Simpson – Correspondence Inward, 1843, McLoughlin to
       Simpson, 20 March 1843.
132   HBCA, B.223/c/1, Fort Vancouver – Correspondence Inward, 1826-50, Simpson to
       McLoughlin, 21 June 1843.
133   HBCA, B.223/c/1, Fort Vancouver – Correspondence Inward, 1826-50, Governor and Com-
       mittee to McLoughlin, 27 September 1843.
134   HBCA, B.188/a/12, Fort St. James – Post Journal, 1828, 1 April 1828.
135   Ibid., 4 April 1828.
136   Lamb, *Letters and Journals of Simon Fraser*, 239.
137   HBCA, B.188/a/1, Fort St. James – Post Journal, 1820-21, 17 April 1820.
138   HBCA, B.188/a/5, Fort St. James – Post Journal, 1825-26, "Report of New Caledonia Dis-
       trict 1826," 154.
139   HBCA, D.4/119, Governor George Simpson – Correspondence Book Inwards, 1824-26, Con-
       nolly to the Governor and Council of the Northern Department, 1 May 1826; also see ibid.,
       Connolly to Simpson, 30 April 1826.
140   HBCA, B.188/a/5, Fort St. James – Post Journal, 1825-26, 8 April 1826.
141   Ibid., 12 April 1826.
142   HBCA, D.4/119, Governor George Simpson – Correspondence Book Inwards, 1824-26, Con-
       nolly to the Governor and Council of the Northern Department, 1 May 1826.
143   HBCA, B.188/a/10, Fort St. James – Post Journal, 1827, 7, 10, 12-13, 24-25 April 1827.
144   HBCA, B.188/a/12, Fort St. James – Post Journal, 1828, 4 May 1828.
145   The post was rechristened Fort Simpson with a "flagon of Spirits" on 1 May 1824 (HBCA,
       B.119/a/4, McLeod's Lake – Post Journal, 1824, 1 May 1824). The new name did not last
       long, however.
146   HBCA, B.119/a/1, McLeod's Lake – Post Journal, 1823-24, 25 October 1823; also see B.74/a/1,
       Fraser's Lake – Post Journal, 1822-24, 25 July 1823 and B.188/e/3, Fort St. James – District
       Report, 1824-25, fo. 15v.
147   HBCA, B.188/a/2, Fort St. James – Post Journal, 1823-24, 20 July 1823.
148   HBCA, B.74/a/1, Fraser's Lake – Post Journal, 1822-24, 25 July 1823.
149   HBCA, B.188/a/3, Fort St. James – Post Journal, 1824-25, 27 October 1824.
150   HBCA, B.188/a/5, Fort St. James – Post Journal, 1825-26, "Report of New Caledonia Dis-
       trict 1826," 146.
151   Rich, *Part of Dispatch from George Simpson*, 17.
152   Wallace, *John McLean's Notes*, 144.
153   In the month of June 1818 in Stuart's Lake the NWC caught twenty-one sturgeon eight to
       twelve feet in length and "superior in flavour" (Lamb, *Sixteen Years in the Indian Country*,
       192). Not infrequently during the first half of the 1820s, sturgeon measuring eight feet in
       length and weighing 200 pounds and more were taken in the post's nets.
154   HBCA, B.188/e/3, Fort St. James – District Report, 1824-25, fo. 15v.; HBCA, B.119/a/2,
       McLeod's Lake – Post Journal, 1824, 22 February 1824.
155   HBCA, B.188/a/2, Fort St. James – Post Journal, 1823-24, "Summary Report of Saint James
       Western Caledonia," 25 April 1824; HBCA, B.188/a/5, Fort St. James – Post Journal, 1825-
       26, "Report of New Caledonia District 1826," 146.
156   HBCA, B.188/a/5, Fort St. James – Post Journal, 1825-26, "Report of New Caledonia Dis-
       trict 1826," 146. The post's returns totalled eighteen packs in 1823-24 and twenty-one packs
       and seventy-eight pounds of castoreum in 1824-25 (HBCA, B.188/a/4, Fort St. James – Post
       Journal, 1824-25, 27 April 1825).
157   HBCA, B.188/a/3, Fort St. James – Post Journal, 1824-25, 9 November 1824.
158   HBCA, B.188/a/2, Fort St. James – Post Journal, 1823-24, "Summary Report of Saint James
       Western Caledonia," 25 April 1824.
159   Ibid. Fraser's Lake was the "best provision Post in the Country, and the most conveniently

situated for furnishing supplies for the General business of the District, and for the maintenance of Stuarts & McLeods Lakes"; the fort, "being in a ruinous Condition," was renovated in 1825-26 (HBCA, B.188/a/5, Fort St. James – Post Journal, 1825-26, "Report of New Caledonia District 1826," 146). Babine Lake was a "continual source of expenses and vexation to the District" (ibid., 148).

160 HBCA, B.188/a/2, Fort St. James – Post Journal, 1823-24, "Summary Report of Saint James Western Caledonia," 25 April 1824.

161 Ibid.

162 Ibid.

163 HBCA, B.188/e/3, Fort St. James – District Report, 1824-25, fo. 14v. By the 1840s the brigade was leaving earlier (the third week of April) and returning earlier (the middle of September) than in the 1820s, perhaps because of climatic warming. In 1820 the NWC had decided that New Caledonia's returns would have to leave for Fort George in February in order to allow enough time for the brigaders to return with the outfit and distribute it before freeze-up, but in 1821 John Stuart took "an opportunity of proving, the Idea circulated the year before [1820], erroneous, that the Ne[w] Caledonians of themselves could never bring home their Outfit, and now I flatter myself that it is ascertained, the people of Ne[w] Caledonia can after conveying their Returns to [the] place of embarkation, can leave their wintering ground in Canoe[s] and reach Fort George [in] time enough to effect all the purposes they could have done by leaving it in February as agreed upon in 1820" (HBCA, B.188/b/1, Fort St. James – Correspondence Book, 1821-22, Stuart to Cameron, 8 July 1822).

164 HBCA, B.188/a/1, Fort St. James – Post Journal, 1820-21, 16 April 1821.

165 HBCA, B.188/a/19, Fort St. James – Post Journal, 1840-46, 19 April 1843.

166 HBCA, B.188/a/10, Fort St. James – Post Journal, 1827, 22 August, 3 November 1827.

167 HBCA, B.188/b/1, Fort St. James – Correspondence Book, 1821-22, Stuart to Leith, 24 April 1822.

168 HBCA, B.119/e/1, McLeod's Lake – District Report, 1824.

169 HBCA, B.188/e/3, Fort St. James – District Report, 1824-25, fo. 10.

170 HBCA, B.188/e/4, Fort St. James – District Report, 1826-27, fos. 2v.-3.

171 HBCA, D.4/119, Governor George Simpson – Correspondence Book Inwards, 1824-26, Connolly to the Governor and Council of the Northern Department, 1 May 1826; also see Fleming, *Minutes of Council*, 144.

172 HBCA, D.4/120, Governor George Simpson – Correspondence Book Inwards, 1826-27, McLoughlin to Simpson, 20 March 1827.

173 HBCA, B.45/z/1, Fort Colvile – Miscellaneous Items, 1828-56, "Distribution of Men at Fort Colvile 18th April 1828."

174 Rich, *Part of Dispatch from George Simpson*, 240.

175 HBCA, B.188/a/3, Fort St. James – Post Journal, 1824-25, 11 November 1824.

176 Ibid., 13 December 1824.

177 Ibid., 21 March 1825.

178 Cullen, "Outfitting New Caledonia 1821-58," 238.

179 Ross, *Adventures of the First Settlers*, 1986 edition, 42.

180 Wilkes, *Narrative*, 4:371.

181 Ibid., 329, 433.

182 Wallace, *John McLean's Notes*, 167.

183 HBCA, B.188/a/8, Fort St. James – Post Journal, 1826-27, 5 May 1826. According to Connolly, the spring navigation that year was "later than is in the remembrance of any Man in this country"; spring arrived three weeks later in 1826 than in 1825 (HBCA, B.188/a/5, Fort St. James – Post Journal, 1825-26, "Report of New Caledonia District 1826," 144, 154-5).

184 HBCA, B.188/a/10, Fort St. James – Post Journal, 1827, 1, 4 May 1827.

185 HBCA, B.188/a/12, Fort St. James – Post Journal, 1828, 30 April, 1, 2, 4, 5 May 1828.

186 HBCA, B.188/a/14, Fort St. James – Post Journal, 1829-30, 1-7 May 1829.

187 HBCA, B.188/a/17, Fort St. James – Post Journal, 1831-32, 7, 10-12 May 1831.

188 HBCA, B.188/e/5, Fort St. James – District Report, 1834, fo. 1; HBCA, D.4/126, Governor George Simpson – Correspondence Book Inwards, 1833-34, Dease to the Chief Factors and Chief Traders of the Athabasca District, 19 September 1833.

189 Rich, *Part of Dispatch from George Simpson*, 28-9.

Chapter 5: Packhorsing over the Mountain

1   Rich, *Part of Dispatch from George Simpson*, 29-30.
2   Ibid., 189-90.
3   HBCA, D.4/116, Governor George Simpson – Correspondence Book Inwards, 1821-22, Stuart to the Governor and Council [of the Northern Department], 27 April 1822.
4   HBCA, B.188/a/5, Fort St. James – Post Journal, 1825-26, "Report of New Caledonia District 1826," 148.
5   HBCA, B.5/e/1, Fort Alexandria – District Report, 1827-28, fo. 5v.
6   Rich, *Part of Dispatch from George Simpson*, 193-4.
7   HBCA, B.188/a/3, Fort St. James – Post Journal, 1824-25, 7 March 1825.
8   HBCA, B.188/a/10, Fort St. James – Post Journal, 1827, 26 July 1827.
9   HBCA, B.5/e/1, Fort Alexandria – District Report, 1827-28, fo. 2.
10   Wallace, *John McLean's Notes*, 161.
11   HBCA, B.5/e/1, Fort Alexandria – District Report, 1827-28, fo. 4.
12   HBCA, B.188/a/5, Fort St. James – Post Journal, 1825-26, "Report of New Caledonia District 1826," 148. Whenever there was a shortfall of salmon, the natives resorted to rabbits (HBCA, B.5/e/1, Fort Alexandria – District Report, 1827-28, fo. 4).
13   HBCA, B.5/a/1, Fort Alexandria – Post Journal, 1824-25, 31 December 1824.
14   HBCA, B.188/a/4, Fort St. James – Post Journal, 1824-25, 17 October 1825.
15   HBCA, B.5/e/1, Fort Alexandria – District Report, 1827-28, fo. 7.
16   Ibid., fo. 4.
17   HBCA, B.188/a/8, Fort St. James – Post Journal, 1826-27, 8 September 1826.
18   HBCA, B.5/e/1, Fort Alexandria – District Report, 1827-28, fos. 8v., 11v.-12.
19   HBCA, B/5/a/5, Fort Alexandria – Post Journal, 1842-43, 26 September 1842.
20   HBCA, D.4/120, Governor George Simpson – Correspondence Book Inwards, 1826-27, Connolly to the Governor and Council of the Northern Department, 15 March 1827.
21   HBCA, B.188/a/8, Fort St. James – Post Journal, 1826-27, 7 September 1826. The journal added in the middle of the month, however, that "the returns have failed throughout the Department [district], owing it appears to the uncommon height of the waters during the most favourable period for Hunting Beaver" (ibid., 16 September; also see 23 September).
22   HBCA, B.188/a/10, Fort St. James – Post Journal, 1827, 4 May 1827.
23   HBCA, B.188/b/1, Fort St. James – Correspondence Book, 1821-22, Stuart to Leith, 24 April 1822.
24   HBCA, B.5/a/1, Fort Alexandria – Post Journal, 1824-25, 23 June 1824.
25   Pack horses had also been brought to New Caledonia earlier, when the brigade route had been temporarily shifted from the Peace to the Fraser-Columbia. There were fifty-two horses at Fort Alexandria in 1821, for instance (HBCA, B.188/d/1, Fort St. James – Account Book, 1821-22, "Distribution of New Caledonia Outfit 1821").
26   HBCA, B.188/e/3, Fort St. James – District Report, 1824-25, fos. 11v.-12.
27   Ibid., fo. 12v.
28   HBCA, B.188/a/3, Fort St. James – Post Journal, 1824-25, 11 November 1824, 18 February, 7 March 1825; HBCA, B.188/a/4, Fort St. James – Post Journal, 1824-25, 10 May 1825. Eight horses were kept at Stuart's Lake in the summer of 1829 (HBCA, B.188/a/14, Fort St. James – Post Journal, 1829-30, 16 September 1829).
29   HBCA, D.4/5, Governor George Simpson – Correspondence Book Outwards (General), 1824-25, Simpson to Dease, 11 April 1825.
30   Ibid., Simpson to McLoughlin, 10 April 1825.
31   Ibid., Simpson to McLoughlin, 11 July 1825.
32   HBCA, D.4/119, Governor George Simpson – Correspondence Book Inwards, 1824-26, McLoughlin to the Chief Factors and Chief Traders of the Columbia Department, 20 June 1825; also see HBCA, B.223/b/1, Fort Vancouver – Correspondence Book, 1825, McLoughlin to the Chief Factors and Chief Traders of the Columbia Department, 20 June 1825. John Warren Dease was the brother of the better-known Peter Warren Dease, who was to replace William Connolly in 1830 as *homme d'affaires* of New Caledonia.
33   HBCA, D.4/119, Governor George Simpson – Correspondence Book Inwards, 1824-26, Dease to the Governor, Chief Factors, and Chief Traders of the Northern Department, 21 July 1825; [Work], "Journal," 1-18, 24 July 1825.

34 HBCA, B.223/b/1, Fort Vancouver – Correspondence Book, 1825, McLoughlin to Dease, 5 September 1825.

35 HBCA, D.4/119, Governor George Simpson – Correspondence Book Inwards, 1824-26, Dease to the Governor, Chief Factors, and Chief Traders [of the Northern Department], 7 April 1826.

36 HBCA, B.188/a/5, Fort St. James – Post Journal, 1825-26, 25 November 1825; HBCA, B.188/b/4, Fort St. James – Correspondence Book, 1825-26, Dease to Connolly, 30 August 1825 and McLeod to Connolly, 10 October 1825; HBCA, D.4/199, Governor George Simpson – Correspondence Book Inwards, 1824-26, Connolly to Simpson, 30 April 1826. In mid-June McLoughlin had ordered Work at Spokane House to trade 100 apichimons – "pieces [of] Buffaloe Robes to serve instead of saddle Cloths" – for New Caledonia and forty apichimons and 200 fathoms (1,200 feet) of pack cords for Thompson's River for use in 1826 (HBCA, B.223/b/1, Fort Vancouver – Correspondence Book, 1825, McLoughlin to Work, 19 June 1825).

37 HBCA, B.188/a/5, Fort St. James – Post Journal, 1825-26, 25 November 1825; HBCA, D.4/119, Governor George Simpson – Correspondence Book Inwards, 1824-26, Connolly to Simpson, 30 April 1826, Connolly to the Governor and Council of the Northern Department, 1 May 1826.

38 HBCA, B.188/b/4, Fort St. James – Correspondence Book, 1825-26, Connolly to McDonnell, 30 November 1825, no. 14.

39 Ibid., Connolly to McDonnell, 30 November 1825, no. 15.

40 HBCA, B.188/a/5, Fort St. James – Post Journal, 1825-26, 28 November 1825; HBCA, D.4/119, Governor George Simpson – Correspondence Book Inwards, 1824-26, Connolly to Simpson, 30 April 1826.

41 HBCA, B.188/a/5, Fort St. James – Post Journal, 1825-26, 28 November 1825 and 26 January 1826; HBCA, B.188/b/4, Fort St. James – Correspondence Book, 1825-26, McLeod to Connolly, 15 December 1825, Connolly to McLeod, 5 February 1826; HBCA, D.4/119, Governor George Simpson – Correspondence Book Inwards, 1824-26, Connolly to McLeod, 7 February 1826, Connolly to Simpson, 30 April 1826. Three years earlier McBean had experienced even more difficulty driving horses from Alexandria to Thompson's River. At the beginning of December 1822 he left Alexandria with four men and sixty-five horses but reached Thompson's River with only fifty animals, ten having drowned (including his own horse), two having strayed, two having broken their necks in a fall from a cliff, and one having been abandoned because it was unable to continue (HBCA, B.97/a/1, Fort Kamloops – Post Journal, 1822-23, 9 December 1822; HBCA, B.188/b/3, Fort St. James – Correspondence Book, 1823-24, McLeod to Stuart, 12 December 1823).

42 HBCA, D.4/119, Governor George Simpson – Correspondence Book Inwards, 1824-26, Connolly to McLeod, 7 February 1826.

43 Ibid., Connolly to Simpson, 30 April 1826.

44 HBCA, B.188/a/5, Fort St. James – Post Journal, 1825-26, 27 January 1826.

45 HBCA, B.188/a/5, Fort St. James – Post Journal, 1825-26, 25 February 1826; HBCA, B.188/b/4, Fort St. James – Correspondence Book, 1825-26, McDougall to Connolly, 1 February 1826; HBCA, D.4/119, Correspondence Book Inwards, 1824-26, Connolly to Simpson, 30 April 1826.

46 HBCA, D.4/119, Correspondence Book Inwards, 1824-26, Connolly to Simpson, 30 April 1826.

47 HBCA, B.188/a/5, Fort St. James – Post Journal, 1825-26, 25 February, 5, 6, 15, 27 March 1826.

48 HBCA, B.188/a/5, Fort St. James – Post Journal, 1825-26, 9 March 1826; HBCA, D.4/119, Governor George Simpson – Correspondence Book Inwards, 1824-26, Connolly to Simpson, 30 April 1826.

49 HBCA, B.188/a/5, Fort St. James – Post Journal, 1825-6, 9 March 1826.

50 HBCA, D.4/119, Governor George Simpson – Correspondence Book Inwards, 1824-26, Connolly to Simpson, 30 April 1826; also see HBCA, B.188/a/5, Fort St. James – Post Journal, 1825-26, "Report of New Caledonia District 1826," 154-5.

51 HBCA, A.12/1, London Inward Correspondence from Governors of H.B.C. Territories – Sir George Simpson, 1823-32, Simpson to the Governor and Committee, 20 August 1826;

HBCA, D.4/119, Governor George Simpson – Correspondence Book Inwards, 1824-26, Connolly to Simpson, 30 April 1826 and fos. 59v. and 63-63v.

52   HBCA, D.4/119, Governor George Simpson – Correspondence Book Inwards, 1824-26, McDonald to Connolly, 10 April 1826.

53   HBCA, D.4/119, Governor George Simpson – Correspondence Book Inwards, 1824-26, McDonald to Connolly, 14 March, 10 April 1826.

54   HBCA, D.4/119, Governor George Simpson – Correspondence Book Inwards, 1824-26, McDonald to Connolly, 10 April 1826.

55   Ibid., McDonald to the Governor, Chief Factors, and Chief Traders of the Northern Department, n.d.

56   HBCA, B.188/b/4, Fort St. James – Correspondence Book, 1825-26, Ermatinger to Connolly, 5 April 1826.

57   HBCA, B.188/a/5, Fort St. James – Post Journal, 1825-26, 1 May 1826.

58   HBCA, B.188/a/8, Fort St. James – Post Journal, 1826-27, 8 May 1826; however, see HBCA, B.188/b/5, Fort St. James – Correspondence Book, 1826-27, fos. 3-5, where it is stated that Alexandria received only thirty horses.

59   HBCA, D.4/119, Governor George Simpson – Correspondence Book Inwards, 1824-26, Connolly to the Governor and Council of the Northern Department, 1 May 1826.

60   HBCA, A.12/1, London Inward Correspondence from Governors of H.B.C. Territories – Sir George Simpson, 1823-32, Simpson to the Governor and Committee, 20 August 1826.

61   HBCA, D.4/6, Governor George Simpson – Correspondence Book Outwards (General), 1825-26, Simpson to Connolly, 5 July 1826.

62   HBCA, B.188/a/5, Fort St. James – Post Journal, 1825-26, 9 March 1826.

63   HBCA, B.223/b/2, Fort Vancouver – Correspondence Book, 1826, Black to McLoughlin, 23 March, 15 August 1826, McDonald to McLoughlin, 22 August 1826; [Work], "Journal," 17, 30-1 July, 3 August 1826.

64   HBCA, B.188/b/5, Fort St. James – Correspondence Book, 1826-27, fo. 12. As late as 1834 the brigade horses were still being kept at Alexandria, although an indeterminate number were also being held at Thompson's River.

65   HBCA, D.4/119, Governor George Simpson – Correspondence Book Inwards, 1824-26, Connolly to the Governor and Council of the Northern Department, 1 May 1826; also see ibid., Connolly to Simpson, 30 April 1826.

66   HBCA, B.188/a/8, Fort St. James – Post Journal, 1826-27, 9 September 1826.

67   Ibid., 15 October 1826.

68   Ibid., 5 November 1826.

69   Ibid., 7 January 1827.

70   HBCA, B.5/a/3, Fort Alexandria – Post Journal, 1833-34, 3 August 1833.

71   HBCA, B.188/a/14, Fort St. James – Post Journal, 1829-30, 20 August 1829.

72   HBCA, B.5/a/7, Fort Alexandria – Post Journal, 1845-48, 3 May 1848, "Instructions in regard to the post, during my absence."

73   HBCA, B.188/a/11, Fort St. James – Post Journal, 1828, 14 February 1828; HBCA, B.188/a/12, Fort St. James – Post Journal, 1828, 27 March, 3 May 1828.

74   Rich, *Part of Dispatch from George Simpson*, 238.

75   HBCA, B.188/a/14, Fort St. James – Post Journal, 1829-30, 28 March 1829.

76   HBCA, B.5/a/1, Fort Alexandria – Post Journal, 1824-25, 5 August 1824.

77   HBCA, B.5/a/2, Fort Alexandria – Post Journal, 1827-28, 9 May 1827.

78   HBCA, B.188/a/8, Fort St. James – Post Journal, 1826-27, 8 May 1826.

79   HBCA, B.188/a/14, Fort St. James – Post Journal, 1829-30, 7 May 1829.

80   HBCA, B.188/a/17, Fort St. James – Post Journal, 1831-32, 13 May 1831.

81   HBCA, B.188/a/14, Fort St. James – Post Journal, 1829-30, 1, 3, 6 May 1829.

82   HBCA, E.12/3, Duncan Finlayson – Journals, 1831-38, "Journal," n.p., n.d.

83   Carl Landerholm, ed., *Notices & Voyages of the Famed Quebec Mission to the Pacific Northwest* ... (Portland: Oregon Historical Society 1956), 155.

84   HBCA, B.188/a/8, Fort St. James – Post Journal, 1826-27, 8, 10 May 1826.

85   HBCA, B.188/a/10, Fort St. James – Post Journal, 1827, 4, 5, 6 May 1827.

86   HBCA, B.188/a/12, Fort St. James – Post Journal, 1828, 5, 6, 7 May 1828.

87   HBCA, B.188/a/14, Fort St. James – Post Journal, 1829-30, 6, 7, 8, 9 May 1829.
88   HBCA, B.188/a/17, Fort St. James – Post Journal, 1831-32, 11, 14 May 1831.
89   HBCA, B.5/a/3, Fort Alexandria – Post Journal, 1833-34, 7, 15, 18 May 1834.
90   HBCA, B.5/a/4, Fort Alexandria – Post Journal, 1837-39, 28 April, 2 May 1838, 25, 28 April 1839; HBCA, B.5/a/5, Fort Alexandria – Post Journal, 1842-43, 25 April, 1 May 1843; HBCA, B.5/a/6, Fort Alexandria – Post Journal, 1843-45, 25, 29 April 1844.
91   [John Tod], "Journal Thompson River John Tod," BCARS, MS AB20 K12A 1841-43, 4 August 1841.
92   Ibid., 11 October 1843.
93   HBCA, B.5/e/1, Fort Alexandria – District Report, 1827-28, fo. 3.
94   HBCA, B.188/a/17, Fort St. James – Post Journal, 1831-32, 20 May 1831.
95   HBCA, B.188/a/8, Fort St. James – Post Journal, 1826-27, 18, 19 May 1826.
96   HBCA, B.188/a/10, Fort St. James – Post Journal, 1827, 8 May 1827.
97   HBCA, B.188/a/8, Fort St. James – Post Journal, 1826-27, 21 May 1826.
98   HBCA, B.188/a/17, Fort St. James – Post Journal, 1831-32, 24 May 1831.
99   HBCA, B.5/a/6, Fort Alexandria – Post Journal, 1843-45, 30 April 1844.
100 HBCA, B.188/a/8, Fort St. James – Post Journal, 1826-27, 13-14 May 1826.
101 HBCA, B.188/a/12, Fort St. James – Post Journal, 1828, 8 May 1828.
102 HBCA, B.188/a/8, Fort St. James – Post Journal, 1826-27, 13-14 May 1826.
103 HBCA, B.188/a/10, Fort St. James – Post Journal, 1827, 6, 7, 17 May 1827.
104 HBCA, B.188/a/14, Fort St. James – Post Journal, 1829-30, 10, 17, 18-19 May 1829.
105 HBCA, B.188/a/17, Fort St. James – Post Journal, 1831-32, 17, 21, 22, 23 May 1831.
106 HBCA, B.188/a/8, Fort St. James – Post Journal, 1826-27, 11 May 1826.
107 HBCA, B.188/a/10, Fort St. James – Post Journal, 1827, 7 May 1827.
108 HBCA, B.188/a/17, Fort St. James – Post Journal, 1831-32, 18 May 1831.
109 Ibid., 15 May 1831.
110 HBCA, B.188/a/8, Fort St. James – Post Journal, 1826-27, 8, 13-14, 15, 20 May 1826; HBCA, B.188/a/12, Fort St. James – Post Journal, 1828, 7 May 1828; HBCA, B.188/a/14, Fort St. James – Post Journal, 1829-30, 9 May 1829.
111 HBCA, B.188/a/8, Fort St. James – Post Journal, 1826-27, 13-14 May 1826.
112 HBCA, B.188/a/17, Fort St. James – Post Journal, 1831-32, 15 May 1831.
113 HBCA, B.188/a/8, Fort St. James – Post Journal, 1826-27, 20, 21, 23 May 1826.
114 HBCA, B.97/a/2, Fort Kamloops – Post Journal, 1826-27, 8 March 1827.

Chapter 6: Packhorsing between the Fraser and the Columbia

1   Rich, *Part of Dispatch from George Simpson*, 30-1.
2   HBCA, B.97/a/2, Fort Kamloops – Post Journal, 1826-27, foreword; HBCA, B.188/a/10, Fort St. James – Post Journal, 1827, 18 May, 15 July 1827.
3   HBCA, D.4/5, Governor George Simpson – Correspondence Book Outwards (General), 1824-25, Simpson to McLeod, 1 November 1824.
4   HBCA, B.97/e/1, Fort Kamloops – District Report, 1827, fos. 2v., 3; also see Rich, *Part of Dispatch from George Simpson*, 30.
5   HBCA, B.223/e/3, Fort Vancouver – District Report, [1825-26], fo. 2v.
6   HBCA, B.97/e/1, Fort Kamloops – District Report, 1827, fo. 3.
7   [Tod], "Journal Thompson River," 2 May, 11 August 1843.
8   HBCA, B.97/a/2, Fort Kamloops – Post Journal, 1826-27, 30 September 1826.
9   See the August 1841 entries in [Tod], "Journal Thompson River."
10   Ibid., 11 October 1843.
11   McLeod, *Peace River*, 114.
12   HBCA, B.97/e/1, Fort Kamloops – District Report, 1827, fo. 4.
13   [Tod], "Journal Thompson River," 9 May 1842.
14   HBCA, B.97/a/1, Fort Kamloops – Post Journal, 1822-23, 26 August 1822.
15   HBCA, B.97/a/2, Fort Kamloops – Post Journal, 1826-27, 3 December 1826.
16   HBCA, B.97/e/1, Fort Kamloops – District Report, 1827, fo. 2v.
17   Rich, *Part of Dispatch from George Simpson*, 31.
18   HBCA, B.97/e/1, Fort Kamloops – Post Journal, 1827, fo. 2v.

19   HBCA, B.97/a/2, Fort Kamloops – Post Journal, 1826-27, 25 December 1826.

20   HBCA, B.97/e/1, Fort Kamloops – District Report, 1827, fo. 2v.

21   HBCA, B.97/a/2, Fort Kamloops – Post Journal, 1826-27, 28 September, 11 October, 27 November 1826.

22   Ibid., 15, 17 October, 8 November, 4 December 1826.

23   [Tod], "Journal Thompson River," 5-7 December 1841.

24   HBCA, B.97/a/1, Fort Kamloops – Post Journal, 1822-23, 16 August, 14 December 1822, 5 January 1823.

25   Ibid., 6, 22 January, 22 February 1823.

26   Ibid., 8 January 1823.

27   HBCA, B.97/a/2, Fort Kamloops – Post Journal, 1826-27, 9 September 1826.

28   Ibid., 22 August, 17 September, 17 October, 10, 15 November, 3, 23 December 1826, 4, 29 January, 2, 14 February 1827; HBCA, B.223/b/2, Fort Vancouver – Correspondence Book, 1826, McDonald to McLoughlin, 22 August 1826.

29   At an uncertain date just before or right after 1847, the horse trail from Thompson's River to Okanagan Lake may have been shifted from Fort Kamloops southwards along the route of Highway 5A to Nicola Lake and then up the Nicola River, past Douglas Lake, and perhaps down Lambly Creek to Okanagan Lake – thereby avoiding the steep ascent of Monte Creek and part of the rugged lakeshore.

30   For the details of this route I am much indebted to Harris, Hatfield, and Tassie, *The Okanagan Brigade Trail*, 1989 and Holt, Jahnke, and Tassie, *The Okanagan Brigade Trail*, 1986.

31   HBCA, B.97/a/1, Fort Kamloops – Post Journal, 1822-23, 1, 18, 31 March 1823.

32   HBCA, B.188/a/8, Fort St. James – Post Journal, 1826, 25 May, 3, 4 June 1826; [Work], "Journal," 3 June 1826.

33   HBCA, B.188/a/10, Fort St. James – Post Journal, 1827, 18, 26 May 1827.

34   HBCA, B.188/a/12, Fort St. James – Post Journal, 1828, 19, 27 May 1828.

35   HBCA, B.188/a/14, Fort St. James – Post Journal, 1829-30, 21, 29 May 1829.

36   HBCA, B.188/a/17, Fort St. James – Post Journal, 1831-32, 25, 26 May, 3 June 1831.

37   HBCA, B.188/a/8, Fort St. James – Post Journal, 1826, 29 May, 1 June 1826.

38   HBCA, B.188/a/14, Fort St. James – Post Journal, 1829-30, 26, 27 May 1829.

39   HBCA, B.188/a/17, Fort St. James – Post Journal, 1831-32, 30 May 1831.

40   HBCA, B.188/a/12, Fort St. James – Post Journal, 1828, 22, 27 May 1828.

41   HBCA, B.188/a/8, Fort St. James – Post Journal, 1826, 28 May 1826.

42   HBCA, B.188/a/14, Fort St. James – Post Journal, 1829-30, 24 May 1829.

43   HBCA, B.188/a/8, Fort St. James – Post Journal, 1826, 2 June 1826.

44   HBCA, B.188/a/14, Fort St. James – Post Journal, 1829-30, 22 May 1829.

Chapter 7: The Easy Leg from Okanagan to Walla Walla

1   Hiram Martin Chittenden and Alfred Talbot Richardson, eds., *Life, Letters and Travels of Father Pierre-Jean De Smet, S.J. 1801-1873* (New York: Kraus Reprint 1969), 1:384.

2   Ross, *Adventures of the First Settlers*, 1986 edition, 154, 158-9.

3   Wilkes, *Narrative*, 4:433.

4   HBCA, B.223/e/3, Fort Vancouver – District Report, [1825-26], fo. 2v.

5   HBCA, B.97/a/2, Fort Kamloops – Post Journal, 1826-27, [foreword].

6   Rich, *Part of Dispatch from George Simpson*, 227.

7   Ibid., 50.

8   Ibid., 227.

9   HBCA, B.223/a/3, Fort Vancouver – Post Journal, 1826, Amelius Simpson, "Journal of a Voyage Across the Continent of North America in 1826," 25 October 1826.

10   [Henry Warre], "H.F. Warre Papers," NAC, MS MG 24, F 71, 15:1,090-1.

11   HBCA, B.223/e/3, Fort Vancouver – District Report, [1825-26], fo. 3v.

12   Wilkes, *Narrative*, 4:444.

13   On 24 August 1824, for instance, John Work left the forks for Spokane with two servants and several Indians and more than one hundred horses – including eighty carrying the outfit – "to bring up the property & for the people to ride" ([Work], "Journal," 24, 26 August 1824).

14   HBCA, B.76/e/1, Fort George (Columbia River) – District Report, 1824-25, fo. 4v.; HBCA,

D.4/5, Governor George Simpson – Correspondence Book Outwards (General), 1824-25, Simpson to McLoughlin, 10 April 1825.

15 HBCA, B.45/a/1, Fort Colvile – Post Journal, 1830-31, 24 April 1830, 13 April 1831.
16 Ibid., 10, 12 July 1830, 12 February, 23 March 1831; HBCA, D.4/101, Governor George Simpson – Official Reports to the Governor and Committee in London, 1834, Simpson to the Governor and Committee, 21 July 1834; MacLaren, "Journal of Paul Kane's Western Travels," 37.
17 Wilkes, *Narrative*, 4:445.
18 Ibid., 434.
19 HBCA, B.223/z/4, Fort Vancouver – Miscellaneous Items, 1824-60, Warre and Vavasour to the Secretary of State for the Colonies, 1 November 1845.
20 HBCA, B.45/a/1, Fort Colvile – Post Journal, 1830-31, 12, 23, 24, 28 April, 4, 7, 10, 21 May, 15, 19, 22, 24 November 1830.
21 Ibid., 20 April, 22, 23, 24 May, 14, 25, 27, 31 July, 3 August, 25 September, 21, 22, 23 October 1830.
22 William A. Lewis and Jacob A. Meyers, eds., "Journal of a Trip from Fort Colvile to Fort Vancouver and Return in 1828," *Washington Historical Quarterly* 11 (1920): 104-6.
23 [Work], "Journal," 3, 6 June 1826.
24 HBCA, B.188/a/12, Fort St. James – Post Journal, 1828, 26, 27 May 1828.
25 Ogden, "Notes on Western Caledonia," 55.
26 Clarence B. Bagley, ed., *Early Catholic Missions in Old Oregon* (Seattle: Lowman & Hanford 1932), 1:76.
27 Cullen, "Outfitting New Caledonia," 238.
28 HBCA, B.76/e/1, Fort George (Columbia River) – District Report, 1824-25, fo. 2v.
29 T.C. Elliott, ed., "Journal of John Work [1825-26] …," *Washington Historical Quarterly* 5 (1914): 175.
30 Lewis and Meyers, "Journal of a Trip," 106.
31 Wilkes, *Narrative*, 4:380.
32 HBCA, B.76/e/1, Fort George (Columbia River) – District Report, 1824-25, fo. 2v.
33 George B. Roberts, "Recollections of George B. Roberts," BLUC, MS P-A 83, 42.
34 Lewis and Meyers, "Journal of a Trip," 105-6.
35 Wilkes, *Narrative*, 4:381.
36 Franchère, *Journal of a Voyage*, 157, n. 3.
37 J.B. Tyrrell, ed., *David Thompson's Narrative of His Explorations in Western America 1784-1812* (Toronto: Champlain Society 1916), 452.
38 Ibid., 454-5.
39 Ibid., 469.
40 Spaulding, *On the Oregon Trail*, 52.
41 Ross, *Fur Hunters of the Far West*, 55.
42 Merk, *Fur Trade and Empire*, 38.
43 HBCA, D.4/121, Governor George Simpson – Correspondence Book Inwards, 1827-28, Connolly to the Governor, Chief Factors, and Chief Traders of the Northern Department, 25 February 1828.
44 Peter H. Burnett, *Recollections and Opinions of an Old Pioneer* (New York: D. Appleton 1880), 128.
45 HBCA, B.223/z/4, Fort Vancouver – Miscellaneous Items, 1824-60, Warre and Vavasour to the Secretary of State for the Colonies, 1 November 1845; [Warre], "Papers," 15:1,083. Subsequently, Vavasour reported that batteaux were "expressly adapted to this dangerous River navigation," and he added: "These boats are built of Cedar after the model of a bark Canoe, the planks being rivetted to the ribs, having no knees, and the seams filled with pitch and gum, they are propelled with the oars by 5 men and steered with a paddle (HBCA, B.223/z/4, Fort Vancouver – Miscellaneous Items, 1824-60, Vavasour to Holloway, 1 March 1846).
46 Wilkes, *Narrative*, 4:371.
47 Ibid., 378.
48 HBCA, B.223/b/2, Fort Vancouver – Correspondence Book, 1826, McLoughlin to Connolly, 18 November 1826.

49   Ibid., McLoughlin to Work, 18 November 1826.
50   HBCA, B.223/b/3, Fort Vancouver – Correspondence Book, 1827-28, McLoughlin to Dease, 21 November 1827, 20 March 1828, McLoughlin to Connolly, 20 March 1828.
51   HBCA, B.223/b/15, Fort Vancouver – Correspondence Book, 1836-37, McLoughlin to McDonald, 10 May 1836, McLoughlin to Ogden, 10 May 1836; HBCA, B.223/b/17, Fort Vancouver – Correspondence Book, 1837, McLoughlin to Ogden, 10 May 1837.
52   HBCA, B.223/b/17, Fort Vancouver – Correspondence Book, 1837, McLoughlin to Ogden, 10 May 1837.
53   HBCA, B.223/b/3, Fort Vancouver – Correspondence Book, 1827-28, McLoughlin to Connolly, 20 April 1827.
54   HBCA, B.223/b/17, Fort Vancouver – Correspondence Book, 1837, McLoughlin to Ogden, 10 May 1837.
55   HBCA, B.223/b/18, Fort Vancouver – Correspondence Book, 1837-38, McLoughlin to Black, 21 April 1838.
56   HBCA, B.223/b/3, Fort Vancouver – Correspondence Book, 1827-28, McLoughlin to Dease, 21 November 1827, 20 March 1828.
57   HBCA, D.4/85, Governor George Simpson – Official Reports to the Governor and Committee in London, 1822, Simpson to the Governor and Committee, 31 July 1822.
58   [Douglas], *Journal*, 179-80.
59   Wilkes, *Narrative*, 4:372.
60   Ibid., 391-2. For more on Ogden, see Gloria Griffen Cline, *Peter Skene Ogden and the Hudson's Bay Company* (Norman: University of Oklahoma Press 1974).
61   William Fraser Tolmie, "History of Puget Sound and the Northwest Coast," BLUC, MS P-B 25, 12.
62   Ross, *Fur Hunters of the Far West*, 194. For the context, see Theodore J. Karamanski, "The Iroquois and the Fur Trade of the Far West," *Beaver* 312 (Spring 1982): 4-13.
63   Ross, *Fur Hunters of the Far West*, 194, 195.
64   Ibid., 193, 194.
65   Ibid., 194; Franchère, *Journal of a Voyage*, 70, 114.
66   Wilkes, *Narrative*, 4:392.
67   Kane, *Wanderings of an Artist*, 181; also see ibid., 102.
68   McLeod, *Peace River*, 29.
69   Wilkes, *Narrative*, 4:371, 391.
70   HBCA, B.223/z/4, Fort Vancouver – Miscellaneous Items, 1824-60, Warre and Vavasour to the Secretary of State for the Colonies, 1 November 1845.
71   [Warre], "Papers," 15:1,091-2, 1,096-8.
72   [Work], "Journal," 3 May 1824.
73   Ibid., 1, 2, 4 May 1824.
74   HBCA, B.188/a/1, Fort St. James – Post Journal, fos. 5v.-6.
75   HBCA, B.188/a/8, Fort St. James – Post Journal, 1826-27, 7-9 June 1826; [Work], "Journal," 7, 9 June 1826. According to Work, however, from Fort Nez Percés the brigade comprised fifty-five men ([Work], "Journal," 9 June 1826).
76   HBCA, B.188/a/10, Fort St. James – Post Journal, 1827, 25-31 May, 1-2 June 1827.
77   HBCA, B.188/a/12, Fort St. James – Post Journal, 1828, 28-29 May 1828; Lewis and Meyers, "Journal of a Trip," 106; [Work], "Journal," 20-23, 27-28 May 1828.
78   HBCA, B.188/a/14, Fort St. James – Post Journal, 1829-30, 29-31 May, 1 June 1829.
79   HBCA, B.188/a/17, Fort St. James – Post Journal, 1831-32, 2-6 June 1831.
80   Paul Kane reported that the Kettle Falls portage was two miles in length, but he probably exaggerated the distance (MacLaren, "Journal of Paul Kane's Western Travels," 36).
81   As in Lac des Chicots (Stump Lake) just south of Fort Kamloops.
82   HBCA, B.76/e/1, Fort George (Columbia River) – District Report, 1824-25, fo. 1v.
83   HBCA, B.223/z/4, Fort Vancouver – Miscellaneous Items, 1824-60, Warre and Vavasour to the Secretary of State for the Colonies, 1 November 1845.
84   Kane, *Wanderings of an Artist*, 113.
85   HBCA, D.5/7, Governor George Simpson – Correspondence Inward, 1842, McDonald to Simpson, 26 May 1842.

86   Gough, *Journal of Alexander Henry*, 2:635.
87   [Warre], "Papers," 15:1,087-9.
88   De Smet, *Oregon Missions*, 235.
89   MacLaren, "Journal of Paul Kane's Western Travels," 36, 44.
90   HBCA, B.223/a/3, Fort Vancouver – Post Journal, 1826, Amelius Simpson, "Journal of a Voyage Across the Continent of North America in 1826," 26, 27 October 1826.
91   Ross, *Adventures of the First Settlers*, 1986 edition, 144.
92   Ibid.
93   [Douglas], *Journal*, 160.
94   HBCA, B.223/a/3, Fort Vancouver – Post Journal, 1826, Amelius Simpson, "Journal of a Voyage Across the Continent of North America in 1826," 23 October 1826.
95   De Smet, *Oregon Missions*, 235.
96   HBCA, E.12/2, Duncan Finlayson – Journals, 1831-38, "Journal," 25 October 1831.
97   Glazebrook, *Hargrave Correspondence*, 293. For a firsthand account of this accident by a survivor, see Kane, *Wanderings of an Artist*, 233-4.
98   HBCA, B.223/c/1, Fort Vancouver – Correspondence Inward, 1826-50, Governor and Committee to McLoughlin, 31 December 1839.
99   [Warre], "Papers," 15:1,087.
100 HBCA, D.4/125, Governor George Simpson – Correspondence Book Inwards, 1829-31, Harriott to Simpson, 16 March 1831.
101 Rich, *Letters of John McLoughlin*, 2:57.
102 HBCA, B.188/a/12, Fort St. James – Post Journal, 1828, 29 May, 1 June 1828; HBCA, D.4/122, Governor George Simpson – Correspondence Book Inwards, 1828-29, Connolly to the Governor and Council of the Northern Department, 28 February 1829; Lewis and Meyers, "Journal," 107; Rich, *Letters of John McLoughlin*, 1:56-7; [Work], "Journal," 29 May, 1 June 1828.
103 HBCA, D.4/123, Governor George Simpson – Correspondence Book Inwards, 1829-30, Connolly to the Governor and Council of the Northern Department, 4 March 1830.

Chapter 8: The Hard Leg from Walla Walla to the Sea

1   HBCA, B.223/a/3, Fort Vancouver – Post Journal, 1826, Amelius Simpson, "Journal of a Voyage Across the Continent of North America in 1826," 31 October 1826.
2   Ibid., 1 November 1826.
3   Thompson, *Columbia Journals*, 152.
4   For an authoritative treatment by an anthropologist of the fort's history of relationships between the natives and the white fur traders, missionaries, and settlers before 1856, see Theodore Stern, *Chiefs & Chief Traders: Indian Relations at Fort Nez Percés, 1818-1855* (Corvallis: Oregon State University Press 1993) and idem, *Chiefs & Change in the Oregon Country: Indian Relations at Fort Nez Percés 1818-1855* (Corvallis: Oregon State University Press 1996).
5   Ross, *Fur Hunters of the Far West*, 121.
6   HBCA, A.12/1, London Inward Correspondence from Governors of H.B.C. Territories – Sir George Simpson, 1823-32, Simpson to the Governor and Committee, 20 August 1826.
7   HBCA, B.223/b/3, Fort Vancouver – Correspondence Book, 1827-28, McLoughlin to Connolly, Dease, and Black, 3 June 1826.
8   HBCA, B.223/e/3, Fort Vancouver – District Report, [1825-26], fos. 2-2v.
9   HBCA, B.146/e/1, Fort Nez Percés – District Report, 1827, fo. IV.
10   Rich, *Part of Dispatch from George Simpson*, 50-1.
11   Glazebrook, *Hargrave Correspondence*, 427.
12   HBCA, B.223/z/4, Fort Vancouver – Miscellaneous Items, 1824-60, Warre and Vavasour to the Secretary of State for the Colonies, 1 November 1845.
13   [Warre], "Papers," 15:1,101.
14   MacLaren, "Journal of Paul Kane's Western Travels," 41.
15   HBCA, B.146/a/1, Fort Nez Percés – Post Journal, 1831, 1 June 1831.
16   HBCA, D.4/117, Governor George Simpson – Correspondence Book Inwards, 1822-23, Ross to the Governor and Council of the Northern Department, 27 April 1823.
17   Ross, *Fur Hunters of the Far West*, 125.

18 HBCA, B.188/b/1, Fort St. James – Correspondence Book, 1821-22, Stuart to Garry, 20 April 1822.
19 [Work], "Journal," 22 August 1830, 20 July 1831.
20 HBCA, B.223/e/4, Fort Vancouver – District Report, [1845?], fo. 1.
21 HBCA, D.4/5, Governor George Simpson – Correspondence Book Outwards (General), 1824-25, Simpson to McLoughlin, 10 April 1825.
22 Ross, *Fur Hunters of the Far West*, 118, 119.
23 HBCA, D.4/117, Governor George Simpson – Correspondence Book Inwards, 1822-23, Dease to the Governor and Council of the Northern Department, 12 April 1823.
24 Ibid., Ross to the Governor and Council of the Northern Department, 27 April 1823.
25 HBCA, B.146/a/1, Fort Nez Percés – Post Journal, 1831, passim. Numerous skunks were another pest.
26 Ross, *Fur Hunters of the Far West*, 119, 146.
27 HBCA, B.146/a/1, Fort Nez Percés – Post Journal, 1831, 25 May 1831.
28 MacLaren, "Journal of Paul Kane's Western Travels," 41.
29 HBCA, B.146/a/1, Fort Nez Percés – Post Journal, 1831, 14 April 1831.
30 Ibid., 29 March 1831.
31 Ibid., 19 May 1831.
32 Ibid., 22 May 1831.
33 HBCA, D.4/119, Governor George Simpson – Correspondence Book Inwards, 1824-26, Dease to the Governor, Chief Factors, and Chief Traders of the Northern Department, 21 July 1825.
34 HBCA, B.146/e/1, Fort Nez Percés – District Report, 1827, fos. 1, 1v.
35 HBCA, B.146/a/1, Fort Nez Percés – Post Journal, 1831, 27 September 1831.
36 Ibid., 22 October 1831.
37 HBCA, E.12/2, Duncan Finlayson – Journals, 1831-38, "Journal," 25 October 1831.
38 [Warre], "Papers," 15:1,108.
39 Cox, *Columbia River*, 86.
40 According to Father De Smet, "*Dalle* is an old French word, meaning a trough, and the name is given by the Canadian voyageurs to all contracted running waters, hemmed in by walls of rocks" (De Smet, *Oregon Missions*, 214).
41 Moulton, *Journals of the Lewis & Clark Expedition*, 5:331.
42 Cox, *Columbia River*, 83.
43 Ross, *Adventures of the First Settlers*, 1849 edition, 122.
44 HBCA, B.223/a/3, Fort Vancouver – Post Journal, 1826, Amelius Simpson, "Journal of a Voyage Across the Continent of North America in 1826," 31 October 1826.
45 Bagley, *Early Catholic Missions*, 1:40.
46 Wilkes, *Narrative*, 4:387.
47 HBCA, B.223/a/3, Fort Vancouver – Post Journal, 1826, Amelius Simpson, "Journal of a Voyage Across the Continent of North America in 1826," 31 October 1826.
48 Moulton, *Journals of the Lewis & Clark Expedition*, 7:129.
49 Bagley, *Early Catholic Missions*, 1:41. According to Ross Cox, however, the Little Dalles were "one deep rapid" from four to five miles in length (Cox, *Columbia River*, 80).
50 Franchère, *Journal of a Voyage*, 148.
51 Cox, *Columbia River*, 80.
52 Ross, *Adventures of the First Settlers*, 1849 edition, 119.
53 HBCA, B.223/a/3, Fort Vancouver – Post Journal, 1826, Amelius Simpson, "Journal of a Voyage Across the Continent of North America in 1826," 1 November 1826.
54 John Kirk Townsend, *Narrative of a Journey Across the Rocky Mountains to the Columbia River* (Fairfield, WA: Ye Galleon Press 1970), 285.
55 Bagley, *Early Catholic Missions*, 1:41.
56 Wilkes, *Narrative*, 4:384 5.
57 [Warre], "Papers," 19:1,573-5.
58 Ross, *Adventures of the First Settlers*, 1986 edition, 126, 128. According to Wilkes, however, the portage was only a mile long and "very rugged" (Wilkes, *Narrative*, 4:385). Perhaps the two men used the portage at different times of the year or the route of the portage had been changed in the intervening thirty years.

59 Ross, *Adventures of the First Settlers*, 1986 edition, 129, 130.
60 Wilkes, *Narrative*, 4:383-6.
61 HBCA, B.223/z/4, Fort Vancouver – Miscellaneous Items, 1824-60, Warre and Vavasour to the Secretary of State for the Colonies, 1 November 1845.
62 Cox, *Columbia River*, 79.
63 Bagley, *Early Catholic Missions*, 1:42.
64 HBCA, B.223/a/3, Fort Vancouver – Post Journal, 1826, Amelius Simpson, "Journal of a Voyage Across the Continent of North America in 1826," 1 November 1826.
65 [Warre], "Papers," 15:1,115.
66 Ibid., 1,113.
67 Moulton, *Journals of the Lewis & Clark Expedition*, 5:363.
68 Ross, *Adventures of the First Settlers*, 1986 edition, 123.
69 Cox, *Columbia River*, 79.
70 Townsend, *Narrative of a Journey*, 290-1.
71 [Warre], "Papers," 19:1,562-4.
72 Bagley, *Early Catholic Missions*, 1:41; HBCA, B.223/z/4, Fort Vancouver – Miscellaneous Items, 1824-60, Warre and Vavasour to the Secretary of State for the Colonies, 1 November 1845. David Douglas, however, stated that the river fell 147 feet in 2 miles ([Douglas], *Journal*, 127).
73 Moulton, *Journals of the Lewis & Clark Expedition*, 7:104, 105, 108.
74 Cox, *Columbia River*, 77.
75 Ross, *Adventures of the First Settlers*, 1986 edition, 122.
76 Wilkes, *Narrative*, 4:380, 381, 385.
77 Kane, *Wanderings of an Artist*, 180.
78 Ross, *Adventures of the First Settlers*, 1986 edition, 123; Ross, *Fur Hunters of the Far West*, 146.
79 [Warre], "Papers," 15:1,117-18.
80 HBCA, E.12/2, Duncan Finlayson – Journals, 1831-38, "Journal," 25 October 1831.
81 [Douglas], *Journal*, 127.
82 [Work], "Journal," 5, 8-13 May 1824.
83 HBCA, D.4/119, Governor George Simpson – Correspondence Book Inwards, 1824-26, McLoughlin to the Chief Factors and Chief Traders of the Columbia Department, 20 June 1825; Rich, *Letters of John McLoughlin*, 1:5.
84 HBCA, B./188/a/8, Fort St. James – Post Journal, 1826-27, 11 June 1826.
85 Ibid., 9-11, 15-16 June 1826; Elliott, "Journal of John Work," 286, 287; [Work], "Journal," 9-11 June 1826.
86 HBCA, B.188/a/10, Fort St. James – Post Journal, 1827, 2-5 June 1827.
87 HBCA, B.188/a/12, Fort St. James – Post Journal, 1828, 1-3, 5-9 June 1828; [Work], "Journal," 5 June 1828.
88 HBCA, B.188/a/14, Fort St. James – Post Journal, 1829-30, 2-3, 6-7 June 1829.
89 HBCA, B.146/a/1, Fort Nez Percés – Post Journal, 1831, 4-7 June 1831; HBCA, B.188/a/17, Fort St. James – Post Journal, 1831-32, 7-9, 11 June 1831.
90 Elliott, "Journal of John Work," 85-6.
91 HBCA, B.223/e/1, Fort Vancouver – District Report, 1826-27, fo. 2.
92 Elliott, "Journal of John Work," 29.
93 Moulton, *Journals of the Lewis & Clark Expedition*, 7:104.
94 Ross, *Adventures of the First Settlers*, 1986 edition, 240.
95 Ross, *Fur Hunters of the Far West*, 94, 111.
96 Ross, *Adventures of the First Settlers*, 1986 edition, 129.
97 Ross, *Fur Hunters of the Far West*, 90.
98 [Douglas], *Journal*, 142, 143.
99 HBCA, A.12/1, London Inward Correspondence from Governors of H.B.C. Territories – Sir George Simpson, 1823-32, Simpson to the Governor and Committee, 20 August 1826.
100 HBCA, D.4/121, Governor George Simpson – Correspondence Book Inwards, 1827-28, McLoughlin to Simpson, 20 March 1828.
101 HBCA, D.4/5, Governor George Simpson – Correspondence Book Outwards (General), 1824-25, Simpson to McLoughlin, 10 April 1825. Instead, Work took Josette Legacé, a

Spokane mixed blood, as a "country wife" (native common-law wife); he married her in 1849 in Victoria.

102   Rich, *Letters of John McLoughlin*, 2:118.
103   [Warre], "Papers," 15:1,112.
104   Wilkes, *Narrative*, 4:403.
105   Ibid.
106   Rich, *Letters of John McLoughlin*, 1:85-6.
107   Glazebrook, *Hargrave Correspondence*, 68; HBCA, D.4/125, Governor George Simpson – Correspondence Book Inwards, 1829-31, Kittson to Rowand, 12 August 1830.
108   HBCA, D.4/125, Governor George Simpson – Correspondence Book Inwards, 1829-31, Harriott to Simpson, 16 March 1831.
109   Isaac Cowie, ed., *The Minutes of the Council of the Northern Department of Rupert's Land, 1830 to 1843* ... (Bismarck, ND [?]: State Historical Society of North Dakota, n.d.), 787.
110   Cox, *Columbia River*, 166-7, 228.
111   HBCA, E.12/2, Duncan Finlayson – Journals, 1831-38, "Journal," 25 October 1831.

Chapter 9: At the Sea

1   HBCA, B.223/a/3, Fort Vancouver – Post Journal, 1826, Amelius Simpson, "Journal of a Voyage Across the Continent of North America in 1826," 2 November 1826.
2   Corney, *Early Voyages in the North Pacific*, 175-7.
3   Fort George's district report for 1824-25 stated that in summer abundant salmon and "large & excellent" sturgeon were bought from the natives at a "cheap rate," the former being salted down for winter consumption and the latter being eaten fresh; also, potatoes were grown at the fort in "great abundance," and in winter a "good many" swans, geese, and ducks were bought from the natives, as well as some venison (HBCA, B.76/e/1, Fort George [Columbia River] – District Report, 1824-25, fo. 4v.).
4   Jones, *Astorian Adventure*, 148.
5   Gough, *Journal of Alexander Henry*, 2:674-5.
6   Ibid., 672-3, 678.
7   Jones, *Astorian Adventure*, 148.
8   HBCA, B.76/e/1, Fort George (Columbia River) – District Report, 1824-25, fos. 5, 8-8v.
9   John Stuart, "Letter Books and Journals," OHS, MS 1,502, reel 1, n.p.
10   HBCA, B.223/e/3, Fort Vancouver – District Report [1825-26], fo. 1.
11   Ibid., fo. 2; HBCA, B.223/e/1, Fort Vancouver – District Report, 1826-27, fo. 2.
12   See John A. Hussey, *The History of Fort Vancouver and Its Physical Structure* ([Tacoma]: Washington State Historical Society n.d.).
13   [Warre], "Papers," 15:1,119-23, 1,126.
14   HBCA, D.4/6, Governor George Simpson – Correspondence Book Outwards (General), 1825-26, Simpson to McLoughlin, 10 July 1826.
15   Rich, *Part of Dispatch from George Simpson*, 68.
16   Ibid., 69.
17   HBCA, D.4/119, Governor George Simpson – Correspondence Book Inwards, 1824-26, McLoughlin to the Governor, Chief Factors, and Chief Traders of the Northern Department, 20 March 1826.
18   HBCA, B.188/a/10, Fort St. James – Post Journal, 1827, 5 June 1827.
19   Rich, *Part of Dispatch from George Simpson*, 69.
20   HBCA, D.4/125, Governor George Simpson – Correspondence Book Inwards, 1829-31, fos. 77, 78v.
21   Dunn, *History of the Oregon Territory*, 151.
22   HBCA, D.4/101, Governor George Simpson – Official Reports to the Governor and Committee in London, 1834, Simpson to the Governor and Committee, 21 July 1834.
23   HBCA, B.223/b/18, Fort Vancouver – Correspondence Book, 1837-38, McLoughlin to Douglas, March 1838.
24   Wilkes, *Narrative*, 4:329, 331.
25   Ibid.
26   [Warre], "Papers," 15:1,126.

27 [Douglas], *Journal*, 127.
28 Gibson, *Farming the Frontier*, 69.
29 Rich, *Letters of John McLoughlin*, 1:228; also see HBCA, D.4/125, Governor George Simpson – Correspondence Book Inwards, 1829-31, Kittson to Rowand, 12 August 1830.
30 HBCA, B.223/b/27, Fort Vancouver – Correspondence Book, 1840, McLoughlin to A. Simpson, 13 June 1840.
31 Wilkes, *Narrative*, 4:336, 337.
32 Ibid., 205.
33 Ibid., 5:140.
34 Ibid.
35 Ibid.
36 Ibid., 88. Some sources (e.g., John Dunn and Paul Kane) assert that malaria first appeared in 1829 and that the natives blamed its introduction on Captain John Dominis of the American coaster *Owhyhee*.
37 Burt Brown Barker, ed., *Letters of Dr. John McLoughlin* ... (Portland: Oregon Historical Society 1948), 132.
38 McDonald, *Fur Trade Letters*, 140.
39 McLeod, "Papers," 1:297.
40 Rich, *Letters of John McLoughlin*, 1:233.
41 HBCA, B.146/a/1, Fort Nez Percés – Post Journal, 1831, 8-9, 18 October 1831.
42 Glazebrook, *Hargrave Correspondence*, 87-8.
43 Ibid., 103.
44 HBCA, B.223/b/8, Fort Vancouver – Correspondence Book, 1832-33, McLoughlin to Simpson, 12 September 1832.
45 Work, "Correspondence," 36.
46 McLeod, "Papers," 1:353.
47 De Smet, *Oregon Missions*, 22-3; Landerholm, *Notices & Voyages*, 18.
48 [Warre], "Papers," 16:1,285.
49 Even without malaria, white morbidity at Fort Vancouver could still be high. At one time during the winter of 1826-27 every fifth man at the post was hospitalized (Rich, *Letters of John McLoughlin*, 1:46).
50 HBCA, B.223/b/11, Fort Vancouver – Correspondence Book, 1834-36, McLoughlin to Governor, Chief Factors, and Chief Traders of the Northern Department, 29 August 1835; HBCA, B.223/b/15, Fort Vancouver – Correspondence Book, 1836-37, McLoughlin to Simpson, 5 September 1836; HBCA, B.223/b/17, Fort Vancouver – Correspondence Book, 1837, McLoughlin to Simpson, 30 August 1837.
51 Governor Simpson in 1825 assured Beaver House that the Columbia outfit for the inland trade amounted to only about fifty tons of goods, leaving ample room in the supply ship for cargo for the coast trade (HBCA, D.4/7, Governor George Simpson – Correspondence Book Outwards [General], 1824-26, Simpson to the Governor and Committee, 10 March 1825). According to Commander Wilkes of the United States Exploring Expedition, in 1841 the London ship returned three-quarters empty ([Charles Wilkes], *Diary of Wilkes in the Northwest*, ed. Edmond S. Meany [Seattle: University of Washington Press 1926], 38), owing, apparently, to the decrease of returns.
52 [Wilkes], *Diary*, 39.
53 HBCA, B.223/b/17, Fort Vancouver – Correspondence Book, 1837, McLoughlin to Simpson, 30 August 1837.
54 HBCA, B.223/b/3, Fort Vancouver – Correspondence Book, 1827-28, McLoughlin to Connolly, 17 November 1827.
55 James Cooper, "Maritime Matters on the Northwest Coast ...," 1878, BLUC, MS P-C 6, 1.
56 HBCA, A.6/25, London Correspondence Book Outwards – H.B.C. Official, 1838-42, Governor and Committee to Simpson, 1 March 1841.
57 Finlayson, "History of Vancouver Island," 37.
58 HBCA, D.4/116, Governor George Simpson – Correspondence Book Inwards, 1821-22, Leith to the Governor of the Northern Department, 11 February 1822.

59 HBCA, D.5/1, Governor George Simpson – Correspondence Inward, 1821-26, Governor and Committee to Simpson, 2 June 1824.
60 Ibid.
61 HBCA, C.4/1, Book of Ships' Movements, 1719-1929, fos. 25v.-27. It was the custom to give one sea otter and two beaver skins to the captain of a London ship upon reaching the Columbia depot (HBCA, D.4/6, Governor George Simpson – Correspondence Book Outwards [General], 1825-26, McLoughlin to the Governor and Committee, 6 October 1825).
62 Rich, *Letters of John McLoughlin*, 1:71-3.
63 HBCA, B.188/a/14, Fort St. James – Post Journal, 1829-30, 6 May 1829.
64 Rich, *Letters of John McLoughlin*, 1:73.
65 Ibid., 83-4.
66 HBCA, B.76/e/1, Fort George (Columbia River) – District Report, 1824-25, fos. IV.-2.
67 HBCA, B.223/a/3, Fort Vancouver – Post Journal, 1826, Amelius Simpson, "Journal of a Voyage Across the Continent of North America in 1826," 2 November 1826; HBCA, B.223/z/4, Fort Vancouver – Miscellaneous Items, 1824-60, Warre and Vavasour to the Secretary of State for the Colonies, 1 November 1845.
68 Wilkes, *Narrative*, 4:327.
69 "Papers Relative to the Expedition of Lieuts. Warre and Vavasour to the Oregon Territory," PRO, MS F.O. 5/457, 45v.
70 Merk, *Fur Trade and Empire*, 94.
71 Ross, *Adventures of the First Settlers*, 1849 edition, 56-7.
72 Cox, *Columbia River*, 155.
73 Captain William Black, "A Description of the Mouth of Columbia River, North West Coast of America," OHS, MS 1,574, n.p.
74 Landerholm, *Notices & Voyages*, 143n.
75 Wilkes, *Narrative*, 4:293.
76 William James Morgan, David B. Tyler, Joye L. Leonhart, and Mary F. Loughlin, eds., *Autobiography of Rear Admiral Charles Wilkes, U.S. Navy 1798-1877* (Washington, DC: Department of the Navy 1978), 508-9.
77 Wilkes, *Narrative*, 4:305.
78 HBCA, B.223/c/1, Fort Vancouver – Correspondence Inward, 1826-50, Governor and Committee to McLoughlin, 8 December 1835.
79 [Nathaniel Wyeth], *The Correspondence and Journals of Captain Nathaniel J. Wyeth 1831-6*, ed. F.G. Young, Sources of the History of Oregon, vol. 1, nos. 3-6 (Eugene: University Press 1899), 180.
80 Thomas J. Farnham, *Travels in the Great Western Prairies, the Anahuac and Rocky Mountains, and in the Oregon Territory* (London: Richard Bentley 1843), 2:193; Joel Palmer, *Journal of Travels over the Rocky Mountains ...* (Cincinnati: J.A. and U.P. James 1847), 174.
81 HBCA, D.4/59, Governor George Simpson – Correspondence Book Outwards (General), 1841-42, Simpson to the Governor and Committee, 25 November 1841.
82 HBCA, D.4/67, Governor George Simpson – Correspondence Book Outwards (General), 1845-46, Simpson to McLoughlin, Ogden, and Douglas, 16 June 1845.
83 "Papers Relative to the Expedition of Warre and Vavasour," 45v.; [Warre], "Papers," 16:1,195.
84 Landerholm, *Notices & Voyages*, 143.
85 "Papers Relative to the Expedition of Warre and Vavasour," 45v.
86 HBCA, B.223/b/2, Fort Vancouver – Correspondence Book, 1826, McLoughlin to the Governor and Committee, 1 September 1826.
87 HBCA, D.4/6, Governor George Simpson – Correspondence Book Outwards (General), 1825-26, McLoughlin to the Governor and Committee, 6 October 1825; Rich, *Letters of John McLoughlin*, 1:1.
88 HBCA, B.223/b/2, Fort Vancouver – Correspondence Book, 1826, McLoughlin to the Chief Factors and Chief Traders of the Northern Department, 4 July 1826, McLoughlin to the Governor and Committee, 1 September 1826; Rich, *Letters of John McLoughlin*, 1:25.
89 HBCA, D.4/125, Governor George Simpson – Correspondence Book Inwards, 1829-31, McLoughlin to Rowand, 3 August 1830.

90 Ibid., Connolly to the Chief Factors and Chief Traders of the Athabasca District, 2 September 1830; HBCA, B.223/b/8, Fort Vancouver – Correspondence Book, 1832-33, McLoughlin to Simpson, 12 September 1832.
91 Rich, *Letters of John McLoughlin*, 1:137.

Chapter 10: The Hard Leg from the Sea to Walla Walla

1   Kane, *Wanderings of an Artist*, 178.
2   HBCA, D.4/5, Governor George Simpson – Correspondence Book Outwards (General), 1824-25, Simpson to McLoughlin, 11 July 1825.
3   HBCA, B.223/b/1, Fort Vancouver – Correspondence Book, 1825, McLoughlin to Simpson, 20 June 1825; HBCA, D.4/6, Governor George Simpson – Correspondence Book Outwards (General), 1825-26, McLoughlin to the Governor and Committee, 6 October 1825; HBCA, D.4/119, Governor George Simpson – Correspondence Book Inwards, 1824-26, McLoughlin to Simpson, 20 June 1825.
4   Rich, *Part of Dispatch from George Simpson*, 241.
5   HBCA, B.188/a/12, Fort St. James – Post Journal, 1828, 15 July 1828.
6   Rich, *Part of Dispatch from George Simpson*, 241.
7   HBCA, B.188/a/14, Fort St. James – Post Journal, 1829-30, 7 June 1829; Rich, *Letters of John McLoughlin*, 1:71-3.
8   HBCA, D.4/123, Governor George Simpson – Correspondence Book Inwards, 1829-30, Connolly to the Governor and Council of the Northern Department, 4 March 1830.
9   HBCA, B.146/a/1, Fort Nez Percés – Post Journal, 1831, 3 July 1831.
10 In 1824, however, the brigade inexplicably did not leave Fort George "to proceed to the interior" until 2 August ([Work], "Journal," 2 August 1824); nevertheless, it still avoided high water and reached its destination well before the end of summer.
11 Occasionally more than one brigade was dispatched inland from the depot in the same year. In 1822, for example, a brigade of six boats with 240 pieces departed Fort George on 23 February for Walla Walla and returned on 16 March (HBCA, D.4/116, Governor George Simpson – Correspondence Book Inwards, 1821-22, Cameron to Simpson, 3 April 1822), and on 8 July another brigade of ten boats (plus four more from Walla Walla) left Fort George for Fort St. James, which was reached on 16 August (HBCA, B.188/b/1, Fort St. James – Correspondence Book, 1821-22, Stuart to Cameron, 8 July 1822).
12 HBCA, B.5/a/2, Fort Alexandria – Post Journal, 1827-28, McLoughlin to Connolly, 17 November 1827; HBCA, B.223/b/3, Fort Vancouver – Correspondence Book, 1827-28, McLoughlin to Connolly, 17 November 1827.
13 Wilkes, *Narrative*, 4:364, 370.
14 Ibid., 371-2.
15 Ibid., 379.
16 HBCA, D.4/120, Governor George Simpson – Correspondence Book Inwards, 1826-27, McLoughlin to Simpson, 20 March 1827.
17 HBCA, B.223/b/2, Fort Vancouver – Correspondence Book, 1826, McLoughlin to the Governor, Chief Factors, and Chief Traders of the Northern Department, 4 July 1826.
18 Wilkes, *Narrative*, 4:379.
19 [Warre], "Papers," 19:1,559.
20 Corney, *Early Voyages in the North Pacific*, 177.
21 Kane, *Wanderings of an Artist*, 179.
22 Ibid.
23 Wilkes, *Narrative*, 4:379.
24 Thompson, *Columbia Journals*, 152, 153, 163.
25 Wilkes, *Narrative*, 4:381.
26 Ibid., 387, 389.
27 McLeod, *Peace River*, 100.
28 [Warre], "Papers," 19:1,577.
29 Wilkes, *Narrative*, 4:380.
30 Kane, *Wanderings of an Artist*, 184.
31 Wilkes, *Narrative*, 4:388.

32   Ibid., 390.
33   Ibid., 379.
34   Ibid., 380.
35   Rich, *Letters of John McLoughlin*, 1:74.
36   Ibid., 230; Anonymous, "Documents," *Washington Historical Quarterly* 1 (1907): 43; HBCA,
     B.146/a/1, Fort Nez Percés – Post Journal, 1831, 9 July 1831.
37   Rich, *Letters of John McLoughlin*, 2:108, 128.
38   Ibid., 1:6.
39   HBCA, B.188/b/6, Fort St. James – Correspondence Book, 1828-29, 49.
40   HBCA, B.223/b/34, Fort Vancouver – Correspondence Book, 1846, Ogden and Douglas to
     Governor and Committee, 28 July 1846.
41   HBCA, B.188/b/1, Fort St. James – Correspondence Book, 1821-22, Stuart to Cameron, 8
     July 1822.
42   [Work], "Journal," 2-7, 9-10 August 1824.
43   Elliott, "Journal of John Work," 84, 85, 87; HBCA, B.223/b/1, Fort Vancouver – Correspon-
     dence Book, 1825, McLoughlin to Simpson, 20 June 1825; HBCA, D.4/6, Governor George
     Simpson – Correspondence Book Outwards (General), 1825-26, McLoughlin to the Gov-
     ernor and Committee, 6 October 1825; HBCA, D.4/119, Governor George Simpson –
     Correspondence Book Inwards, 1824-26, McLoughlin to the Chief Factors and Chief Traders
     of the Columbia Department, 20 June 1825, McLoughlin to Simpson, 20 June 1825; Rich,
     Letters of John McLoughlin, 1:5-6; [Work], "Journal," 21-26, 29 June 1825.
44   HBCA, B.76/e/1, Fort George (Columbia River) – District Report, 1824-25, fos. 2v., 5.
45   HBCA, D.4/5, Governor George Simpson – Correspondence Book Outwards (General),
     1824-25, Simpson to McLoughlin, 10 April 1825.
46   Elliott, "Journal of John Work," 27, 30; HBCA, B.188/a/8, Fort St. James – Post Journal,
     1826-27, 5-10, 12-13, 15 July 1826; HBCA, D.4./120, Governor George Simpson – Corre-
     spondence Book Inwards, 1826-27, Connolly to the Governor, Chief Factors, and Chief
     Traders of the Northern Department, 18 July 1826; [Work], "Journal," 5, 8, 12 July 1826.
47   HBCA, B.188/a/10, Fort St. James – Post Journal, 1827, 5 June 1827; HBCA, D.4/121, Governor
     George Simpson – Correspondence Book Inwards, 1827-28, McLoughlin to the Governor, Chief
     Factors, and Chief Traders of the Northern Department, 17 August 1827, Connolly to the Gov-
     ernor, Chief Factors, and Chief Traders of the Northern Department, 20 September 1827.
48   HBCA, B.188/a/10, Fort St. James – Post Journal, 1827, 14, 23 June 1827. According to another
     company source, the brigade comprised nine boats with fifty-four men and about 325 pieces
     (HBCA, D.4/120, Governor George Simpson – Correspondence Book Inwards, 1826-27,
     McLoughlin to Simpson, 20 March 1827).
49   HBCA, B.188/a/12, Fort St. James – Post Journal, 1828, 9 June 1828; HBCA, D.4/122,
     Governor George Simpson – Correspondence Book Inwards, 1828-29, Connolly to the Gov-
     ernor and Council of the Northern Department, 28 February 1829.
50   HBCA, B.188/a/12, Fort St. James – Post Journal, 1828, 9 June 1828; Lewis and Meyers,
     "Journal of a Trip," 110; [Work], "Journal," 23 July 1828.
51   HBCA, B.188/a/12, Fort St. James – Post Journal, 1828, 9 June, 23, 26-8, 31 July 1828; [Work],
     "Journal," 24, 27, 30 July 1828.
52   HBCA, B.188/a/14, Fort St. James – Post Journal, 1829-30, 7 June, 10-12, 14, 19, 21 July 1829.
53   HBCA, B.146/a/1, Fort Nez Percés – Post Journal, 1831, 8-9, 11-12 July 1831; HBCA, B.188/a/17,
     Fort St. James – Post Journal, 1831-32, 11, 27-30 June, 4-5, 8 July 1831.
54   Wilkes, *Narrative*, 4:379, 381, 385, 387, 390.
55   Townsend, *Narrative of a Journey*, 344.
56   Bagley, *Early Catholic Missions*, 1:76; Landerholm, *Notices & Voyages*, 28.
57   Wilkes, *Narrative*, 4:379.
58   Kane, *Wanderings of an Artist*, 178; MacLaren, "Journal of Paul Kane's Western Travels," 39, 41.

Chapter 11: The Easy Leg from Walla Walla to Okanagan

 1   HBCA, D.4/5, Governor George Simpson – Correspondence Book Outwards (General),
     1824-25, Simpson to Dease, 11 April 1825.
 2   HBCA, B.146/e/2, Fort Nez Percés – District Report, 1829, fo. 5v.

3   Franchère, *Journal of a Voyage*, 150-1.
4   Moulton, *Journals of the Lewis & Clark Expedition*, 9:241, 297.
5   [Warre], "Papers," 15:1,106-7; also see HBCA, B.223/z/4, Fort Vancouver – Miscellaneous Items, 1824-60, Warre and Vavasour to the Secretary of State for the Colonies, 1 November 1845.
6   HBCA, D.4/5, Governor George Simpson – Correspondence Book Outwards (General), 1824-25, Simpson to McLoughlin, 10 April 1825.
7   Ibid.
8   HBCA, B.223/b/2, Fort Vancouver – Correspondence Book, 1826, McLoughlin to Dease, 8 August 1826; Merk, *Fur Trade and Empire*, 255.
9   HBCA, B.223/b/1, Fort Vancouver – Correspondence Book, 1825, McLoughlin to Dease, 5 September 1825; HBCA, B.223/b/2, Fort Vancouver – Correspondence Book, 1826, McLoughlin to Black, 31 March 1826.
10 HBCA, B.223/b/2, Fort Vancouver – Correspondence Book, 1826, McLoughlin to Black, 17 July 1826.
11 HBCA, B.97/a/2, Fort Kamloops – Post Journal, 1826-27, McDonald to McLoughlin, 22 August 1826.
12 HBCA, B.223/b/2, Fort Vancouver – Correspondence Book, 1826, McLoughlin to Dease, 8 August 1826.
13 Rich, *Part of Dispatch from George Simpson*, 51.
14 HBCA, B.146/a/1, Fort Nez Percés – Post Journal, 1831, 30-31 March, 11, 13-14 April, 9, 20 August, 29-30 November 1831.
15 HBCA, B.188/a/8, Fort St. James – Post Journal, 1826-27, 15, 17 July, 1, 10, 13 August 1826; HBCA, B.188/b/5, Fort St. James – Correspondence Book, 1826-27, Connolly to the Northern Department, 7, 9; HBCA, B.223/b/2, Fort Vancouver – Correspondence Book, 1826, Black to McLoughlin, 15 August 1826, McDonald to McLoughlin, 22 August 1826; HBCA, D.4/120, Governor George Simpson – Correspondence Book Inwards, 1826-27, Connolly to the Governor, Chief Factors, and Chief Traders of the Northern Department, 18 July 1826, McDonald to Simpson, 30 July 1826, Connolly to the Governor and Council of the Northern Department, 15 March 1827.
16 HBCA, B.188/a/10, Fort St. James – Post Journal, 1827, 2, 24 June, 3 July 1827.
17 HBCA, B.188/a/12, Fort St. James – Post Journal, 1828, 1, 11 August 1828.
18 HBCA, B.223/b/15, Fort Vancouver – Correspondence Book, 1836-37, McLoughlin to Pambrun, 23 June 1836.
19 HBCA, B.223/b/17, Fort Vancouver – Correspondence Book, 1837, McLoughlin to Pambrun, 23 June 1837, 15 July 1837.
20 [Work], "Journal," 21, 29 June, 28-31 July 1825.
21 HBCA, B.188/a/8, Fort St. James – Post Journal, 1826-27, 18-19 July, 2, 10 August 1826; HBCA, D.4/120, Governor George Simpson – Correspondence Book Inwards, 1826-27, Connolly to the Governor, Chief Factors, and Chief Traders of the Northern Department, 18 July 1826, Connolly to the Governor and Council of the Northern Department, 15 March 1827; [Work], "Journal," 7 August 1826.
22 HBCA, B.188/a/10, Fort St. James – Post Journal, 1827, 24 June, 3-4 July 1827; HBCA, D.4/121, Governor George Simpson – Correspondence Book Inwards, 1827-28, Connolly to the Governor, Chief Factors, and Chief Traders of the Northern Department, 20 September 1827.
23 HBCA, B.188/a/12, Fort St. James – Post Journal, 1828, 1, 10-11 August 1828; [Work], "Journal," 31 July, 1, 3, 5, 9-10 August 1828.
24 HBCA, B.188/a/14, Fort St. James – Post Journal, 1829-30, 21-22, 30-31 July 1829.
25 HBCA, B.146/a/1, Fort Nez Percés – Post Journal, 1831, 11-12 July 1831; HBCA, B.188/a/17, Fort St. James – Post Journal, 1831-32, 12, 21 July 1831.

Chapter 12: Packhorsing between the Columbia and the Fraser

1   McLeod, *Peace River*, 114.
2   HBCA, B.188/b/1, Fort St. James – Correspondence Book, 1821-22, Stuart to Cameron, 9 August 1822.
3   McLeod, *Peace River*, 100. McLeod seems to have been given to exaggeration, saying, for example, that from 200 to 300 pack horses were used between Fort Okanagan and

Thompson's River (ibid.), whereas only half that number were employed, and that 250 horses were kept in the "stockades" at Thompson's River (ibid., 114), whereas it is doubtful that even half that number were corralled there.

4   HBCA, B.97/a/1, Fort Kamloops – Post Journal, 1822-23, 1 February 1823.

5   HBCA, B.97/a/2, Fort Kamloops – Post Journal, 1826-27, McDonald to McLoughlin, 22 August, 3 December 1826, McDonald to Connolly and McGillivray, 30 December 1826; HBCA, B.223/b/2, Fort Vancouver – Correspondence Book, 1826, McDonald to McLoughlin, 22 August 1826.

6   HBCA, B.97/a/2, Fort Kamloops – Post Journal, 1826-27, 17 October, 8 November 1826. Also see HBCA, B.223/b/2, Fort Vancouver – Correspondence Book, 1826, McDonald to McLoughlin, 30 September 1826.

7   HBCA, B.188/a/10, Fort St. James – Post Journal, 1827, 18 July 1827.

8   HBCA, B.97/e/1, Fort Kamloops – District Report, 1827, fo. 1; Rich, *Part of Dispatch from George Simpson*, 224.

9   HBCA, B.188/b/1, Fort St. James – Correspondence Book, 1821-22, Stuart to Lewis [Lewes], 19 July 1822, Stuart to Cameron, 9 August 1822; HBCA, B.188/d/1, Fort St. James – Account Book, 1821-22, "Invoice of Sundries Supplied by the Columbia to New Caledonia on A/c of Outfit for 1821."

10 HBCA, B.188/a/8, Fort St. James – Post Journal, 1826-27, 10, 13-25 August 1826; HBCA, B.188/b/5, Fort St. James – Correspondence Book, 1826-27, Connolly to the Northern Department, 9; HBCA, D.4/120, Governor George Simpson – Correspondence Book Inwards, 1826-27, Connolly to the Governor and Council of the Northern Department, 15 March 1827.

11 HBCA, B.97/a/2, Fort Kamloops – Post Journal, 1826-27, 9 September 1826.

12 HBCA, B.188/a/10, Fort St. James – Post Journal, 1827, 4-6, 15 July 1827.

13 HBCA, B.188/a/12, Fort St. James – Post Journal, 1828, 12-13 August 1828.

14 HBCA, B.188/a/17, Fort St. James – Post Journal, 1831-32, 21-22, 26-27, 30-31 July, 1-3, 5 August 1831.

Chapter 13: Packhorsing over the Mountain

1   HBCA, B.5/a/2, Fort Alexandria – Post Journal, 1827-28, 18 July 1827.

2   Rich, *Part of Dispatch from George Simpson*, 169-70.

3   HBCA, B.97/a/2, Fort Kamloops – Post Journal, 1826-27, McDonald to McLoughlin, 30 September 1826; HBCA, B.188/a/8, Fort St. James – Post Journal, 1826-27, 5 November 1826; HBCA, B.223/b/2, Fort Vancouver – Correspondence Book, 1826, McDonald to McLoughlin, 30 September 1826.

4   HBCA, B.97/a/2, Fort Kamloops – Post Journal, 1826-27, 22, 27 November 1826, McDonald to Dease, 3 December 1826.

5   HBCA, B.188/a/8, Fort St. James – Post Journal, 1826-27, 9 September, 5 November 1826, 7 January 1827.

6   HBCA, B.188/e/4, Fort St. James – District Report, 1826-27, fo. 3.

7   HBCA, B.188/b/1, Fort St. James – Correspondence Book, 1821-22, Stuart to Cameron, 9 August 1822, Stuart to McMillan, 15 August 1822.

8   HBCA, B.188/a/8, Fort St. James – Post Journal, 1826-27, 26-31 August, 1-9 September 1826.

9   HBCA, B.5/a/2, Fort Alexandria – Post Journal, 1827-28, 26 July, 12, 22 August 1827; HBCA, B.188/a/10, Fort St. James – Post Journal, 1827, 15-19, 26 July 1827.

10 HBCA, B.188/a/12, Fort St. James – Post Journal, 1828, 24-25, 31 August, 3 September 1828.

11 HBCA, B.188/a/14, Fort St. James – Post Journal, 1829-30, 12-15, 22 August 1829.

12 HBCA, B.188/a/17, Fort St. James – Post Journal, 1831-32, 6, 12, 18 August 1831.

13 HBCA, B.5/a/3, Fort Alexandria – Post Journal, 1833-34, 17 August 1833; HBCA, B.5/a/4, Fort Alexandria – Post Journal, 1837-39, 20 August 1837; HBCA, B.5/a/5, Fort Alexandria – Post Journal, 1842-43, 24 August 1842; HBCA, B.5/a/7, Fort Alexandria – Post Journal, 1845-48, 1 September 1846, 26 August 1847.

Chapter 14: Canoeing up the Fraser

1   HBCA, B.5/a/2, Fort Alexandria – Post Journal, 1827-28, Connolly to Joseph McGillivray, 22 August 1827.

2   Ogden, "Notes on Western Caledonia," 54.
3   HBCA, B.188/a/1, Fort St. James – Post Journal, 1820-21, 1 June 1820.
4   HBCA, B.188/d/1, Fort St. James – Account Book, 1821-22, "Invoice of Sundries Supplied
     by the Columbia to New Caledonia on A/c of Outfit for 1821"; HBCA, D.4/116, Governor
     George Simpson – Correspondence Book Inwards, 1821-22, Brown to unknown, 4 Novem-
     ber 1821; HBCA, D.4/117, Governor George Simpson – Correspondence Book Inwards, 1822-
     23, Brown to Simpson, 3 December 1822, McDougall to Simpson, 22 October 1823.
5   HBCA, B.188/a/8, Fort St. James – Post Journal, 1826-27, 8, 10, 13, 23-28 September 1826;
     HBCA, D.4/120, Governor George Simpson – Correspondence Book Inwards, 1826-27, Con-
     nolly to the Governor and Council of the Northern Department, 15 March 1827.
6   HBCA, B.5/a/2, Fort Alexandria – Post Journal, 1827-28, 26-29 July 1827; HBCA, B.188/a/10,
     Fort St. James – Post Journal, 1827, 27-29, 31 July, 13 August 1827; HBCA, D.4/121, Gover-
     nor George Simpson – Correspondence Book Inwards, 1827-28, Connolly to the Governor,
     Chief Factors, and Chief Traders of the Northern Department, 20 September 1827. Accord-
     ing to the post journal of Fort Alexandria, five canoes and twenty-four men constituted the
     brigade; according to the post journal of Stuart's Lake, kept by the brigade leader, the brigade
     comprised four canoes, each bearing four men.
7   HBCA, B.188/a/12, Fort St. James – Post Journal, 1828, 2-6, 18 September 1828; HBCA,
     D.4/122, Governor George Simpson – Correspondence Book Inwards, 1828-29, Connolly to
     the Governor and Council of the Northern Department, 28 February 1829.
8   HBCA, B.188/a/14, Fort St. James – Post Journal, 1829-30, 23 August, 16, 29 September 1829.
9   HBCA, B.188/a/16, Fort St. James – Post Journal, 1830-32, 14 September 1831; HBCA,
     B.188/a/17, Fort St. James – Post Journal, 1831-32, 18, 20, 24, 26, 29 August 1831.
10   HBCA, B.5/a/3, Fort Alexandria – Post Journal, 1833-34, 17, 26 August 1833; HBCA, B.5/a/4,
     Fort Alexandria – Post Journal, 1837-39, 20, 25 August 1837; HBCA, B.5/a/5, Fort Alexan-
     dria – Post Journal, 1842-43, 24, 29 August 1842; HBCA, B.5/a/7, Fort Alexandria – Post
     Journal, 1845-48, 1 September 1846, 26 August, 6 September 1847.
11   HBCA, B.188/a/19, Fort St. James – Post Journal, 1840-46, 30 September 1844.
12   HBCA, B.188/a/20, Fort St. James – Post Journal, 1846-51, 11 October 1848.

Conclusion

1   HBCA, D.4/116, Governor George Simpson – Correspondence Book Inwards, 1821-22,
     Stuart to the Governor and Council [of the Northern Department], 27 April 1822.
2   HBCA, B.188/b/1, Fort St. James – Correspondence Book, 1821-22, Stuart to Garry, 20 April
     1822.
3   Fleming, *Minutes of Council*, 17.
4   Merk, *Fur Trade and Empire*, 37, 72.
5   Cullen, "Outfitting New Caledonia," 233.
6   HBCA, D.4/5, Governor George Simpson – Correspondence Book Outwards (General),
     1824-25, Simpson to Brown, 4 April 1825.
7   Cullen, "Outfitting New Caledonia," 236-7.
8   Fleming, *Minutes of Council*, 75, 105; HBCA, B.188/a/3, Fort St. James – Post Journal, 1824-
     25, 30 October 1824; HBCA, B.188/a/4, Fort St. James – Post Journal, 1824-25, 7 November
     1825; HBCA, B.188/a/8, Fort St. James – Post Journal, 1826-27, 10, 23 September 1826; HBCA,
     B.188/a/17, Fort St. James – Post Journal, 1831-32, 20, 24 August, 13 September 1831; HBCA,
     B. 188/e/4, Fort St. James – District Report, 1826-27.
9   See Cullen, "Outfitting New Caledonia," 236.
10   HBCA, D.4/85, Governor George Simpson – Official Reports to the Governor and Com-
     mittee in London, 1822, Simpson to the Governor and Committee, 15 August 1822; Wilkes,
     Narrative, 4:328.
11   The longer distance of transport to the Columbia than to Hudson Bay from London was
     reflected in the fact that the markup on HBC goods at Fort Vancouver was twice that at
     York Factory, at least until 1829, when the advances were equalized (Merk, *Fur Trade and
     Empire*, 317).
12   [William Fraser Tolmie], *The Journals of William Fraser Tolmie: Physician and Fur Trader*, ed.
     Howard T. Mitchell (Vancouver: Mitchell Press 1963), 176; Wilkes, *Narrative*, 4:328.

13   Richard Somerset Mackie, "Geopolitics and Commercial Strategy: A Study of the Hudson's Bay Company on the Pacific, 1821-1843," doctoral dissertation, Department of History, University of British Columbia, 1993, 364-5.

14   See Gibson, *Farming the Frontier*, Table 30, 201.

15   Wilkes, *Narrative*, 4:364.

16   HBCA, B.188/b/1, Fort St. James – Correspondence Book, 1821-22, Stuart to Garry, 20 April 1822.

17   HBCA, D.4/116, Governor George Simpson – Correspondence Book Inwards, 1821-22, Lewes to Simpson, 2 April 1822.

18   HBCA, B.74/a/1, Fraser's Lake – Post Journal, 1822-24, 13 May 1822, 15 June 1823; HBCA, B.119/b/1, McLeod's Lake – Correspondence Book, 1823-24, [Stuart] to Brown, 12 May 1824; HBCA, B.188/a/2, Fort St. James – Post Journal, 1823-24, 10 June 1823, B.188/a/3, Post Journal, 1824-25, 3 May 1825, B.188/a/4, Post Journal, 1824-25, 17 May 1825, B.188/a/5, Post Journal, 1825-26, 2, 3 May 1826, B.188/a/8, Post Journal, 1826-27, 8 March 1827, B.188/a/12, Post Journal, 1828, 5 May 1828, B.188/a/13, Post Journal, 1828-29, 28 February 1829, B.188/a/14, Post Journal, 1829-30, 7 May 1829, B.188/a/17, Post Journal, 1831-32, 5, 8, 13 May 1831; HBCA, D.4/119, Governor George Simpson – Correspondence Book Inwards, 1824-26, Connolly to Brown, 4 May 1826; HBCA, D.4/127, Governor George Simpson – Correspondence Book Inwards, 1833-35, Dease to the Governor and Council of the Northern Department, 14 February 1835; Rich, *Part of Dispatch from George Simpson*, 24-5; Wallace, *John McLean's Notes*, 151.

19   Glazebrook, *Hargrave Correspondence*, 256; HBCA, E.12/4, Duncan Finlayson – Journals, 1831-38, "Journal," 1835, 1836, 1837-38, fos. 40v.-41.

20   Merk, *Fur Trade and Empire*, 341.

21   Gibson, *Farming the Frontier*, Table 30, 201.

22   James Douglas, "Correspondence Outward, 1844-1857," BCARS, MS B40, Douglas to Ross, 12 March 1844, pt. 1.

23   HBCA, B.223/e/4, Fort Vancouver – District Report [1845?], fos. 3v., 4, 7.

24   HBCA, E.12/2, Duncan Finlayson – Journals, 1831-38, "Journal," 1831, fo. 24v.

25   HBCA, B.223/z/4, Fort Vancouver – Miscellaneous Items, 1824-60, Warre and Vavasour to the Secretary of State for the Colonies, 1 November 1845.

26   HBCA, D.5/7, Governor George Simpson – Correspondence Inward, 1842, McDonald to Simpson, 23 April 1842.

27   MacLeod, *Letters of Letitia Hargrave*, 116-17.

28   HBCA, D.4/2, Governor George Simpson – Correspondence Book Outwards (General), 1822-23, Simpson to the Chief Factors of the Columbia River District, 12 July 1823.

29   Tod, "History of New Caledonia," 21.

30   MacLeod, *Letters of Letitia Hargrave*, 199.

31   HBCA, B.223/c/1, Fort Vancouver – Correspondence Inward, 1826-50, Governor and Committee to McLoughlin, 27 September 1843.

32   Ibid., Governor and Committee to McLoughlin, 8 October 1845.

33   Ibid., Simpson to Ogden, Douglas, and Work, 28 June 1847; Rich, *Part of Dispatch from George Simpson*, 218.

34   MacLeod, *Letters of Letitia Hargrave*, 290.

35   Work, "Letters," Work to Ermatinger, 23 November 1847.

36   McLeod, "Papers," 1:365.

37   [Tolmie], *Journals of William Fraser Tolmie*, 334.

38   Glazebrook, *Hargrave Correspondence*, 317, 332.

39   Ibid., 332.

40   Ibid., 382. Simpson saw promise in diversification, asserting that "in the fur returns of the country, we cannot expect very material improvement, but by availing ourselves, as at Fort Langley, of the other resources of the Country [fish, timber], the affairs of the West Side of the Mountains, I think, are susceptible of amendment" (HBCA, B.223/c/1, Fort Vancouver – Correspondence Inward, 1826-50, Simpson to Ogden, Douglas, and Work, 28 June 1847).

41   Glazebrook, *Hargrave Correspondence*, 384.

42   Ibid., 426.

43   Ibid., 423. Also see the comments of Dugald Mactavish (ibid., 383).

44   Ibid., 422.
45   Ibid., 426. For more on McDonald, see Jean Murray Cole, *Exile in the Wilderness: The Biography of Chief Factor Archibald McDonald 1790-1853* ([Toronto]: Burns & MacEachern 1979).
46   HBCA, A.11/72, London Inward Correspondence from H.B.C. Posts – Fort Victoria, 1845-50, Douglas and Work to Governor and Committee, 7 December 1846; HBCA, B.223/b/34, Fort Vancouver – Correspondence Book, 1846, Douglas and Work to Governor and Committee, 7 December 1846.
47   HBCA, D.4/60, Governor George Simpson – Correspondence Book Outwards (General), 1842, Simpson to the Governor and Committee, 1 March 1842.
48   HBCA, A.11/70, London Inward Correspondence from H.B.C. Posts – Fort Vancouver, 1840-51, Douglas to Barclay, 29 April 1847, Ogden and Douglas to Governor and Committee, 20 September 1847.
     In the autumn of 1846 Douglas, Ogden, and Work (the Board of Management that had replaced McLoughlin at Fort Vancouver) reported to the Governor and Committee that in the spring of that year Chief Trader Alexander Anderson with five men had explored two land routes – via "Harrisons River" and via the "Quequealla [Coquihalla] River" – between New Caledonia and Fort Langley north of the new boundary "for carrying on the business of the Interior, in the event of our being deprived of the Columbia, or other circumstances rendering it advisable to remove our principal depot to the Straits of de Fuca, and Fort Langley becoming the rendezvous of the Interior Brigades." The first route was found to "not answer our purpose, and ought never to be attempted," since the "natural difficulties by that route are great [particularly over Pavilion Mountain], and ... the communication would at best be tedious and dangerous." The second route, however, proved to be a "practicable communication throughout," the sole objection being "the depth and duration of snow in the mountains [the Coquihalla Pass reaching 1,245 metres, or 4,050 feet, in elevation]," so that the brigades would not be able to return to Thompson's River before the end of August, "about two weeks later than by the Columbia route." The board concluded that "beyond this detention which will not cause any important derangement in the interior districts, we see no serious objection to the new route, and it is our opinion that the business may be carried on by it with advantages: we will therefore take measures to clear the road in course of next summer (1847)" (HBCA, B.223/b/34, Fort Vancouver – Correspondence Book, 1846, Ogden, Douglas, and Work to Governor and Committee, 2 November 1846). That summer of 1847 saw the last Fraser-Columbia brigade in the face of American import and transit duties. The Coquihalla route was explored again in the fall of 1847 (HBCA, B.223/b/36, Fort Vancouver – Correspondence Book, 1847, Douglas and Work to Governor and Committee, 20 September 1847). Finally, in 1848 Governor Simpson wrote the Board of Management that "it is most fortunate that we have been successful in our endeavours to find a practicable route to the interior via Frasers River, and we are very much pleased to learn that, the outfits and returns of the interior are this season to be conveyed by that route." He added that "the communication will, as a matter of course, be improved from year to year, and now that it has been once adopted, we think it may be advisable to continue our transport by that channel, abandoning the Columbia altogether as a means of communication with the interior" (HBCA, B.223/c/1, Fort Vancouver – Correspondence Inward, 1826-50, Simpson to Ogden, Douglas, and Work, 24 June 1848).

Appendix 1

1   This account has survived in two variants with different handwriting and similar wording. The longer variant, printed here, is from the "Journal of Occurrences New Caledonia District 1826/27," in HBCA, B.188/a/8, Fort St. James – Post Journal, 1826-27, pp. 1-53; the shorter variant is from "New Caledonia Journal 1826," in HBCA, B.188/a/9, Fort St. James – Post Journal, 1826, fos. 1-22v. In both versions capitalization and punctuation are sometimes indeterminate, as well as inconsistent, so the transcription should be used with caution; scrupulous readers should consult the originals. Published with the permission of the Hudson's Bay Company Archives, Provincial Archives of Manitoba, Winnipeg.
2   Regrettably, Chief Factor Peter Skene Ogden, who conducted the brigade for a decade between the middle 1830s and the middle 1840s and consequently undoubtedly knew the

system better than anybody, apparently never kept a journal; or if he did, it has yet to come to light or has not survived. Additionally, in 1822 Chief Trader William Brown of the Babine Post had intended to write a "Journal of the Voyage to and from the Columbia" but unfortunately dropped the idea in the wake of the decision at the beginning of that year to shift the supply route back to the Peace (HBCA, D.4/118, Governor George Simpson – Correspondence Book Inwards, 1822-23, Brown to Simpson, 25 April 1823). David Douglas, who accompanied a cattle drive over the brigade trail in the spring of 1833 from Fort Okanagan to New Caledonia, drew a series of sketch maps of the route (see David Douglas, ["Book of sketch maps of journey from the junction of the Columbia and Okanagan rivers to Quesnel and north; April-May, 1833"], BCARS, MS CM A291).

Appendix 2

1   HBCA, B.188/a/17, Fort St. James – Post Journal, 1831-32, fos. 6-17. Published with the permission of the Hudson's Bay Company Archives, Provincial Archives of Manitoba, Winnipeg.
2   At this point in the margin of the original there is the following notation, written transversely: "The Frasers Lake returns amount to near 19 Pks & 1 Keg Castorum 4000 Salmon sent down for the voyage & Lower Posts."

Bibliography

PRIMARY SOURCES

Unpublished

Allan, George. "Journal of a Voyage from Fort Vancouver, Columbia to York Factory, Hudson's Bay, 1841." British Columbia Archives and Records Service. MS

"Astor Papers." Beinecke Rare Book and Manuscript Library, Yale University. Western Americana Collection. MS

Black, Captain William. "A Description of the Mouth of Columbia River, North West Coast of America." Oregon Historical Society. MS 1,574

[Connolly, Henry]. "Reminiscences of one of the last descendants of a Bourgeois of the North West Company." National Archives of Canada. MS MG29 B15, vol. 61, file 34

Cooper, James. "Maritime Matters on the Northwest Coast ..." 1878. Bancroft Library of the University of California at Berkeley. MS P-C 15

Douglas, David. "Book of Sketch Maps of Journey from the junction of the Columbia and Okanogan Rivers to Quesnel and North, April-May, 1833." British Columbia Archives and Records Service. Add. MSS 0622

Douglas, James. "Correspondence Outward, 1844-1857." British Columbia Archives and Records Service. MS B40

――――. "Journal of a Journey from Fort Vancouver to York Factory and Back 1835." British Columbia Archives and Records Service. MS

Ermatinger, Edward. "Edward Ermatinger Papers 1820-1874." National Archives of Canada. MS 19, series A2(2)

[Ermatinger, Edward and Francis]. "Ermatinger Papers." British Columbia Archives and Records Service. MS AB40 Er62.3

Finlayson, Roderick. "The History of Vancouver Island and the Northwest Coast." 1878. Bancroft Library, University of California at Berkeley. MS P-C 15

Harriott, John Edward. "Memoirs of Life and Adventure in the Hudson's Bay Company's Territories, 1819-1825." Beinecke Rare Book and Manuscript Library, Yale University. Western Americana Collection. MS 245

Hudson's Bay Company Archives, Provincial Archives of Manitoba. A.6/25, London Correspondence Book Outwards – H.B.C. Official, 1838-42; A.11/70, London Inward Correspondence from H.B.C. Posts – Fort Vancouver, 1840-51; A.11/72, London Inward Correspondence from H.B.C. Posts – Fort Victoria, 1845-50; A.12/1, London Inward Correspondence from Governors of H.B.C. Territories – Sir George Simpson, 1823-32; B.5/a/1, Fort Alexandria – Post Journal, 1824-25; B.5/a/2, Fort Alexandria – Post Journal, 1827-28; B.5/a/3, Fort Alexandria – Post Journal, 1833-34; B.5/a/4, Fort Alexandria – Post Journal, 1837-39; B.5/a/5, Fort Alexandria – Post Journal, 1842-43; B.5/a/6, Fort Alexandria – Post Journal, 1843-45; B.5/a/7, Fort Alexandria – Post Journal, 1845-48; B.5/e/1, Fort Alexandria – District Report, 1827-28; B.45/a/1, Fort Colvile – Post Journal, 1830-31; B.45/e/3, Fort Colvile – District Report, 1830; B.45/z/1, Fort Colvile – Miscellaneous Items, 1828-56; B.74/a/1, Fraser's Lake – Post Journal, 1822-24; B.76/e/1, Fort George (Columbia River) – District Report, 1824-25; B.97/a/1, Fort Kamloops – Post Journal, 1822-23; B.97/a/2, Fort Kamloops – Post Journal, 1826-27; B.97/e/1, Fort Kamloops – District Report, 1827; B.119/a/1, McLeod's Lake – Post Journal, 1823-24; B.119/a/2, McLeod's Lake – Post Journal, 1824; B.119/a/4, McLeod's Lake – Post Journal, 1824; B.119/b/1, McLeod's Lake – Correspondence Book, 1823-24; B.119/e/1, McLeod's Lake – District Report, 1824; B.146/a/1, Fort Nez Percés – Post Journal, 1831; B.146/e/1, Fort Nez Percés – District Report, 1827; B.146/e/2, Fort Nez Percés – District Report, 1829; B.188/a/1, Fort St. James – Post Journal, 1820-21; B.188/a/2,

Fort St. James – Post Journal, 1823-24; B.188/a/3, Fort St. James – Post Journal, 1824-25; B.188/a/4, Fort St. James – Post Journal, 1824-25; B.188/a/5, Fort St. James – Post Journal, 1825-26; B.188/a/6, Fort St. James – Post Journal, 1825-26; B.188/a/8, Fort St. James – Post Journal, 1826-27; B.188/a/10, Fort St. James – Post Journal, 1827; B.188/a/11, Fort St. James – Post Journal, 1828; B.188/a/12, Fort St. James – Post Journal, 1828; B.188/a/14, Fort St. James – Post Journal, 1829-30; B.188/a/16, Fort St. James – Post Journal, 1830-32; B.188/a/17, Fort St. James – Post Journal, 1831-32; B.188/a/19, Fort St. James – Post Journal, 1840-46; B.188/a/20, Fort St. James – Post Journal, 1846-51; B.188/b/1, Fort St. James – Correspondence Book, 1821-22; B.188/b/2, Fort St. James – Correspondence Book, 1822-23; B.188/b/3, Fort St. James – Correspondence Book, 1823-24; B.188/b/4, Fort St. James – Correspondence Book, 1825-26; B.188/b/5, Fort St. James – Correspondence Book, 1826-27; B.188/b/6, Fort St. James – Correspondence Book, 1828-29; B.188/d/1, Fort St. James – Account Book, 1821-22; B.188/d/15, Fort St. James – Account Book, 1836-37; B.188/e/1, Fort St. James – District Report, 1822-23; B.188/e/3, Fort St. James – District Report, 1824-25; B.188/e/4, Fort St. James – District Report, 1826-27; B.188/e/5, Fort St. James – District Report, 1834; B.201/a/1, Fort Simpson (Nass River) – Post Journal, 1832; B.223/a/3, Fort Vancouver – Post Journal, 1826; B.223/b/1, Fort Vancouver – Correspondence Book, 1825; B.223/b/2, Fort Vancouver – Correspondence Book, 1826; B.223/b/3, Fort Vancouver – Correspondence Book, 1827-28; B.223/b/8, Fort Vancouver – Correspondence Book, 1832-33; B.223/b/11, Fort Vancouver – Correspondence Book, 1834-36; B.223/b/15, Fort Vancouver – Correspondence Book, 1836-37; B.223/b/17, Fort Vancouver – Correspondence Book, 1837; B.223/b/18, Fort Vancouver – Correspondence Book, 1837-38; B.223/b/27, Fort Vancouver – Correspondence Book, 1840; B.223/b/34, Fort Vancouver – Correspondence Book, 1846; B.223/b/36, Fort Vancouver – Correspondence Book, 1847; B.223/c/1, Fort Vancouver – Correspondence Inward, 1826-50; B.223/e/3, Fort Vancouver – District Report, [1825-26]; B.223/e/4, Fort Vancouver – District Report, [1845?]; B.223/z/4, Fort Vancouver – Miscellaneous Items, 1824-60; C.4/1, Book of Ships' Movements, 1719-1929; D.4/2, Governor George Simpson – Correspondence Book Outwards (General), 1822-23; D.4/5, Governor George Simpson – Correspondence Book Outwards (General), 1824-25; D.4/6, Governor George Simpson – Correspondence Book Outwards (General), 1825-26; D.4/7, Governor George Simpson – Correspondence Book Outwards (General), 1824-26; D.4/59, Governor George Simpson – Correspondence Book Outwards (General), 1841-42; D.4/60, Governor George Simpson – Correspondence Book Outwards (General), 1842; D.4/67, Governor George Simpson – Correspondence Book Outwards (General), 1845-46; D.4/85, Governor George Simpson – Official Reports to the Governor and Committee in London, 1822; D.4/86, Governor George Simpson – Official Reports to the Governor and Committee in London, 1823; D.4/87, Governor George Simpson – Official Reports to the Governor and Committee in London, 1824; D.4/88, Governor George Simpson – Official Reports to the Governor and Committee in London, 1825; D.4/99, Governor George Simpson – Official Reports to the Governor and Committee in London, 1832; D.4/101, Governor George Simpson – Official Reports to the Governor and Committee in London, 1834; D.4/106, Governor George Simpson – Official Reports to the Governor and Committee in London, 1839; D.4/116, Governor George Simpson – Correspondence Book Inwards, 1821-22; D.4/117, Governor George Simpson – Correspondence Book Inwards, 1822-23; D.4/118, Governor George Simpson – Correspondence Book Inwards, 1822-23; D.4/119, Governor George Simpson – Correspondence Book Inwards, 1824-26; D.4/120, Governor George Simpson – Correspondence Book Inwards, 1826-27; D.4/121, Governor George Simpson – Correspondence Book Inwards, 1827-28; D.4/122, Governor George Simpson – Correspondence Book Inwards, 1828-29; D.4/123, Governor George Simpson – Correspondence Book Inwards, 1829-30; D.4/124, Governor George Simpson – Correspondence Book Inwards, 1830-31; D.4/125, Governor George Simpson – Correspondence Book Inwards, 1829-31; D.4/126, Governor George Simpson – Correspondence Book Inwards, 1833-34; D.4/127, Governor George Simpson – Correspondence Book Inwards, 1833-35; D.5/1, Governor George Simpson – Correspondence Inward, 1821-26; D.5/7, Governor George Simpson – Correspondence Inward, 1842; D.5/8, Governor George Simpson – Correspondence Inward, 1843; E.12/2-4, Duncan Finlayson – Journals, 1831-38

Lee, Daniel. "Articles on the Oregon Mission." Oregon Historical Society. MS 1,211, pt. 5

[McDonald, Archibald]. "McDonald Correspondence." British Columbia Archives and Records Service. MS AB40 M142A

McLeod, John. "John McLeod Papers 1811-1837." National Archives of Canada. MS 19, series A23. Vol. 1

National Archives of Canada. Map VI-700

"Papers Relative to the Expedition of Lieuts. Warre and Vavasour to the Oregon Territory." Public Record Office. MS F.O. 5/457

Roberts, George B. "Recollections of George B. Roberts." Bancroft Library of the University of California at Berkeley. MS P-A 83

Stuart, John. "Letter Books and Journals." Oregon Historical Society. MS 1,502, reel 1

Tod, John. "History of New Caledonia and the Northwest Coast." 1878. British Columbia Archives and Records Service. MS

_____. "Journal Thompson River John Tod." British Columbia Archives and Records Service. MS AB20 K12A 1841-43

Tolmie, William Fraser. "History of Puget Sound and the Northwest Coast." Bancroft Library of the University of California at Berkeley. MS P-B 25

[Warre, Henry]. "H.F. Warre Papers." National Archives of Canada. MS MG 24, F 71. Vols. 15-16, 19

Work, John. "Journals" and "Letters." Oregon Historical Society. MS 319

_____. "Journal of John Work." British Columbia Archives and Records Service. MS AB40 W89.1

_____. "Work Correspondence." British Columbia Archives and Records Service. MS AB40

Published

Anonymous. "Documents." *Washington Historical Quarterly* 1 (1907): 40-3, 256-66

Bagley, Clarence B., ed. *Early Catholic Missions in Old Oregon*, vol. 1. Seattle: Lowman & Hanford 1932

Barker, Burt Brown, ed. *Letters of Dr. John McLoughlin* ... Portland: Oregon Historical Society 1948

Burnett, Peter H. *Recollections and Opinions of an Old Pioneer*. New York: D. Appleton 1880

Chittenden, Hiram Martin, and Alfred Talbot Richardson, eds. *Life, Letters and Travels of Father Pierre-Jean De Smet, S.J. 1801-1873*. New York: Kraus Reprint 1969

Corney, Peter. *Early Voyages to the North Pacific 1813-1818*. Fairfield, WA: Ye Galleon Press 1965

Cowie, Isaac, ed. *The Minutes of the Council of the Northern Department of Rupert's Land, 1830 to 1843* ... Bismarck [?]: State Historical Society of North Dakota n.d.

Cox, Ross. *The Columbia River: Or scenes and adventures during a residence of six years on the western side of the Rocky Mountains among various tribes of Indians hitherto unknown* ... Ed. Edgar I. Stewart and Jane R. Stewart. Norman: University of Oklahoma Press 1957

De Smet, Pierre-Jean. *Letters and Sketches: With a Narrative of a Year's Residence Among the Indian Tribes of the Rocky Mountains*. Philadelphia: M. Fithian 1843

_____. *Oregon Missions and Travels over the Rocky Mountains, in 1845-46*. New York: Edward Dunigan 1847

[Douglas, David.] *Journal Kept by David Douglas during his Travels in North America 1823-1827* ... New York: Antiquarian Press 1959

Drury, Clifford Merrill, ed. *First White Women Over the Rockies*, vol. 1. Glendale, CA: Arthur H. Clark 1963

Dunn, John. *History of the Oregon Territory* ... 2nd ed. London: Edwards and Hughes 1846

Elliott, T.C., ed. "Journal of John Work [1825-26] ..." *Washington Historical Quarterly* 5 (1914): 83-115, 163-91, 258-87; 6 (1915): 26-49

Ermatinger, C.O., and James White, eds. "Edward Ermatinger's York Factory Express Journal, Being a Record of Journeys Made Between Fort Vancouver and Hudson Bay in the Years 1827-1828." *Proceedings and Transactions of the Royal Society of Canada*, 3rd series, vol. 6, sect. II (1912): 67-132

Farnham, Thomas J. *Travels in the Great Western Prairies, the Anahuac and Rocky Mountains, and in the Oregon Territory*. London: Richard Bentley 1843

Fleming, R. Harvey, ed. *Minutes of Council Northern Department of Rupert Land, 1821-1831*. Toronto: Champlain Society 1940

Franchère, Gabriel. *Journal of a Voyage on the North West Coast* ... Trans. Wessie Tipping Lamb. Toronto: Champlain Society 1969

Glazebrook, G.P. de T., ed. *The Hargrave Correspondence 1821-1843*. Toronto: Champlain Society 1938

Gough, Barry M., ed. *The Journal of Alexander Henry the Younger 1799-1814,* vol. 2. Toronto: Champlain Society 1992

Jones, Robert F., ed. *Astorian Adventure: The Journal of Alfred Seton 1811-1815.* New York: Fordham University Press 1993

Kane, Paul. *Wanderings of an Artist Among the Indians of North America from Canada to Vancouver's Island and Oregon Through the Hudson's Bay Company's Territory and Back Again.* Edmonton: M.G. Hurtig 1968

Lamb, W. Kaye, ed. *The Journals and Letters of Sir Alexander Mackenzie.* Cambridge, UK: Cambridge University Press for the Hakluyt Society 1979

———, ed. *The Letters and Journals of Simon Fraser 1806-1808.* Toronto: Macmillan 1960

———, ed. *Sixteen Years in the Indian Country: The Journal of Daniel Williams Harmon 1800-1816.* Toronto: Macmillan 1957

Landerholm, Carl, ed. *Notices & Voyages of the Famed Quebec Mission to the Pacific Northwest ...* Portland: Oregon Historical Society 1956

Lewis, William A., and Jacob A. Meyers, eds. "Journal of a Trip from Fort Colvile to Fort Vancouver and Return in 1828." *Washington Historical Quarterly* 11 (1920): 104-14

MacLaren, I.S., ed. "Journal of Paul Kane's Western Travels, 1846-1848." *American Art Journal* 21 (1989): 23-62

MacLeod, Margaret Arnett, ed. *The Letters of Letitia Hargrave.* Toronto: Champlain Society 1947

McDonald, Lois Halliday, ed. *Fur Trade Letters of Francis Ermatinger ... 1818-1853.* Glendale, CA: Arthur H. Clark 1980

McLeod, Malcolm, ed. *Peace River: A Canoe Voyage from Hudson's Bay to Pacific by Sir George Simpson (Governor, Hon. Hudson's Bay Company), in 1828. Journal of the late Chief Factor, Archibald McDonald (Hon. Hudson's Bay Company), who accompanied him.* Edmonton: M.G. Hurtig 1971

Merk, Frederick, ed. *Fur Trade and Empire: George Simpson's Journal ...* Rev. ed. Cambridge, MA: Belknap Press 1968

Morgan, William James, David B. Tyler, Joye L. Leonhart, and Mary F. Loughlin, eds. *Autobiography of Rear Admiral Charles Wilkes, U.S. Navy 1798-1877.* Washington, DC: Department of the Navy 1978

Moulton, Gary E., ed. *The Journals of the Lewis & Clark Expedition,* vols. 5-7, 9. Lincoln: University of Nebraska Press 1988-91

Ogden, Peter Skene. "Peter Skene Ogden's Notes on Western Caledonia." Ed. W.N. Sage. *British Columbia Historical Quarterly* 1 (1937): 45-56

Palmer, Joel. *Journal of Travels over the Rocky Mountains ...* Cincinnati: J.A. and U.P. James 1847

Rich, E.E., ed. *Colin Robertson's Correspondence Book, September 1817 to September 1822.* Toronto: Champlain Society 1939

———, ed. *Journal of Occurrences in the Athabasca Department by George Simpson, 1820 and 1821, and Report.* Toronto: Champlain Society 1938

———, ed. *Letters of John McLoughlin from Fort Vancouver to the Governor and Committee,* vols. 1-2. London: Hudson's Bay Record Society 1941-3

———, ed. *Part of Dispatch from George Simpson Esq' Governor of Ruperts Land to the Governor & Committee of the Hudson's Bay Company London March 1, 1829 ...* Toronto: Champlain Society 1947

Ross, Alexander. *Adventures of the First Settlers on the Oregon or Columbia River.* London: Smith, Elder 1849

———. *Adventures of the First Settlers on the Oregon or Columbia River, 1810-1813.* Lincoln: University of Nebraska Press 1986

———. *The Fur Hunters of the Far West.* Ed. Kenneth A. Spaulding. Norman: University of Oklahoma Press 1956

Spaulding, Kenneth A., ed. *On the Oregon Trail: Robert Stuart's Journal of Discovery.* Norman: University of Oklahoma Press 1953

Thompson, David. *Columbia Journals.* Ed. Barbara Belyea. Montreal: McGill-Queen's University Press 1994

[Tolmie, William Fraser]. *The Journals of William Fraser Tolmie: Physician and Fur Trader.* Ed. Howard T. Mitchell. Vancouver: Mitchell Press 1963

Townsend, John Kirk. *Narrative of a Journey Across the Rocky Mountains to the Columbia River.* Fairfield, WA: Ye Galleon Press 1970

Tyrrell, J.B., ed. *David Thompson's Narrative of His Explorations in Western America 1784-1812.* Toronto: Champlain Society 1916

Wallace, W. Stewart, ed. *Documents Relating to the North West Company.* Toronto: Champlain Society 1934

———. ed. *John McLean's Notes of a Twenty-Five Year's Service in the Hudson's Bay Territory.* Toronto: Champlain Society 1932

Warre, H.J. *Overland to Oregon in 1845: Impressions of a Journey across North America.* Ed. Madeleine Major-Frégeau. Ottawa: Public Archives of Canada 1976

Wilkes, Charles. *Narrative of the United States Exploring Expedition,* vols. 4-5. Philadelphia: Lea & Blanchard 1845

Williams, Glyndwr, ed. *Hudson's Bay Company Miscellany 1670-1870.* Winnipeg: Hudson's Bay Record Society 1975

Williams, Glyndwr, and John S. Galbraith eds. *London Correspondence Inward from Sir George Simpson 1841-42.* London: Hudson's Bay Record Society 1973

Wolfenden, Madge, ed. "John Tod: Career of a Scotch Boy." *British Columbia Historical Quarterly* 28 (1954): 132-238

[Wyeth, Nathaniel]. *The Correspondence and Journals of Captain Nathaniel J. Wyeth 1831-6.* Ed. F.G. Young. Vol. 1, nos. 3-6 of *Sources of the History of Oregon.* Eugene: University Press 1899

SECONDARY SOURCES

Books and Pamphlets

Adney, Edwin Tappan, and Howard I. Chapelle. *The Bark Canoes and Skin Boats of North America.* Washington, DC: Smithsonian Institution Press 1983.

Brown, Jennifer S.H. *Strangers in Blood: Fur Trade Company Families in Indian Country.* Vancouver: University of British Columbia Press 1980

Cline, Gloria Griffen. *Peter Skene Ogden and the Hudson's Bay Company.* Norman: University of Oklahoma Press 1974

Gibson, James R. *Farming the Frontier: The Agricultural Opening of the Oregon Country, 1786-1846.* Vancouver: University of British Columbia Press 1985

———. *Otter Skins, Boston Ships, and China Goods: The Maritime Fur Trade of the Northwest Coast, 1785-1841.* Montreal: McGill-Queen's University Press 1992

Harris, Bob, Harley Hatfield, and Peter Tassie. *The Okanagan Brigade Trail in the South Okanagan 1811 to 1849: Oroville, Washington to Westside, British Columbia.* N.p.: n.p. 1989

Holt, Roberta, Alfred Jahnke, and Peter Tassie. *The Okanagan Brigade Trail: Central and North Okanagan. A Field Guide to the Remaining Sections of the Trail.* Vernon: Vernon Branch of the Okanagan Historical Society 1986

Hussey, John A. *The History of Fort Vancouver and Its Physical Structure.* [Tacoma]: Washington State Historical Society n.d.

Innis, Harold A. *The Fur Trade in Canada: An Introduction to Canadian Economic History.* Rev. ed. Toronto: University of Toronto Press 1970

Irving, Washington. *Astoria; or, Anecdotes of an Enterprise beyond the Rocky Mountains.* Ed. Edgeley W. Todd. Norman: University of Oklahoma Press 1964

Porter, Kenneth Wiggins. *John Jacob Astor: Business Man,* vol. 1. New York: Russell & Russell 1966

Ronda, James P. *Astoria & Empire.* Lincoln: University of Nebraska Press 1990

Stern, Theodore. *Chiefs & Change in the Oregon Country: Indian Relations at Fort Nez Percés 1818-1855.* Corvallis: Oregon State University Press 1996

———. *Chiefs & Chief Traders: Indian Relations at Fort Nez Percés, 1818-1855.* Corvallis: Oregon State University Press 1993

Van Kirk, Sylvia. *"Many Tender Ties": Women in Fur Trade Society.* Winnipeg: Watson and Dwyer 1980

Articles and Chapters

Brown, William C. "Old Fort Okanogan and the Okanogan Trail." *Oregon Historical Quarterly* 15 (1914): 1-38

Buckland, F.M. "The Hudson's Bay Brigade Trail." In *The Sixth Report of the Okanagan Historical Society 1935,* 11-22. Vancouver: Wrigley Printing 1936

Creech, E.P. "Brigade Trails of B.C." *The Beaver* 231 (Spring 1953): 10-15

Cullen, Mary. "Outfitting New Caledonia 1821-58." In Carol M. Judd and Arthur J. Ray, eds. *Old Trails and New Directions: Papers of the Third North American Fur Trade Conference*, 231-51. Toronto: University of Toronto Press 1980

Harris, Cole. "Towards a Geography of White Power in the Cordilleran Fur Trade." *Canadian Geographer* 39 (1995): 131-40

Karamanski, Theodore J. "The Iroquois and the Fur Trade of the Far West." *The Beaver* 312 (Spring 1982): 4-13

Mackie, Richard Somerset. "Geopolitics and Commercial Strategy: A Study of the Hudson's Bay Company on the Pacific, 1821-1843." Doctoral dissertation. Department of History, University of British Columbia 1993

Ormsby, Margaret A. "The Significance of the Hudson's Bay Brigade Trail." In *The Thirteenth Report of the Okanagan Historical Society 1949*, 29-37. N.p.: n.p. n.d.

Smyth, David. "The Yellowhead Pass and the Fur Trade." *BC Studies* 64 (1984-5): 48-73

Index

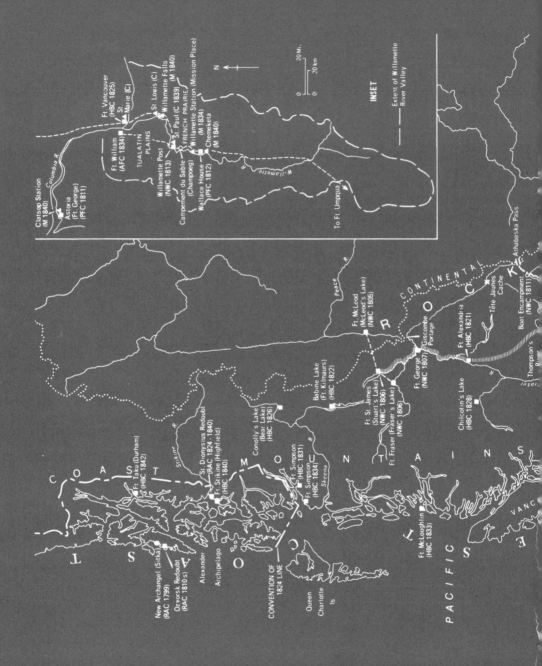

New Archangel (Sitka)
(RAC 1799)

Ozvorsk Redoubt
(RAC 1810s)

Alexander

Archipelago

Queen
Charlotte
Is.

CONVENTION OF
1824 LINE

Ft. Taku (Durham)
(HBC 1842)

St. Dionysius Redoubt
(RAC 1824-1840)

Ft. Stikine (Highfield)
(HBC 1840)

Conolly's Lake
(Bear Lake)
(HBC 1826)

Ft. Simpson
(HBC 1831)

Ft. Simpson
(HBC 1834)

Ft. McLoughlin
(HBC 1833)

Chilcotin's Lake
(HBC 1828)

Ft. Fraser (Fraser's Lake)
(NWC 1806)

Ft. St. James
(Stuart's Lake)
(NWC 1806)

Babine Lake
(Ft. Kilmaurs)
(HBC 1822)

Ft. McLeod
(McLeod's Lake)
(NWC 1805)

Ft. George
(NWC 1807)

Giscombe
Portage

Ft. Alexandria
(HBC 1821)

Tête Jaunes
Cache

Boat Encampment
(NWC 1811)

Athabaska Pass

Thompson's
River

COAST

COAST

ROCKY

CONTINENTAL

MONTCOAST

PACIFIC

BELT

Peace R.

Stikine R.

Skeena R.

Fraser R.

VANC.

VANCO

INSET

Clatsop Station
(M 1840)

Astoria
(Ft. George)
(PFC 1811)

Columbia R.

Ft. Vancouver
(HBC 1825)

St.
Marie (C)

Ft. William
(AFC 1834)

TUALATIN
PLAINS

Willamette Post
(NWC 1813)

Campement du Sable
(Champoeg)

Wallace House
(PFC 1812)

St Louis (C)

St. Paul (C 1839)

Willamette Falls
(M 1840)

FRENCH PRAIRIE

Willamette Station (Mission Place)
(M 1834)

Chemeketa
(M 1840)

Willamette

To Ft Umpqua

N

20 Mi.

20 km

Extent of Willamette
River Valley